# Selected Exaggerations

ISBN
978-0-7456-9165-7

W0008784

# Peter Sloterdijk

## Selected Exaggerations

### Conversations and Interviews 1993–2012

Edited by Bernhard Klein

Translated by Karen Margolis

polity

First published in German as *Ausgewählte Übertreibungen. Gespräche und Interviews 1993-2012* © Suhrkamp Verlag, Berlin, 2013
This English edition © Polity Press, 2016

Polity Press
65 Bridge Street
Cambridge CB2 1UR, UK

Polity Press
350 Main Street
Malden, MA 02148, USA

All rights reserved. Except for the quotation of short passages for the purpose of criticism and review, no part of this publication may be reproduced, stored in a retrieval system, or transmitted, in any form or by any means, electronic, mechanical, photocopying, recording or otherwise, without the prior permission of the publisher.

ISBN-13: 978-0-7456-9165-7
ISBN-13: 978-0-7456-9166-4 (pb)

A catalogue record for this book is available from the British Library.

Library of Congress Cataloging-in-Publication Data

Names: Sloterdijk, Peter, 1947- author.
Title: Selected exaggerations : conversations and interviews, 1993-2012 / Peter Sloterdijk.
Description: English edition. | Malden : Polity, 2016. | Includes bibliographical references.
Identifiers: LCCN 2015024410| ISBN 9780745691657 (hardback) | ISBN 9780745691664 (pbk.)
Subjects: LCSH: Sloterdijk, Peter, 1947---Interviews. | Philosophers--Germany--Interviews. | Philosophy, German--21st century.
Classification: LCC B3332.S254 A5 2016 | DDC 193--dc23 LC record available at http://lccn.loc.gov/2015024410

Typeset in 10.5 on 12 pt Times NR MT by
Servis Filmsetting Ltd, Stockport, Cheshire
Printed and bound in the UK by CPI Group (UK) Ltd, Croydon, CR0 4YY

The publisher has used its best endeavours to ensure that the URLs for external websites referred to in this book are correct and active at the time of going to press. However, the publisher has no responsibility for the websites and can make no guarantee that a site will remain live or that the content is or will remain appropriate.

Every effort has been made to trace all copyright holders, but if any have been inadvertently overlooked the publisher will be pleased to include any necessary credits in any subsequent reprint or edition.

For further information on Polity, visit our website:
politybooks.com

# Contents

# IN PLACE OF A PREFACE[1]

*Bernhard Klein in conversation with Peter Sloterdijk*

**Karlsruhe, 17 December 2012**

KLEIN: Mr Sloterdijk, after extensive research I have compiled a selection of your interviews over the past two decades, a very compact selection from an enormous wealth of material, but still a weighty volume. I am aware that interviews are only a small part of your publishing activity – the phrase 'tip of the iceberg' is very apt here. You have more than forty books to your name, and have also written a large number of essays for a wide range of newspapers, periodicals and anthologies. You have held professorships in Karlsruhe and Vienna for the past twenty years, and you only resigned from the position in Austria quite recently. Aside from this you have had a full timetable as a speaker at all kinds of events, and you have participated in numerous conferences, conventions and symposia. You have given readings from your latest books, and held seminars, ceremonial addresses and after-dinner speeches. You have done interviews in many media and for over ten years you moderated your own TV programme.

According to the general wisdom, 'less is more'. Why, in your case, is *more* more? Does your almost frantic creative energy express something of the powerlessness every writer feels when faced with the silence of the library?

[1] *Translator's Note:* Some of the original interview titles have been changed in the German edition of this book and in the present English translation.

All notes are by the translator, with the exception of those marked with an asterisk, which are provided by the German editor.

SLOTERDIJK: I think the real answer to the question of the main impetus for my work is connected more to an inner state rather than an actual motive. Looking back over the years these interviews cover, my first impression of myself is defencelessness, or the ability to be enticed. The cliché of the born writer's endogenous, ebullient productivity certainly doesn't apply to me, and nor does the model of committed literature. What people see as productivity in my case is usually only my inability to defend myself against suggestions from other people. It starts from a degree of over-compliance. This is ultimately responsible for the constant transition from passivity to production. But this state would not be sustainable without some cockiness. If I took on an additional task, it meant I was prepared to say I could manage that. In the process I sometimes got exhausted, of course, but that was superseded by an incredibly reckless trust in my powers of regeneration. That, incidentally, is the only difference worth mentioning between my earlier life and the present: for a while now, I have noticed that regeneration demands its own time.

KLEIN: Take us into your creative workshop. Can you describe your working technique and explain how you organize your library? How do you remember things?

SLOTERDIJK: Nobody can really know how his memory works. I only know I must have a well-organized internal archive even if it might seem chaotic to other people. My inner archivist finds access to the important files fairly regularly. He is one collaborator who has never disappointed me. He fortuitously retrieves documents I didn't even know had been filed ready for reference. Sometimes he unwittingly discovers nearly finished pieces of writing that I only have to copy up.

KLEIN: To what extent does your relation to language enhance your zest for writing and publishing?

SLOTERDIJK: Language is generally seen as a medium for understanding – an assumption that writers shouldn't accept unquestioningly. A critical minority sees language as the starting point of all misunderstandings. Wittgenstein even thought that philosophical problems arose when language goes on holiday – although he didn't reveal to us what he meant by 'going on holiday'. Does it mean being nonsensical? Or poring over pseudo-problems, firing excessive volleys into the air? Anyway, he toyed with the idea that one could just as well do without language; the deflationary tendency is clearly evident. Reading that, I can imagine a wrinkled janitor entering the scene who wants to put an end to the silliness of youth. Statements like that seem narrow to me. You really don't know what might happen if you get involved in going on holiday. I prefer the opinion of Wittgenstein's fellow Austrian, Egon Friedell, who said: 'Culture is a wealth of problems.' We can try to economise on everything, but not on problems.

KLEIN: So far I have managed to trace around 300 of your interviews in various newspaper archives and on the Internet. Staying with the iceberg image, if we present over thirty selected pieces in this book, this is indeed only the part of the iceberg visible above water. What role do the interviews play in your work as a writer and media personality? Are they there to promote the 'management of your own name', as you yourself once expressed it?

SLOTERDIJK: You know, some highly reputable authors never gave interviews, and some did so only rarely. But there are others who accept interview proposals easily. I count myself among the latter. It involves brand-name management, and that is an offshoot one accepts. With most interviews the reader will notice that even if I thought about that aspect beforehand, I forgot it after a minute at most. The interview is one form of literary production among others, and I see it as a subgenus of the essay. I have practised it frequently since the time I overcame my reluctance and accepted the role of public intellectual that ensued from my first publications. As you can see, I enjoy formulating things and making propositions, and once I am immersed in the flow of speech I stop worrying about the effect. My worries only become acute in the reworking phase. I'm sensitive about failed expressions.

KLEIN: True, your interviews are not one-to-one live publications. You always check them over.

SLOTERDIJK: Let's say they are a mixed form composed of improvisation and edited work. In some cases the editing is limited to just one or two slight touches, but others involve a completely new version.

KLEIN: Over the years, the young, shy Sloterdijk we see in old videotapes has become a star. To me he is like a colossus of expressive force, verbally and in writing. This creative energy, it seems to me, can't be explained by normal standards. It is still a mystery how you have managed this.

SLOTERDIJK: I admit that I have felt many things blowing through me. Now and then I enjoy the powerful cross-draughts, but by no means always. My basic feeling, as I have said, is not of excessive productivity but of receptiveness to evidence from all directions, what I just called defencelessness. In the early stage I usually like the things I am doing, but I quickly lose sight of them. It might sound odd, but if a major work is in the making I only have brief feelings of achievement, and they only happen rarely. I am incapable of developing such emotions, or of holding on to them. I am always faced with the blank sheet of paper that shows I haven't done anything yet. So I put out my feelers and start from scratch. It may sound absurd, but I usually suspect myself of not doing enough. This probably shows I am lacking in hindsight intelligence. As I don't see my past, I have no choice but to keep moving. Maybe that would be the next lesson: slowing down and returning to the moment. But I'm still wary of such suggestions and dismiss them scornfully as ideas for retired folk.

KLEIN: I have heard you shared a communal apartment when you were younger. How did you manage to be creative in the midst of the chaos? Many people would say in that kind of environment they could never put anything down on paper.

SLOTERDIJK: I didn't actually live in that apartment in Munich but I visited it every day. What I noticed about myself then was the ability not to let anything put me off course. I always had intense relationships, I had close ties to women and male friends, and we went out a lot and travelled frequently. For the past twenty years the family has been my main form of life, and that's not pure solitude either. I can well remember the time when a boisterous toddler ran around my study. It was entertaining for me – I couldn't be disturbed. Today I find it odd that I get irritated more easily. In the past the telephone didn't disturb me, nor did workmen or Jehovah's Witnesses. I saw everything as inspiration, not interruption. A miraculous superstition was at work: whatever happened would immediately be transformed into part of the production. In that middle phase I seemed to be living in a protective shell; I was sure of my own topics, or the topics were sure of me. Nothing could distract me.

KLEIN: When you say 'defencelessness', it suggests being tired and giving up. Evidently you have constantly used the creativity of writing to banish this eventuality.

SLOTERDIJK: Old working animals know that even tiredness can become a motive force if it activates regeneration. Once you have really rested, let's say for a whole day, it feels as if you have gained the energy for three new lives. In the past I used to emphasize the difference between regeneration and a vacation. I saw the latter as illegitimate and thought it had no reason to exist. To put it arrogantly, I used to think you only need a vacation from the wrong life. Today I have changed my mind. Gradually I am coming round to admitting that vacations are justified.

KLEIN: Let me return to your interviews again. At the moment, Suhrkamp Verlag, which has been your publishing house since your first book thirty years ago, is in the headlines.[2] There was a time at Suhrkamp when its authors were horrified at the idea of publishing anything in a Springer Press newspaper. Now, however, you publish in practically every medium that asks you, almost at random it seems, and you even published something once in *Bild-Zeitung* and *Playboy*. How do you judge yourself in this context? How has the Suhrkamp author changed over the years since the time it was unthinkable to give interviews to Springer Press newspapers?

SLOTERDIJK: One thing is clear: the typical Suhrkamp author no longer exists, if he or she ever did. Actually, the publishing house used to be the imprint for a collection of highly idiosyncratic characters. What do you suppose Bloch and Beckett had in common? Or Hesse and Luhmann? By now the diversity has increased, if anything. Some Suhrkamp authors have retained the spirit of the sixties or seventies and represent softer versions of latter-day Marxism. You can see they are children of the zeitgeist as well because, almost unnoticed, they have changed their topic from utopia to justice – this is where the remnants of the Frankfurt School of civil theology live on. On the other hand, many new shades of personality have emerged in the spectrum, both at the literary and the scholarly ends.

The success of my book in 1983 was a signal for me to look at future fields of action elsewhere. Why not in the previously unthinkable media? Over time I have increasingly discarded inherited aversions. I have met with interview partners from the most politically heterogeneous media without having a hidden agenda of ideological criticism, and, wherever possible, on an equal footing. The only exception is the press of the neo-nationalist strand – in that case my personal background had an influence. Perhaps I should have cast off this inhibition as well, and made occasional home visits to confused extreme right-wing souls.

KLEIN: Many of the interviews in the present volume relate to your new publications at the time, while others take their cue from topics in the air at that particular juncture. Do you remember interviews that especially influenced you?

SLOTERDIJK: Most of the conversations and interviews in the present book happened so long ago that I can't remember the situations they occurred in or, at best, only vaguely. I still have a vivid memory of the circumstances of the wide-ranging two-part interview with Ulrich Raulff, the director of the German Literature

[2] Klein is referring to developments in a lengthy legal battle over ownership and editorial control of Suhrkamp Verlag that began in 2002 and was finally resolved in 2015.

Archive. The theme was 'Fate', and it took place about two years ago, the first part in Karlsruhe and the second in Marbach, where Raulff sat opposite me as the host and guardian of his treasures. Those were moments of pure intellectual happiness. At such points one realizes more keenly than usual what literature can be, including in the form of the spoken word. It is a syntactic technique of happiness. The levitation begins with combining two or three words in a non-prosaic fashion.

KLEIN: The present volume is an anthology of trenchant formulations. We get the impression that, for you, dialogue is always a metalogue as well. Many voices come and go in it. The interviews take the form of conversations between two people, but it seems to me you would be most comfortable in conversation with several partners.

SLOTERDIJK: True, I experience dialogue as a polylogue, a conversation with many people. After all, aside from their own voice, good interviewers usually bring all kinds of other voices with them. They are already a chorus of subjectivity themselves. This inevitably creates echoes in the interviewee. If there is anything I really don't like, it is an exchange of empty phrases that sound like official pronouncements.

KLEIN: We can guarantee there are no empty phrases to be found anywhere in this book.

SLOTERDIJK: Let me explain where my aversion to empty phrases comes from. For as long as I can remember, I have had a childish fear of boredom. I have always thought the most boring things possible are the kind of set speeches you hear in the academic discourse market, not to mention the chipboard sheets from the political DIY store. To avoid misunderstandings, I should say I know a good kind of boredom that is calming and integrating. You can entrust yourself to it like to an old nursery school teacher. I am thinking of the subtle boredom of a landscape, the liberating boredom of the sea, the lofty boredom of the mountains and the boredom of great narrative literature when it sometimes demands patience. An evil boredom emanates from the intrusive bigotry of conceited empty phrasemongers – it is just as deadly as it is reputed to be. Do you know this kind of situation? You exchange a few words with somebody whom you may not even dislike a priori. After three or four sentences back and forth you feel incredibly world-weary. It is as if your vitality battery has been used up within seconds and you don't know why. I avoid that sort of boredom like the plague. It is a pathological condition that takes away your pleasure in speaking, in expressing opinions, in being able to say what you see, indeed, in life itself. The symptom of severe boredom is speech breakdown. All at once the words refuse to come out in the right order, you barely manage to squeeze out a noun but the verb doesn't follow, there is an overwhelming, awful feeling of not wanting to say anything else – which should definitely not be confused with the good state of just having nothing to say. Sometimes I almost hit the danger point when I notice a conversation partner is digging up totally hackneyed questions, questions that are essentially ways of dumbing down. They always have the subtext: come and share our misery! I have made a great effort to learn to evade such attacks by reformulating the questions until I regain the desire to react to them.

KLEIN: Do you mean there are questions like vampires that suck the life out of the respondent?

SLOTERDIJK: There are questions like that and questioners like that. In theosophical circles such negatively charged people are called prana suckers, vampires of life's breath. Sometimes the questioner's mental exhaustion is clear from the start. In the best case I try to answer like a tour director or an emergency doctor.

KLEIN: I am absolutely sure there are no interviews in the present book in which you had to play the role of emergency doctor, and nobody who reads these pieces would think of speech breakdown. But I wonder whether we can sense a kind of respect, not to say awe, in your interview partners now and then.

SLOTERDIJK: If it were ever the case, it would have been wrong to leave it like that. Interviews in public are a form of sport in which the point is not to win, but to play for a draw on a higher plane. In every sophisticated question–answer flow the discussion partners remind each other of their more intelligent options. One discovers the pleasure of being able to navigate in a problem space.

KLEIN: I'd like to refer again to the enthusiasm that's often discernible in what you say, whether we call it youthful or not. Your drive for expression started exploding after your India trip in early 1980. Could it be that, after India, you experienced a quasi-archaic pre-lingual enthusiasm that converged with later academic influences? You have probably often been asked this question. I am fascinated that, from then on, there seemed to be no way back for you. Suddenly the only open road led towards productivity.

SLOTERDIJK: It would be better to say, the road to practical testing of a presentiment. I was latently aware that I was living on the quiet. After 1980, the time was ripe for me to start striking out. Back then I found the right note for myself, if one can put it so naively. It was as if I had discovered the instrument for making my kind of music. The instrument was tuned at the moment I realized what my opportunity consisted in.

KLEIN: Naturally, we'd like you to explain that in more detail.

SLOTERDIJK: Let me try. I was born in 1947 and as a young man I grew up almost without any paternal influence. At the right moment I realized I should decide to be a sort of father to myself. I already had a good idea of what mothering is, whether pre-existing or chosen, and how one gradually leaves it behind. I had no idea what fathering meant. I had to find my fathers and mentors, which meant I had to look in the world around me. Fathers are models we seek to have something to conquer later on, aren't they? So I set off, with admiration as my guideline. Nobody who had something to say was safe from my admiration – or from my disappointment either. The breakthrough came when I understood that I had to explain the world to myself. In my case it could only happen by taking myself in hand – as teacher and student in one. Somehow I managed to duplicate myself into a bigger and a smaller part. So I took myself by the hand and explained the world and life to myself. Evidently this made sense to many observers who enjoyed reading what I said to myself. They probably laughed at how I slipped into the role of the wise old man for the sake of the junior. I still think this method wasn't the worst way to approach the philosophical sphere. It was particularly useful in my case because it fitted the situation of a young person who, like many of his generation, grew up with a strong sense of cultural insecurity.

KLEIN: What made you go East after you finished your dissertation under the professors in Hamburg? What did you learn from the Bhagwan Shree Rajneesh, or Osho, as he was also known? Why did you go to India at that time instead of staying at the university?

SLOTERDIJK: That is a long story I can only sketch briefly here. In 1974 I was offered a post as a temporary assistant professor at Hamburg University. I accepted, and moved to Hamburg. The following year in Hamburg was a very fruitful time for me, a watershed in my life. I was very lucky to become a close associate of Klaus Briegleb, the tenured professor for modern German literature. I knew him from Munich and in my opinion, and not only mine, he was the foremost literary scholar in the country and at the peak of his art in his years in Hamburg. The constellation with my older colleagues was equally auspicious, an intellectual spiral nebula with enormous energy. It was also interesting in terms of group eroticism. As regards the university, from then on I knew it was not my kind of patch. I went back to Munich when my contract expired. Then the wild years of groups began: communes, psychotherapy, meditation groups, the New Left, the New Man. Topics like that were constantly bandied about. Back then, we believed in theory as if it had messianic power. The period between 1974 and 1980 was the experimental phase of my life. I had written my doctoral dissertation, I had many options open to me, and the only thing I knew clearly was that I wouldn't go back to the university. If there is such a thing as suffering from doubt, I wasn't aware of it then. I felt inspired by having the freedom of several years ahead to find my feet without having to commit myself.

KLEIN: But that still doesn't explain why you decided to go to India.

SLOTERDIJK: The Indian trip had been a preordained choice in the spiritual curriculum of the West since the days of the blessed Hermann Hesse. You might have read Marx, Lenin and Marcuse, but the Orient was still missing. One day the time was ripe. It embodied everything that mattered back then, the therapeutic awakening, the spiritual awakening and the countercultural awakening. What is more, the whole enterprise was headlined by the topic of the day, 'free love', like a neon sign on Times Square. You would have had to be an idiot not to give it a try. Anyway, in India you met half of Frankfurt and half of Munich. I experienced my best Adorno colloquia on the fringes of the ashram in Poona. This was the start of an incredibly intensive period, because in India you just met people who were brave in their own fashion, aggressive, confrontational, and generous with feelings, observations and touching. The mood there today is largely defined by the need for safeguards, which was unknown back then. Of course, everybody was crazy at that time; you realize it when you look back soberly, but you have to admit they were brave to the point of excess. To go to India under the conditions at that time was really a big leap, a breach with the culture we came from.

KLEIN: Replaying old videos in which the eyes of Osho are looking at us, we can still feel the pulse of a dimension beyond European academia. How did this guru come to play such a major role at that time?

SLOTERDIJK: Nowadays he doesn't mean anything to me any more, aside from a rather remote feeling of gratitude. Remember, I was one of the people who returned from the East intending to stay here. I had changed, for sure, but I hadn't become Indianized. On the contrary, it was only since then that I consciously became a European. I have built the impulses from there discreetly into my life. They are only present now in an altered form, as elements of gentle vibrations.

KLEIN: Have you lived 'under a brighter sky' since then?

SLOTERDIJK: That's how I once expressed it. After I came back from India I developed my own private meteorology. I no longer felt personally affected by the weather forecast for Central Europe.

KLEIN: Can you explain how we get to the brighter sky in our region? Are there directions for people beset by crises and looking for inner strength?

SLOTERDIJK: I don't want to embark on a discursive essay about the interconnection of individual and society, but it should be clear that the brightening up of feeling for the world is linked to a change in the mode of socialization. At the end of the Second World War, Arthur Koestler wrote a lucid essay, 'The Yogi and the Commissar', in which he typologically contrasted the two fundamental responses of the twentieth century to the misery of the world, the response of the yogi, who chooses the path inwards without asking about external conditions, and the response of the commissar who never tires of repeating the thesis that the social structures first have to be completely changed before we can think about emancipation of individuals. Towards the end of the 1970s the social revolutionary illusions of the decade collapsed, leaving a gap that offered fresh scope for the yogi option.

Most people don't remember that today. At the moment we are going through an era of commissars again, even if they are no longer the type of communist Koestler had in mind. Today's protagonists of social democracy are convinced that expanding the authority of the state is the cure for all of life's evils. The absolutism of the social sphere is seeping into the smallest cracks once again. The commissar's approach is not compatible with the classical Indian conception of the world. People in India tend to think that while each individual carries the potential for a revolution within himself or herself, it is a revolution in the first person. I returned from India to Europe with this lesson in my baggage without paying duty on it, and I have never completely renounced it. The ensuing conflict with the commissars was predictable. Overall, this happened in a rather weird way, perhaps partly because I didn't take the floor as a phenotypic yogi, turned away from the world, idealistic and esoteric, but as a person very much of this world yet with a different concept of the world. This contradiction has hung in the air, more or less unexplained, for around thirty years. Now and then, new commissars ganged up against some of my interventions – think of the strange failed debate two years ago about democratically redefining taxation in the spirit of giving. One way or another, that was an odd scene. A grand coalition of commissars bludgeoned an idea that obviously came from the yogi region. People still don't understand that there is more than one kind of progress, more than one revolution, more than one anthropology.

KLEIN: How does it affect you as a person when, aside from criticism, you also get a great deal of admiration? How do you cope with all the projections of your readers and fans?

SLOTERDIJK: Now I'm going to say something very odd: I often don't feel appreciation from outside. When it comes to applause, I'm afraid I am mentally blind. It hasn't escaped me that some readers value my work, just as it hasn't escaped me that attempts have been made to devalue it. I haven't been deaf to the applause but it doesn't distract me, and individual readers' opinions have only rarely touched me deeply.

KLEIN: That sounds very paradoxical. After all, at the same time you claim to react very sensitively to external stimuli.

SLOTERDIJK: Maybe I should explain that in more detail. I am talking about the public impact of books. You see, before a new work leaves my workshop I first have to accept it myself. At that moment I am my own audience, and I want to be convinced as such. My approval is not given for nothing. At the moment I hand over a piece of work I must have an idea of its place on the scale of values. If the author doesn't know that, who should? I don't believe in the cliché of the writer who produces work automatically or while sleepwalking, who creates works at his desk like a pure fool and only knows they are worth something when others react excitedly. Many artists nowadays adopt the camouflage of 'I don't know' games, acting as if the sophisticated public alone can pass judgement on a work of art. I think the self-evaluation of any author worthy of the name is usually just as accurate as the readers' verdict, and often better. Maybe a certain percentage should be deducted for the usual self-overestimation and then we would get a realistic value.

KLEIN: In other words, in cases where the inner power of judgement is sufficiently well developed, excessive self-overestimation wouldn't occur at all. Then one would not be overly surprised by other people's common judgement. But the ability to see beyond the narrow confines of one's own work seems to be an art not everybody is endowed with.

SLOTERDIJK: Let's say that publication means deciding whether something you have written passes the test. It presupposes an internal verdict about whether a construction has made the grade. You don't make a decision like that because you are so blindly narcissistic as to think everything of yours is magnificent. On the contrary, you are more likely to feel intense self-doubt. Only a little is allowed to pass through the barrier. If you conclude the work can remain as it is, the pre-censorship is complete. That doesn't exclude other people with other standards making other judgements. The author is only the person who says 'finished'. Anything else can be done by other people as well, but the author is the one who breaks off the work on a thing. An intimate sense of evidentness decides when the time is right.

KLEIN: Your fans and critics agree that your style is baroque and not infrequently brilliant. How far does clarity play a role in your conception of philosophical prose?

SLOTERDIJK: My judgement on this is biased. I believe my own writings are completely clear. I often work with abbreviations and exaggerations or, technically speaking, ellipses and hyperbole, two stylistic methods that are indisputably useful for working out ideas. Some colleagues accuse me of sprinkling metaphors too liberally, but I always respond that concepts and metaphors are not necessarily opposed, and metaphors often represent a higher state of concepts. There are, of course, theoreticians who were socialized in a different culture of rationality and have difficulty understanding associative language. They are accustomed to discussing whether a statement such as 'All bachelors are unmarried men' should be regarded as an analytical judgement. They are suspicious of my hopping and jumping and are inclined to cry 'thought poetry!' or 'metaphor-spouting!'

KLEIN: Do you mean 'live' thinking should rate higher than edited thinking because it is more difficult?

SLOTERDIJK: It is not necessarily more difficult, but rarer. 'Live' is a term from broadcasting technology that allows us to participate in events elsewhere. In general, we are not present when thinking is happening somewhere. And it is usually a long time since thought took place. With luck, it is recorded in writing and we can read it later.

KLEIN: The idea of reading something later raises an important question for me. I have the impression that some time ago you began the phase of reappraisal of your work as a whole, still hesitatingly, but we can recognize the beginnings. The section of your oeuvre published in book form so far represents less than half of your works. The present interview collection provides an initial, extremely selective indication of what you have produced along the way in the everyday business of *Zeitkritik*, critique of our times. In relation to the lectures and essays you have produced in the past twenty-five years, as far as I know there is no plan for a collected edition, which would involve a series of big volumes. From what I can see, the majority of your unknown works consists of your academic lectures, and only those who attended have an idea of them. Great treasures of live thinking are probably buried among them. What are you going to do with them?

SLOTERDIJK: For twenty years I gave lectures at the Academy of Fine Arts in Vienna on many topics without repeating them. The audiotapes of those lectures must be lying around in various private and university archives. Most of the public lectures in

Karlsruhe, and the seminars there, are also documented but not catalogued. Only one complete lecture, the final lecture of the cycle on classical Greek theatre in the auditorium of the state library in Karlsruhe, was published in 1999 by supposé. It is an interpretation of Sophoclean drama with the title *Ödipus oder Das zweite Orakel* [Oedipus or the Second Oracle]. That piece shows roughly what it was like when I could act freely in a live situation. Some time ago Auer Verlag issued an audio cassette with six recordings of lectures, but as far as I remember they were based on written scripts. There are probably around 1,500 hours of speech tapes in the archives. Regrettably, Suhrkamp Verlag couldn't decide to take on management of the documents. Meanwhile the Centre for Art and Media Technology in Karlsruhe has taken the first steps towards collecting and archiving the material. A considerable proportion of the documents has been digitized and listened to for indexing purposes with the aim of deciding, using selected key words, which pieces are suitable for transcription. I suspect most of them can simply be forgotten with no loss, but perhaps some things are worth producing. It seems this project could move forward in the next few years. Incidentally, in the period when I lectured in Vienna and Karlsruhe there was a loyal audience composed of people from the university and local residents in the city whose presence gave me the illusion of not talking entirely to the wind. Sadly, I have never been in the position of Meister Eckart when he claimed he was so full of God that he would have preached to the offertory box if there had been nobody to hear him. I was happy to have an audience and let their presence inspire me.

KLEIN: Let's not forget that the *Philosophische Quartett* is still available in the ZDF archives.[3]

SLOTERDIJK: According to my calculations, we produced sixty-three programmes in ten and a half years. My appearances in my own TV programme constitute a special category that has practically nothing to do with the rest of my work. In the *Quartets* I was always very reserved, aside from a few exceptions when I indulged in spinning yarns a little more freely. Usually I played the discreet moderator whose main concern is to offer the guests the

[3] *Das Philosophische Quartett (The Philosophical Quartet)* was a cultural talk show on German television hosted by philosophers Peter Sloterdijk and Rüdiger Safranski, who were joined for every edition by two different guests, usually prominent German intellectuals. Broadcast every two months on ZDF, the second German public TV channel, the show ran for ten years from 2002 to 2012.

best possible frame. You could call it the achievement of being lacklustre, which has its own attraction.

KLEIN: Let me briefly quote from Kant's *Groundwork of the Metaphysics of Morals*:

> This descending to popular concepts is certainly very commendable, provided the ascent to the principles of pure reason has first taken place and has been carried through to complete satisfaction. That would mean that the doctrine of morals is first *grounded* on metaphysics and afterwards, when it has been firmly established, is provided with *access* by means of popularity.[4]

Could you identify with this statement in your work as a public intellectual?

SLOTERDIJK: I can't shake off the impression that Kant is expressing himself much more simply here than he really thought. He is pretending to believe philosophy is a result-based science that stops short of the last insights. They can naturally be popularized without difficulty. But that's not how things are. I assume that if philosophers knew something relevant with absolute certainty it would have seeped through by now. Since Kant, philosophers have had 200 years to reach agreement. But they disagree more than ever. The model of ex-cathedra popularization of metaphysically certified doctrines can't be applied to today's intellectual situation. Nobody knows any more what generally compelling 'fundamental metaphysical principles' might be. Theoreticians can't even agree whether the word 'fundamental' is a meaningful term. The whole business of 'making something fundamental' has become problematic. One gets the impression all the fundamental rule-makers are going round in circles. Incidentally, the symptomatic metaphorical mistake in the comment by Kant you just quoted shows that he couldn't decide himself in which area to look for the so-called principles. He says, first we should 'ascend' to them, and then, two lines later, we find the same principles have descended again to become the secure ground on which popular teaching should be 'firmly grounded'. The debate over 'grounding' ran dry some time ago. I think it was best summed up in the maxim attributed to Le Corbusier that the ground is the foundation of the basis.

[4] Quoted from Immanuel Kant, *Practical Philosophy*, ed. Mary J. Gregor (Cambridge: Cambridge University Press), 1999, p. 63.

KLEIN: But then, what can a philosopher still share with the wider public?

SLOTERDIJK: I tend to regard philosophy not as a specialized subject but as the mode of working on a topic. Anybody who thinks *more philosophico* locates positive knowledge against the background of unknowing and in the context of general concerns. This creates an oscillation between affirmations and sceptical moments. If this is done over a lengthy period, when we share thoughts and ideas we can see for ourselves that we have much more unknowing in common than effective knowledge. Over time, the non-professional participants in such exercises can adopt this mode of thinking. In the process one learns how to be sure-footed on shaky ground. This kind of modal philosophical behaviour can go in many directions. In the future it can even touch a larger public, whereas it would be unrealistic to expect philosophy as an academic subject to emerge from its conclave again. Fortunately, there is a series of well-established disciplines such as anthropology, linguistics, ethnology, psychology, systemics and, more recently, neurology and particularly cultural theory that, in terms of the logic of their objects, operate more or less close to philosophy, or could do so. Their actors know quite precisely what they can do and where the borders of their art lie. We can pick up on these findings. In the disciplines I have mentioned the archives are full of knowledge suitable for post-sceptical representation to the public. That is all I have been doing for a long time now.

# 1

# THE HALF-MOON MAN

*Interview with Elke Dauk**

DAUK: Mr Sloterdijk, ten years ago the *Critique of Cynical Reason* seemed like a tremendously bold call. How do you explain that extraordinary impact?

SLOTERDIJK: The book was not a call – it was a performance. It celebrated what it discussed in its own pages. It was, and still is, a very cheerful book, unusually provocative in a context where one doesn't expect it. The critique lies in the tone. Considering its subject, it is astonishingly funny; it contains a kind of phenomenology of all the jokes that can ever be made about humans in the nine major fields of humour, which are spelled out in detail in the second volume.

Above all, it contributed to blasting open the conspiracy of disenchantment, the left-wing mawkishness in the year 1983. The *Critique of Cynical Reason* was the attempt to reconstruct the super-ego disaster of European culture in a phenomenologically broad study – a super-ego disaster that began with people having to live up to unattainably high ideals. Today we are living through the break-up of a process of constructing the super-ego that had already begun in antiquity. What Europeans experience today as a universal feeling of demoralization, right down to the tiny ramifications of political incorrectness that have such a deep influence on the zeitgeist, are

* This interview between Peter Sloterdijk and Elke Dauk appeared under the title 'Der Halbmondmensch', in the *Frankfurter Rundschau* (29 September 1993, supplement): 2.

Elke Dauk's book about life forms in the Western world, *Der Griff nach den Sternen. Suche nach Lebensformen im Abendland*, was published in 1998 by Insel Verlag, a division of Suhrkamp Verlag.

remote effects of a process of idealization that took root with Greek philosophy and the later Christian doctrine of virtue and inexorably led to an unparalleled history of destruction.

DAUK: To what extent was the *Critique of Cynical Reason* a critique of the Enlightenment?

SLOTERDIJK: It is not a critique of the Enlightenment, but rather a continuation of the Enlightenment in a self-reflective stage. It is enlightenment about the Enlightenment. Reflections across borders that necessarily emerge in a first attempt are recognized at the second attempt and are already part of the picture by the third attempt. The third attempt is social education after the bad experiences society had made with its own naivety. We have still not learned the art of convincing humans to live together in large communities. It has become so questionable whether it can succeed at all, via the paths of classical idealism and conceptions of sacrifice first developed in antiquity, that we have to expect new attempts.

DAUK: Wasn't it also the attempt to create an opposing model to sublate the destructive reason represented by kynicism and Diogenes?

SLOTERDIJK: It is not about sublating destructive elements. I focused on kynicism as a sort of existential revolt that had already become formulated in antiquity against the city and the state, that is, against the two major repressive forms, against the 'political monsters' of ancient times. Even today, people can use this model for guidance if they understand that humans must first be brought into life before the state can use them. Modern education, the modern Enlightenment and the modern state system have always assumed humans as given and don't consider how humans are born, how they engender themselves. In my opinion, ancient kynicism was an attempt, perhaps with inappropriate means, to defend a sphere in which humans are not delivered to the state too quickly, and don't become agents of big structures too quickly. The aim of kynicism was to recall a life form that was linked to the concept of self-assertion at that time, a life form in which human beings emerge first of all, and are not already exploited and given missions.

DAUK: Did you want to go beyond social theory towards an art of living or, more precisely, eroticism?

SLOTERDIJK: What I do is not only social theory; it is a philosophical-existential approach that per se observes the social world as a fragmented landscape of obsessions. The book is a manifesto of liberation; it is the continuation of a strand of German philosophy insofar as it was a philosophy of emancipation. It was probably most successful in Germany because it played language games in a new way on a sophisticated level of possibilities.

DAUK: Back then, using the example of the atom bomb, you characterized the subject as the pure will to annihilate himself and the world. Does this analysis still hold today?

SLOTERDIJK: In principle, yes. But the social parameters have shifted very considerably. Nowadays we no longer face the paranoid duel that pitted two exemplary political mega-centres against each other in the Cold War era. Today the issue is not so much to disarm two such subjects or to give information about them, although this is still relevant, but to reform them and inform them in such a way that they can live with their own magnitude, with their own potential for violence, and their own paranoia. This might sound paradoxical, but it is not about smashing up these great subjects but about helping them to function successfully. By 'successfully', I mean beyond self-destruction.

DAUK: Is the kynical-cynical impulse still the motive force of your thought?

SLOTERDIJK: Kynical-cynical impulses do not lead to thought; they lead to formal rejection of unreasonable demands. Forces that drive thought are not found on the level of kynical and cynical impulses because these impulses have something to do with defensive movements, defensive feelings. The cynical impulse is the feeling of rejection that powerful persons have when people demand that they humbly submit to morality or a norm. They feel too strong for that and become cynical. And the kynical impulse is the resistance produced by the vitality of 'poor suckers' when they are required to keep to norms that were created for others. In their own way, they are also too strong to let themselves be castrated by a sort of normativism that tries to co-opt them for a social game that nobody ever asked if they wanted to play. In both cases it is a sort of individualist *résistance* that operates on the borders of moralism, in the one case from above, in the other from below. There are records of this from various world cultures since the beginning of cities and empires. One can see that this kind of *résistance*, this rejection of the imperial ethos, from above as from below, has been known for around 2,500 years, and particularly in the West where there has always been special licence for speaking out defiantly, that is, where the truth oracle has functioned better, and even in a cheeky, immoral tone, than in China or other places, where the political pressure to gloss over and say the required things operates much more tightly. Returning to your question, for me, and I think for most philosophers, what drives thought lies at a deeper level. It is not resistance, but riddles, that make one think. Having a big 'No' inside you leads to therapy, at best. But if you have a riddle inside you, you arrive either at art or philosophy. I see my work being located at the intersection of these fields.

DAUK: You have been interested in Gnosis in recent years. Whereas the kynic insists on a fulfilled life, the disciple of Gnosticism seeks flight from the world. Isn't this a path from 'life as risk' to 'life as mourning'?

SLOTERDIJK: Quite the contrary. I am much more optimistic now than I was in my book *Critique of Cynical Reason*, because that book only spoke the language of cheerful protest. You can declare war and you can declare a holiday, and that book declared a holiday. It did so intentionally and polemically against a society that had declared war and troubles. Today my eyes see other horizons and my thinking stems from a different centre that is more thoroughly worked out and differently informed about its reasons for cheerfulness. My reasons for cheerfulness go much deeper than those of the *Critique of Cynical Reason*. The result is that I no longer work on a theory of protest but on a fundamental theory of the absent person. That means I use anthropological arguments to develop the thesis that humans have turned away from the world to a large degree, and they always exist also in the mode of absence, in the mode of unknowing, in a nocturnal relation to the world. Consequently I see no reason, at least not in terms of anthropology, to continue the forcible co-option of individuals for the sake of a totality called 'reality'. That's what contemporary media do when they keep on agitating about troubles, showering people constantly with unpleasant news, inspired by a degree of informative sadism, as if to say, 'We have recorded this awful stuff to pass on and you are the right recipients.' Everybody tries to be the medium, not the filter. The filters and the end buyers are always the others. I think it's possible to show that people never have to be end buyers of misfortune. Their inherent nature makes them like half-moons, only half turned towards the world, and their other half belongs to a different principle that can't be reached by that agitation about troubles.

DAUK: Is the relationship between the ego and the world the basic theme of your work?

SLOTERDIJK: The relationship between humans and the world has been the theme of philosophy for 2,500 years, but classical metaphysics included a third element that gets a bad press today. However, the metaphysical triangle in which thought was practised via the major questions – the triangle consisting of God, man and the soul – still exists as a rump. Elsewhere it is replaced by a monist view of the world, that is, by positing the world as absolute, and treating human beings only as a function of the world, as a local function of the cosmos or a local function of society. This makes us slip back into the bad old conditions because we urge each individual to live his or her life in a way that is symptomatic of a society that doubts its own existence. There are good reasons to reject this imposition. I am beginning to present a very different kind of anthropology, one that eliminates the automatic relation of man and the world. Humans don't belong to the world like your thumb to your hand. They also stand with their backs to the world – as children of the night or of vacant nothingness.

DAUK: Were you interested in Gnosticism because the Gnostics practised opposition to the agents of the material world?

SLOTERDIJK: I saw Gnosis as an exercise ground on which one can study the a-cosmic dimension, the components of the human psyche that are turned away from the world. It was an interdisciplinary project between the philosophy of religion and anthropology. The results are now available, first of all in a big collection of documents titled *World Revolution of the Soul*, a documentation of nearly a thousand pages that proves how people in the Western tradition have recorded their deregistration – if I can put it like that – at the residency registration office of the cosmos. Another result of the project is my forthcoming book, *Weltfremdheit* [World Estrangement]. This is not documentation – it is a discursively written account that develops the above-mentioned thesis in relation to music, sleep, drugs, religions, the death drive, self-awareness, meditative phenomena and many other things. The whole point is to show that we can't get any further with a primitive face-to-face relationship between 'man and the world'. It shows that we only describe a human being properly when we show that he or she lives at a sharp angle to reality and is sometimes here and sometimes not, and usually not.

DAUK: How is *Weltfremdheit* related to your thesis that hominization, humanization itself, is the disaster per se?

SLOTERDIJK: I don't say that on my own account; rather, I adopt a thesis that emerged around 2,000 years ago in the context of a dissident branch of Judaism during a self-critical phase of Jewish Genesis theology, and that people in our cultural sphere have never forgotten since then. The secret rumour says that there was a clumsy Creator and that this earth is not the best achievement of the world beyond, and certainly not optimal, and that the fundamental Catholic decision to save God by burdening man isn't the only meaningful possibility for distributing the burden in this context. We could also burden God and thus save the truth by regarding the Creation as second-best, maybe even as a botched effort, or one with a built-in tendency to fail. That is quite a different philosophical approach and it has created a breakthrough in anthropology and made negative anthropology possible, that is, teachings about a person's absence from the world as a kind of theory of the night and of sleep, of absence. As soon as that is formulated in enough detail we shall see that it generally offers a better way to describe humans than positivist anthropologies do.

DAUK: Isn't the dark side of man only half the truth?

SLOTERDIJK: It is the forgotten half of the truth. What matters now is to continue thinking about the cognitive insights of anthropology in such a way that we remain within the continuum of Western learning processes and can still discuss and debate on an equal footing with a Taoist sage, an Indian sadhu and an ecstatic Hasid.

# 2

# WHY ARE PEOPLE MEDIA?

*Interview with Jürgen Werner**

WERNER: We usually think of media as apparatuses that transmit pictures and sound – but you argue that people are media. Why?

SLOTERDIJK: To be a medium means to occupy the middle in a field of at least three elements. That is a phenomenon people are aware of nowadays particularly in relation to technical media. We have radio receivers. We have television receivers. If Mr A. wants to send Mr B. a quick message he uses what we call a new medium, a telephone or a fax machine. Now, cultural anthropology has shown that media are not originally apparatuses, but people. It is modernism that first led us to shift the role of transmitter from people to apparatuses. This displacement drama hides the business secrets of modernity.

WERNER: When people act as transmitters, what are they transmitting between?

SLOTERDIJK: Firstly, as with the apparatuses, they are transmitting between two communicating sides. This is easy to explain if you think of travelling salesmen, who played an enormous role in antiquity because they fulfilled the function of international commuters. They were people who commuted between self-contained cultures. It would be wrong to imagine the world of that time as it is today, a world of tourists. Reconstructing the age of settled life

* This interview between Peter Sloterdijk and Jürgen Werner appeared under the title 'Warum sind Menschen Medien, Herr Sloterdijk?' [Why are People Media, Mr Sloterdijk?], in the *Frankfurter Allgemeine Zeitung Magazin* (9 September 1994): 54f.

Jürgen Werner was an editor at the *Frankfurter Allgemeine Zeitung* until 1998, first in the Sports section, then at *FAZ-Magazin.*

requires people of our times to envisage a bygone form of life that was largely shaped by what Benedictine monks called *stabilitas loci*, being settled in one place. This makes the people in settled cultures who saw more than one village or town extraordinarily important. They seemed like a prefiguration of messengers from the world beyond. In antiquity there was a social class of itinerant preachers, philosophers, educators and rhetoricians who travelled from village to village and from town to town and tried to communicate their worldly wisdom, their tricks and their doctrines to different audiences. They are the actual ancestors of those we call 'experts' or 'consultants' today. At the same time they are representatives of what I call 'personal mediumism'. Incidentally, the phenomena of personal mediumism are totally rational. That is a very important point for me. Since the nineteenth century, the concept of the personal medium has been consigned to the occult sphere, the idiot's corner. Nowadays people who hear voices quickly receive generous doses of psychiatric treatment. This makes it very difficult for anybody to use the term 'medium' in ordinary speech today. I am interested in developing mediumism as an anthropological term with such broad scope that it will be impossible to make a statement about a person without saying in which medial system he or she lives.

WERNER: Being a medium means being able not to oppose something but to be open towards something different. Can you also oppose things you are enthusiastic about? Musil once said a man can't be angry at his own time without suffering some damage. Are we damaged if we don't let ourselves be affected by the flow of our times?

SLOTERDIJK: Yes, seriously damaged, in fact. 'Going against the flow' is merely a metaphor for withdrawing from the flow – drying out. It is a way of describing the fundamental schizophrenic disturbance that applies to the whole situation of modern people, to the extent that they typically represent the results of a centuries-long history of de-spiritualization. The de-spiritualized individual stands at the edge of everything like an absolute onlooker, a final consumer. The sum of de-spiritualized persons amounts to the contemporary population of last people. That is something that justifies the phrase, 'to forfeit his soul'.[1]

WERNER: Do we have to give up the ideal of independence if we see man as a medium?

[1] 'For what does it profit a man to gain the whole world and forfeit his soul?' (Mark 8:36, ESV).

SLOTERDIJK: We have to conceive independence very differently. Independence only happens by stepping up our participation, not by continuing to invest in the ideal of coolness. Coolness is the meta-symptom of a post-religious situation. It is the major symptom of a generation that doesn't even bother to dip its feet into the stream it emerged from to test how the temperature was. This investment in not letting the intellect flow, sitting coolly on the riverbank as the last man or woman, influences the conditions under which we as teachers find our students today, but also under which we meet with adults in our role as consultants. De-spiritualization is the lowest common denominator of contemporary 'spiritual' life.

WERNER: Couldn't we see it as a reaction to being overchallenged, related to the present generation seeing and hearing so much through electronic media that it raises the sensation threshold?

SLOTERDIJK: I'm very sensitive to any discussion about being overchallenged, because the term has become a universal excuse for people, and actually misses the point. The idea nowadays is that people shouldn't be spurred on any more; instead, they should be reassured they shouldn't feel guilty for not being the way they are supposed to be. But in fact people need challenges, they can't stand being unchallenged any longer, and they rebel against being expected to reduce their existence to a state of stupidity and lack of achievement. Basically the whole society, with very few exceptions, is in a kind of psychological strike against the world. We don't want to use our intelligence. Even our brains carry the message: work to rule. That is the real disaster of this period, the 1990s.

WERNER: Can electronic media help people to stop this strike or do they hamper this?

SLOTERDIJK: The electronic media are actually very counterproductive. They foster the cool, half-moronic, smiling person who is on strike. But that is not their ultimate definition. They are not defined by their use. I don't know what is in the technological nature of television that condemns it to broadcast programmes of the quality it does. If we gave humans another hundred years, I think we would reach a new state of balance between our personal media and electronic media. The latter are obviously profoundly necessary for evolution. They synchronize people in large political spaces. We have been able to observe this principle at work since the beginning of the written word, which should be interpreted as a form of rational telepathy. If an imperial decree was written in Rome and a courier took it out of the palace, it was intended to be decipherable in Carthage and capable of being translated into some kind of action or ideas. This rational telepathy organized communication of power in large areas. The social synthesis through writing is, of course, preceded by another synthesis, namely that arising through imperial power, military power. And if we pursue this and place the need for synthesis at the basis of modern society, then we also understand why the media are like they are.

WERNER: If the media develop as we are told, in a few years we will have more than a hundred TV channels. In other words, instead of global synthesizing, people will be completely separated from each other. Does that mean nobody will look at what anybody else has watched, and each person will only be aware of his or her own programme?

SLOTERDIJK: I think all these scenarios are wrong. Even with multiple channels, an interesting niche will emerge here and there. We shouldn't worry too much about how this is developing. It is more likely that society will revert to the experience of de-spiritualization in an even harsher form than is already the case. But the tendency towards the electronic kiosk will also open up a field of additional gadgets. This is where the big opportunity lies. Many people in our culture have nothing to do any longer; there is high unemployment, even more inside people themselves than in the outside world, and this creates an immense need for micro-dramas.

WERNER: What would a society look like in which basic forms of sensitivity, openness and the right kind of independence could be strengthened? And what role would electronic media play in this?

SLOTERDIJK: I think electronic media will simply replace schools. I have high hopes of this.

WERNER: But wouldn't that be alienation from personal encounters again?

SLOTERDIJK: Yes, but it would be alienation from personal teaching that is already alienated anyway. For today's generation, their teachers' outlook is an initiation into stupidity as a normal state. The average teacher represents the result of an education process that fosters parroting. Those thirteen years of classes are such an obscene spectacle that it's actually a miracle anybody gets through that kind of teaching by example. It would be a good thing if everything in school teaching that relies on spreading the word, on the syllabus and on academic subjects, were to disappear. All of that is a major assault on human intelligence. The electronic media are an excellent barrier against that. In ten years all subjects could be computerized in a fantastic, lively, entertaining way. Teachers will not be able to keep up. The coolness system is also related to the institutionalization of stupidity through state schools. The children sit around in those compulsory classes becoming increasingly defeatist, increasingly defeated and increasingly listless. Of course, as a new father, I must worry about things that never bothered me before. I'm already horrified at the thought of teachers I know. If I imagined having to hand my child over to people like that for five hours a day I would become a crazed killer – or somebody who wants to change the world for the better. And as long as my relationship to violence remains as tenuous as it is now I will probably opt for the ludicrous task of improving the world.

WERNER: What has to happen for modern people to rediscover themselves as a medium?

SLOTERDIJK: Cultural criticism always attacks the mass media. I don't think that makes sense. We should look more closely at the work of deformation that starts deeper down, especially because it involves so much demoralization. Something gets destroyed there that should not be destroyed under any circumstances – the awareness that knowledge is born out of euphoria and that intelligence is a relationship of the happy consciousness with itself. And that intelligence partly consists in the ability to find our own ways of overcoming the boredom that develops in an under-used brain. Across society as a whole, the most disturbing symptom is that people are no longer ambitious enough to plumb the limits of understanding within themselves. Intelligence is the last utopian potential. The only *terra incognita* humankind still owns are the galaxies of the brain, the Milky Ways of intelligence. And there is hardly any convincing space travel in them. Incidentally, this internal astronautics is the only alternative to a consumerist perspective. It is the only thing that could explain to people in the future that their intelligence space is so immense that they can experiment with themselves for millennia without becoming exhausted. The really good news is that there is something breathtakingly great that is called intelligence and is uncharted. Who is willing to volunteer? The volunteers of intelligence are *eo ipso* its media.

3

# WORLD ESTRANGEMENT AND DIAGNOSIS OF OUR TIMES

*Interview with Andreas Geyer**

GEYER: Professor Sloterdijk, looking at your publications, for some time now two opposite extremes have been discernible. On the one hand, there is your intense focus on Gnosis or mysticism. Three years ago you compiled a practical reader with commentaries on Gnosis. Last year you published a comprehensive book with the title *Weltfremdheit* [World Estrangement], in which you attempt to redevelop forgotten Gnostic themes. Yet we can hardly assume you have become an unworldly mystic. In fact, we could say you seem to be trying harder than ever to keep your finger on the pulse of the time. In the past year alone you have published three volumes of essays in which you take positions on concrete political and social questions. This polarity, of introspection on the one hand and contemporary diagnosis on the other – is it coincidental, or is there something behind it, perhaps even a major new theme of your philosophy?

SLOTERDIJK: To begin with, I agree with how you describe the alternating movement of my work in recent years, a rhythmic alternation in which an introversion is followed by an extroversion and an extroversion by an introversion. The internal structure of the book about world estrangement contains something of this alternation and reflects on it.

It is the slumbering, or forgotten, topic of European philosophy, which is, of course, essentially a philosophy of verification

* This interview between Peter Sloterdijk and Andreas Geyer was originally broadcast on Bayerischer Rundfunk (Bavarian Radio) on 2 December 1994.

Andreas Geyer heads the Medical Affairs section at Bayerischer Rundfunk in Munich.

or philosophy of situations, with no understanding of events and rhythms. The fact that humans are beings in the process of coming into the world and departing from it, that humans are beings who awaken and whose attention breaks down, creatures able to withstand stress but only up to a certain limit: these topics are largely overlooked in philosophy in favour of visions of structure.

I think the kind of philosophy that has a certain anthropological realism in proposing a new language for mankind has no choice but to address this elementary rhythm in which humans are described as really coming-into-the-world and departing-from-the-world. Indeed, this holds not only for the greatest metaphysical pulsation, for expressions of birth and death, but also for the micro-rhythm that characterizes every single hour of every day. In this respect I would say it is merely a continuation of a feature that philosophy has generally exhibited since the nineteenth century, namely getting down off the high horse of absolute reflection and orienting towards the low ground of precise self-observation and merging of logical motifs with anthropological motifs. The place where the intersection of these currents occurs is where, for me, the wave movement develops with a certain inevitability: once outward, once inward, once with one's back to the world, monologues of the soul, attempts to turn off the world's main switch. It is an old saying that the last one out turns off the light. The same applies to thinking: the last one turns off the light of existence. And what remains after turning off the light is a voice, a world remainder that is still capable of self-examination – while it is true, of course, that there will never be a self that does not contain deposits of world remainders.

GEYER: You have written that your latest book, *Weltfremdheit* [World Estrangement], is 'a phenomenology of the worldless intellect, or the intellect turned away from the world'. Could we start by clarifying what you understand by the term 'world estrangement' in this context?

SLOTERDIJK: 'Weltfremdheit' [World estrangement] is one of those marvellous words that make the German language appear to be philosophizing of its own accord. My ambition – rather like that of Ernst Bloch in relation to the word 'utopia' – was to skim off the negative element of this formulation and take the expression seriously for long enough for it to be finally accepted as a positive term, actually as a basic concept of philosophy. 'World' is not something we live in with no alternative; rather, 'world' designates that which we continually turn towards, under the precondition that we have turned away from it previously.

In other words, this involves a rhythmological world concept: 'world' is everything that rises and that falls, and in between are phases of balance and the present and duration. But these phases are all momentary and, of course, the original moment of abstraction of classical philosophy – or of any theory at all – consists in it attempting to create durable propositions and durable discourses. This means that in a particular way it starts off by missing the elementary truth about humans as beings that are sometimes here and sometimes not – and mostly not. Theory is also a form of world estrangement, namely, it is the sleep of reason that believes it is always here. Philosophy and ascesis were two closely related quantities, and philosophy has always been a sort of discipline of permanent wakefulness. Like ancient asceticism, it toyed with the illusion that there was a possibility of imitating God, insofar as this is a God that is ever-wakeful, never sleeping, all-knowing, all-accompanying, a God facing every event. I think it is entirely necessary for philosophy, and for people in general, to develop a language and to propose a form of theory which would make it clear that humans are beings standing by and large with their back to reality. Turning towards reality is the exception, and turning away from everything that is a part of that reality is the rule. That is why I am now using the term 'world estrangement' with the assumption it is a basic concept.

GEYER: In other words, you mean that until now in Western philosophy it is exclusively the world-oriented mind that has been socially acceptable, and this has resulted in an important component of the human mind getting lost – or at least, being barely acknowledged.

SLOTERDIJK: Mind has always been world spirit in a way. This is not just a terminological speciality of Hegel's – he merely uses it to define the latent trend of all theories of mind. The mind has always been world-oriented and has always been the light spread over things of the world. Knowledge has always been a knowledge of the positive. But it is a non-wakeful knowledge. That is my point. Knowledge and consciousness or, more precisely, knowledge and wakefulness, are two different quantities, and European philosophy was passionate about confusing them. This leads to philosophy being increasingly incompetent in some way to deal with questions of wakefulness and, incidentally, also questions of topicality. A philosopher who touches on topicality is still regarded very much as an unserious member of the discipline. It is a late consequence of the preliminary decision made in very early times that privileged the unambiguous correlation of knowledge and world. But the fact there is a waking that has no world as yet, and that consequently only 'eavesdrops' on the world, a waking that somehow derives from the night the idea of the morning – to describe things with metaphors that meant a lot to Martin Heidegger – those are circumstances that we can see much better by looking at them from this kind of rhythmic viewpoint, and that we can also convey much better in language after having decided on the positive concept of world estrangement.

GEYER: The point of your argument is that the mind turned away from the world as an essential component of human beings has not simply vanished, but is forging ahead today on new paths. Which paths?

SLOTERDIJK: To start with, we should mention the classical paths to what I would call an officially created world estrangement, or turning away from the world. After all, we live in a culture, in a cultural moment, when we can look back on 3,000 years – perhaps even 4,000 years in India – of organized escape or distance from the world. We shouldn't forget that, until quite recently, intellectual history was essentially the narrative of life forms and thinking of people who lived in retreat. It is a relatively novel idea that intellectual history should be the history of a mind oriented towards the world. What we call intellect – and that is why most people turn up their noses when such things are mentioned – is located on a terrain where we are usually confronted with world escapism, ascesis, retreat to the wilderness, and with monasteries, monastic forms of life, etc. …

GEYER: But surely those were also the classical paths, weren't they?

SLOTERDIJK: Those were the main routes, the paths created by an official and noble – this is very important – a noble escape from the world. The world is everything, in a way, that encourages humans to turn their back on it. This has been concealed up to now in the traditions of our mental philosophy. One could get the impression that the deconstruction, or the dismantling, of the great systems of mental philosophy has brought human beings into a more wretched situation than ever before, because they were forcibly incorporated with no alternative into a world that was always presented as positive. We must object to that from the modernist position too: humans remain estranged from the world or turned away from the world to a large extent – even at a time when people no longer interpret themselves as intellectual beings and where the opposition of world children and intellectual humans seems to have ultimately collapsed. Today, even intellectual persons sign a certificate attesting their reality fitness. We have run out of ontological excuses for world escape in the classical sense. We cannot retreat to God during our lives like the saints in the wilderness in Syria in the third and fourth centuries. Some rather vain poets and writers, in particular, put themselves up on pillars; usually they place their pillars in densely populated areas, as Bertolt Brecht once joked in relation to Stefan George.

GEYER: But where are these 'pillars' today? Where do they stand?

SLOTERDIJK: Everybody has his or her private pillar in the bedroom. Now, this may not be a lofty philosophical topic, but the human being as the sleeper is the unknown quantity per se in the history of thought. Not that there hasn't been a great deal of meaningful and valuable empirical research on sleep in recent years – but that is a matter for psychologists. Philosophy itself seldom crosses the threshold to this perception of the human constitution. Philosophers do not want to know that they sleep. At most, philosophers admit that they know that they do not know. But they hardly admit that they are only rarely awake. They don't realize that, because they usually express themselves, speak and think when they are here. But they seldom think at twilight. And this temporal shift of the philosophical moment: not thinking at noon, not thinking in the harsh light of the morning, but at twilight, very early in the morning or very early in the evening, this gives rise to other tones and other perceptions. Nowadays, a kind of Janus position is possible: we can look forward and backward at the same time and know that we are a disappearing person or an arriving person, depending on the direction. If we think on entering or leaving, if we think at those moments and not in the overcrowded middle, and not on this positivist bright day, then we have the view on either side and know that thinking is also a coming and a going. This makes twilight the authentic time of day for a philosophy that has got wise to itself or can look over its own shoulder.

GEYER: We can also artificially induce this sleeping state by using drugs. What can be said about drugs in this context?

SLOTERDIJK: A chapter is devoted to this question in the book *Weltfremdheit* that you mentioned earlier. I answer the question why humans, from the earliest times of cultures that we know, have been drug users, even if under quite different terms. The term 'drug' is a pharmacist's term and a police term …

GEYER: A term we associate today with addiction!

SLOTERDIJK: A term linked to addiction, and the associations seem to hold. They are associations for a phenomenon that first arose in relation to this description. I think the so-called drugs didn't make people addicted in the past – because they were not drugs, but psychedelic, psychotropic substances, we could almost say 'theotropic' substances. In other words, they opened the door to the Sacred, the door to the gods, chemicals that …

GEYER: Were used as part of rituals …

SLOTERDIJK: Bound up with rituals, rooted in a cult, in which the plant and the god and the person were mutually correlated in a holy triad. The more elaborate the use of drugs in a ritual culture, the more impossible it is to abuse them in the sense of private intoxication. People who took drugs in ancient times did it to give their lives existential and metaphysical input, as some people still do nowadays, whereas today's drug addicts are people who have fallen into the hands of a dealer who exploits their weakness. They no longer have a metaphysical informer, but a thoroughly empirical trader instead.

GEYER: Does this mean modern drug consumers have nothing more in common with the mystic?

SLOTERDIJK: Well, they still do in a certain way, because everything perverted has something in common with things that are the right way round. I think modern drug addicts are also in search of God to some extent, or in search of fulfilment, to put it more cautiously. Drug addicts also have ideas – we don't know where they come from, but they have these ideas – of what would satisfy them, what would lighten the load of their existence, and particularly what would release them from their hatred of the situation their existence condemns them to. And to the extent they are absolute seekers, that is, people with a manic drive or a manic desire, we might say they probably do have something in common with traditional seekers of God. I think it wouldn't be totally wrong to say that successful drug therapy occurs mainly where people are not sobered up or dried out in a trivial way and sentenced to a dry reality, but where they can be offered alternative feelings of being high, where they are shown a different kind of vitality and different stimulation, and the ecstasies of withdrawal successfully outweigh the ecstasies of addiction. If that works, then such therapies will work as well. If not, it is difficult to break the vicious circle of repetition compulsion in addiction.

GEYER: I was surprised that in your progress through the different forms of flight from the world and quest for God there is one mass phenomenon you did not mention at all. I am thinking of the 'esoteric wave' that has been around for some time now. It has lasted too long to be just a passing phenomenon …

SLOTERDIJK: You are right. But I must say I do touch on it – indirectly. The tone and choice of subject in my book are at a certain level. It may be arrogant or not, but I overfly the stomping grounds of vulgar esoteric people. That is absolutely right. Anyway, I never wanted – how shall I phrase it? – to produce an encyclopedia of flight from the world and forms of world escape. I was more interested in the classical forms of flight from the world. I thought that if I could include a good chapter on Indian spirituality in the book, and if I could find a place for a good chapter on the Freudian theory of the death drive and, above all, if I could give a reasonably adequate account of Platonism and the Socratic art of dying in the book, then I would have dealt in advance, in exemplary form, with everything esotericism talks about, usually as vulgar rehashing. Most of esotericism is nothing but bad philosophy. It is usually an overgrowth of late Platonism that has slunk back into modern publications on a digression via Islam, on a detour via Greek Orthodox and Russian Orthodox religiosity and on the path via theosophy. Let's consider the *corpus hermeticum*, the much-quoted construct that speaks of Hermes Trismegistos, with its legends and sagas. You just have to glance at the texts to see it is degraded stuff from trivial Platonism that simply can't be compared with the magnificent constructs of Christian Gnostics or the theology of Origenes, not to mention Plotin. If you know the originals, the highest forms, this spoils you for the type of esotericism sold in bookshops, because the authors of those works are all merely propounding degraded forms of Platonic monotheism, sometimes mixed with Indian-polytheist religiosity.

GEYER: I would go even further in my verdict on 'esotericism'. It is true that it attracts the most absurd combinations of astrology, tarot cards, the study of German runes, etc., and usually with a bit of pop psychology as well. But what always makes me wonder, is: how can so many people fall so easily for the most bizarre rituals on the modern esoteric market, but when it comes to the rituals of the Catholic Church the same people suddenly come to their senses and find them absolutely ridiculous? How does that fit together?

SLOTERDIJK: That's because Christianity is not a religion of being able to let yourself go. This is the whole problem! The only Christians who can let go are the enthusiastic theologians themselves, the very small number of inspired priests and pastors who experience similar medial ecstasies in the pulpit to the esoteric types. But this is a very, very small minority. Christianity is a religion of dryness. As I describe in a passage in my book, it is based on a sacrament of withdrawal. In fact, the Eucharistic Communion wafers are not psychedelic substances, and do not have – or, if they ever did, no longer have – the power to cause a reaction like rapture in those who eat them. The sacrament of withdrawal basically aims to make a sober person out of the Christian, a person who shoulders the cross of reality and postpones the ecstasy problem for later, as a post-mortal matter. That is the big difference between esoteric people and mainstream Christians.

In the United States, incidentally, there are a whole lot of

Protestant sub-sects of Christianity that would not fit the description you just gave. They are even more esoteric than esoteric people here in Germany, in one respect particularly: they communicate much more to people, attribute more medium-type powers to them and address them even more clearly as possessed by the Holy Spirit. That is what the whole of esotericism ultimately leads to. People want to be possessed again, and they claim something like a natural right to being possessed, or obsession. They don't tolerate the despiritualizing effect of enlightened, scholarly education forever. This explains the mass exodus to the various branches of esotericism. People reach for the first best obsession. They are far from choosy in this respect.

GEYER: It's a fast-food obsession, of course! Yet it can't really be an alternative in the long run.

SLOTERDIJK: You're right, it's a fast-food obsession. But in the first place it's not about quality but about the basic experience of being swept away by something or other. People who are not fired by enthusiasm can't bear themselves for long, and only a very few people achieve the self-admiration that appears in philosophy as a borderline possibility. Consequently, people have to buy cheap enthusiasm off the rack. By now these racks are the crammed shelves in any random bookshop, even in the smallest towns in Germany. I don't know if you have ever been to the United States and had the opportunity to look at the bookstores over there. The situation there is much more extreme. There are big bookstores in which nothing is sold except that type of literature and you get the impression that those are the most prosperous ones. The conclusion I draw is that people are no longer prepared to put up with being disenchanted by the reality definition of mainstream culture. There are a very large number of 'pirate routes' into the new obsessiveness, and people practically claim a birthright to being overpowered by something they hope will be stronger at wrestling the devil than they are themselves.

GEYER: Sometimes I suspect that the tendency towards turning away from the world as you define it occurs where we least expect it, namely in modern theoretical physics. If extrapolated, these new cosmological attempts at explanation certainly have mystical and mythical qualities ...

SLOTERDIJK: I prefer the term 'mythical' here ...

GEYER: But I think 'mystical' also applies!

SLOTERDIJK: You are right that natural scientists also infer a sort of mystical dimension as a marginal value. Why? – Because their investigations lead into an area where the possibility of giving positive answers comes to a complete halt. This is the operation that the mystics of monotheist religions utilized to focus on the abyss. We know about that from positive theology, which attempted to focus thinking on God by means of the *via eminentiae*, the way of eminence: think of the biggest thing you can imagine and then think of something even bigger. Conceive God as that which transcends your power of explanation. By analogy, physicists who seek the most powerful explanation for the world and then say, 'That's not enough, either', are doing the same thing. Basically, the sheer madness of reasoning has brought you to dissolution, and that is the procedure of mystical thought. As long as it is not an emotional mysticism but a logical mysticism, you arrive in the abyss by way of a pathos of reasoning that has reached a conclusion. We can study that in the case of Meister Eckhart, we can already see it for Plotin, and for Dionysius Areopagita – in fact, for everybody for whom mysticism was not about intoxication and feelings, but a question of taking matters to their logical conclusion. These people exhibit phenomena comparable to the limiting states in natural science in which thought tapers off.

You are absolutely right. This is a neo-mystical trend, even in the strictest form of theory. We should add, however, that the people who propound these theories today are not the strictest characters – they tend to be crossover types. Outstanding physicists are nearly always people who can't bear working in an office. They share this trait with other eccentrics, not least certain kinds of philosophers. Incidentally, the well-known modern philosophers happily put up with working in offices – that's exactly what they can be reproached for. In negotiations for job appointments they talk mostly about their office and hardly say anything about their mission.

GEYER: Well, you certainly take swipes at established philosophy. For instance, you have written, 'Anybody who wants to learn to talk over people's heads in a complex way can't do better than become a player in the contemporary philosophy business.' What do you think is going wrong? What must philosophy do to reach people again?

SLOTERDIJK: Let's take modern medical recruitment as an example. We have a grading system that results in Grade A students and children from families that aspire to high living standards being favoured for the healing professions because they can expect special advantages. Unsuitable people are being systematically selected on the wrong basis. I think every discipline today in the whole spectrum of sciences is going similarly in the wrong direction. It would be a miracle if philosophy were an exception to this. Of course, academic philosophy is hugely misdirected because the academy as it exists today no longer has any academic spirit but a spirit of competition for qualifications. We're talking about big contests for avoiding mistakes. It creates neurotic-compulsive careers, and people who get through that only remain philosophers in exceptional cases. Philosophy is dying as a result of its academic representatives, just as religion – hasn't yet died, I would say, but has wasted away because of its theologians. We are entitled to claim this rather broad generalization if we are prepared to accept the exceptions. And God knows, in this century there has been a whole series of splendid exceptions – particularly in German philosophy – that still confirm the rule. Heidegger was also an important figure as a university teacher. After the war there were lively figures who breathed new life into the subject. Thank God that happens over and again. In fact, it would be dishonest to scold philosophy in general if we were not prepared to begin with the exceptions. But it's your fault, you started me off on this topic! Personally I only make such comments in brackets and as asides. I'm not a polemical author at all. My kind of polemics is indirect.

GEYER: Well then, let's drop this tiresome topic. It seems to me you essentially want to achieve two kinds of synthesis – in your latest book and, I think, in your thought as a whole. In the first stage you tried to reunite widely different faculties such as philosophy, religion, mysticism and psychoanalysis. In the second stage you also crossed cultural borders and tried, for example, to integrate Eastern mysticism and philosophy into your thought. Are you ultimately interested in showing that this Eastern way of looking at the world and people, which is usually more mystical, is not only compatible with the Western way, but possibly even complementary to it?

SLOTERDIJK: My idea is rather different, namely, that the people on earth who now discover they belong to the same species all share a common difficulty. They are gradually working out the 'disadvantage of being born' at this point of the planet in different ways and means. Carrying the weight of the world is an art that can be practised in many different ways. I think it is right to say that it is fundamentally the same art. It consists of answers to the burdensome nature of life …

GEYER: But you are trying to translate these answers into the same language, to synchronize them …

SLOTERDIJK: Not into the same language. All I'm saying is that there is an ecumene, a concentrated area of high culture in relation to problems, but not an ecumene of answers. It's not so much that the big differences between people are national and cultural; it's rather that they are very, very deeply idiosyncratic. You have to be more of a novelist than a cultural morphologist to discover these differences. An idiot has different strategies for mastering life than the cleverest person in the same culture. I'm convinced we should look for the great gap that yawns between people on the level of individual strategies.

One thing is true, however: in every human culture there are people who have an easy life and people who have a hard life. And in every culture those who have an easy life and those who have a hard life have to create a lowest common denominator. The person with the easiest life lives in a group and the person with the hardest life lives in a group and they have to meet somewhere in a shared symbolic continuum. The moment that happens is the moment when something that we call culture today starts to emerge: a totality is created that is self-centred and potentially independent from the outside world, a pandemonium of life arts and life forms. The Indians developed such an incredibly rich culture that they spelled out nearly everything humans could be in their own forms. That would be true even if they had not been flanked in the East by the Chinese, to whom exactly the same statement applies, and in the West by the Europeans, to whom the same also applies to the very highest degree. The pandemonic character of culture actually relies on the fact that cultures are precisely these continua: that the hardest life and the easiest life contribute to the symbolic system of their respective cultures, and that we find a common symbolic shell for the easiest and for the most difficult life, for the most casual frivolity and for the deepest passion. People can live in this shell; these are the famous 'houses of Being' that Heidegger spoke of, unfortunately in the singular, not the plural – houses of Being that are the containers in which people make their own sense of the enormous size and expanse of the world.

GEYER: Your book on world estrangement ends with something I would almost call pathos, a conciliatory pathos unusual for philosophy today. You write: 'The duty to be happy applies more than ever in times like ours. The true realism of the species consists in not expecting less than is demanded of its intelligence.'

In other words, you have obviously not lost your faith in human beings. We could even get the impression that you have become more optimistic since the *Critique of Cynical Reason* …

# 4

# UTERUS ON WHEELS

## *Interview with Walter Saller from* Der Spiegel*

SPIEGEL: Why is modern man so obsessed with cars?

SLOTERDIJK: It is an obsessive relationship. The person and the vehicle form a unity in which the vehicle can assume the role of the better ego. It is the faster and more kinetically powerful self that imagines itself in the automobile. I see the unity of person and vehicle as already prefigured in Plato. In general, in every culture that invented the wheel, the wagon and riding, and developed the centaur motif, man with his small strength rides on a bigger animal energy, transformed into a hybrid creature with a human front and the lower body of a horse.

SPIEGEL: Do you mean that traffic planners who only see the car in terms of transportation haven't understood its real nature?

SLOTERDIJK: Any theory that characterizes cars as a means of transport leaves out a whole dimension: the car is a means both of intoxication and regression. It is a uterus on wheels that has the advantage over its biological model of being linked to independent movement and a feeling of autonomy. And this goes even further: a car is a Platonic cave built around the individual driver, but we don't sit welded into it. Instead, this private travelling cave offers us the view of a world passing by. The car also has phallic and anal components – the primitive-aggressive competitive behaviour, and the revving up and overtaking which turns the other, slower person, into an expelled turd, almost like in defecation.

* This interview between Peter Sloterdijk and Walter Saller appeared under the title 'Rollender Uterus', in *Der Spiegel* magazine 8 (1995): 130.
Walter Saller is a German journalist.

SPIEGEL: Does that make the catalyser the nappy of anal pleasure?

SLOTERDIJK: The catalyser represents a form of hygiene education of the automobile self. Civilized people suddenly erupt with all kinds of sinister things when they are sitting at the wheel. In fact, in the car people pass through stages of gradual regression of the adult ego going right back to the intra-uterine mollusc. And at every level of psychological development the car reproduces tensions and aggressions in the process of individuation.

SPIEGEL: To put it more simply: why are so many people aggressive behind the wheel?

SLOTERDIJK: In traffic, regressed egos that often feel attracted by 'king of the road' myths and childish projections of royal power clash with each other. Weak people in particular tend to act out such myths aggressively and use the car to express themselves.

SPIEGEL: In other words, the myth of the car must be shattered. How can this be done?

SLOTERDIJK: I don't see any chance at the moment. We have been conducting an ecological debate for the past twenty years, and the car is still here in all its glory. Its aesthetic and technological development has been explosive. This suggests that cars are connected with a kind of archetypal violence that is completely immune to enlightenment.

SPIEGEL: And where is the enlightenment-resistant car heading for?

SLOTERDIJK: It is on the ride to nowhere, on the ride to the ride. In a sense cars are circus vehicles, vehicles of futility – but an enthusiastic kind of futility. We enjoy the ride as a ride and this overrides the issue of destinations. Car driving is a religion. Modernism as a whole resembles an arena, a self-contained circuit. That's why Formula One races are so important. They are the modern proof of what St Paul the Apostle wrote: the godless go round in circles. The circular rides in the circus contradict the elementary hope, the key theme of the modern age: the primacy of the journey out, opening up new spheres. If technology is the perfect control of sequences of movement, this leaves us with only one progressive function: braking.

# 5

# FIRE YOUR SHRINK!

## *Interview with Martin Frischknecht**

FRISCHKNECHT: 'Fire your shrink; hire a philosopher' is the latest trend in the United States, where more and more people looking for cures seem to be dropping out of psychotherapy and turning to philosophy. Therapy is generally defined as a healing art, whereas philosophy is seen as love of wisdom. Why should philosophers suddenly be able to heal?

SLOTERDIJK: Philosophers can't heal anything, not even themselves. They aren't competent to heal, unless the ability to heal is somehow equivalent to the claim to heal. A suspicion has haunted all therapy systems for a long time now: that the most important thing about any method is a therapist who believes in him- or herself and his or her method. In other words, that people can be convincingly tricked into health. Many people get healthy or describe themselves as healthy simply because they would be ashamed to upset a persuasive therapist like theirs by not getting better. The therapist appears before the client and commands the illnesses to leave the body. They should turn round and go, and in general they do just that.

FRISCHKNECHT: How does the philosopher react to these demands?

SLOTERDIJK: No differently. He or she falls in line with a tradition that began with Mesmer's magnetic healing 200 years ago, and has been continually revived since then without people knowing

* This interview between Peter Sloterdijk and Martin Frischknecht was originally published under the title 'Interview mit dem Philosophen Peter Sloterdijk', in *Spuren – Magazin für Neues Bewußtsein* 45 (1997).

Martin Frischknecht is the publisher of the magazine *Spuren – Das Leben neu entdecken*, Winterthur (Switzerland).

how the therapeutic success actually works. If philosophers start being active in this field as well now, it is merely one brief incident in the long history of the riddle of why a particular kind of closeness in encounters between people benefits the person on the receiving end. For 200 years there has been a very diverse history of experimenting with such relationships of closeness – organized encounters with people who listen to each other, lay hands, hug each other, cry their eyes out, etc. These are arrangements that inherently release a specific therapeutic potential and we don't really know who to attribute this to.

It doesn't matter, for however this arrangement is set up it evidently works – unless the so-called helpers are obviously vampires or sadists who can only get what they want by leading people in that direction. But if a halfway clear standard for the code of encounters in such fields of intimacy is observed, we almost always see some kind of therapeutic productivity.

FRISCHKNECHT: In that case, everything else would be superstructure. It doesn't really matter whether the healing person involved is oriented to Rogers, Jung or Heidegger.

SLOTERDIJK: The important thing is for people to enter a kind of healing retreat together, to create a little conspiracy, to get together as two persons who say, 'As long as our relationship lasts, we are the craziest people ever. We are living as conspirators for a time, extra-territorials in relation to the rest of the world, in the land of "us", and we're regenerating ourselves there. That's all.' And it works. People are animals that need a complementary other. They can't survive in the way they are supposed to be according to the modern world's basic individualist ideology. People can't really become what individualist ideology demands of them. There is no such thing as autonomy, and it is even doubtful whether adulthood in the true sense of the word really exists. There is no genuine independence and, even if there were, it wouldn't be desirable. People are always twins but they usually do not know the other complementary individual, yet during their lives they fill the role or place of the other in various guises, and they are happier and healthier if they cast the role right. In allocating the twin role, the role of the essential inner other, they decide what they are going to become. Constant miscasting at this point, constantly under-filling this position, leads to human atrophy. You can give the role to a dachshund, of course, or even a whisky bottle; you can fill this position with almost anything, from a lifeless object to the God of St Augustine. Depending on whom you choose as your counterpart, your own self forms in resonance with it. I see this resonance between an individual and his or her twin, or double, as a fundamental secret of psychology. The way this resonance occurs determines whether the person's existence is a success or a failure. This account seems to me a good way to reconstruct the whole field of therapy. The therapist is an optional casting choice for the vacant twin position. If he or she does it well, if he or she behaves adequately like a good twin for a while, and is sufficiently discreet and encouraging, the subject of the therapy will flourish.

FRISCHKNECHT: You recently advocated tackling the so-called sect question again and discussing the topic under different auspices. At the moment there is scaremongering about how easy it is to seduce the masses, and about the coming millennium. What perspectives do you think are missing from that?

SLOTERDIJK: The most important thing people forget is that all good human groups are sects. Regrettably, the term 'sect' currently has a bad reputation. This is related to the fact that we don't have any ideological opponents at the moment. Our society can't hunt down socialists, communists and anarchists any more. All those groups have either become well-behaved or silent. Who is left to hunt down? Only terrorists and sect members, that is, people who throw physical or mental bombs.

The discussion as it runs today says more about the whole ideological field than about individual groups. Of course there are quite disgusting groupings whose members one has to feel sorry for from any angle. But focusing on those groups hardly helps to explain the problem of sects for society as a whole.

Some organizations are certainly criminal and show nasty tendencies to psychological slavery. But that doesn't alter the fact that whenever people get together, whenever they form an association or, let's say, if they form a couple, they do things other people don't like. First, because they don't invite us to join them and, second, because outsiders imagine that it's hot and exciting inside those groups and people outside are missing something. We get the feeling that sect members indulge in a life in the psychological tropics while we decent folk living on the edges of the Alps are resigned to permafrost with short summers. This represents a provocation that leads to constant trouble. Moreover, sect leaders give their followers such brazen answers to the question of meaning that non-members of the sect can't even laugh about it.

I interpret sects as substitute forms of the extended family. As such, first and foremost they have very good functions of the kind church congregations have always had. And because sects are psychological incubators they run the risk of overheating. If that happens, they are no longer beneficial to their members but make them dependent on the benefits.

Such dependence falls under a wider definition of drugs. The typical sect leader behaves like a dealer – he takes more from people than he gives them. Incidentally, that is also the definition of an average businessman, and actually of anybody who thinks in terms of capital, for whom taking more than they give is self-evident. Particularly in psychic exploitation this rule is immediately clear in an ugly way.

FRISCHKNECHT: I am trying to avoid the word 'sect', if possible, because it is generally used in a derogatory fashion. The term covers a wide variety of groups, from Seventh Day Adventists to Hare Krishna disciples and drinking clubs. They are all lumped together and ostracized by methods that increasingly resemble inquisitions. You have spoken of latent totalitarianism in this context.

SLOTERDIJK: I use the term 'sect' to mean the relationship of an inclusive majority towards an exclusive minority, which is what a sect is. Our society is trying, at least at points where liberal thinking occurs, to move from totalitarian inclusiveness to a pluralism of exclusive groups. That is, society is dissolving into a patchwork of exclusive minorities that are not easy to enter.

I am talking of groups that are formed on the basis of specific characteristics and shut themselves off from the outside world. In many respects religious groups act similarly. Mostly they settle into a victim cliché, and they end up fairly often as something approaching a structure of self-sacrifice, clearly because they realize the best way to get a voice in society today is as a group of victims and targets of discrimination.

FRISCHKNECHT: We can see how groups suddenly start gaining members just because they are despised and persecuted.

SLOTERDIJK: The Scientologists are a particularly good example. They pursue a totally schizophrenic programme. On the one hand, Scientology is a religion of winners, while, on the other, Scientologists are also persecuted, and to some extent defeated winners. The American leaders of this sect (note they are American) realized that their biggest social success lay in being obstructed, discriminated against and misunderstood. This combination is the *non plus ultra*: a religion that is utterly shameless and rejects any kind of solidarity, in which people have recognized that the status of loser is actually more profitable.

FRISCHKNECHT: In fact, the first Christians had great success with that particular mixture.

SLOTERDIJK: That was a different constellation. The first Christians triumphed over the competing systems of religion because they founded an authentic form of building congregations and a culture of friendship unprecedented in antiquity. Early Christian theology was partly the attempt to combine the experiences of people at that time into a common language. This brought a current of basic democracy into the story that has still not totally disappeared today. You could almost say that the Europeans have Greek urban culture to thank for pretty much everything, as do the Christian sects that later became the official Church. That is the European mix: Greek urban culture plus good Christian sectarianism. By that I mean communication forms used by people who found a new reason to talk to each other because they belonged to the same system of religious delusion – and that is actually a good kind of delusion. The system of Christian delusion made them humanly and morally superior to the manic system and increasingly naked nihilism of the Romans, who had manoeuvred themselves into an ideological tunnel with their barbaric games and entertainments, and couldn't get out again.

FRISCHKNECHT: But where does such a strong reaction come from? Why does a society feel so deeply challenged by a few groups?

SLOTERDIJK: It comes from the fact that the Europeans established a culture built on the distinction between civil society and religious congregation. In principle this means our states are religiously neutral. Since the end of the Thirty Years War, Europe has moved a step further from each generation to the next. Religion was increasingly forced out of the state sector and consigned to the private sector. It was the opposite in earlier times, when the state was religious and citizens had to seek their freedoms elsewhere. Today the state is liberal and reacts hysterically towards a society that is more religious at certain points than it would like. Part of this hysteria is dealt with under the heading of 'fundamentalism'.

FRISCHKNECHT: It just takes a few Muslim girls to wear headscarves in school to plunge Europe into a debate about the basic values of its society. And alongside this is a semi-private area where people are subjected to inquisitorial examination about their membership of a religious group to determine, for instance, if they are suitable for public office.

SLOTERDIJK: This is the point where the state realizes it can no longer blindly depend on its members' loyalty as it could in a homogeneous, neutral mass culture where religion was restricted to a private issue. Today we can no longer rely on society not becoming a battlefield of religious partisan fighting. Some religious groupings are suspected of latent hegemonic ambitions, and are believed to be subversive. But this has been a basic element of European paranoia for a couple of hundred years: that there could be people among us of different faith, who watch us and pay lip service to things that sound just like what we believe in. In fact, such people are following the orders of the Pope, an Indian guru or American mafia bosses. They have secretly conspired with a gang leader for souls and have entered a pact with the devil, which means that although those people are still here, they are already somewhere else. It is such images of fear that give society a glimpse of its own disintegration.

FRISCHKNECHT: You allot sects an important role in the lives of many people as incubators and boilers. What happens to people who get caught in those containers? What decides whether somebody passes through a sect phase or becomes imprisoned by it?

SLOTERDIJK: It depends on the membership rules. If sects are primarily what they have every right to be in our times, that is, helpers for psychological transition, places where people can do emotional and spiritual apprenticeships, then they are very beneficial institutions. That is because we are increasingly heading towards a form of society in which becoming an adult is portrayed as a difficult process. Looking at the clock or a birth certificate tells us little about when a person has reached adulthood. In this situation a society needs spaces that offer scope for episodes of extended maturing.

This is something one must almost suggest. Whether you think sects are appropriate for carrying out these functions or not, it is a fact that people with delayed or fragmented development towards adulthood would be well advised to attend such schools of emotion. Not everybody leaves high school or its equivalent as a well-rounded personality, and not everybody has developed the functioning of the essential, inner other to such a level of maturity in their twenties that we can say society has no need of something like that. The opposite is the case. Many people only start the process of maturing at that age. Many have had enough of the zombies they have met until then and finally want to see real people. That is exactly what can happen in a psychological and spiritual subculture: one finally sees real people. It is a fantastic and essential demand. It is understandable that people may be rather indiscriminate in that situation.

FRISCHKNECHT: Indiscriminate! This begs the question as to how we are supposed to have learned to be choosy!

SLOTERDIJK: Absolutely. Where are we supposed to have met those kinds of people before, and how could we have trained the ability to choose between them? From this perspective there is a human right to fall for charlatans, and that right has to be respected within certain limits.

FRISCHKNECHT: And what about the people who get hooked?

SLOTERDIJK: That's a different issue. Of course, in many cases a milieu is created and what should have been a useful expedient becomes a subculture and assumes a life of its own. But which criteria do we want to apply to criticize people who get caught? There are people who are still Christians even 2,000 years after Christ. We are just more careful about using the idea of 'getting hooked' in relation to them. There are people who are still trying, 2,500 years after Buddha, to get closer to enlightenment with Buddhist techniques and teachings. Are they hooked? Maybe.

Every organized form of psychological needs inevitably suffers the fate of creating a milieu. The phenomenon of getting hooked arises as soon as a need takes on an organizational form. But I think we should look at this in a wider context. Nations are full of people who got caught. A newborn baby is not yet a Swiss, or a German, or a Chinese citizen. Because they are where they are, they are socialized as locals. In sects and religious communities something like a second generation emerges, and the institutionalized religion then develops from its midst. It is a phenomenon we can observe elsewhere, for example, in psychotherapy. There are people who are still in therapy and have their own children meanwhile. Until the parents announce: 'We're not hooked any more!' should the children be taken into state care?

FRISCHKNECHT: You can talk. You became a father a few years ago and you turned fifty a few days ago.

SLOTERDIJK: I have chosen to get caught on hooks that are less tricky than the nails of sects. The philosophy hook was hammered into the wall 2,400 years ago by a magnificent madman, and hanging from it today is regarded as fairly honourable.

FRISCHKNECHT: If that hook were called 'Scientology' you would be ruined and your reputation would be down the drain.

SLOTERDIJK: True. It's not good that people are discriminated against for being members of a supportive group. It is a paradox that people looking for help in particular should not have to deal with. They go to a helper because they want to reach greater psychological maturity and find themselves, a process they haven't achieved properly yet. This drags them into a whirlpool of discrimination, which means they now have two problems instead of just one: at the same time as the guru helps them, he takes them into social isolation, which means they can only have rewarding contact with him and people like him, and a doubly hostile world begins right outside the door of the therapeutic space.

In this respect I admire societies like the United States, where the sect is a constituent part of society itself, so to speak. Unlike in Europe, sects can't be ostracized in the USA, because the people who wanted to exclude them would expose themselves as sectarians the moment they tried to do it. Under those conditions I don't even need to have an opinion about sects I don't like. That's a genuine expression of freedom. We don't have that freedom in Europe right now. We must have an opinion about Scientology. In my opinion they are a gang of criminals, but it would be much better to live in a world in which we weren't obliged to have such opinions. I wouldn't say they are nice people. But I would like to say their crimes are unimportant compared with other things that go on. Ideally, I would prefer to be able to say that I really don't care what they do.

FRISCHKNECHT: Meanwhile there are groups that are so literal about following the agenda of not being part of this world that they collectively take their own lives. How do you interpret this phenomenon?

SLOTERDIJK: They are not people who practise meditation or who live in a state of awareness. They live in a comic. They were never there; they always dropped out. For them, departure would be structured as arrival to show there are places where people can arrive. The people in San Diego who killed themselves were typically bright intellectuals, New Celibates, well-dressed, high-income children of the middle class who were only apparently integrated into their society, but were actually always on board the space station.[1]

[1] Sloterdijk is referring to Heaven's Gate, a millenarian group devoted to UFO religion in San Diego, USA. Thirty-nine members of the group committed mass suicide on 26 March 1997, apparently to reach what they believed was an alien spacecraft.

# 6

# PHILOSOPHICAL RETUNING

## *Interview with Felix Schmidt**

SCHMIDT: Mr Sloterdijk, only a few months ago you were complaining that philosophy had abdicated and the discourse on philosophical topics was dead. The reaction to your book *Regeln für den Menschenpark* [Rules for the Human Zoo][1] must have made you think again.

SLOTERDIJK: I am impressed at the scale of public discussion and the great improvement in the level of argument. What began with sheer rabble-rousing in the *Süddeutscher Zeitung* newspaper and in *Der Spiegel* magazine has turned into an authentic debate overnight. After a long period when the German public seemed paralysed by rhetoric about beliefs and the inevitable counterpart, the flight into stupidity, it is suddenly clear that one can still talk to people on an intellectual level, perhaps more than ever. People are fed up with organized hypocrisy and boring speeches, and want to

* This interview between Peter Sloterdijk and Felix Schmidt appeared under the title 'Meine Arbeit dreht sich um das Zur-Welt-Kommen' [My work revolves around coming-into-the-world], in *Die Welt* newspaper (6 October 1999): 35.

Felix Schmidt was cultural editor of *Der Spiegel* magazine, and editor-in-chief of the *Welt am Sonntag* newspaper and of the magazines *Stern* and *Hörzu*. He was also director of television for the broadcasting authority Südwestfunk Baden-Baden and managing director of AVE television production companies.

[1] Peter Sloterdijk. 'The Elmauer Rede: *Rules for the Human Zoo.* A Response to the *Letter on Humanism*', trans. Mary Varney Rorty, *Environment and Planning D: Society and Space* 27/1 (2009): 12–28. Available at: <http://web.stanford.edu/~mvr2j/sloterdijk.html>.

use their intelligence freely again without perpetual intimidation by discourse police.

SCHMIDT: Your critics, particularly Jürgen Habermas's journalistic disciples, accused you of 'fascist rhetoric' and 'selection fantasies' in this debate because your *Human Zoo* lecture apparently advocated a new stylistic breed of the human species.

SLOTERDIJK: The word 'apparently' should be underlined. If you read my text carefully line by line alongside the so-called interpretations, you can only talk of hallucinations and a deliberate attempt to ruin my reputation. Every author dreams of people reading his writings like mind-enhancing drugs, but in this case the side effects have got out of control. As usual in Germany, some of those involved have projected their own National Socialist nightmares into the text and want to be lauded as good citizens for that. My letter to Jürgen Habermas, published in *Die Zeit*, said what was necessary about the background to this deliberate misreading. Journalists had already followed this up and found confirmatory evidence by the time Habermas himself indirectly admitted in his placatory letter to *Die Zeit* that I had been justified in accusing him. In the meantime, Habermas's incriminating letter instructing his faithful pupils what to write has turned up in the media.

SCHMIDT: Not everybody can tolerate it when the universal thinker cuts a swathe through the obscurity of the epoch with one great blow, and actually has success doing it.

SLOTERDIJK: If you wanted to be mean, you could say I have a megalomaniac streak that has defied therapy so far and allows me to jump lots of hurdles. In the long run, I can't do my work if I'm expected to apologize constantly for my best options.

SCHMIDT: Isn't the main reason for your success that the philosophy you practise and describe is a kind of life aid?

SLOTERDIJK: I would answer the question positively if I were sure we could agree that this description is partly ironical.

SCHMIDT: We can do that.

SLOTERDIJK: My viewpoint is not edification, but what we call the fundamental problems in relation to existentialist philosophy: the problems we do not have to create artificially in order to have them, as is done in every academic research discipline, for example. By definition, researchers are people who solve problems that only exist because they have created them – with the exception of doctors. By the way, I have been involved in debates with doctors more and more often recently. One of my forthcoming books will be a collection of medico-philosophical essays in which I discuss the relationship between catharsis, healing, suggestion and immunity. The term 'immunity' has become a key focus of my work over the past few years. From this aspect, which is a kind of immune-anthropology, I have actually developed a style of thinking that no longer accepts the dominant role of non-edifying philosophy as criticism.

SCHMIDT: You have always been a therapist of our times, a diagnostician of our times. Your first major work, the *Critique of Cynical Reason*, was greeted as 'the summing-up of our age'.

SLOTERDIJK: The concept, 'diagnosis of our times', brings us close to a cultural-medical approach, because where a diagnosis is made, the therapy shouldn't be far away. But this is difficult for us because, seen as a whole, time and life represent incurable relationships, or at least they create an overall situation in which the incurable has the edge over the curable.

SCHMIDT: Should the *Critique of Cynical Reason* be understood as a cheerful riposte against the Enlightenment that has been frozen stiff in sad, miserable scholarship?

SLOTERDIJK: It is more of an attempt at retuning – including in the sense of changing the strings on the instrument we used for playing the song of the bad world. I come from the circle around the Frankfurt School in which we learned a special kind of virtuous lamentation. You were allowed to be wrong in an argument but not in the tone of it. If you broke the consensus of lamentation you were a bigger traitor than if you disagreed with the masters' opinion in judging a philosophical issue. In concrete terms, you were a traitor if you dared have a different opinion of jazz than Adorno's. My book really did precipitate the major breach.

SCHMIDT: How did it happen?

SLOTERDIJK: It brought a change of key in two respects. First, it was tuned to a more cheerful and playful key, and, second, it broke up the alliance between critical philosophy and academicism. The result was that my work started to reach a general audience, as you can see from the book's enormous success in terms of reviews and sales. We are already into the fourteenth edition, with 120,000 copies sold so far.

SCHMIDT: Do you think you ushered in the demise of critical theory, whose death you certify in the present debate?

SLOTERDIJK: That is doubtless the case, even if we weren't clearly aware of it yet in 1983. Back then, it seemed briefly as if Habermas wanted to accept my approach as the first declaration of an independent third generation of the Frankfurt School, and I didn't see any reason to correct that mistake myself. Quite the opposite: I had achieved something that looked like the fulfilment of a plan that the young Habermas had charted for himself and then forgotten or repressed. 'Thinking with Heidegger against Heidegger' was the motto of a 1953 essay of his. And hadn't I done just that?

But in time it became clear that not all roads lead to Frankfurt, and, what is more, it became evident that the Frankfurt Road wasn't leading anywhere itself. Finally, I got the chance to test in a conflict what Habermas understands by 'communicative action' and what he means when he talks about the 'ideal speech situation' and 'including the Other'. I pronounced Critical Theory dead when all that was left of the critique was hypocrisy. The autopsy will show it was ailing for longer than people had believed.

SCHMIDT: Could Habermas's verdict be connected with the fact that you abandoned the Frankfurt sickbed? You come from the left-wing movement of 1968, the camp of the Frankfurt School. In which range of thought do you position yourself today?

SLOTERDIJK: I would dearly like to find a good answer to that question. Most of all, I would like to have a good topography or a political map on which I could plot where I stand now. I still see myself as a product of the critical movement of 1968, but I seriously believe that I understand the left better today than they understand themselves. If it were still possible to be a leftist, I would be happiest describing myself as such. But it wouldn't exactly be true.

SCHMIDT: Are you hurt by the accusation that you have drifted very far to the right?

SLOTERDIJK: No. I think there are maturing processes that don't fit into that conventional pattern. The more experience I gain, the less time I have for the eternally badly behaved, hyper-moralistic lefties to whom I once belonged. The stage of maturity – and that concept means more to me today than a definition of political position – doesn't allow space for that any more. Generally, I think people today are wrong in debating about values at the expense of a debate about maturity and processes of maturing. If you say 'values', you should always make maturity a condition or admit openly: 'I stand for values that I don't turn into reality.' If the debate were held like that, I would join in. But I can't stand the whole annoying present trend towards thinking in terms of norms and values that comes mainly from crazy jurists and philosophers who believe jurists are the men of the moment. This is a new form of correct hypocrisy nowadays and it already shows signs of tomorrow's excess. Philosophy has the right to make this a topic.

SCHMIDT: How did you discover philosophy as your elixir of life?

SLOTERDIJK: To be honest, I don't really know. I can only describe it psychologically. The job is there and you invent the motive for it. In other words, it is a particular kind of thoughtfulness, a particular talent for absorbing books very easily and talking about them just after reading them as if they were part of your native language. In my case this was evident relatively early on. It may sound odd, but at the age of fourteen I was already using the vocabulary of Kantian philosophy when talking to myself. At fourteen I read Kant's first *Critique* and Nietzsche's *Zarathustra* for the first time, and at the same age I wrote a summary of philosophical proofs of the existence of God for my school homework. All that gave me the rather unusual qualification of having learned to speak the standard language of philosophy like ordinary speech. Growing up without a father, I didn't waste any time on false anti-authoritarian dialectics. I didn't have to submit to any paternal authority trying to force me to do something I didn't want. And I was enormously greedy in devouring anything that seemed best to me at that time: the philosophy and language of Max Bense, Foucault, Adorno, Benn and Gotthard Günther, whose philosophy of cybernetics is still underrated today.

SCHMIDT: The part of you that loves word games never tires of experimenting with new forms of description to extend the borders of possible expression. In your latest work, *Spheres*,[2] you use language that sounds rather strange to describe immaterial objects.

SLOTERDIJK: That's right. *Spheres I* and *Spheres II* are both written in a non-existent language – a language I invented specially for that book.

SCHMIDT: How do you invent a language?

SLOTERDIJK: In the course of developing an individual philosophical position it is quite natural to end up creating one's own language as a precision instrument for a problem you have just discovered. It is, indeed, a foreign language within my native language, and it characterizes me as long as I speak it. A person who conducts cross-border operations, as I do, can't achieve anything with newsreader's German.

SCHMIDT: You expressed that in *Der Zauberbaum* [*The Magic Tree*] your only published novel to date.[3]

SLOTERDIJK: *Der Zauberbaum* is the book I had to work hardest on because I first had to capture a freedom I would never have imagined possible before I experienced it myself.

SCHMIDT: *Der Zauberbaum* is about the discovery of the

[2] Peter Sloterdijk, *Sphären I*, 1998; *Sphären II*, 1999; *Sphären III*, 2004 (Berlin: Suhrkamp Verlag).

English editions: *Spheres I: Bubbles*, 2011; *Spheres II: Globes*, 2014; *Spheres III: Foam*, forthcoming (Los Angeles: Semiotexte/ MIT).

[3] Peter Sloterdijk, *Der Zauberbaum* (Berlin: Suhrkamp Verlag), 1987. (No English translation.)

unconscious. Did you ever do psychoanalysis yourself to help you dig so deeply?

SLOTERDIJK: I didn't invent anything in the book. Everything in it is self-analysis distilled in a literary fashion. It is an interpreted autobiography. In the period between 1975 and 1985 my life was strongly motivated by self-awareness. My Indian trip was part of this.

SCHMIDT: Do you mean the months you spent in a guru community?

SLOTERDIJK: It was inspired less specifically by cultural criticism than one might say in retrospect. I didn't go to India as a romantic. It was a very specific fascination I wanted to explore in depth. It emanated from a guru who gave me the impression I would benefit by letting him beguile me. This spiritual impulse and my experience in America directly afterwards prevented the shy, introverted parts of me from defining my life – otherwise things would have worked out differently. I would probably have failed early on.

SCHMIDT: Was it the crucial experiences of the psychoanalytic experiments and the Indian adventure that finally silenced your sarcastic approach attuned to catastrophes?

SLOTERDIJK: I think at least two things were responsible. Firstly, I started defining myself professionally as a writer and philosopher. That wasn't the case to begin with, when I saw philosophizing as an expressive act, and only published my excesses or my arrogance, as it were.

SCHMIDT: And secondly?

SLOTERDIJK: When I was young I was not exactly a loner, but I was certainly not somebody who felt my emotional partnerships should lead to starting a family. That has changed fundamentally. Parallel to affirming philosophy as a profession I made what you could call an affirmation of the family as a way of life. You can trace that in my books from the 1990s. The texts suddenly show awareness of children, and you can hear fatherly tones – I was forced to learn a lesson I had previously rejected. The experience that children define reality and that you have to experience the possibility of reality from that point was related to the fact that I became a father.

SCHMIDT: In *Spheres* you actually revealed yourself as a kind of midwife. Birth, or to put it another way, coming-into-the-world, seems to have assumed a central place in your thought.

SLOTERDIJK: I had already made the hero in *Der Zauberbaum* dream of his own birth. The book was published in 1985, and quite correctly understood as my agenda. The basic features haven't changed at all. I have just understood better that birth as a type of event and coming-into-the-world as another type of event are not the same thing, because for creatures of our kind, being born is not enough to come into the world. The fact that a birth is a coming-into-the-world at all is the key to the whole mystery, and that is what my work is about.

SCHMIDT: Isn't a person like you, a highly motivated athlete in the fields of thought and writing, so absorbed physically and psychologically by a work like the three volumes of *Spheres* that he has no time for anything else?

SLOTERDIJK: Although I occasionally call myself a failed Bohemian, working boosts my energy. When you are writing and you realize that the text is going to be successful, you get back more energy than you put into producing it. Of course, the precondition for a successful text is that you don't torture yourself. And the readers can feel that the texts have been written without torture, that they flow and are carried along by a happy feeling all the way through. Even if one or two texts are wrong, it doesn't affect the whole thing.

SCHMIDT: Concerning that happy feeling: I've heard that you also get it from enjoying a fine Bordeaux wine. You're quite a connoisseur, are you?

SLOTERDIJK: That's all self-taught! In the field of philosophy I never had a proper teacher, at least not in the complete sense of the word, and to some extent I learned things auto-didactically. It's just the same with Bordeaux. But by the time we reach the point of understanding something about Bordeaux we can't afford to pay for it any more. Now we have to make do as best we can with Australian and Italian wines. It's really awful. The only aspect of globalism I seriously deplore is that ignorant Japanese and Americans sour the enjoyment of the few Europeans who really understand something about their own wine because they buy up everything we have come to cherish.

# 7

# WE'RE ALWAYS RIDING DOWN MATERNITY DRIVE

## *Interview with Mateo Kries**

KRIES: Is mobility a fundamental human constant?

SLOTERDIJK: From a philosophical viewpoint, we can think of the characteristic mobility of humans as coming-into-the-world. The formula of coming-into-the-world says that more happens at the birth of a human being than the biological exit from the mother. The meaning of birth in general is probably that beings which come from inside achieve a change of place from an absolutely intimate protected space to an outer, less protected space that, regardless of its openness, still has to retain some characteristics of a protected space if it is to remain habitable. In other words, the particular attribute of the human birth is the exodus from the interior world into the real world, an experience of openness, freedom and danger. On my basic analysis, human mobility, as far as it interests philosophers, depends on this movement. Of course there are also extra-philosophical aspects of mobility that develop completely in the physical, sociological or economic dimensions. But as soon as we examine human mobility using instruments of philosophical and depth psychology, we arrive directly at the field where this natal discrepancy comes into play.

KRIES: Is the urge to keep moving inborn, or is it like a primal element, something unstoppable?

* This interview between Peter Sloterdijk and Mateo Kries appeared under the title 'Wir fahren immer auf dem Maternity Drive . . .', in the exhibition catalogue *Automobility – Was uns bewegt* (Weil am Rhein: Vitra Design Museum), 1999, pp. 102–13.

Mateo Kries is chief curator at the Vitra Design Museum in Weil am Rhein.

SLOTERDIJK: We should always be very careful with anthropological generalizations. All the same, it is a fact that the great majority of human beings invested too much in the past 10,000 years in an experiment hostile to mobility – the all-embracing attempt to halt the initial nomadic flow of human movement. This, the greatest attack ever made on mobility, has the lovely name 'settledness', and occurred in the same timespans as the agrarian and the agrosophical or agraro-ontological periods of human cultural history. The soil on which the farmer sits tight, the clod of earth that transforms humans themselves into a second plant, is an incredibly intense and durable force, and we are far from having freed ourselves of it completely.

Yet the soil has not remained the epitome of superior power; it has not defined humans everywhere for all time. As we can see, the age of settledness and of fixed ties to the soil ended in Europe with the beginning of the modern age, and a neo-nomadic epoch staked its claim. The underlying trend of the twentieth century consists of ending the era of settledness and liberating the kinetic potential in humans that has been tied down for over 10,000 years.

KRIES: At the same time the urge for mobility repeatedly occurs in the mythologies of almost all peoples, even during settled periods ...

SLOTERDIJK: Because the old settledness contained an element of excess by which humans were expected to accept being bound in a way that belied their kinetic truth. Consequently, this had to emerge elsewhere, and particularly in the psychological evasions and flights of imagination typical of those times – leaving aside discussion of war and pilgrimage, the two formalized compensations for settledness, for the moment.

We could certainly claim that humans, in terms of metaphysical and imaginary mobility, were more mobile in the 10,000 years of great pacification than we are today with our trains, planes and cars. The reason is that people of that bygone era had internal maps charting movements over a very wide area. Their most important means of transport was the soul, which, as we know, travels faster and more appreciatively than the modern car user.

KRIES: Can you give concrete examples of myths or soul journeys? How did they occur?

SLOTERDIJK: The culture of soul journeys begins with the observation that individuals can lose their souls. In depression some people become separated from the principle that animates them. They become stiff and weary, they seem to be soulless and don't move to the group's rhythm any more. This makes the little society of the group realize that one of its members is having a crisis and losing their soul, or – to use an anachronistic modern expression – is suffering from depression. This suggests that the soul must have lost its way. Shamans become important here because they know the art of looking for the depressed person's lost free soul somewhere at the edge of the world, and bringing it back to its owner. The early movement experiments and shamanic soul journeys were meant to revive the alliance between humans and their animators, that is, their companion spirits, the forces that help to arouse enthusiasm. This involves a truth that was in force long before all philosophies, and before the major religions: that humans can only move properly when their moving principle, their true motor, their soul, is with them. No good movement exists without enthusiasm.

KRIES: Does this imply that the invention of the automobile or of mobile devices and their use is a kind of anti-depressant?

SLOTERDIJK: Definitely, for the car is a machine for increasing self-confidence. The difference is that an external engine causes the movement. The car gives its driver additional power and reach. Today, regrettably, we have a predominance of naïve theories of sociology of traffic that see cars mainly as a means of transport. But as long as people stick to simple transport studies we won't get to the essential layers of modern automobility. I think we have to see the vehicles of humans in the first place as a means of idealization and intensification, and consequently as a kinetic anti-depressant. The big demand for automobility certainly comes from people who want the vehicle for increasing their radius of action and capability. The statistics tell us clearly that only one in three car trips is connected with work and with what we call transportation in the economic sense. Two out of three movements are escapes: people drive to their lovers, they take trips to the countryside and on holiday, they go visiting, or they use the car for letting off steam. We could almost think people use the car as revenge on the heavy demands of settledness.

KRIES: Does this explain the desire for locomotion?

SLOTERDIJK: Yes, in a way. But if we want to talk like that, we have to derive the meaning of desire correctly. We have to be able to say how people came to feel desire, or how desire found us. Desire is the material the movements are made of; it builds the bridge to goals we have not reached. But I think we shouldn't talk of desire if we don't talk beforehand and at the same time about settledness, and about how the wishes of people who have been made static are organized, and therefore about the system of frustrations that shapes the desires that are typical of our form of life.

KRIES: Today the car actually has its own mythology.

SLOTERDIJK: This is revealing because, according to my working hypothesis on the theory of religion, myths only evolve where people try to speak about what complements them. Humans are beings that understand themselves in terms of their complementary principle – we could say, in terms of their invisible partner. In the mythical period of consciousness those partners were seen primarily as gods and spirits, whereas today they are seen as technical adjuncts to the human body, that is, as machines and media. All cultures work at spinning themselves into their symbolic husks and these husks are first woven by the companion spirits. The car seems capable of a mythological development precisely because it is a kind of materialized companion spirit. We can baptize cars, we can talk to cars, and they have something common to all religious spheres – we can go inside them, immerse ourselves in them. As we noted at the start of this discussion, at least indirectly, people are beings that can't help constantly asking about the difference between inside and outside. They can't suppress the question about the difference between being born and not being born. Because this difference will never be completely clear, and because the ideal interior cannot be totally cast off or totally reproduced, people face the persistent question: how do we succeed in being as good outside as we are inside? The car is a suggestive answer to this. It is the most perfect solution to the following riddle: how can I move with masterful control although I don't venture out?

Modern humans are customers who voice a demand for methods of demonstrating supreme control. That is the basic cultural market. People who offer means of representing or simulating supreme control can always count on enormous demand. That is just what car manufacturers do. They offer one of the most convincing means of demonstrating supreme control in today's world, and we are incapable of not demanding that. Personally, I sometimes ask myself how so many friends in my circle happen not to have a driving licence. I'm like a magnet that pulls nails out of a rotten old ship – I have the curious ability to attract people from the intellectual scene who function completely as non-drivers. I think not one of my close friends, or maybe only one or two, has a driving licence. We obviously play different kinds of mastery games, which don't involve driving around the neighbourhood. I'm the only tacky automobilist in this select clique. We have constructed a congenial system that makes driving our own car unimportant. I think all of us are people who belong more to the old shamanic culture where people still achieved their exalted feelings with soul journeys, and no driving licence exists for that.

KRIES: Many people feel they don't exist at all without a car. The physical experience of having these machines available is totally fundamental to their identity.

SLOTERDIJK: Those people have their antecedents in the horse cultures of the past 3–4,000 years. The symbiosis between an animal as a means of transport and the rider already existed once in the case of the centaur. The horse as a complement to humans has also produced its own mythology. The typical human rider has faded into the background today, although he or she still exists, usually embodied by young women, with the girl in front and the horse behind. Those are the animal centaurs of today, whereas the technical centaurs are represented by the people at the wheel inside with the car outside surrounding them. Incidentally, there are almost as many horses today as there were in the eighteenth or nineteenth centuries, but they have all been reassigned. They are almost all leisure horses, hardly any workhorses nowadays. Isn't it an odd comment on today's society that only horses have achieved emancipation? Humans are still work animals just as they always were, even if they are miserable jobless people, but the horses standing in German paddocks today are all horses of pleasure, post-historic horses. Children stroke them and adults admire them, and we feel very sorry for the last workhorses we see now and then at the circus and at racecourses. Some are used in psychotherapy for children with behavioural problems, but they are treated well and respectfully. All the other European horses have managed to do what humans still dream of – horses are the only ones for whom historical philosophy's dream of a good end to history has become reality. They are the happy unemployed that evolution seemed to be moving towards. For them, the realm of freedom has been reached, they stand in their paddock, are fed, have completely forgotten the old drudgery and live out their natural mobility.

KRIES: What does the car mean for our mobility?

SLOTERDIJK: From the philosophical perspective we have to pose the question of the 'real' meaning of the automobile as follows: do we make new movements with the car – that is, trips to places where we have never been before? Or do we use the new vehicle for old movements, that is, for journeys that we always repeat on the oldest patterns and for which the vehicle only provides a new setting? In the latter case I am speaking of Platonic movements, in the former of exodus-type movements.

In terms of Platonic explanation we believe we have understood a movement when we recognize its old pattern, when we can say, for example: the natal breakthrough is repeated here by other means. In Platonic traffic analysis, the trip always goes backward to the origins, and all vehicles are aids for retrospective yearning. On this view all vehicles ultimately serve only the journey home. The return journey has priority everywhere. All the wheels are set in motion to seek the mother, and the word 'maternity' is on every street sign.

We're always riding down Maternity Drive. If we adopt this level of analysis, the vehicle is understood as a means to carry out an old movement with a new medium. If we choose this romantic, psychoanalytic theory of travelling, the answer to the question, 'Where are we going?' is: 'Always home'. But I would be interested in working out the difference between old and new movements. New movements require non-Platonic kinetics, that is, a theory of exodus. The primacy of the journey out applies here. I think we should also develop an argument for the outward journey that can match the power of Platonic and psychoanalytic regressions. We have to make room in theory for trips to new terrain, and award the vehicle an appropriate function in such exodus-type movements. The automobile can also take us to places we have never visited before. It is not just the means of regression we suspect it to be in our most interesting theories – it can also give us access to new, open places, it can also be a medium of coming-into-the-world.

We have to grant the car the two potentials that belong to basic human mobility – exodus and regression. Philosophically speaking, whenever people make an outward movement, it brings into play a movement of coming-into-the-world. When people are born they discover not only their mother, who was the first vehicle and will remain so for some time to come; they also discover the world in which they move on without the mother. For us, perhaps learning means, above all, understanding the difference between mother and world on a deeper level. It is from this starting point that vehicles acquire their meaning. If they were only a means to re-create a womblike situation and to return to an inner world, then they would merely be 'homecoming vehicles'. But I want to emphasize the other direction of movement: what about an 'outward-bound vehicle'? Where are the means of transportation that bring us into the open? To be able to give a convincing answer, it seems important to me to point to a profound lack of contemporary debate on automobility. Everybody suffers from being much too 'car-centric' and restricted to movements on land. This results in not thinking through the difference between the ship and the car thoroughly enough. The reason is trivial: most people who talk about the car today are incorrigible landlubbers, and consequently use inland terms to explain mobility as a whole, and this leads to one-sided concepts.

Anybody looking for the truth about the vehicle for which the outward journey has primacy simply has to consider the ship – from the *Argo* of Theseus to Columbus's *Santa Maria*. We do the car too much honour if we make it the exclusive focus of the mobility question. In a comprehensive theory of mobility we have to appreciate ships, particularly the ocean-going ships of the age of discovery, much more than we usually do. Even today, the ship is much more magical than the car in many respects, and the actors and spectators of the great age of ocean travel felt this magic very strongly. As a whole, the mythology about ships is more powerful than the mythology of automobiles, which has barely existed for a hundred years. The poetry of shipping space is much more extensive than the poetry of the automobile – in its first century the automobile failed to find its Herman Melville. It is no coincidence that the setting for the greatest novel of world literature is a whaling ship. We are still waiting for the book that raises the automobile to the status of a world metaphor as Melville's peerless book has done for ship's navigation. The twentieth century, especially the second half, liquidated the primacy of ships, leaving a hazy memory of the most powerful of all vehicles so far. The result is that our thoughts about traffic are dominated by the paradigm of road travel, and we understand almost nothing any longer about movements related to outward journeys, exodus and the ocean.

KRIES: The conquest of the world by the ship is fascinating in a different way from the conquest by the car. One reason is probably that the automobile has become a mass phenomenon and the aspects of adventure that are still associated with ocean voyages, or are associated in our imagination, obviously can't be transferred to four-wheeled vehicles.

SLOTERDIJK: But automobility has democratized the privilege of movement. Today we forget too easily that mobility was an aristocratic privilege until the beginning of the twentieth century. Rulers were those who advanced faster and more successfully. The lord was reflected in his vehicle. Nowadays we have produced kinetic democracy through the mass distribution of means of mobility. That is the real reason why people today feel equal – not because they are equally talented or educated, or have the same voting rights, but because they are equally fast and because the little person can overtake the rich lord at any time. Kinetic emancipation has happened on the streets, and therefore the truth is on the highway. The United States shows us that mass culture is largely automobile culture. Harking back to sailing vessels, on the other hand, would return the focus to a more aristocratic and maritime-nomadic type of mobility. Incidentally, you have to admit that a port has a different kind of magic than a parking lot. What is more, the means of propulsion, the wind, has a deeper relationship to imaginative power, to the processes of ensoulment that stimulate the imagination, than the jet engine of a modern aircraft.

KRIES: Convertible drivers or motorcyclists argue the same way.

SLOTERDIJK: Motorcyclists are returning sailors who can't forget the storm and don't want to miss the ecstasy of the open sea. But since we are dependent today on replaying maritime ecstasies in a different medium, we are left with the full-throttle experience.

KRIES: The current discussion about mobility is also defined by the question as to which means of transportation is right for which purpose …

SLOTERDIJK: Respectable transport scholars and the gentlemen from urban transportation companies usually get their ideal of mobility from railway vehicles. The dream of safe movement is only realized on the tracks. Only rail traffic allows implementation of the ideal of completely reversible movement – outward journey minus return journey equals zero. From the underlying structural perspective, we can see a battle in today's transport system between mad and rational transporters, in which the rational ones opt for the railways and the mad ones for the roads, because only the roads can serve as a substitute for air, ocean and primordial waters. On the roads all the intoxicating, excessive potential of the urge for mobility can be acted out in the progressive as well as the regressive mode. The railways, on the other hand, put an end to the kinetic delirium.

KRIES: All the same, sensible transport scholars cite a very concrete and palpable risk involved in our mobility today. You have talked about the kinetic utopia yourself …

SLOTERDIJK: We can reformulate this kinetic utopia in a language of critique of religion and of victim theory. Then the question is: 'How many victims is such a high level of mobility worth to us?' In fact, everything that costs human life is usually prohibited today because we have abolished human sacrifice. Still, eight or ten thousand road deaths annually are not sufficient reason to demand a ban on road traffic. In this case we make an offset calculation, and because mobility is actually the occult kinetic religion of modernity, there is not the slightest chance of restricting or suppressing the demands for mobility. Quite the opposite: we have to consider how we approach the demands for even greater increases. Anybody trying to impose restrictions on mobility today would unleash a civil war.

KRIES: Are automobiles female or male?

SLOTERDIJK: Automobiles are male outside and female inside, as befits amphibian or hermaphrodite constructs. Femininity plays a role here in terms of the characteristic 'accessibility' – we can go inside. Masculinity is expressed in the characteristic 'good for moving forward'. As automobiles have ideally synthesized these two attributes, they are also the perfect realization of the desire for the hermaphrodite. Since the beginning of this century, mass culture has tended towards dissolving gender difference and producing unisex subjects. Cars are ahead of people in this respect. While convincing bisexuals have yet to be created, cars have already reached this goal.

# 8

# TACKLING THE UNSPOKEN THINGS IN CULTURE

## *Interview with Felix Schmidt**

SCHMIDT: Mr Sloterdijk, people see you as one of the nation's intellectual heroes. They even call you a star and award you the vacant seat next to Schopenhauer. Do you feel right and comfortable sitting there?

SLOTERDIJK: Sitting next to great dead men is always very uncomfortable. A living person should try to avoid such comparisons because the price is too high. Basically, as an author one wants to resemble the dead rather than the living. One of the paradoxes of an author's existence is that very often – and in philosophy, without exception – one looks for idols in the ranks of the great and glorious. But I can accept being identified in the sense of a family resemblance, because there is a direct line between my work and my kind of philosophizing and that of certain nineteenth-century authors. I mean Kierkegaard, Schopenhauer and particularly Nietzsche.

SCHMIDT: Your unusual popularity as a scholar of the humanities owes a great deal to the scandal caused by your lecture, 'Rules for the Human Zoo'. What is the situation after that scandal?

SLOTERDIJK: Your question has a paramilitary undertone. I will try to respond in a similarly serious tone. My personal situation has changed in that the so-called 'human zoo' affair has given me

* This interview appeared under the title, 'Ich weiß viel vom Wahnsinn' ['I know a lot about madness'], in *Frankfurter Rundschau Magazin* (30 June 2001): 18f.

Felix Schmidt was chief editor for culture at *Der Spiegel*, editor-in-chief of *Welt am Sonntag*, *Stern* and *Hörzu*, and was director of television at Südwestfunk Baden-Baden before becoming managing director of the TV production company AVE.

a new social position. I have become more of a classical political intellectual again. I had previously created an aura of marginal philosophy, an atmosphere of artistic philosophy around myself, and in general there were many advantages to staying that way. Meanwhile I have come to terms with the new definition of myself as a public intellectual.

SCHMIDT: Doesn't the public intellectual sometimes feel he has to influence the nation's image of itself?

SLOTERDIJK: Yes. In such crises of meaningfulness it is advisable either to retreat into rational work or go to a conference, where you realize that the fantasy idea of intellectuals representing the interests of the state has absolutely no connection with reality, and is at best a nice delusion.

SCHMIDT: Have you had your mental state examined recently?

SLOTERDIJK: Should I?

SCHMIDT: I read an allegation somewhere that disappointment sent you on a flight into madness.

SLOTERDIJK: I am always amazed by the diagnoses people dream up for free. German journalism sees itself as a sort of continuation of the Spanish bullfight by other means, and believes it has to present the slaughter of an intellectual at regular intervals. People who talk like that evidently perceive their role in the arena as *banderilleros*, the little gadflies that are intended to annoy the bull if he doesn't want to fight as required. That kind of amateur psychology merely amuses me. It is blatantly obvious what these people are up to.

SCHMIDT: Those attacks still bear the after-effects of the big 'human zoo' debate, which is only gradually calming down. People somehow got the fixed idea that you were advocating a joint venture between philosophy and genetic engineering and, as part of this, a new elite to be formed by selection.

SLOTERDIJK: The accusation that I wanted to replace education by breeding is absolutely stupid. However, it shows up those who enjoy denouncing me as even more stupid. As we well know, the cultural field begins where the biological ends. In the debates around the 'human zoo' I never hid the fact that I stand for culture. It follows that the idea of the elite comes from the educational field, not from biology.

SCHMIDT: Is the debate that has been shifted to the biological sphere a substitute for the complete lack of discussion about deficits in education and training?

SLOTERDIJK: We must underscore this even more: It is a substitute for the dreaded debate that probably can't be postponed any longer – the debate about a socio-psychological disaster in the most real sense of the word, a debate that has forced its way into modern society from the school system. The deliberate silence about the educational disaster is the reason people believe that somebody could abolish school in favour of some kinds of biological mechanisms. But this imaginary scenario is interesting because it demonstrates there is really a need to abolish school.

SCHMIDT: Is there an alternative to school?

SLOTERDIJK: There is no convincing answer to society's question about what could replace the failing education system. One thing is certain: we can't find alternative answers in biotechnology. We urgently need an educational alternative this side of biology.

SCHMIDT: What explains our reluctance to engage in a substantial debate on this?

SLOTERDIJK: There are three or four themes that humans a priori don't like talking about: death, school and their mothers. And school is probably the most unpleasant in this triad.

SCHMIDT: As you have already talked about school, let's talk about your mother.

SLOTERDIJK: Talking about that topic means talking about a strange tragedy I have never publicly revealed anything about before. It still troubles me today.

SCHMIDT: A mother complex?

SLOTERDIJK: My mother was a very gifted woman. She was born in the middle of the First World War, and her father was one of the first soldiers to fall on the Western Front. She had to grow up with the question, 'Where is my real father?' To some extent this question drove her destiny because all her life she never got along well with people, especially not with men.

SCHMIDT: Not with her son either?

SLOTERDIJK: It's not easy to be the son of a woman like her. It created a series of complications that were built into my life trajectory from the very beginning. It took decades of brooding and experimenting with life for me to understand and process those interrelationships. The resurrection of the dead in the child and the grandchild is an uncanny thing, and I have only worked through that phantom history in the past few years. I have, so to speak, laid out my own personal hero's graveyard for my grandfather, and I am in the process of burying him there on behalf of my whole family. Those experiences have taught me how heavy psychological legacies are, and how powerful histories of the soul are. I know that beneath the official history, the daytime history, there is also a nocturnal side, a dark side to history.

SCHMIDT: How far has that influenced your work?

SLOTERDIJK: My entire work so far has been a kind of

history writing like underground mining, in which I tried to weave the history of riddles, the history of injuries and the history of the unconscious quest into the official version of philosophy. This means my concept of philosophy is always starkly defined together with psychology, which has led to some misunderstandings. Philosophy is supposed to philosophize instead of being occupied with psychoanalysis. Generally speaking, philosophy is either a form of happy ontological mathematics without any ulterior motive, and that is quite reasonable, or it is a form of defence, a very rare form of stupidity that has managed to assume a socially respectable front. Only in very rare cases is it salutary work on the things culture leaves unsaid.

From 1975 on, my life was totally devoted to self-awareness. My Indian excursion was part of that. I think my life story is typical of our times – a kind of biography of the age. I know a fair amount about the radicalism, the extremism, the madness and the traumas of the twentieth century. All of that belongs to a single system of communicating vessels circulating the message that something is wrong with life. That's why I am so fascinated by the present, because I am observing something not only in my own feeling of life, but also in society as a whole, that makes me extraordinarily curious, perhaps even joyful. I mean that the social climate has been changing for a while now, and we are emerging from the shadows of madness that hung over us since 1914. More and more people are no longer directly affected by those old communicating vessels of madness.

SCHMIDT: Do you mean society is doing therapy on itself?

SLOTERDIJK: I would rather say it is normalizing itself. But this normalization is a fascinating process, and in the case of Germans, an almost uncanny one. The question of what constitutes German normality is not normal in itself, because none of us will live long enough to meet a normal German. The German forms of life and prevailing moods are changing now – and occasionally I try to play something of an active role in that. Perhaps this is the only exception I have to make to my negative answer to your question as to whether I sometimes feel tempted to become a kind of philosophical National Moderator. I would like very much to link my name with a comprehensive normalization story for this country, which has been sick in some sense up until now. I am optimistic enough to believe the recuperation process can work.

SCHMIDT: We will have to get used to your performance as a philosopher with an optimistic outlook. Have you finally given up being the herald of catastrophe sarcasm?

SLOTERDIJK: I want to confirm that my basic attitude has

changed. The crucial factor in this process was something which had not played a dominant role in my life previously, and which can be described by the conventional concept of responsibility. The catastrophe sarcasm was a contradictory attitude, a kind of sly black humour. I felt instinctively that Marx must have meant something similar when he said we must force the relations to dance by singing their own tune to them. This is a bitter form of revolutionary powerlessness. It gave rise to the catastrophe sarcasm. I was trapped in a pattern of thought that is known from the therapy world but actually depends on a false calculation in human and psychological terms, namely, the view that one can handle doubt as a means to an end, based on the motto: 'I will begin by doubting so that I can be properly reborn later on.' I wouldn't accept that frivolous attitude today. It was an instance of malpractice I wouldn't want to repeat.

SCHMIDT: In some ways you were picking up on your pre-Adorno phase again.

SLOTERDIJK: Anyway, I got rid of the exaggerated critical attitude and remembered a very early phase of my work in which I was influenced by authors from the Protestant tradition, such as Kierkegaard and Bonhoeffer.

SCHMIDT: In the first volume of your *Spheres* trilogy you outed yourself as a kind of birthing assistant, a midwife. You seem deeply impressed by the theme of birth.

SLOTERDIJK: I am one of those unfortunate people whose remembrance of their birth has never been erased from their bodily memory. I know there is a specific form of birth stress that is reproduced throughout one's life.

SCHMIDT: Your daughter is seven years old now, and I'm sure she is a curious child. How do you explain to her what holds the world together in its innermost depths?

SLOTERDIJK: I'm impressed by the natural poetry of her questions. Her way of asking doesn't put pressure on me because it has its own poetic mechanism. I don't know where that comes from. Sometimes it seems to me she has a special aptitude for calming down at the right moment to stop her thoughts from going in cryptic directions. It is fascinating how she plays with mythological imagination and constantly restructures her picture of the world without her very knowledgeable father and omniscient mother setting the agenda.

SCHMIDT: When did you first ask the question as to how the universe, Planet Earth and life arose?

SLOTERDIJK: I don't know if I ever asked myself that question because the answers came much earlier than the questions.

SCHMIDT: How did that happen?

SLOTERDIJK: Like so many other people, I'm a typical victim of the school that permanently answers questions that haven't been asked yet. But it's still possible to recover from that at an advanced age. Last summer I had a moment of deep emotion on the plane of natural philosophy when I saw the wonderful total eclipse of the sun. Suddenly a physical feeling of reality appeared in the tone of natural philosophy. Up until then my concept of reality was defined very closely in relation to humanism, the social sciences, linguistics and culture. I was convinced only oddballs could be interested in physics. Today I think our exaggerated culturalism has probably made us blind to physics. However, I would like to describe the wondrous moment of eclipse of the sun that I enjoyed as an exceptional state, from which point on something changed for me.

SCHMIDT: In any case, philosophy begins in wonder.

SLOTERDIJK: At least, that was the original thesis of Aristotle and Plato. Looking at this thesis more closely, it is very cleverly constructed and actually says something quite different from what is usually associated with it. People probably marvelled for tens of thousands of years without ever beginning to philosophize in the formal sense like the Greeks. Plato developed wonder and questioning to a special form of competition. He made philosophy attractive as a contest in astonishment. Just as we act stupid, we can act astonished – which for many, incidentally, is the same thing. We play at wondering, and can then develop the unnatural questions that philosophers ask.

SCHMIDT: Have you ever vacillated in your life between philosophy and literature?

SLOTERDIJK: No. Never. But for a long time now I have felt the need to change emphasis and cross over to the narrative genre. That is the form I need today as a free phrasemaker in order to realize what is in my imagination.

SCHMIDT: So you keep on crossing between philosophy and literature, between the arts and scholarship.

SLOTERDIJK: I'm sure it will go on like that. But I would be pleased if there were more people who could acknowledge things done well, not only serious functional things but also things achieved in the sense of philosophy as a profession. I think my work has reached the point where it doesn't get further without a degree of collaborative assistance from competent people.

SCHMIDT: That could happen soon if, as planned, you start moderating your own talk show in ZDF, a kind of 'Philosophical Quartet'. Will that mean a TV commission offering guidance, something to give disoriented humankind stability and comfort?

SLOTERDIJK: I would put it a shade more cautiously, although

I think the desire for orientation is absolutely legitimate. For now, we can be content with Nietzsche's definition of philosophy as a project 'for harming stupidity'. My mission in this venture is to situate philosophy in a medium that begins by being completely unsuitable, or practically in an opposite world. It is important to create a really informative and exhilarating context, a fruitful atmosphere for the intelligence. This is created merely by it happening at all.

SCHMIDT: By placing philosophy in the mass medium of television, aren't you worried about making your own contribution to the mediatizing of society that you have compared to public degradation in the arenas of ancient Rome?

SLOTERDIJK: I certainly won't contribute to closing off the arena of the totalitarian mass media even more. I would like to promote a form of public culture that never bothers with distinguishing between winners and losers but, on the contrary, consistently defers this distinction. The point is to remix victor's truth with loser's truth and, by doing so, to force a real widening of perspective. Not knowing who has won and who has lost is a good way to foster open discussion.

SCHMIDT: What do you want to achieve by this?

SLOTERDIJK: My plans are very far from the usual talk-show chitchat and are not intended to add to the trend towards gathering an audience that is sentimental, excitable, cruel, forgetful, and curiously good-natured and nasty at the same time – just as if we were back in the days of the manhunts in the Circus Maximus in Rome.

SCHMIDT: Are you proposing a kind of anti-television?

SLOTERDIJK: Philosophy on television is the anti-circus in the circus. Let's see if it works.

# 9

# ON WEALTH AND SELF-RESPECT

*Interview with Klaus Methfessel and Christian Ramthun**

METHFESSEL/RAMTHUN: Professor Sloterdijk, let's talk about *Menschenpark* [*Rules for the Human Zoo*]. Two years ago you sparked off a debate on genetic engineering that took place mainly in the features pages of newspapers. Are you pleased that politicians are taking up this topic now?

SLOTERDIJK: In tackling this, politics is simply fulfilling its role as provider of a system of norms in a deregulation process that is confusing society at the moment.

METHFESSEL/RAMTHUN: What do you mean by deregulation? The issue here actually concerns new technical possibilities.

SLOTERDIJK: That's right. We have become familiar with the concept of deregulation mostly in relation to retrospective abolition of state control of services. But deregulation has a much wider meaning. Deregulation through innovation is basically our motive force of history per se. The whole modern age is a gigantic experiment in the cultural introduction of technologies that have not been tested before in human history.

METHFESSEL/RAMTHUN: What is your position on this?

* This interview between Peter Sloterdijk, Klaus Methfessel and Christian Ramthun appeared under the title 'Reichtum muß Selbstachtung erzeugen' [Wealth Must Create Self-Respect], in the weekly magazine *Wirtschaftswoche* (19 July 2001): 22–6

Klaus Methfessel is director of the Georg von Holtzbrinck-Schule für Wirtschaftsjournalisten. Christian Ramthun has worked for *Wirtschaftswoche* since 1997 and is deputy chief of the magazine's Berlin office.

Two years ago some critics saw you as an advocate of genetic eugenics.

SLOTERDIJK: That was a misunderstanding, to put it mildly. A philosopher never sees things in terms of being for or against a technology. It is all about trying to understand the technology at a deeper level. In my talk, *Regeln für den Menschenpark* [*Rules for the Human Zoo*], I advocated channelling the mega-trend of genetic engineering in a responsible way. We must be guided by the principle of caution.

METHFESSEL/RAMTHUN: Morality dominates in the genetic debate. The German President is worried about human dignity, while the Chancellor sees opportunities for gainful employment.

SLOTERDIJK: There is not just one single morality. We always behave as if morality were the last word, and only exists in the singular. But morality is just as pluralist as society.

METHFESSEL/RAMTHUN: That sounds almost as if morality is arbitrary.

SLOTERDIJK: No, but it has several roots or sources that give rise to our system of norms. One is the area of domestic life forms, the ethics of the vicinity, so to speak, that regulates communication between people in neighbourly categories. The loftiest generalization of this source of morals is humanism, which is currently trying to establish itself as a world ethos – without admitting that it only interprets one segment of the moral space. Another source is the state's aesthetics. The state has a remit *sui generis*. Its regulatory obligations are not reducible to the general family ethos. Moreover, the moralities of ascetic religions have an independent source that can't be traced back to humanism or the logic of the state.

METHFESSEL/RAMTHUN: And the sources of morality creation are clashing with each other in the genetic engineering debate?

SLOTERDIJK: That happens at the moment when society is forced to discuss the unsupervised introduction of major new technologies that cause social upheaval. From a theoretical viewpoint, we are living in the middle of a fantasy world in which we are following a running experiment on how the stuff of reality is woven and how a society makes new rules for itself in a continuing process of justice and self-discovery.

METHFESSEL/RAMTHUN: Could this discovery process also lead to a renaissance of morality?

SLOTERDIJK: Not to a renaissance of morality as the great mystical singular concept I mentioned earlier – as if humans would be good again because times are bad.

METHFESSEL/RAMTHUN: The Chancellor [Gerhard

Schröder][1] has set up a national ethical council. Is this the right approach, or does it also fall into the category of hyper-consensus?

SLOTERDIJK: The ethical council probably won't work because it was set up by a putsch-type procedure, bypassing Parliament in a way that is far too transparent. The committee seems like a case of blatant manipulation. It gives the impression that the government is buying in expert opinions. Those who participate must ask themselves whether they have reflected closely enough on their own corruptibility.

METHFESSEL/RAMTHUN: All the same, the ethical council hasn't stopped citizens and politicians from conducting excellent debates on genetic engineering . . .

SLOTERDIJK: Which I am very pleased about. For a while it seemed we might have seen the end of a society that engages in debate. But now, on the verge of introducing an important new technology, we are being treated once again to the spectacle of society discussing issues in depth.

METHFESSEL/RAMTHUN: The dispute about genetic engineering seen as a fountain of youth?

SLOTERDIJK: Modern society is being brought back to its origins. It is a birth of society out of the battle of consciousness or the battle of genuine parties.

METHFESSEL/RAMTHUN: Don't we have any proper parties any more?

SLOTERDIJK: Genuine parties only exist where real conflicts of interest occur. At the moment we are seeing parties reforming in a relatively passionate way again, and not along parliamentary lines. We are witnessing the formation of morality parties, an informal party landscape with a technophobic and a technophile party. Right now the technophobic party is in power, although the Chancellor belongs to the technophile tendency.

METHFESSEL/RAMTHUN: Schröder is trying to bridge the gap for the Social Democratic Party with the slogan 'Security in a changing world'.

SLOTERDIJK: That's very smart because it involves balancing out the atmospheric extremes to prevent society plunging into a patently semantic civil war about the intolerable fundamental trends.

METHFESSEL/RAMTHUN: In relation to genetic engineering, this civil war seems to have had more impact on the CDU

[1] Gerhard Schröder, Social Democratic politician and Federal Chancellor of Germany, 1998–2005.

[Christliche Demokratische Union – the conservative Christian Democratic Party].

SLOTERDIJK: There is also a serious conflict within the Green Party, although the great majority of Greens are naturally technophobic. But in the course of the conversion to realpolitik that has been going on in the party for the past ten to fifteen years, some Greens have converted to a rather moderate technophile attitude.

METHFESSEL/RAMTHUN: The SPD [Sozaldemokratische Partei Deutschlands – German Social Democratic Party] is also going through that process.

SLOTERDIJK: Yes, because the SPD, the traditional party of redistribution of wealth, is reconsidering its fateful alliance with a prospering market and has to follow the Chancellor for pragmatic reasons.

METHFESSEL/RAMTHUN: Does the informal evolution of moralist parties as part of the genetics debate have an effect on the traditional party landscape?

SLOTERDIJK: The results show, first of all, that we have four Social Democratic parties and one party of liberal economics in Parliament. The PDS [Partei für Demokratische Sozialismus – Democratic Socialist Party] contains a left-wing fascist opposition bloc that is unpredictable because it gathers resentful anti-capitalist feelings that are difficult to identify as right or left. Basically, all politics that stems from resentment corresponds to what we wrongly describe as right-wing radicalism. In fact, it is an emotional radicalism or a rejectionist radicalism that could just as well be left wing as right wing. But the PDS as a whole is on the path to becoming Social Democratic.

METHFESSEL/RAMTHUN: What will happen now? Is it possible for the genetic engineering debate to create a climate that would result in a social-liberal coalition?

SLOTERDIJK: That wouldn't surprise me. After all, social democracy, since its conversion to the ideology of the third way, has become Blairite, and Blairism is the product of the marriage of Labour and Thatcherism. That, in turn, means the long overdue re-enactment of the working formula that was valid for the twentieth century: the market economy moderated by the welfare state. This turn by social democracy means it has admitted that it is dependent on industry prospering in an infinite economic game, an endless lottery of the markets. Liberalism and social democracy are two sides of the same coin – because both are infinitists.

METHFESSEL/RAMTHUN: Do you mean they don't recognize any limits?

SLOTERDIJK: Yes, they both pursue a policy of exceeding

limits – growth policy. Growth is merely a neutralizing term for crossing boundaries, shifting boundaries. In modern society the upward processes are open because there are no income limits, no limits to satisfaction and no limits to personal fulfilment. In contrast to the ancient hypothesis that humans can be satisfied – which is, of course, the anthropological principle of the ancient world – humans in the modern age are pursuing goals insatiably.

METHFESSEL/RAMTHUN: And the Social Democrats want to continue this insatiable policy of dissolving boundaries?

SLOTERDIJK: It is naturally harder to do that in coalition with the Greens than with the Liberals.

METHFESSEL/RAMTHUN: Aren't Social Democrats very resolute about redistribution?

SLOTERDIJK: They support redistribution; they realize that it depends on endlessly creating value. It is not surprising that Social Democratic prime ministers spearhead advances towards new technologies. It may be rather distasteful that this is occurring in such a sensitive area as human biotechnology, but in the end it is completely consistent.

METHFESSEL/RAMTHUN: In the age of globalization it is probably impossible to avoid the temptations of new technologies.

SLOTERDIJK: Globalization is based on the very successful export of European methods of improving living standards. For the past 200 years Europeans have been developing a range of products that dramatically changes the way of life of people nearly everywhere as soon as the utility value of these new products is recognized. There is a regular jealousy competition about access to these resources.

METHFESSEL/RAMTHUN: What do you mean by 'jealousy competition'?

SLOTERDIJK: All competitions are processes driven by jealousy. The great competition is not about goods but about non-material gratification. Hegel talks about the struggle for recognition as the actual motive force of history.

METHFESSEL/RAMTHUN: And why isn't envy the motive force of competition?

SLOTERDIJK: Both variants exist, of course. 'Jealousy' is the more positive term because jealous people believe in the opportunity of being ahead of their rivals in the race for a particular commodity, even if they first learned from their rivals to covet what the latter already have. In the case of envy, jealousy is deprived of its creative edge, and disparagement of others becomes important: if I don't have something, they shouldn't have it either.

METHFESSEL/RAMTHUN: Do you mean jealousy is linked

more closely with opportunity and freedom, and envy more with equality?

SLOTERDIJK: Yes. It is easier to make a general case for the unreasonable demand that people should do without something.

METHFESSEL/RAMTHUN: It follows that envious societies are typified by more redistribution, but a larger state share. Does this make Germany an envious society and the United States a jealous society?

SLOTERDIJK: That's certainly true.

METHFESSEL/RAMTHUN: Nowadays globalization necessitates the retreat of the state, indirectly fostering the creation of a civil society.

SLOTERDIJK: On condition we can trust traditional state services, that is, provided new management can be found for these large communitarian systems. In other words, the enterprises would become the workers' new fatherlands. The only problem is, there is hardly any evidence to show it works here in Germany.

METHFESSEL/RAMTHUN: Why doesn't it work?

SLOTERDIJK: Because the state is, and continues to be, an enormous service provider for which there is no substitute. Here in Germany, *Homo oeconomicus* is not created by the economy but is born in state-run hospitals, grows up in families, is educated in state schools, trained in state universities, and then emerges at age twenty-five or thirty and is returned to the wild, let loose in the market arena and given a second chance to qualify, as it were – the opportunity to begin a second life to learn the criteria and moral judgements that are part of making the person roadworthy in this other scene.

METHFESSEL/RAMTHUN: Is our society structured in such a way that it can't emancipate itself from state tutelage?

SLOTERDIJK: At any rate, it won't happen soon. Our regulatory state services are so comprehensive and detailed that trying to do it alone would overburden market forces in the long run. It would make sense, however, to reduce state control of schools to some extent, and the same applies to universities and the sciences. It would not a priori be a cultural disaster if the university became more like a privately run company and if academics were somewhat less dependent on the bureaucracy.

METHFESSEL/RAMTHUN: Why do we Germans in particular believe so strongly in the state, in contrast to Anglo-Saxon countries?

SLOTERDIJK: This is related to the fact that, in common with all continental peoples, our notion of the state is strongly influenced by territorialism. That is a very tragic notion of the state. It means the state exists for us to be able to die for it. In the end, the nation is a sacrificial entity, and that is something countries based more on maritime cultures, those neo-nomadic collectives of Britons and Americans, are reluctant to understand. But meanwhile we continentals are also increasingly abandoning the lofty state that gives death and demands sacrifice.

METHFESSEL/RAMTHUN: If we look at the growth of tax evasion and illegal labour, Germans are becoming increasingly unwilling to make financial sacrifices for the state.

SLOTERDIJK: From a historical perspective, the tax rate is extremely high. People in the so-called higher-income bracket have realized they have the comparative in terms of earnings, but the superlative in terms of taxation. We are punished for success, and that is sending out the wrong signal – it emanates from the lofty state that still exists with a lofty idea of community and a lofty ideology of redistribution, and that justifies the harm done to middle-class households and the interference in citizens' property. But the population is becoming less tolerant of these interventions because people always feel that taxation is just a matter of sufferance and nothing else.

METHFESSEL/RAMTHUN: How do we achieve the situation of citizens suffering less and giving gladly?

SLOTERDIJK: It depends on seeing the levies, the taxes subjectively, so that we don't just mindlessly hand over part of what we have earned, but we can dedicate it to a goal. Sponsoring is an ideal example of what could be possible here.

METHFESSEL/RAMTHUN: That would be a systemic breach: taxes are not supposed to serve a specific end but to finance state activity as a whole.

SLOTERDIJK: Of course. But if the state merely acts as the imaginary pimp of the whole society and extracts everything it can, but doesn't explain convincingly what it is doing with it, that results in taxation passivity and citizens end up fleeing as tax exiles. Anybody who understands anything about the economy and intelligent allocation can't agree with the way those mass redistributions take place. If governments here in Germany don't handle it more cleverly, we will observe the strange socio-psychological outcome that people who are getting richer all the time are getting more discontented all the time.

METHFESSEL/RAMTHUN: In that case, would the state be threatening its own existence by destroying the trust society is based on?

SLOTERDIJK: Precisely. There are countless areas of redistribution that could be organized much more intelligently and efficiently by alternative means. I am thinking of unemployment benefits, of the whole welfare state that should be organized more in terms of incentives, much more in terms of entrepreneurship and less in terms of the consumer state.

METHFESSEL/RAMTHUN: Are you saying that entrepreneurial thinking is supposed to save the welfare state?

SLOTERDIJK: Yes, entrepreneurs will raise the banners of hope again. Without a movement of entrepreneurs, as there was once a workers' movement, the economy can no longer explain itself adequately to society.

METHFESSEL/RAMTHUN: And what will be written on the banners?

SLOTERDIJK: 'Entrepreneurs of the world, unite' – what else? At the moment only entrepreneurs can convincingly represent the interests of the industries and services that produce the hardware, that is, the real value of productive industry, against the phantom superstructure of speculative finance economy. Only an entrepreneurs' movement can act in the anti-capitalist way that is needed now. It is time for entrepreneurial anti-capitalism.

METHFESSEL/RAMTHUN: The entrepreneur as alternative to the distorted picture of globalization, of the anonymous flow of money around the globe?

SLOTERDIJK: Entrepreneurs must show that an operative economy, not the dictatorship of the lottery bosses, is the foundation of the market economy. Entrepreneurs are the social democracy of tomorrow.

METHFESSEL/RAMTHUN: Are you serious?

SLOTERDIJK: Of course. At the moment entrepreneurs may describe themselves in neoliberal terms, but this is becoming increasingly false as the years go by, because in the end they can only justify themselves as producers of the net value that serves the other side of redistribution.

METHFESSEL/RAMTHUN: And this results in the economy itself stabilizing society?

SLOTERDIJK: Exactly. We have three mechanisms of redistribution: taxation, the stock market and foundations. Redistribution must take place because statehood and civil laws will suffer if they are not sufficiently well grounded. The first platform for redistribution, social democracy, is no longer convincing in the long run, and alongside it the economy has developed another platform for redistribution – the shareholder system.

METHFESSEL/RAMTHUN: In other words, shareholder capitalism alongside state redistribution. And what is the third platform?

SLOTERDIJK: I call that 'subjective tax'. There are beautiful examples from the Anglo-Saxon world, where gentlemanly capitalism has a certain tradition. Calvinism's strength was that it produced a type of person who was willing to earn 5 million pounds as a capitalist and then spend 4 million pounds in foundations as a member of Christian society. We have to remould our rich people from a cultural perspective and explain to them that just being rich is not good enough.

METHFESSEL/RAMTHUN: Are you advocating a new Calvinism?

SLOTERDIJK: A new Calvin? No, he was a weird, unpleasant fellow. I would rather have a mixture of an opera director and Albert Schweitzer – I mean somebody who adds charisma and gives hope to millionaires again.

METHFESSEL/RAMTHUN: So that giving can be fun?

SLOTERDIJK: Wealth must be fun – in such a way that the fun turns serious of its own accord. Wealth is too serious to leave to envy and fear. Unfortunately, people here in Germany don't know that the only feeling that makes life worthwhile is generosity. Too many people in this country haven't been rich for long enough to attain this wisdom and make the move towards generosity.

METHFESSEL/RAMTHUN: That could explain why the Germans have never been as affluent as they are today, but are still not happier.

SLOTERDIJK: Indeed, people in this country are caught in a socio-psychological dilemma. The only possibility of getting out of it would be to reclaim the public arena lustfully, turning it into a culture of public generosity. Then wealth would be justified again …

METHFESSEL/RAMTHUN: … and people would be in a better mood?

SLOTERDIJK: I won't claim that their bad mood will vanish; it is too deeply entrenched in the system. After all, we are dealing with a jealousy and envy machine of huge dimensions. That basic tension can't be eliminated. But we can make the whole issue less acute if people feel more freedom at the point where money is spent, if they experience more generosity and get back the euphoria of a celebratory donation. We should break through the spiritual isolation of the rich.

# 10

# LEARNING IS JOYFUL ANTICIPATION OF ONESELF

*Interview with Reinhard Kahl**

KAHL: A new education debate is in the air. What's brewing?

SLOTERDIJK: Potential disturbance is in the air for the whole society. You can compare it to how individuals feel physical pain. Debates and scandals form a nervous system of topics by which society perceives itself.

KAHL: Education debates could be a way for society to explore itself. But the promising debate often breaks off at the last moment. Why?

SLOTERDIJK: We usually try to suppress questions about education. They are some of the most uncomfortable questions. Compared to that, the hospital system is almost pleasant and fascinating, as we can clearly see from the mass media. We have endless film series about hospitals and consultant surgeons. The gentlemen in green who snip around on bodies have become heroes. Intuitively we could say it doesn't make sense – we don't actually want to see anything unpleasant like an operating theatre in our living room in the evening. But in fact, that's just what people want. The really unpleasant thing is school.

KAHL: There are some school soaps on television nowadays. But their equivalent of the operating theatre in hospital series would be lessons and exams, and you don't see them in school series.

SLOTERDIJK: School exams are so unpleasant because they

* This interview between Peter Sloterdijk and Reinhard Kahl appeared under the title 'Lernen ist Vorfreude auf sich selbst', in *Pädagogik* 53 (2001): 40–5 (Beltz, Weinheim).

Reinhard Kahl is a journalist and film-maker.

remind many people of birth. In schools, people are not interned for nine months but incubated for at least nine years. Then they have to fight their way out in written exams, in other words, closed situations. Modern people don't want to be reminded that they were ever incarcerated.

KAHL: School isn't seen as a prenatal paradise – that would be asking too much – but it isn't seen as the joyful event of coming-into-the-world either. Can we think of school as pressure in the birth canal?

SLOTERDIJK: School is what people always want to leave behind them. People rarely look back at school with affection.

KAHL: It wasn't always as clear-cut as that.

SLOTERDIJK: Romanticism about school, as expressed in the famous film *Die Feuerzangenbowle* [*The Punch Bowl*],[1] evokes memories of situations that were not yet emergencies. Today the school has become a necessity of its own.

KAHL: A curious necessity, like a military exercise that uses live ammunition. On the other hand, there is a lack of resonance for taking any action that might have a serious effect. The school wryly adopts an attitude of necessity and claims, 'all this is required later in life'.

SLOTERDIJK: The famous saying that we don't learn for school, but for life, was an attempt at justification from the very beginning. The original school allowed pupils to learn for school because the Graeco-Roman view was that there was no need to learn for life. Life is its own teacher; it is self-explanatory. School, however, meant leisure for the Greeks, and leisure was regarded as the quintessence of life. Funnily enough, the Greeks formed their word for 'to work' or 'to do business' from the negation of the word 'to be idle'. Anybody learning for leisure was engaging in free activity.

KAHL: How did the intrinsic value of a leisure education become a means to other ends?

SLOTERDIJK: When the modern nation-state took over the school service, the necessity principle was transferred to learning in school. It became pre-professional: school is preparation for employment. The German concept of education was shaped by Prussian neo-humanism around 1800 and still tries to find a balance between

[1] *Die Feuerzangenbowle* [*The Punch Bowl*] was a popular German film released in 1944. Set in a school in Germany, it was famous for its praise of schooldays as the best days of life, and for its light-hearted escapism during the grim last year of the Second World War.

the classical and the modern concept: we learn for school and for life. The society of work is already at the door, but the school still holds its own as an autonomous life form. *Die Feuerzangenbowle* symbolizes this compromise. Meanwhile the migration of necessity into the classroom has advanced considerably. We're not going to see any new punch bowls.

KAHL: School means something traumatic for most people. What is it? You mentioned the birth analogy. Does school make people feel unwelcome?

SLOTERDIJK: Perhaps. For most children today, school is the initiation into a situation that they feel is not about them personally. It's an inoculation programme that administers grievances until they have passed through every kind of grievance – and then they get their narcissistic school-leaving certificate. The message is: 'Whatever you may think of yourself, you're not that important.' People don't like being reminded of such exams.

KAHL: In the old school where people supposedly learned for life, they experienced being a small cog in a big machine. The oppositional movement, 'do whatever you want', didn't get far either. Today we have school students who end up without any idea of what they want.

SLOTERDIJK: That is undoubtedly related to the fact that today's educationists don't know themselves what they are educating children for. Modern society's confusion about its own goals is more clearly reflected in the confusing school system than anywhere else – except, perhaps, the area of visual arts, which is also a great world stage for mental disturbance. The school and the art business are nervous systems of sensitive issues in society in which the confusion about what will happen next is very clearly articulated. On average, teachers can't be different from the society they come from.

KAHL: Twenty or thirty years ago many people said they wanted to affect things by playing a key part in social change, and they became teachers. By now there are many other options for people with ideas. The teaching profession has become a second choice. How are refugees from life supposed to represent the world to the next generation?

SLOTERDIJK: Teachers are people who often believe it is better to explain something than do something. The cowardly and the theoretical decisions about life don't necessarily converge, but often do. The result is schools as socio-psychological biotopes with an atypical concentration of timid, under-motivated people concerned with private issues. The only answer is to de-professionalize schools. We have to enhance their social skills and leave them free on the factual side. It is increasingly clear that you don't get to the core of learning with classic schooling methods. All the people who turned out to be special in school didn't do it because of the school but because the school left them alone. When things went well it offered protection under which intensive learning processes, which have always been intrinsically autodidactic, could flourish. Sometimes the autodidactic element was able to evolve under cover of didactics. But I think this particular constellation has passed its optimal point. New optimal situations have to be created for autodidactics. The school is probably no longer part of these optimal conditions.

KAHL: Aren't didactic teachers – there are other kinds as well, of course – representatives of an ailing priestly class nowadays? Who else still believes knowledge can be passed down from above?

SLOTERDIJK: Priesthood: that's a convincing analogy. Today, armies of world clerics appear before their flock and appeal to the good in human beings. Meanwhile they have discovered that their appeals result in evil developing all the more. Then people pretend to naivety and ask what's going wrong.

KAHL: Teachers don't encourage new knowledge 'from below'. They lack the combination of action and experience.

SLOTERDIJK: Teachers live with false descriptions – more so, in fact, than any other group in society, aside from nihilists, who know what they're doing and still keep on doing it. Nihilists are always on target with any possible enlightenment. They are already on the baseline of total lack of illusions about themselves and others. They think and act on the damaging assumption that entropy always wins. This is precisely what we people on the creative side have been fighting against with the methods of art and philosophy since way back when. The point is to inspire people to enthusiasm and get them involved.

KAHL: So let's give school one more chance! How could it become a venue, or even a hothouse, for autodidactic experiments? After all, people learning of their own accord are not autistic. They need other people to inspire them, people who are curious but don't lecture them or 'mediate' the lessons in a boring way.

SLOTERDIJK: Yes, we need schools that emphasize young people's pertinacity and don't colonize them for the sake of 'necessity'. We must shut the school doors to business, fashion and other such terrifying menaces, and reconstruct a living space for people to engage in a libidinous relationship with their own intelligence. What is clear to see in a small child usually gets lost in the school pupil. The rescue of the cognitive libido must become the school's core project.

KAHL: School as a space of dense atmospheres swelling with possibilities? You have been occupied for years with understanding what spheres are and not getting stuck with congealed substances like knowledge.

SLOTERDIJK: My theory of enthusiasms, that is, of public spirits, tries to reduce overblown romantic-nationalist concepts to the level of specific groups. Schools must become boarding schools! Not literally, of course, but rather in the sense of emphasizing the intrinsic character of school life. I'm seeing that with my daughter, who is lucky to be in an excellent schooling situation. In her case, you can see clearly what it means to spend time in an environment for encouraging enthusiasm.

KAHL: What grade is she in?

SLOTERDIJK: She is in the second year at the Montessori branch of an ordinary elementary school. You can see how a different climatic policy in the school encourages a different way of speaking to the pupils and a different language among the pupils themselves. This school begins by assuming that the learning libido is the real capital. The children bring their curiosity, their enthusiasm, that priceless medium of happy anticipation of their own self, into the learning process. What matters is expectation of the next state to be reached. A form of didactics that respects this operates quite differently and with better results than a school where teachers have the attitude: you're going to be astonished, and I'm the one who is going to show you how things are.

KAHL: That's what nourishes the evil eye, which is probably related to the frustration of teaching staff. They basically remain like school pupils from the ages of six to sixty-five, and that's really mortifying.

SLOTERDIJK: I think it's time for teachers to carry on the work Nietzsche did for priests. Teachers are an authority that is under-criticized and deserves to be given liberating and destructive criticism. In fact, people mostly accuse teachers of the wrong things.

KAHL: The accusation of laziness, for example.

SLOTERDIJK: That's lazy itself.

KAHL: It may apply to some people who are already practically retired from the job, usually due to mental overload. But isn't the teaching profession a case of overload in structural terms?

SLOTERDIJK: That's why teachers should be helped with adequate criticism. The analysis of job-specific mortification and experiences of failure is needed just as much as the analysis of resentment against the profession. That would be the most valuable kind of enlightenment. We must link up with teachers to revitalize the school starting from its strongest position. Where is its renewable, enthusiastic source point? Schools must come forward energetically and say: we offer opportunities, here is our knowledge, here is our art of living – we are inviting you to all that. The gesture of invitation is perhaps the most important thing. It turns schools into guesthouses of knowledge and places for the intelligence to go on outings, so to speak.

KAHL: You mean the end of compulsory school, which insists, like a surreal restaurant, on forced feeding and pupils being compelled to eat everything on their plate?

SLOTERDIJK: We have to break with the most harmful of all ancient European concepts: the idea of knowledge transfer. This idea of instilling is wrong in terms of system theory, it is morally wrong ...

KAHL: Unsustainable in terms of cognitive psychology ...

SLOTERDIJK: And despite that, the school is built around that idea, around the truly accursed and harmful idea of transfer.

KAHL: They are still distributing Communion wafers.

SLOTERDIJK: The institution of school is based on the perverse communion that says: 'We have and we share out.' But learning just doesn't function that way. We have to respect that we're always dealing with people who are accomplished in their own personal way. Up until now they have been complete and without any real deficiency. The next state or condition can only be constructed on the basis of the work the person has already done. Teachers can only disturb the process, unless they become something like a host, a coach or – in a good sense – a seducer who is already at the place the child's next step leads to. In such 'guesthouses' the principle of happy anticipation could seal the pedagogical pact. Watching my daughter, I am fascinated by this. At the age of two, she already strikes me as a person who has something I have never seen properly described, either in psychoanalysis or any other kind of psychological description. I discovered from her that the libido of wakefulness is shown by the fact she is excited about her next state. She is happy about her own becoming. It is as if she were wearing a safety lamp on her head that lights up the next chapter of life for her discreetly and always auspiciously. She always sees light at the end of the tunnel. It is the light from her own inbuilt projector.

KAHL: What a drama it would be if the safety lamp were blown out and only the gaffer on set switched the lights on and off! Maybe blowing out one's own light was a systemic compulsion of old industrial capitalism, against which it was futile to rebel. Enterprises today are also increasingly unable to cope with burned-out cases. They can deal with them as consumers, but not in the role of 'staff members'.

SLOTERDIJK: Professional teaching must forge the link again with the dynamic libido that illuminates one's own ability to become. Instead of that, I have heard that teachers of German-language classes invited staff from the Employment Office in Karlsruhe to visit schools to teach school students how to fill in unemployment benefit forms. I know it's an extreme example, but it illustrates where the problem lies. Many teachers, when they operate as creators of the bad climate, practise the didactics of discouragement. They often do it, even without wanting to, when they secretly project their own failure or their self-pity on to their young clients.

KAHL: That provokes running battles and power struggles.

SLOTERDIJK: Most of all, the latent message comes through: 'You'll be astonished. I myself stopped being astonished a long time ago.' These two pieces of lethal information turn people into first-class climate polluters. Children should be protected against adult pessimism with their own special anti-pollution law. To refer to my daughter again, she has the advantage of an exceptional situation: she has a teacher with an amazing way of tapping the source that generates happiness. Like a good demon, he links into the children's love of learning. He lights up when he sees the children's faces lighting up. This is awesome, and sets a standard. But along come the parents with their concept of realism, their pessimism and their fearful projections, and try to curtail this space of didactic miracles and to colonize it from outside.

KAHL: What do the parents say?

SLOTERDIJK: 'Aren't you giving the children the wrong picture of life?' 'Can't you make things more structured?' 'Can't you be a bit stricter?' Statements like that show how 'realists' try to impose their climatic monopoly. We have to create a counter-climate to oppose this. Basically, in my work as a university teacher and as a writer, I see myself mainly as a creator of spheres and a didactic proponent of atmospheres. What people learn is not all that important in the first place; far more important is for them to enter a climate that makes them aware that being able to learn is, in itself, the best opportunity of their life. In my opinion, this work of climate creation that some people attack as unjustified shamanism is indispensable for the moral regeneration of our community.

KAHL: If using productive atmospheres works, something could develop that we never experience when only standard results are presented and the special atmospheres are sacrificed to the requirements of rigid purity rules.

SLOTERDIJK: That's when the poison of boredom starts to spread. The school is an epicentre of boredom and is run by professional bores who daub, gum up and insult children's intelligence. Many people never recover. That is the real educational disaster. In the end, atmospheres must be seen as the most real things of all.

Today, we create situations for young people in which they have everything to hand and no desire for anything. We lose more than ten years in the elementary education process, and the best students need another ten years after the first educational experience to find their own second chance. By then, if all goes well, we have an original thirty-year-old who, after the process of school and regeneration, can start his or her own career as a creative person attuned to atmospheres.

KAHL: Most people in Germany would think it is a strange idea that everything else depends on atmospheres in institutions and around people.

SLOTERDIJK: The problem is more acute in Germany. The catastrophe of National Socialism with its monstrous perversion of collective enthusiasm has resulted in a super-abstinence of communal energy in this country. In French and Anglo-Saxon culture, and in the USA, the school system is governed by different climatic factors. There is much more emphasis on the relation between the institution and the public spirit that animates people. In Germany, we have a very bureaucratic school atmosphere, always combined with resignation and dogmatic scepticism.

KAHL: The German preference for being victims – or anything rather than active players because that could make them perpetrators – is particularly widespread in teachers' staff rooms.

SLOTERDIJK: It's not only victim passion that exists, but also victim didactics and victim simulation. At our university we recently experienced the problem of individual students having to put up with restrictions and inconveniences because of reorganization in some subjects.

KAHL: You are referring to the School of Design in Karlsruhe, to which you were appointed rector this year.

SLOTERDIJK: That's right. And what happened? We had 120 students applying for credits for two semesters of their course because they feel they are victims of the move to the new centre, which offers them access to one of Europe's most impressive university buildings, not to mention one of the best teaching bodies and fabulous teacher–student ratios. The temptation to describe our own life in the light of discrimination has become so strong that even young people have now developed this resigned, senior-citizen-type attitude, combined with an aggressive kind of moralist demanding, as if it were perfectly natural. To counter this, we must try to interest them in the idea of entrepreneurial life so that they don't already behave like social security clients at the age of twelve. In any case, victim hysteria relates back to childish patterns – to over-dramatization of minor injuries.

KAHL: The foundling, exposed, all alone in the world.

SLOTERDIJK: Betrayed by all – and besides, my parents are not my real parents. My teachers are not my real teachers. Everyone abandoned me. I'm only looking for the mailbox where I can post my complaints letter …

KAHL: The agony column …

SLOTERDIJK: … the world's agony column. This attitude can only be corrected by activating a conspiracy of knowing better. Philosophy, literature and art must be the starting point for putting an end to the era we have lived in for fifty, sixty years now, handing in our homework as a model nation with collective depression. We are at the beginning of a generational change. It should be interpreted openly and energetically.

KAHL: Couldn't a new education debate be a medium for that? We must transpose to society as a whole the image of 'joyful anticipation of oneself' as the heart and soul of the learning process.

SLOTERDIJK: Yes, we should have this debate, because societies have no centre and no ego, they only have the public as a medium for giving wake-up calls and creating disturbances. We must finally abandon the dangerous spectres that have driven the twentieth century into disasters, the idea that society is totally itself at some point. After all, the crazy illusion of a Führer is nothing but the political interpretation of a fallacy that our culture has blithely fostered for centuries, namely, that there is a place where it could be completely itself. This realization is the entrance charge we have to pay if we want to attain the second wave of sociological enlightenment. We must understand that societies use atmospheres to control and climatize themselves. The topics we are talking about form a semantic air-conditioning system. Right now, all the signs are that we are programming it wrongly.

KAHL: Humans are, so to speak, the subtenants of the world, responsible for small precincts, but not for the atmosphere, not for the intermediate parts. We hold 'the state' and 'society' responsible for that.

SLOTERDIJK: And that leads to running away, disablement or avoidance panic. We feel trapped in the 'system'. This is the basis for the psychology of employees and public servants today. Instead, we must start with a good understanding of the perspective of an entrepreneur, an entrepreneur of life, and use this kind of thinking to reanimate the public service as well. Perhaps this will lead to the emergence of a new generation of teachers. I think the impulse for this has to come from artists and from independent media. Philosophy and art set the tone – they retune the general atmosphere.

KAHL: Maybe we should begin by imagining a school with different architecture. Looking at classrooms where everybody sits in rows leaves me speechless.

SLOTERDIJK: The nineteenth century built schools, museums and barracks – three atmospheric conditioning systems that preform social synthesis with the aid of state techniques for influencing people. Schools must be liberated from this tradition. Hopefully, the idea of a new kind of school will become enough of a political issue in the coming years that a new phase of experimentation can begin. With luck, we could have a really good, productive row about education quite soon …

KAHL: It could happen …

SLOTERDIJK: There's enough tinder for it. Then, after the abreaction phase in which people have collectively got over the duty and the tendency to complain, we could start a productive discussion and try to design a school that fits the level of our knowledge and experience. Given the amount of accumulated discontent, the time is ripe. As far as positive forces are concerned, we will first have to reorganize what little we have left to see if it is enough for an offensive.

KAHL: How shall we start? Isn't it important first of all to bring other adults into schools instead of only lifelong teachers? This could evolve into a kind of co-evolution. If teachers work as people gatherers, bringing 'third parties' into schools, they will become more adult themselves. It will be good for them and for the school.

SLOTERDIJK: That would be a first step. At the same time, a new viewpoint on people has to be constructed in the media. I don't think it would be too difficult to show that interesting people are more fascinating than the average entertainment. If the fascination value of being involved with a living person who has become an adult can't compete with regression programmes offered by sex, crime and co., we have lost the game. Windows should be opened in the media …

KAHL: And 'third parties' should be brought in everywhere.

SLOTERDIJK: Exactly. We don't know the interesting people in our own society. That means our society doesn't know itself and doesn't know that it doesn't know itself. If the media can successfully convey this enthusiasm for interesting people, they will also trigger a new learning process in schools of bringing in remarkable people with interesting jobs. That would be a broad move to de-professionalize curricula.

KAHL: Parents would worry that their children wouldn't learn anything any more.

SLOTERDIJK: You can deal with the panic aroused by the

suspicion that competency is being compromised by emphasizing that nothing is more educational than the opportunity to see successful people at close quarters. By the way, concerning universities of the arts, that is also my response to the outdated master-class principle. If we want to preserve anything of the idea of the master, we have to translate it into the form of watching successful creators of art at work and observing their success curve. That is highly instructive under any circumstances, regardless of whether students react by positive association or by rejection. Both are equally informative, provided that students have an authentic opportunity to see a creative person fully in action. This is precisely the concept of our art school in Karlsruhe.

KAHL: Dialogues worthy of the name consist of finely tuned agreements and refusals.

SLOTERDIJK: Allowing scope for productive scepticism in relation to a successful position is never a waste of time. Even people who react by turning away have learned a great deal from it. Perhaps we live in a period in which people learn more by rejection than by borrowing. The cowardly teacher is the bad teacher. The good teacher is the person who is open to rejection. The same applies to good writers, who must always risk enough that they are worth reading even if we reject them.

KAHL: That brings us to the well-known Sloterdijkian concept of 'de-idiotizing': expending our own stupidity, for how can we get rid of it otherwise?

SLOTERDIJK: How can we get rid of it, if not in dealing with potential imitators who are smart enough to refuse to imitate at the last minute?

# 11

# POSTMEN AND FALLEN TOWERS

*Interview with Arno Frank**

FRANK: Mr Sloterdijk, what mandate do you have for breaking into television?

SLOTERDIJK: Definitely not the mandate of the world spirit. It's more about my feeling that, given the decadence of the universities, philosophy should link up with other media.

FRANK: TV philosopher – is that your mission?

SLOTERDIJK: We can describe every activity a person engages in from two different viewpoints. We can portray it from one side as a mission and from another as a need. If we describe it as a mission, then we believe that the individual has an idea or a master behind him that sends him ahead. In my case it is not as easy. I don't have a master or an obsessive idea that decides for me what I should do. If I did, I would feel much more comfortable at the moment.

FRANK: Why?

SLOTERDIJK: Because then I could say: whether or not it works out, the idea or the sender is responsible. I would only be the messenger, the postman, and could deliver my message without being responsible for its success.

FRANK: What about the other version …?

SLOTERDIJK: We must interpret it as an expressive action – in other words, I don't have to trace the sequence of themes back beyond the author. It can start with the author. That means the

* This interview between Peter Sloterdijk and Arno Frank appeared in the *taz* newspaper under the title 'Ich bin nicht der Postbote' ['I am not the Postman'] (19 January 2002): 3f. Arno Frank is an editor at the *taz*.

author expresses himself or herself. He or she is an energy field that wants to discharge in that direction and no other.

FRANK: A medium within the medium, so to speak. But philosophers don't usually frequent the footlights ...

SLOTERDIJK: The studio has no ramp. In conventional theatre there is a border between the stage and the auditorium. On the TV podium you are surrounded by spectators – the TV situation is like being encircled. The question is: what can motivate people to let themselves be surrounded by spectators?

FRANK: Exhibitionists love situations like that.

SLOTERDIJK: Maybe. But that's really not my concern.

FRANK: Not a trace of vanity?

SLOTERDIJK: I am a person who likes keeping one side hidden, even when I appear in public. I have a mysterious aversion to the idea of people looking at me from the right-hand side.

FRANK: In a metaphorical, political sense?

SLOTERDIJK: No, spatially. In television you can't stand with your back to a pillar like a figure in a Gothic cathedral and imagine that you're drawing strength out of the stone. Television is a cannibalistic medium that devours people optically. We are going to experiment with being eaten.

FRANK: You recently suggested interpreting nations as institutions that maintain concentrated postal and communications systems – with telecommunications firms as secular churches. What do you mean by that?

SLOTERDIJK: Modern media societies have no brain, no central organ, only dense concentrations in the nervous system. How is such a complex and brainless system supposed to control itself? If modern societies were organized like churches, for example, Telekom would be the provider of both the network and the content of democracy. That is a lovely ecclesiological illusion: if we were like churches we could avoid the impression that no genuine internal connection exists in society. We would be limbs of a large communitarian body. I am thinking about a map Dietmar Kamper[1] once showed me. It was drawn by a medieval monk who had projected the body of Christ in the crucifix position on to the map of Europe, so that altogether the points representing the monasteries of Europe formed something like a visualization of the Corpus Christi spectre. A mystical EU.

[1] Dietmar Kamper (1936–2001) was a German writer, philosopher and sociologist. He was professor of sociology at the Free University Berlin from 1979.

FRANK: What is a society today when it isn't a society?

SLOTERDIJK: The question is: how can we envisage social relationships at all if we describe society as a whole as a body without a central organ?

FRANK: And the answer?

SLOTERDIJK: The answer would be a media theory for our times, and a number of people in the contemporary scene are working on that. Think of the work of Norbert Bolz, or Friedrich Kittler, or Jochen Hörisch, to mention only the older ones.[2] Those three men are intellectuals of my generation I feel related to because I am doing analogous work. Each of the three, in his own way, has experienced similar kinds of trouble with their former comrades.

FRANK: The same academic allergy against new approaches?

SLOTERDIJK: These three authors are like litmus tests for the resentment of the social environment. They are cheerful theoreticians who see their intellectual practice additionally as leisure practice. I regard them as partners in crime. We are atmospheric felons in a cultural society that continues to claim a monopoly when it comes to defining moralist smog. In that context such enlighteners or clarifiers are not welcome at first. But I am convinced that within a generation their work will be canonical. It may sound strange, but I believe we have an avant-garde impact even today. Yet the inhabitants of the intellectual field aren't amused when you tell them you are ahead in some way – you get sent to purgatory like a backward pupil.

FRANK: In your major work, *Sphären* [*Spheres*], you develop a theory of 'ensouled spaces', from bubbles to globes to foam ...

SLOTERDIJK: I think foam is the defining metaphor for multiple spaces for which the phrase 'dreams are foam' no longer holds. The substantialist aversion against anything fleeting and fragile – against foam – is also only lack of thought. If you think about multi-chambered systems under the premises of spatial logic, you quickly stop wanting to use foam, or scum, as a metaphor for something despicable. Quite the opposite: we realize that foam is a cosmogonic principle without which life and environmental effects would simply be impossible. But that is a theme I will develop calmly, like the plot of a stage play. If all goes well, we can talk about it again in eighteen months' time.

[2] Norbert Bolz (b. 1953) is a German philosopher, media theorist and design theorist. Friedrich Kittler (1943–2011) was a media theorist and philosopher known as 'the Derrida of the digital age'. Jochen Hörisch (b. 1951) is a German literary and media theorist.

FRANK: In *Spheres II* you wrote that a city shows in the vertical what it plans to do in the horizontal. Following your theory, wasn't the attack on the World Trade Center in New York also an annihilating attack on a semantic level?

SLOTERDIJK: Islamist terror dealt a blow at the level of real existing symbolism, which is why the Americans' counter-attack has been so remarkably flat and helpless. The reason is that the attacker can't be hit symmetrically. The Americans don't dare to attack the strong symbol that belongs to the perpetrators. We simply have to consider what the equivalent, in the Islamists' worldview, is to what they think the World Trade Center means to us. It involves a very small number of objects. The list would be headed by the Dome of the Rock in Jerusalem, followed by the Ka'aba in Mecca. Who could justify military assaults on those two objectives?

FRANK: But a war is already being fought on the symbolic level.

SLOTERDIJK: What the Americans and their friends in the Western world find very difficult to grasp is that they have lost – lost at the first shot. This is about a war that consisted of a single battle and led to a pure defeat that can never be compensated for. The twin towers fell. Everybody saw it and that means, however odd it may sound, that the show is already over, and everything you might want to write as a sequel is playing out on another level. The sight of collapsing tower blocks is doubly painful in a culture whose sources prepare it for such a process. On the one hand, we have the myth of David and Goliath, which has been subverted in the most unpleasant fashion here in Germany. We are used to pitting the small good person against the big bad one, and are suddenly forced to let the big good one enter the ring against the small bad one. That stiffens all the remaining moral feathers on our already well-plucked conscience. Only the fully plucked can unreservedly come to terms with this new situation. The great good against the small bad – will that be the new battle line-up of the twenty-first century? That's really a joke.

FRANK: And the second myth?

SLOTERDIJK: That, on the other hand, concerns the Tower of Babel, which represents the first time theological resentment against a tall building was articulated – in fact, against the Others' tall building. This myth expresses the enslaved Jews' discontent with Babylonian arrogance. It is a lustful destruction fantasy about the text: 'God reduces heathen towers to rubble and ashes.' This is a constitutive theme for our culture. The trauma of September 11 is so big because it concerns an attack on the dominant illusionary system of world power. The people of the United States don't know how to keep on dreaming their neo-Babylonian dream of total security of the inner world by total control of the external world without destroying themselves. An evil virus has indeed infiltrated into the hegemony of the United States. We should realize that it is in our own interests that this virus doesn't cause too much alienation in the American mentality. At the moment I see the greatest danger in terms of global politics of resentment. Thank God, American democracy has a degree of resilience, and American civil society in particular has miraculous moral resources. But it is a severe infection.

FRANK: Because there is no way to compensate for it any longer?

SLOTERDIJK: The message of the towers has already become imprinted in historical memory because in our culture the symbolism of the tower is very deeply imbued with theological and ethno-narcissistic elements. A fallen tower signifies a divine judgement beyond which there is no possibility of return.

FRANK: As the author of spherological theory, do you welcome the introduction of a single currency in Europe as an affluent sphere?

SLOTERDIJK: I see the euro as an admission that the Europeans don't have a unified concept at the moment. The question is: why don't they have it? Are they so united and content with their European existence that they don't demand anything else? Or are they in a condition of malignant weakness whose outcome doesn't look good – a kind of weakness that expresses the extinction of this civilization's power to solve problems? I tend to think the first case is the answer. I think something very unique is emerging in Europe, namely a great structure whose internal constitution no longer has an imperial agenda. That's something we have never seen before in history: the great power that appears imperial without a programme.

FRANK: In contrast to American greatness?

SLOTERDIJK: Yes, American greatness still follows an imperial code. The European structure is post-imperial, and in that respect the far more interesting structure. It gives more scope for thought and is more worthy of imitation. It inspires fewer jealousy conflicts. In fact, at the moment world history has a hot centre, which is the internal monotheistic athletic contest of megalomanias. That is the reason why we are seeing an American–Islamic world war front, at least at the semantic level. A war of jealousy is being fought here. It is about occupying the position of the leading monotheist people. And anybody who is a loyal follower of Mohammed and positions himself or herself like that obviously has a problem with America. The USA is the triumphant ruling theocracy at the moment.

FRANK: A religious state? In which sense?

SLOTERDIJK: America occupies the exact place at God's right hand that can only be occupied once. We could say this results in a Jacob and Esau problem on the global political level, the purest form of a theodrama. We are watching two interconnected crusades – an oriental and a Western crusade are intertwined in astounding symmetry. René Girard, the great analyst of triangular conflicts, tried to show this in an article for *Le Monde*.[3] The struggle of imitative jealousies relates to a property that is first constituted within this competition, namely the privilege of being the culture on which the hand of the One God rests most visibly.

FRANK: How do you recognize this?

SLOTERDIJK: On the one hand, Bush says, 'God is not neutral in the battle between America and its enemies.' The twenty-first century will be an experimental set-up to process the manic content of that statement. On the other hand, Bin Laden's key phrase is, 'What happened in New York is good terror.' The sooner people grasp the symmetry between these statements, the better for us.

FRANK: And in Europe?

SLOTERDIJK: Europe will only thrive if it understands where its advantage and its strengths lie in this situation.

FRANK: What might they be?

SLOTERDIJK: It is an advantage to have no interests in this affair beyond fully conditional, or rather, ironical support of the United States. Europe is already immersed in a post-monotheistic situation. Perhaps that would be the most positive definition we could offer for the introduction of the euro. If we want to venture very far ahead in the beautiful art of positive thinking, we can describe the procedure on 1 January 2002 in these terms: the monetary union is the final step in recognizing that we are already living in a post-imperialist structure in which the idea of cultural or quantitative greatness has become totally decoupled from the manic propulsion programmes of imperial culture. From a long-term perspective, when the situation has stabilized, Europe will outstrip the United States as the homeland of the art of living.

[3] René Girard is a French-born American literary critic, historian and philosopher specializing in social sciences. He is particularly known for his work on mimicry and scapegoats.

# 12

# RAISING OUR HEADS

## Pampering Spaces and Time Drifts

### *Conversation with Thomas Macho**

MACHO: I would like to begin with the idea that the possible improvement, perfection and optimizing of human beings is a project that has been conceived and planned for just a little over 200 years. Time – whether past or present – was not actually a theme in pre-industrial agrarian cultures. Those cultures doubtless had their stories of origin, more or less detailed chronicles and – usually apocalyptic – ideas of the future. But the horizons of remembrance are just as limited as the horizons of planning. Even in the eighteenth century, a scholar could still work with creation dates calculated from biblical texts, such as 7 October 3761 BC. And we learn from the story of Joseph the Egyptian that in a great empire, a high culture of the ancient world based on writing, a man able to plan ahead for a timespan of twice seven years could rise to become the Pharaoh's chief adviser. For agrarian cultures, time is simply a function of destiny. The history of the earth and of life and, most of all, the history of humankind, first became visible in the nineteenth century as a timespan to be calculated in millions of years. Perhaps it was only in the twentieth century that – with the aid of new sciences such as statistics and prognosis – the future could appear spread out as an incalculable open continuum. Politics, economics

* This conversation between Peter Sloterdijk and Thomas Macho appeared under the title 'Den Kopf heben: Über Räume der Verwöhnung und das Driften in der Zeit', in Petra Lutz, Thomas Macho and Gisela Staupe (eds), *Der (im)perfekte Mensch: Metamorphosen von Normalität und Abweichung* (Vienna, Cologne, Weimar: Böhlau Verlag), 2003, pp. 379–405.

Thomas Macho is a cultural scholar and philosopher. He has been a professor of cultural history at the Humboldt University of Berlin since 1993.

and new technologies whose impact it may only be possible to evaluate after thousands of years impose a kind of thinking in the future without any historical models to rely on. Since the twentieth century we have known in more detail what it means to project the education or improvement of the human race.

SLOTERDIJK: This approach to consciousness of time raises a controversial point right away. In working on the third volume of my *Spheres* project I have developed a new approach in philosophical anthropology with a stronger spatial emphasis. It was surprising, even for me, to see how much this theory of the contemporary age – for that is essentially what *Spheres III* is intended to be – had to delve into anthropology. I would actually go as far as to say that the forms of philosophical anthropology until then had been defined too hastily. At least, as I see it, the shotgun wedding between the concepts 'philosophy' and 'anthropology' didn't result in a lasting alliance, either in the Heideggerian form or in the form of Plessner's or Gehlen's philosophy. I am aware, of course, that Heidegger would be appalled at anybody making such associations with his works – he saw himself as a resolute anti-anthropologist – but at the same time he wouldn't really be able to deny the connections to what Plessner did on the one hand and Gehlen on the other. *Spheres III* has evolved into a book that proposes reshaping philosophical anthropology as topology. My aim was mainly to explain to people by starting from the place where human beings are formed – the surreal place that determines anthropogenesis. I am thinking of *Homo sapiens*' characteristic tendency to premature births, and the permanent incubator situation in which the young grow up. I am also thinking of the extraordinary bonding between mothers and their young that flows into the human condition from the ancient primate legacy. All that gives us the right to speak of an exceptional neurological situation in relation to *sapiens*. Added to that is the exceptional phonotopic situation, life in 'the house of language', to cite Heidegger's great phrase. We realize all too rarely that the house of language is firstly, and usually, a house of nonsense. It is the refuge of redundancy and self-arousal. Its residents live *eo ipso* in the house of self-referentiality, perhaps even in the house of proto-music. In other words, it is the home of a kind of tonality or sound closer to music than to communication. In this case, *Dasein* means something like being heard.

MACHO: The 'house of language' is a mysterious place. Neither linguists nor palaeo-anthropologists know when and how language developed in the first place, and the possible preconditions under which it had to develop. The word 'house' suggests that people first developed grammatically differentiated languages, with subject-predicate relations for example, during the 'Neolithic revolution' when houses and cities were built. We have examples of many different kinds of symbol formation from the period 40,000 to 30,000 BC (in the Spanish and French cave paintings, for example); but if we think about the anatomy of the vocal apparatus among Neanderthals it is still completely unclear whether these images and symbols indicate a sort of language (and it is probably unlikely). Nonetheless, and despite all his criticism of anthropology, Heidegger insisted on the house of language: he argued that humans only became conclusively and unmistakably distinguished from animals through entry into the house of language. On the contrary, I think humans and animals entered the house of language together, and the first things they probably heard – according to Julian Jaynes's thesis – were commands and imperatives.

SLOTERDIJK: According to the latest information from geneticists, *Homo sapiens* shares 99.4 per cent of his genetic make-up with chimpanzees. This is horrifying for anthropocentric people. It follows that the whole anthropological difference induced by the break with animality resides in this tiny remainder – provided it can be biologically located. This fact makes it immediately clear that genetics is not adequate as a basis for the human phenomenon. Rather, we have to take account of a topological difference to explain what actually happened when great apes became human beings. 'Topological difference' means we are dealing with an essential displacement, and that is what leads to culture. As I see it, humanization is a side effect of exceptional pampering. The 'pampering' of humans enables them to move into the house of language. Of course I am aware that the term 'pampering' sounds outrageous to most people – especially those who are generally regarded as poor wretches anyway. Since the eighteenth century, if not before, 'pampering' has been seen as one of the worst statements people can make about other people. Nothing has struck fear into educators and moralists as much as the phenomenon of pampering – and sometimes for good reason, because this fear conceals an insight of great significance. I am actually saying that pampering is the *conditio humana* as such, and those who don't want to talk about pampering should keep silent about human beings. In fact, the anthropologists of the eighteenth century spoke of pampering, although not from a theoretical perspective but in a moralizing, admonitory tone: do anything you want, as long as you never admit to the tendency to pamper! That was almost the categorical imperative of bourgeois educational theory. I am arguing that anthropologists have seen humans as being so seriously at risk from pampering that they can't talk about the human constitution except in terms of admonitions. Once again, in this case the alarm was quicker than the theory. After 200 years of aversive discourse about pampering we have reached the moment when we can neutralize the concept and transform it into a descriptive term. What happens when the block behind which the phenomenology of pampering was hidden up to now collapses? What happens when the scene is no longer dominated by educationalists who want to turn people into diligent citizens, soldiers and subjects? When the traditions of education for toughening people up don't work any more, and militarist alchemy no longer sets the tone? For the first time, we can calmly survey the immense mass of facts about pampering – and we have reached the moment when philosophy really meets anthropology. This is where the encounter between the two happens first, and all the previous attempts of so-called philosophical anthropology were over-hasty and based on false concepts because the core concept, pampering, was either missing or only effective in a distorted way. Gehlen's reference to human abandonment of instincts is still too vague and too negatively formulated. The trend may be right but there is still too much of the teacher calling for the heavy hand of institutions to take charge of this mollycoddled, biologically impossible being and give it support. Plessner's case is very similar, although seen through the lens of liberalism and just as inadequate. It is not enough to say that *Homo sapiens* is his own spectator – however deeply meaningful such a diagnosis may be. Basically, this statement is about transcendental philosophy distilled into anthropology: if humans are their own spectators it means they are always simultaneously agents of their lives and observers of those same lives. They live their life and stand beside themselves. This is all that the formula of eccentric positioning that Plessner propounded means. Because, we are told, life in human form is something that cannot simply be lived, but must be led, one can say of *Homo sapiens* that he represents the union between the leaders and the led. So far, so good. But that's not enough because it doesn't tackle the basic problem – the dynamic of pampering that catapults humans out of nature. Occasionally I use an image of *Homo sapiens* as a space traveller, sitting in a pampering rocket and being catapulted into outer space. We have always lived in a space station of pampering, but usually we don't notice because part of the character of pampering is that it naturalizes itself at every stage and declares itself to be self-evident. Pampering is relegated to the background as self-evident and becomes irrelevant. As a theoretician, you have to be very cold-blooded and try to think in a way that is methodically asocial before you are able to articulate such theses at all.

Incidentally, there is another reason why this is the only way things can be: ancient European influences have accustomed us to describing humans in terms of their misery – we usually see them as animals that lack something. The tradition of the *conditio humana* focuses unequivocally on human beings as broken creatures. We could rename the species *Homo patiens*. This reminds me of the basic text of European miserabilism with the telling title *de humanae conditionis miseria*, written by Lotario de Segni, later Pope Innocent III, around the year 1200. It is quite a remarkable and illuminating text, a veritable litany of misery based on the decision to weigh up human existence completely on the negative side and to fuel arguments about the weariness of life – presumably to eulogize taking refuge with God as the sole alternative to normal existence.

MACHO: Raising the spectre of the misery of human existence is, of course, an essential element of talking about death and mortality that was important for the old cultures – before the advent of humanism – because people believed that 'memento mori' was a mark of the specific human condition. Notwithstanding all the idealization of perfection and beauty of human beings, often with reference to Greek art, we should never forget the fleeting nature of humans, the transience of their existence. The cruellest discussion on the miserable condition of humans that I know of – aside from the text by Innocent III you have just mentioned – is in the medieval dialogue between Death and the Bohemian ploughman, where man is described as a mass of refuse, a churn of filth, a dish for worms, a stink house, a repulsive washtub, a rancid carcass and a reeking flagon of urine, whose cavities exude 'disgusting filth'. This dialogue about death allows us to locate humans in a kind of middle position: on the one hand they are distinguished from animals, on the other from God and the angels. Humans stand in the middle between animals and God: we can also glean that from the Porphyrian tree, the scale of being that gave rise to Neoplatonism, a philosophy full of overflows and emanations. Herder's *Ideas for a Philosophy of the History of Mankind* – even though it argues in terms of universal history – is quite obsessed by the idea that humans are the beings in the middle, not just the 'deficient beings' but the 'beings liberated in the creation' that can develop downwards (towards the animals) or upwards (towards spiritual beings). The principles of 'domestication' are unified in this middle. These principles literally mean the connections between living in the house of being, habituation and pampering.[1] Habituation – along with pampering

[1] Sloterdijk is playing with the German nouns *das Gewöhnen* [habituation] and *das Verwöhnen* [pampering], both of which have their roots in the verb *wohnen* [to live in, or to inhabit].

– is probably an equally interesting process of early human history. Constructing houses, learning to speak, and commanding and obeying, presupposes habituation; without habituation we would be totally incapable of perceiving our pampering – including where it is thwarted by death, hunger and illness. The 'first liberated being in the creation' can habituate himself or herself beyond destiny and coercion. Habituation and pampering, those beginnings of living, can, as you suggest, only be conceived adequately as themes of topology. Actually, time is always presented topologically – even as a miserabilist epitome of an experience of *vanitas*, of the transience of life. Until recently, we never imagined time in any other way except topologically, in concepts of distance or measurable stretches. From the start, time was an epiphenomenon of space, just like memory. Somebody who remembers (or plans) builds spaces, interior palaces we know from the *ars memoriae*. But to get back to pampering: in your view it precedes inhabiting, or even habituation. When and where was the 'pampering rocket' you refer to actually launched?

SLOTERDIJK: The special human variation of pampering arises from the fusion of a favourable situation, in which the early hominoid type of savannah walker emerged, with an old animalist advantage of warmth, already fully developed in hominoids, which is evident in the mother–child relationship among great apes. The formula says: Savannah security effect plus hominoid cosy room. The moment these two factors coincide the special incubator effect occurs, resulting in the emergence of *Homo sapiens*. There is a natural history of pampering that goes back far beyond the human field. Since the time it was defined by Julius Kollmann, a biologist of the late nineteenth century, the phenomenon of retaining juvenile morphologies has been described as neoteny. The neo-characteristics of children and young adults are projected through neoteny, or juvenilization, into the morphology of adults. In other words, a general protraction of juvenile forms occurs – a phenomenon that biologists have noted in numerous animal species. As we know, it is heavily topologically conditioned because, as far as I can see, it can be observed exclusively in nest-building, cave-dwelling or other animal species that have particular technical skills for creating niches. We can see immediately that nest-building animals start a process of enormous security transfer for the benefit of their own brood that will show up sooner or later in the biological appearance of their offspring. This transfer is unknown to flight animals living out in the open, which means they cannot afford such extensive juvenilization of their offspring. Nest-builders, however, generate a spontaneous incubation effect for the benefit of their young. I can see it in cats,

I can see it in dogs, I can see it in countless other mammals, not to mention the famous axolotl. Where the nest security effect occurs, the offspring can be born in a shockingly immature state. The same thing can be observed in marsupials, which have the most interesting life form in terms of developmental history because they seem to embody the compromise solution between live birth and laying eggs. This touches on the topological puzzle of neoteny. As soon as the work of the uterus can be transferred from the maternal body to a nest, nature treats itself to an additional pampering luxury: the children are born much less matured than those in more exposed life forms, without nests. This is where it gets interesting philosophically, because to be born prematurely generally means exposing the nervous system to the venture of postnatal maturing. If the wiring of the nerves occurs largely a priori or prenatally, the result is an animal that learns relatively little because it doesn't need to learn much – a relatively ready animal in a relatively ready environment. Premature babies, however, start with the adventure of not being ready and leave room for a great deal a posteriori. The result is something like a natural history of the a posteriori principle. It could be written as the natural history of openness to experience, of open-mindedness. This is connected with the luxury of pampering, or with the level of unreadiness at which a nervous system becomes fit for the world or open-minded.

But all that is still animal history. It must be narrated in the context of biology – it is not yet human history. The biological extension of the juvenile phase creates animals that play and experiment more, that are essayists by nature and have a prolonged phase of mental maturation. In any case, the relationship between a priori and a posteriori can be described neurologically. This sums up the outline of the first half of my topological argument. In the second half, the anthropological space question is refined using the following idea: as we know, we are descendants of a species of tree-dwelling apes that developed into savannah apes. But how did the tree-dwelling ape arrive in the savannah? And how does a climber become a walker? How did walking upright evolve? How were all these exodus phenomena possible? There are plenty of fairly controversial topics – and, at the same time, something like the *thema probandum* for anthropologists, because somebody who has nothing to say about walking upright hasn't really grasped the issue of human beings. But for the moment we are less interested in the vertical apes problem than in characteristics of the place at which apes can become men. Once again we establish the primacy of topology and we also offer an explanation for why, in the beginning, time could actually appear as integrated into space.

Savannah apes live in a world with a wide horizon – a huge difference to the world of the treetop, which consists of a world of leaf caverns. This cannot be emphasized enough. Before human beings came the apes, and they had a horizon. This situation creates a cognitive pattern that belongs to our a priori equipment as human beings. I am thinking of an inborn schema of alertness that anticipates something like the transcendental unity of mental perception. In Kantian terms, we humans have a red alert that must be able to keep up with everything we imagine. We note first that the savannah ape is comparatively untroubled to begin with, and for most of the time. He sees possible danger coming from afar, so he can relax much more than the tree ape that can't see the danger coming from so far away. His long-sightedness gives him a safety buffer that affects his whole behaviour. Equanimity is a biological attainment from the savannahs. Like some other savannah inhabitants, *Homo sapiens* is a sleepy creature dependent on alerts. His natural behaviour is to hang around and do nothing most of the time. This automatically brings to mind male lions that spend twenty-three hours of the day dozing. These types of idleness and relaxation are typical of the savannah. The safety buffer provided by the wide view enables this. But then time and the event come into play. *Homo sapiens* is not only a sleepy creature ready for alert but also a curious creature driven by appetite. Let's imagine the basic situation of life modified into a wide horizon: what has to happen to raise the level of alertness in a pampered ape? Evidently it is triggered when a stress factor appears on the horizon. Whether aggressor or prey, something has to interrupt the situation – and, in fact, the interruption appears on the horizon. Then the ape raises its head and is immediately 'right there' with its eyes. Raising the head, incidentally, is a metaphor Heidegger used to describe the way a person stands in a clearing. The new event comes in the form of a break in the line of the horizon. The event that fixes the time appears in the space as a disturbance on the horizon. In my view, this provides a further argument to confirm that the time problem could be largely neutralized in the earliest periods of prehistory. The animal with this observational advantage sees things approaching – as eventful interruptions on the horizon. When the alarm is over, peace returns to the horizon. To sum up the two arguments: adding together these two functions, the nest privilege of the neotenized animal and the horizon privilege of the savannah apes, brings into view what I have just described as the launching pad for the pampering process.

MACHO: Savannah apes learned to deal flexibly with the point on the horizon, the disruption on the horizon, the feared or desired appearance on the horizon. It did not always signal danger – more often it meant food. The latest studies show that prehistoric people in the East African savannah lived in blissful harmony with the animals, because they fulfilled their protein needs exclusively with dead animals. They were not 'killer apes' but carrion eaters. Yet how could they find dead animals quickly before they were inedible or devoured by beasts of prey? Only through specific 'signs from heaven' – namely, the circular plummeting of vultures that appeared on the horizon.

SLOTERDIJK: There is a neurobiological argument that illustrates the connection you mention quite well. It recalls the familiar station effect: we are sitting in a train and the train beside us departs. We usually have the impression we are the ones who are moving. Maybe this can be seen as a sign of an inborn expectation that makes us think the horizon is fixed, whereas movement can only be movement within a horizon. On the other hand, if the horizon as a whole moves, our nervous system interprets this as if we ourselves are moving. Given our basic biological make-up, it is inconceivable that the horizon is moving. That is why the station illusion occurs so persistently and makes such an impression. Even if you are aware of the effect, it doesn't change anything in the way you perceive it. Your mind invariably tells you: we are on the move. There is a strong argument for seeing this as a relic of the situation of being in the savannah. From this we can develop a psychology of feeling dizzy: dizziness is the monstrous neurological sensation that the horizon is moving.

MACHO: That's exciting. But I'd really like to go back to the topics of horizon opening, neoteny and pampering. It seems to me that the theory of pampering you suggest denotes a sharp difference to anthropology as it has been practised since the eighteenth century. In fact, this theory of pampering dissolves a fundamental ambivalence that was presumed from Herder to Gehlen or Plessner: the idea that the imperfection of human beings – their openness and deficient nature – is the condition for their perfectibility, their freedom or liberated character. From the pampering perspective, humans are not seen as imperfect beings, either in the negative aspect (as 'deficient beings') or the positive aspect (as 'the beings liberated from the creation'). If we describe people in terms of pampering we don't have to accept the diametrical opposition between imperfection and perfection that troubled Herder when he described humans, on the one hand, as 'middle creatures', and, on the other hand, as 'engines' of an imposing universal history that was supposed to stretch from the star systems to future spiritual beings. A historical philosophy that results in education and perfecting can only develop if pampering – regardless of whether it takes the form of risk or opportunity – is characterized as a primary imperfection. This is the only way for narratives to evolve that portray the wretched life of human beings and lead to a perspective of completion: religious and spiritual, military, educational, political or even, more recently, genetic perfection. In his book on *Sedna*, a wide-ranging speculation about early history, Hans Peter Duerr traced how the abandonment of the prehistoric paradise, the 'Fall', actually happened.[2] Why did the pampered prehistoric humans want to move into houses anyway? Why did they often worsen their living conditions, and then describe them as misery, needing improvement? The question has still not been resolved today. One possible answer points to language, to the possibility not only of inhabiting a space but also of naming and expressing it metaphorically: a space in which a person's own beginning and ending could become an elementary question, a space in which – between the dead and the stars – the desire emerged to change, influence, educate, habituate and improve a 'middle creature' that started somewhere and would end somewhere. If I understand you correctly, you assert that in the beginning there was pampering. How did it come about that this pampering was seen as the origin of misery? Or as the root of the imperfection that virtually provoked an educative, missionary response? I don't quite understand that.

SLOTERDIJK: You already suggested the answer earlier yourself. As long as human beings described themselves as 'middle creatures' they lived in images of the world that let them come to terms with their heritage of imperfection – but from the moment humans couldn't position themselves in a middle place between above and below, they rapidly lost the ability to accept their deficiencies. In a middle creature's picture of the world, humans are topologically saturated, as it were. They see themselves in the right place ontologically because, in a cosmology of essences, *Dasein* means that every thing and every living creature stands only at its designated place and nowhere else. If we are really located in the middle between God and the animals, then any situation assigned to us can be seen as a part of human attributes. The revolt against the middle position is perceived as a transgression against moderation. The Greek idea of hubris means exactly that. The famous phrase 'Know yourself' should really also be understood in this sense: keep to the middle as much as you can; don't mistake yourself for the

[2] Hans Peter Duerr is a German anthropologist. Macho is referring to the book by Hans Peter Duerr, *Sedna oder Die Liebe zum Leben* (Frankfurt: Suhrkamp Verlag), 1984.

animals and certainly not for the gods. The Greeks developed an art of speaking to beings who evidently risked hubris, beings who tended to leap out of their rank, their class and their genus.

MACHO: I think this is very important. If humans are the beings in the middle, only very limited scope exists for trying to improve them. Incidentally, I have noticed that even the humanist texts that first explicitly discussed the educational capability of human beings, such as the work of Pico della Mirandola, do not really openly conceive the perfecting of humans; they focused more on the risk that spawns hubris, a transgression of the lower boundary of the middle position (towards bestiality) or of the upper boundary (towards presumptuous divinity).

SLOTERDIJK: Pico's work, however, clearly includes the recommendation to improvement in an upward direction. In addressing humans as *plastes et fictor* he is appealing to their talent for repairing their own deficiencies and creating out of their own resources. It follows that *Homo sapiens* should make something as divine as possible out of himself – there is a clear pressure to move upward in this early humanist-alchemist discourse. If we speak of the middle position here, it means the starting point of a self-selection process that, it is hoped, will reach for the stars. But this is the exception. Generally the strict classification theories, that really mean middle when they say middle, dominate. For them, the idea of the *conditio humana*, properly understood, is a warning about *humilitas*: truly humble people tend to rank themselves in the lower middle. Incidentally, in the current debate on genetic engineering there is a very vocal *humilitas* party that insists that, firstly, we can't do what we want, and, secondly, we're not allowed to do what we can. The modern *superbia* or hubris party, however, openly champions genetic optimization. But what is optimization, and how can we think about it? The term as such is only meaningful if *Homo sapiens* no longer has a fixed position between above and below. In that case, reminders of the *conditio humana* and sermons about *humilitas* become conservative, if not reactionary gestures – because people liberated from the metaphysical middle position, if they understand their position correctly, are condemned to self-improvement. In this case 'liberated' means having to accept the immanent life as the last chance. This causes a kind of metaphysical panic, because anybody who fails in their mortal life fails completely in everything. This is precisely what makes the enormous difference between the age of classical metaphysics based on personalism and the modern age. The inhabitants of a world complemented by a world above may think and believe that ultimately, before God, the difference between the most successful and the most unsuccessful human life on earth hardly matters. On earth the most blatant differences are between winners and losers, but in God's realm there is a return match played with obscure rules – which means the winners from here can be the losers there, and vice versa. The edifying impact of that idea simply can't be overestimated.

Recently, in Seville, I saw a picture by the painter Valdéz de Leal from the late seventeenth century, hanging in the Church of the Sisters of Mercy. It shows, in the harshest possible terms, the consequences of metaphysical egalitarianism and the equal humiliation of all before God and death. The viewer sees a mortuary containing three coffins; a heap of skulls is visible in the dark background. In the foremost coffin lies a cardinal in the most hideous state of decay. In the second coffin is a high-ranking noble. The first man's head is turned to the left, the other man's head to the right. A little further on, almost in darkness, is the coffin of a bourgeois man without any insignia. A scroll with writing in the foreground gives the picture its telling title: *Finis gloriae mundi*. The painter Murillo is supposed to have commented that you have to hold your nose to look at this picture. Yet it is more than an example of Catholic romanticism about cadavers. In our context I would like to read the painting mainly as a reference to the symbolic economy of metaphysics. If you want to classify people between above and below, sometimes you also have to show the border that divides them from the sphere above in the most drastic fashion. You can't have the image of the great Chain of Being without the rhetoric of death.

MACHO: As you describe it, the picture probably belongs to the magnificent tradition of dances of death in which we are shown, picture by picture, as if they were comics of the early modern age, how all humans, regardless of their origin or status, are dragged off by death, or better still, by the dead. The dance of death directly expresses the egalitarianism of mortality, for example, in the proverb: 'Death strangles all people equally / as he finds them, poor and rich.' Such egalitarianism blocks the upward boundary and at the same time keeps the people in the middle firmly in place. This fixing of the upward boundary may also reduce the fear of transgressing the lower boundary towards the animals. The risks of animalization, of bestialization, can only be revived at the moment the upward boundary is opened (one example of this is Herder, who dreamed, more than 150 years before Teilhard de Chardin, of an evolution of the 'noosphere', the transformation of humans into pure 'spiritual beings'). As soon as the upper boundary is declared open for development and mutation, this brings the fear of reversion and regression. It is often the same philosophers who talk about an upward development and simultaneously express concern about animalization: think of the 'Dialectic of Enlightenment'. I suspect that this is the moment when the humanist programme of fear first gains its importance by always associating miserabilism with reversion to bestiality; it is the same moment in which education is organized as dressage, as animal training, as taming – as you wrote in your response to Heidegger's 'Letter on Humanism'. As long as human beings are considered as middle creatures they can only deviate in two possible directions, in the direction of bestialization or in the direction of hubris – in other words, usurping a superman position. That was the centre of the ethical programme of the Greeks: one reason hubris must be avoided is because in principle it always fails.

SLOTERDIJK: The dance of death and related iconographic forms comment on this failure in macabre ways. Death is the great hubris therapist; it reproduces the original relationships by ensuring that human trees do not grow into heaven. Lotario de Segni portrays death and its herald, *miseria*, as levellers, so to speak. Both ensure that *summa summarum* lord and servant are equally wretched, however different their types of wretchedness may be. In the end, both have the same amount on their misery account.

MACHO: That's a beautiful way of expressing it.

SLOTERDIJK: This traditional topic is at its most interesting when the upper classes bemoan the human condition as miserabilism. I have just finished reading a collection of letters of the Marquise de Pompadour, Louis XV's mistress and confidante. I came across a wistful exchange with one of her lady friends where she repeats the old aristocratic lament that the stable boy is happier than the lord, and the recipient of the letter replies that it can't really be true. What Mme Pompadour meant was a kind of courtly *vanitas* theory: in one of her finest letters, addressed to the philosopher Montesquieu, a text that deserves a place in world literature, she reproaches him with an exquisitely phrased complaint that she only has automatons around her at the court. We always thought the critique of alienation was a by-product of German idealism, but obviously there is a French strand to the critique of alienation, in fact, as early as around 1750, in the form of criticism of court automatons. German criticism laments the loss of the soul, whereas the French realize that automatons don't have a soul and don't need one.

To return to the earlier problem: we were asking under which conditions *Homo patiens* leaves the stage to make room for *Homo compensator*. To answer this adequately, we would have to tell a very complex story – one chapter of which would deal with metaphysical topology and the crisis of finding one's place in an ordered context. Another chapter would cover the psychological and moral side effects of modernization. Since the nineteenth century we have been aiming at a social order in which individuals have stopped identifying with their social situation. Feelings about rank have largely disappeared. Nobody still believes that our personal standing in the outside world is an essential statement about our self or our existential mission. The classical *amor fati* is not a modern idea, despite Nietzsche's attempt to reactivate it. Today, people who believe everything that happens to them is always exactly the right thing for them are either followers of esotericism or radical right-wingers. In other words, we are talking about individualist forms of life and subjectivity. We should preface this by saying that the term 'individualism' is very unfortunate because it unfairly labels the so-called 'individuals' practising this way of life. In fact, they are not indivisible or 'undividable' at all, but highly divisible creatures, in other words, 'dividuals', if you like, who live in permanent distinction from themselves. To be an individual today means occupying the spot where the systematic distinction occurs between the life lived previously and the life to be lived in the future. The individual is the point of experience between our own personal past and our own future. In other words, we become an individual/dividual in the moment we transfer transcendence into ourselves. From then on the person relates to himself or herself as his or her interior, greater other. My life until now has created me as an *individuum revelatum*, an uncovered, known, manifest self – and it is exactly in this capacity that I can relate to myself as an *individuum absconditum*. I am already here and simultaneously I embody my own not-yet. I see myself as an *individuum absconditum* to the extent that I engage with my lack of self-knowledge. I have myself constantly in my mind's eye; I define myself in relation to time as a surprise for myself.

MACHO: Accordingly, modern individuals would be possible only under the precondition that they were ready to break with their own history of pampering, in the sense of taking their own position in relation to the future, in fact. In contrast to the positioning in the middle we discussed earlier, they familiarize the theme of permanent escape from the nest. Modern individuals group themselves in forward movement, in the intersection of many different kinds of pampering situations. They pursue careers that can only advance by continual demolition of houses and 'nests'. In this respect they resemble people of the eighteenth or nineteenth centuries who sold all their possessions before embarking on a big journey.

SLOTERDIJK: That means their own domesticity is absolutely the forbidden option for them.

MACHO: This brings us back to the topic that particularly fascinates me. Where and when does one start conceiving of humans from the perspective of the future, of their potential improvement and perfecting? As we have said, in past centuries or even millennia, metaphysics was a discipline of topology: below, above, middle. If time played any role at all, it was related to this spatial planning. The relationship to the past was influenced by holy texts that people believed could even tell them the date of the world's creation, the absolute beginning. The future, however, remained a matter for God, as St Augustine noted in his *Confessions*. Anyone who tried to take control of that future would always risk degenerating into a particular eschatological form of hubris, which we have already mentioned. *Sub specie mortis* the future is not a topic, either for the individual or for humankind. And, even in eschatology, the issue concerns spatial planning again: the sky is above, hell is below, and in between – since the twelfth century – is purgatory. This reflects the consciousness of an agrarian culture that has no extended planning horizon because it remains dependent on many unforeseeable, contingent factors (symbolized in the famous Horsemen of the Apocalypse). As we have said, with a vision stretching fourteen years into the future one could become the Pharaoh's chief adviser.

SLOTERDIJK: Saving food for seven lean years was an enterprise people still talked about thousands of years later. In that respect Joseph was more successful than Lenin.

MACHO: And now we have been individual for nearly 200 years, but also collective, in a remarkable situation that can only be understood if we see it as the result of a warp of metaphysical topology. The boundaries between above, below and the middle were literally blurred, and that was done in the name of time. Doing evolution theory means being able to agree on experiences that apes in the forest and the savannah had millions of years ago, and means that we can reflect on the origin of language or domestication just as we are doing in this conversation. It's like a game we are playing to manage enormous time periods, retrospectively but also ahead of us. Metaphysical topology has been temporalized. Since then, 'below' is the place of the animals behind us, and 'above' is the place of angels, gods and supermen ahead of us.

The first attempts at universal history have already shown what could lie ahead of us (although Herder and Hegel thought humankind had almost arrived at its goal). Since Marxism, if not before, it has become evident how long it can take until the species has passed right through its predicted stages of development. I suspect we have only just arrived at the point when metaphysical topology was temporalized, following the questioning associated with issues of the education, improvement and domestication of humans, all the types of questions that often plague us today.

SLOTERDIJK: That means constructing contemporary arts of living on the basis of giving patience a positive value. The people who are naturally more open and flexible and easier to recruit for fundamental optimization thinking and, even more, for getting fundamentally impatient with their own situation, are those who have learned to stop identifying with their social status. I mean people who are no longer *status* persons in the sense of the old forms of rank, and who have stopped having faith in the essential cosmos where every creature has its rightful place. As soon as people's trust in the divine taxonomies has been weakened, every individual will become structurally appropriative. True, we can still observe an astonishing amount of modesty, persistence and conservative seriousness, but one of the general features of the present is a rather aggressive and grabbing attitude towards fate. Today it is very easy to convince people to believe they deserve better than they actually get. A strong onwards and upwards thrust is starting to dominate, including, and above all, in relation to fate. Ulrich Sonnemann's famous dictum: 'Enlightenment, an enterprise for sabotaging fate',[3] relates to many more areas than we once believed possible – including manipulation of birth and death. What used to be seen as the worst kind of hubris has become normal behaviour today, and for easily understandable reasons. In fact, if objective ranks still existed we should recommend everybody to stay where they are – except for people with hubris who we would have to try to persuade to return to the middle ground. But if nobody has hubris – and that is the fundamental conviction of modern times – the recommendation will look different. Now people can only look towards better things. To some extent meliorism is the latent metaphysics of the present age. It is impossible to establish an objective good; a relative better is easier. We could almost say that people today are obliged to practise hubris unless they give up altogether. They have to maintain a particular orientation onwards and upwards to keep fit existentially. This leads to a remarkable kind of lurching and sliding, because the evolutionist offence of collecting species in the nineteenth century is also relevant for individuals nowadays. We can't really imagine today how shocking the idea once was that God did not conceive the species, and that neither the archetypal content of a species nor its physical appearance are fixed once and for all. That is the real shock of the nineteenth century: the genetic drift,

[3] Ulrich Sonnemann (1912–93) was a German social philosopher, psychologist and political writer who taught at the universities of Munich and Kassel.

the idea that the original images of humans and beasts, of plants and everything that grows and blossoms, are not permanently fixed but drift in evolution, as we say today. That is worse than the worst seasickness because it affects the ontological forms, as it were. When the species drift we become ontologically seasick – suddenly we have to watch fish becoming amphibians and the latter becoming terrestrial animals; we witness a mammoth transforming into an elephant, and wolves turning into dogs – and all sorts of other monstrosities.

MACHO: Evolution as a freak show …

SLOTERDIJK: And as a vaudeville of forms. If God is dead, one reason is because he is no longer any good as a guarantor of the species. No Catholic defence front can change that, and humanism can only offer a weak alternative in this respect. We can see this quite clearly in the current genetics debate, with Catholics and old-fashioned humanists very heavily over-represented. They think it is a good idea to erect a corral round the human gene and shoot at everybody who tries to change it in some way. The unfortunate thing about this issue is that normal reproduction has long since been exposed for contributing to species drift, and every normal sexual act among humans infinitesimally advances this drifting. We must finally realize that the potential of the genus per se is monstrous. In fact, anthropology is only possible now as a branch of general monstrology.

MACHO: Species slide like cultures. Mammoths become elephants, Egyptians become Greeks, and Greeks become Romans. Such 'slipping processes' were only conceivable at a late stage, perhaps only since Hegel's universal history that presented the first model of an evolutionary history. And when everything starts sliding, individuals also slide, always hoping (with hope that is articulated for me in the appropriative figments of some geneticists' imagination) at least to be able to influence the direction of this slippage.

SLOTERDIJK: The concept of peoples was initially conceived in analogy to the species. Peoples were the animal species of the spirit world, so to speak, and as such they could be seen as ideas from God. The discovery of evolutionary drift put an end to this ontological comfort.

MACHO: That is already clear from Herder's *Ideas on the Philosophy of the History of Mankind.* He tried to localize and register cultures in climatic terms. He argued that Africans fit to Africa, Chinese to China, and Lapps to Lapland. All cultures were directly equal to God and history, provided they remained where they originated. But Herder had already noted that cultures move, they slide and drift. The Romans colonized Gaul; the Europeans colonized America. And because cultures slide and drift, and don't keep to the borders of closed republics of the mind and of habits, the individuals in them also slide and drift. The status of individuals is no longer determined by origin; and the openness of their future motivates them to permanent flight from the nest. It is no coincidence that in the nineteenth century, in the wake of evolutionism, this slippage was discussed totally empirically, theatrically, in fact. This happened in the circus where audiences watched poodles doing arithmetic and apes that could stand upright to become men, like in Kafka's short story 'A Report to an Academy', and in freak shows and side shows that presented elephant men, lion men and snake men, often with the label 'What is it?' or 'Nondescripts'. And, of course, slippage was also the subject and goal of research that seems extremely dubious today but was regarded as self-evident at the beginning of the twentieth century. Eugenics was seen as the great progressive science, by no means only among the right wing or 'pre-fascists'. Eugenic ideals were already proclaimed *avant la lettre* in the great social utopias of Plato, Morus, Bacon and Campanella. In 1910, for example, Otto Neurath, a philosopher of the Vienna Circle and pictorial statistician who was later minister of culture in the Munich Soviet Republic, enthusiastically translated Sir Francis Galton's *Hereditary Genius* and added a euphoric foreword. It included the statement, 'Anyone trying to foresee the development of the future with open eyes can see that the major problems that will affect people increasingly strongly will be the improvement of social order and the improvement of our race, two goals that are very closely interlinked.' And Max Weber formulated it as follows in his inaugural lecture as a professor in 1895: 'We do not want to breed wellbeing in people, but rather those characteristics which we think of as constituting the human greatness and nobility of our nature.'

In 1905, a young Dutch evolutionary biologist first had the idea – which seems crazy to us now – of inseminating female primates with the semen of African men to create the missing link artificially. Ernst Haeckel wrote him a letter confirming that he regarded the 'physiological experiments, especially the crossbreeding of lower human races (negroes) and great apes' by 'artificial insemination' as 'very interesting' and believed that 'these experiments could possibly succeed'. In short, the drift, the slippage, became universal, and perhaps this has a practical implication that our current debate has not focused on enough. Philosophy and metaphysics – in the sense of the topology of the middle or of the nest, the localization of the pampering situation you mentioned earlier – always presuppose that their central concepts, the concept of truth, the concept of goodness, everything, in fact, that Plato called ideas and that scholastics calls transcendentals, are basically timeless and seen as supra-temporal. Truth is subject to time just as little as goodness is, and if anything should not drift, it is these key concepts. For millennia, it was unimaginable that the truth drifted, or the law, or the idea of the good. I think the nineteenth and twentieth centuries were marked by a kind of shock wave following the realization that these concepts also drift. Perhaps people could still bear the fact that human beings suddenly had to be fitted into an evolutionary history and could no longer be traced back to a divine act of creation. Maybe it was also possible to accept constantly expanding notions of future horizons, utopias and dystopias. But that truths drift and are not supra-temporally valid, and that goodness is not a settled thing, but, as utilitarians claim, will probably come to light at some time, is deeply shocking. The true, the good and the beautiful will be established a posteriori, historicized and relativized – that is an incredible, terrifying realization. Suddenly we must ask, as Thomas Jefferson wrote in a letter to John Wayles Eppes on 24 June 1813, whether the laws we passed today have to be voted on again in twenty years' time because half the people who just voted for them will be dead by then. And what gives us the right to enact laws for people who are not yet alive? Can the process of slippage be better expressed than in Jefferson's words, which I shall quote here: 'We may consider each generation as a distinct nation, with a right, by the will of its majority, to bind themselves, but none to bind the succeeding generation, more than the inhabitants of another country'?

SLOTERDIJK: That would certainly result in parents having to treat their children as members of a foreign culture, and all education policy becoming foreign policy. It raises really weird questions. Can basic values be improvisations? Can eternal values be modified over time? Incidentally, there is a famous letter from Jefferson in which he tries to remember the mood in which he edited the wording of the American Declaration of Independence. He speaks totally in the language of an occasionalist, saying he did not want to imitate any other document, but to express exactly what that unique historical occasion demanded. This probably sounds strange to anybody looking for a *fundamentum inconcussum* in morality. But what if there is no such thing? What if even the noblest statements of the Constitution were dictated by the 'occasion' or, as we would say, by the cultural context? The most widespread reaction to this worry is a kind of escape to intrinsic values. We can see a general anti-relativist reaction. What is right for values is reasonable for genetics. Many worried, insecure people want to isolate the human gene like a sanctuary and erect a new temple: you can touch everything, but not that. You shall eat of all the fruits of the tree of Knowledge and Ability, but just not of the Tree of Life. You shall change everything and deem it capable of revision, but as for the gene – leave the gene sweetly in peace for me. Anti-relativist feeling is not squeamish when it comes to denouncing relativists. It starts with the terminology: as soon as the new optimization processes of genetic engineering are linked to the traditional concepts of eugenics, it brings up the permanent contamination attached to this expression as a result of Nazi racism. This probably makes eugenics an irredeemable concept, and the people who sarcastically talk of 'liberal eugenics' today are deliberately calculating on the deterrent effect. The friendly adjective can't redeem the sullied noun, which means people exploit the latter's criminal connotations to make the whole thing seem shady. Because of this we never really get to the problem as it exists. The fact is, firstly, that the general drift involves the genetic premises of the *conditio humana*, but, secondly, that this drifting is increasingly moving from the passive to the active form. Just because of this, through the transition from suffering to doing, the Enlightenment has always moved gradually forward up to now, and anybody who wishes it to keep on advancing has to look very carefully at this sensitive spot. The old paradigm of Baconian scholarship comes into play here: *natura non vincitur nisi parendo*, we can't command nature except by obeying it. By obeying, and obediently understanding, we broaden the scope for active modification. This agenda is, I think, still productive, although meanwhile we are also realizing more and more, not least by reading the ecologists, that we can't use the word 'obey' so lightly. The public debate about ostensible eugenics still largely occurs in a region of hysteria. (I use the word 'ostensible' because genetic engineering is totally different from eugenic breeding in the procedural sense, which involves the hopeless problem of merely 'exploited' intermediate generations.) People still project a completely conventional criticism of the 'seizure of power' on to the sphere of biotechnology. Only a few people have understood that the Baconian *nisi parendo* is becoming an urgent issue, because obeying the nature of the genus is an art, and we are gradually beginning to understand its implications. To obey life and understand its plans is an immensely ambitious agenda. Perhaps we will give up one day because understanding the almost insoluble inherent complexity of the phenomena will show the limits to energetic activism.

MACHO: It is only by seeing the eugenics debate as a 'symptom carrier' that we come to the real problem of drift: the temporalizing of a topological metaphysics and ethics that has been practised and preached for thousands of years. I mean what actually happens at the moment somebody says, 'maybe we will only find out what is good and what is true in the future; the *bonum et verum* is not fixed from the start but will only be visible much later'. Such assertions have tremendous disruptive potential. That brings us to a critical reading of Heidegger. Heidegger introduced time as the basic question of philosophy but he simultaneously twisted the question to rescue the topology – the *Sein* – in the *aletheia* concept of truth, in the concepts of framework (*Gestell*) or of clearing (*Lichtung*). He tried to stop the incredible drift Nietzsche described so impressively in section 125 of *Fröhlichen Wissenschaft* [*The Gay Science*]: 'Where are we moving now? Away from all suns? Aren't we perpetually falling? Backward, sideward, forward, in all directions? Is there any up or down left?' Heidegger remained an agrarian thinker who subsumed the drift under the history of existence (and, incidentally, also had a thoroughly positive relationship to fate). To him, time became merely the 'horizon of existence', unlike Ernst Jünger in his later years, who believed he could foresee a 'metamorphosis of the gods' and future 'battles of the Titans'.

SLOTERDIJK: That's just how I see it. It's very important to understand that Heidegger remained an ontologist of the vegetable essence. His philosophy is situated in the system frame of the plant world, which is why emerging or opening (*Aufgehen*) meant so much to him. This could lead us to ask whether there is any convincing metaphysics of animal being. My impression is that the philosophy of animality is in its very earliest stage. This tallies with the impression that the contemporary debate is being conducted in a hysterical tone. Beginnings provide ample scope for hysteria – it is part of the rebellion of the old and shows that some things have become unstoppable. The representatives of the old get hot flashes from the new. Personally, I believe the bio-philosophical age is just dawning. Our first glimpse into the human genome gave us the impression that only part of the genetic text 'makes sense', to use the common, if problematic, metaphor of textual theory. Our genetic make-up evidently involves many things whose purpose we don't understand. Why is there all that redundancy; what are those empty fields for; what is the purpose of the high morbidity potential? These questions are troubling for medicine and theoretically interesting at the same time. Answering them would probably take us back to the beginning of our discussion because we can also articulate the topic of pampering in genetic terminology. In fact, the genome seems to be anything but an economical text that records only what is absolutely necessary. On the contrary, we get the impression it is travelling in a huge genetic omnibus with a whole array of baggage containing genetic information, and enjoying itself. What are we supposed to think about the pile of mob genes that are apparently being dragged in tow in the context of a luxuriant evolution? Our model biologists are rather puzzled and don't know what they are supposed to do with this junk. What are things like that doing in the genetic material of the crown of creation? How, for example, does the genetic programme for Down's syndrome get into our make-up? Questions like that sound blasphemous, I know – but it's a fairly serious issue. We can see one important aspect of the pampering story in the fact that we have a huge morbidity potential accompanying us. One feature of the pampering dynamic of the *conditio humana* is that selection is largely deactivated in it. Countless genetic characteristics, including morbid or pathological ones, are selectively neutral to a great extent. They simply flow with the genetic current, beyond good and evil. The beautiful, the not-beautiful, the beneficial, the detrimental, everything is passed on, it travels along, meandering through the generations – with the restriction that, all in all, we can observe a certain tendency towards beauty in the *sapiens* species, that we can see, for instance, in the hybrid vigour of female forms. We still know regrettably little about bio-aesthetics. In any case, people must take a position themselves on their potential for pampering – and they know that, because they were aware early on of the risk of getting out of condition. We could combine the main ideas of Sartre and Plessner here: we are condemned to pampering; and we can make something ourselves out of what has been made out of us; we can take charge of our own pampering. This will make the future horizon recognizable, because I am sure the twenty-first century will be a mediocre era. The new ruling class will consist not of the military but of doctors and bio-engineers. To borrow a term from the US author James L. Nolan, the state only has a future as the 'therapeutic state'. In the coming mediocracy there will doubtless be doctors who will cheerfully concur with the basic direction of technological civilization as a whole, and propose extending specific health definitions to the genome. These doctors will suggest that we renounce part of the morbidity potential that many members of the *Homo sapiens* species have. They will suggest we could well do with a rather less luxurious morbidity rate. And if there is a safe method available for eliminating clearly identifiable genetic diseases such as Down's syndrome, there is a lot to be said for implementing this technology some day. Whatever the Catholic and humanist guardians of the genetic reservation may say to the contrary, there is no human right to the risk of suffering from Down's syndrome. I am also convinced that precisely defined prevention is legitimate, just as, conversely, I have no time for the arguments of people who want to ensure today that future generations face the same genetic risks as all the previous generations. This is almost outrageous, as if we wanted to explain that humans as such have an obligation to be ill just because the human condition involves a certain risk of deformity.

The more I look at the conservative scene's arguments, the more I am amazed by their lack of generosity in the guise of caring for humankind and its so-called freedom. Those people have a striking lack of anthropological faith – as if they knew for sure that the present state of *Homo sapiens* represented the terminal station of evolution. This brings me back again to our comments about evolutionary drift: apparently it affects not only the biological forms, the species boundaries and cultural codes, but in future it will also increasingly involve technological life forms and therapeutic possibilities. If the border between the curable and incurable is sliding, it is the task of the actors who cause this drift to react by shifting the borders of what can be done and what is permissible, and to improve the professional ethics of doctors from a historical viewpoint. The sabotage of fate goes on. If somebody can cure and doesn't do so, he or she is guilty of the crime of omission, even if it is covered up by the hypocritical claim to protection of the human species. The whole issue concerns affirmation of modern thinking about therapy, not genetic deregulation, as some alarmists claim.

MACHO: Anyway, the new, much-discussed genetic therapy procedures are proving to be very difficult – more difficult than people thought when the research began.

SLOTERDIJK: The result is once again that therapy isn't achieving miracles. It is clear that the alarmists with their overblown arguments haven't given enough thought to the intransigence of the genetic field. In this situation, Bacon's *nisi parendo* argument has immensely far-reaching implications. We can't have fun controlling the gene – that's a story for regressive science fiction. Future society will be defined in therapeutocratic terms, in relation to the rule of therapy, even more than at present, which is yet another reason to reveal the philosophical conditions of ideas of healing and to spell out the psychosomatics of the 'good life'. I think we'll remain meliorists in this respect. We won't stop improving what there is to improve. Anyone who doesn't accept that is dropping out of the Enlightenment. Anybody who argues polemically today against so-called liberal eugenics must ask themselves whether they are not knowingly saying farewell to the Enlightenment because of humanist hysteria.

MACHO: I agree that the area of truly controversial borderline cases is considerably smaller than often assumed in the public discussion. Many things can't be done anyway, and there are some things absolutely nobody wants to do. In the case of cloning, it became clear only recently that reproduction of genetic identity doesn't really work. People who had been offered cloning of their deceased pets suddenly got animals that looked totally different – instead of a beloved plump tabby cat, the 'copy' they got was an elegant monochrome cat resembling the goddess Bastet. Some interventions, however, have been in practice for a long time already. As far as I know, Down's syndrome can be established by a standard amniotic fluid analysis without embryo screening; admittedly, in cases of doubt, therapy simply means killing, even beyond the established limits for an abortion. And, finally, there are quite different cases in which the assessment more clearly shows the effect of the drift, the slippage of terms as well as operations. What do we think, for example, about 'triage', the spontaneous selection of disaster victims according to how seriously they are injured? What do we think of techniques of prenatal optimization that include the selective killing of weaker or apparently biologically disadvantaged foetuses in multiple pregnancies? What do we think about transplant medicine? Turning life into an experimental field evidently also implies decisions for death that can only be legitimated in terms of ethics of responsibility. But what does an ethics of responsibility actually consist of, if it does not argue in terms of 'goodwill' or the 'right attitude', but uses the idea of a future good, a futurized *bonum*? Weren't older cultures lucky to be able to assume that the good was fixed – not just for subsequent generations but also for myself in twenty years from now?

SLOTERDIJK: That raises a new dilemma. Knowing so much in terms of diagnosis and prognosis, we are doomed to construct an incredible bogey out of the ethics of responsibility. Everyone watching current events will admit we are living in the middle of this wave. The reaction is predictable: a new wave of ethicists will inevitably emerge and advocate the virtue of indifference. You can see it coming – a neo-differentialist school advocating laissez-faire. It will demonstrate that an ethics of irresponsibility is necessary after the ethics of responsibility has gone too far. That, I think, will close the circle. The pampering dynamic in humans is so enormous that it even creates luxury forms of responsibility. Today's ethics professors have long since stopped living in the proverbial ivory tower. (Given the present species protection laws, where is all that ivory supposed to come from?) They tend to live in a hothouse of moral overexcitement. It is difficult to stay in such hyper-moral hothouses for long without getting breathless. If you're interested in a cultured style of living, you should protect the house of being from overheating.

# 13

# GOOD THEORY DOESN'T COMPLAIN

*Interview with Frank Hartmann and Klaus Taschwer**

HARTMANN/TASCHWER: Mr Sloterdijk, you have just completed your trilogy on spheres with the publication of your new book, *Schaum* [*Foam*]. The work is 2,500 pages long. Will it be your magnum opus?

SLOTERDIJK: The trilogy will definitely be a major event in my oeuvre, but the weight of emphasis is very likely to change again. I operate like a writer who conceives a philosopher who keeps getting different thoughts. In my case, the philosopher is an artificial figure who was invented in the writer's workshop.

HARTMANN/TASCHWER: Doesn't that undermine the authority of the philosopher?

SLOTERDIJK: I would find it more difficult if a philosopher confused himself with the author of his writings. As soon as philosophers try to be authorities they turn into what they would dearly like to have been in the twentieth century: literary figures with a worldview. If they act as ideologues and leaders in the crisis, they release harmful emissions into society and produce illusory certainties with which people have identified, often in a naive and violent way. If there has been a learning process in philosophy in the past

* This interview between Peter Sloterdijk, Frank Hartmann and Klaus Taschwer appeared under the title 'Gute Theorie lamentiert nicht' ['Good Theory Doesn't Complain'], in *Telepolis* (8 June 2004). Available at: <http://www.heise.de/tp/artikel/17/17554/1.html>.

Frank Hartmann has been a professor at the Bauhaus University in Weimar since 2009. Klaus Taschwer is a freelance social scientist and scholarly journalist. He lives and works in Vienna.

fifty years, it is probably that we have to stop this kind of ideological emission, if possible.

HARTMANN/TASCHWER: You use particularly soft concepts for your theory, such as bubbles and foam. Aren't you making it too easy for your critics?

SLOTERDIJK: Critics want to have it easy, and a kind author respects that. Unfortunately, I don't always succeed in being kind, which means I sometimes tie the choice of concepts to a character test for the reader. If we talk about foaming, for example, the verbal association of 'whipping up foam' is awfully close. I'm watching the critics to see if they can resist being tempted by the cheapest way to use ideas. Good readers understand it's a matter of letting the images and concepts do their work.

HARTMANN/TASCHWER: Sociologists have recently used the concept of the network to describe contemporary society. Does that make sense to you?

SLOTERDIJK: A great deal, in fact. I am fond of quoting Bruno Latour, who has proposed replacing the concept of society with that of agent networks. The term stands for a post-sociological form of reflection that has much to offer. It allows us to respect the relative autonomy of the individual nodes in relation to the rest of the network far more than if we start with a concept of society defined from above.

HARTMANN/TASCHWER: Why do you use the metaphor of foam?

SLOTERDIJK: I want to correct the reduced character of network metaphors. When talking about nets we are using starkly reductive geometry, that is, simply the one- or two-dimensional forms of the point and the line. The term 'foam', on the other hand, brings a three-dimensional construct into play from the very beginning. Whereas in network models the individual points have no volume, and therefore do not live, the image of foam offers the perspective on a theory of household diversity. A household is a successful structure of life. What I am searching for is a theory of humans as beings living in homes, and a theory of agglomeration of those beings in their diverse forms of living and gathering together.

HARTMANN/TASCHWER: What is your own judgement on your book?

SLOTERDIJK: It is worth something on a scale that doesn't exist yet. Because this type of book is new, we can't judge its value. It would already have to be canonical to have a value, but if it were canonical it would not have any innovative power. You can't have value and novelty at the same time. This is clear in the dynamic of de-valorization that surrounds new approaches. As soon as the owners of shares in older theories notice that a new value has ventured the launch on the stock exchange, they are faced with the question: to buy or not to buy? Anyone who wants to keep the old values appreciates the new ones less.

HARTMANN/TASCHWER: What kind of target audience do you envisage for your theory?

SLOTERDIJK: The spheres project is aimed at members of professions that evolve fundamental reflections out of their own activity. I am thinking particularly of architects, climatologists, sociologists and macro-historians, anthropologists, doctors, teachers and theologians. But I'm not only reaching out to professionals – I'm also very interested in the independent readers we used to call dilettantes. Generally, I'm addressing a group of people interested in therapeutic issues in the widest sense, because the real purpose of my book is to reformulate metaphysical problems as immunological problems. In my opinion, philosophy is only meaningful today as general immunology, which aims at knowing how successes in life can be secured in posterity. This makes *Spheres* generally a book for people who want to get fit with the aid of thinking.

HARTMANN/TASCHWER: And how will academic philosophy react to that?

SLOTERDIJK: Such a heterodox book is probably beyond the scope of established philosophical positions.

HARTMANN/TASCHWER: Would you agree with associating your spherology positions with *A Thousand Plateaus* by Deleuze and Guattari, or *Empire* by Hardt and Negri?

SLOTERDIJK: These books would fit nicely together on the shelves. It is true, my book relates better to this system of thought than to any other. In its own way it is a theory of a world liquefied with money, and in that sense it is close to Deleuze's and Guattari's *Capitalism and Schizophrenia*. Incidentally, my editor, who begged me not to write a fourth volume, is horrified because there will be a topical appendix to *Spheres*, a little dinghy of 400 pages titled *Im Weltinnenraum des Kapitals* [*In the World Interior of Capital*]. It contains my counter-proposal to Negri and Hardt.

HARTMANN/TASCHWER: What does that look like?

SLOTERDIJK: *Empire* is an interesting, radical book, but it is based on a confusing concept because talking about empire actually blurs the difference the authors wanted to discuss. If the present world is treated as 'empire' in the singular, we miss the point that the present world of capital and comfort is a highly exclusive structure. Instead, I adopt Dostoyevsky's image of the Crystal Palace that he used as early as the 1860s to describe the consumerist Western world. *Notes from the Underground* should be reread today – it is the Magna Carta of the resistance to globalization and of anti-modern resentment. From Dostoyevsky we get to both Attac and the Islamists. The great advantage of the Crystal Palace metaphor is that the name describes the key thing: we are dealing here with a building that creates an enormous inside/outside difference. This emphasis is missing in the term 'empire' because it suggests everything has already been covered by the system. That is totally wrong. The effective capital zone is a larger but strictly exclusive space – borrowing from Rilke, I use the term 'the world interior of capital'. If you look closely you can see that Negri uses a Gnostic concept of system opposition. He cultivates a mysticism of being oppositional that needs the whole as an opponent, just as Christ once used the world as a foil for escape from the world. I read that book as a requiem mass for left-wing radicalism.

HARTMANN/TASCHWER: You use concepts like 'affluence bubble' or 'pampering groups' in your book. Is that appropriate in the face of rising unemployment and shrinking social services?

SLOTERDIJK: You can recognize good theory by the fact that it doesn't complain. The present crisis offers us a better view of our affluence bubble from the outside. Since the time the exclusion dynamic became more acute internally, the inclusions have also become more conspicuous for theory. The pampering theory of *Spheres III* has a precise date: it reacts to the crisis of the therapy and nanny state. In the present twilight of prosperity, the differences between the pampering classes in the population are tangible. In other words, I am presenting a crisis theory – but, unlike classical Marxism, it does not derive a tendency towards impoverishment from this. It uses a break in pampering to develop a general theory of human luxury and constitutive pampering.

HARTMANN/TASCHWER: How far will the twilight of affluence go?

SLOTERDIJK: I don't think Germany will witness a dismantling of the welfare state on the model of the United States. The positions of social democracy in Europe are too firmly consolidated, at least on the continental mainland. By social democracy, I mean the structure of welfare policy as a whole rather than the parties of that name.

HARTMANN/TASCHWER: What does that mean?

SLOTERDIJK: I am convinced there can be no democratic party in the parliaments of continental Europe that does not have a social agenda. The CSU [German Christian Social Union] in its Bavarian form, for example, is much more social democratic than the SPD [German Social Democratic Party] under Schröder on the national level.[1] Social democracy describes the understanding of the dynamic of the economy driven by mass purchasing power – and that is at the basis of every kind of modern party democracy. Since the 1980s boom, most people know that economic growth can't occur without a degree of mass frivolity. That's why all politicians have lately settled down to the mix of security and frivolity that fits the system. It would simply be impossible to communicate a policy of mass impoverishment, particularly from the viewpoint of capital interests, which people in system-critical circles often continue to identify with conservative interests, which is increasingly absurd. The present problem involves the public getting accustomed to leaving out a bottom section of the total state benefits . . .

HARTMANN/TASCHWER: . . . in the sense of a two-thirds society?

SLOTERDIJK: To begin with, more of a nine-tenths society or, at worst, a four-fifths society. In this context I'm quoting subversive literature such as the Poverty Report of the Federal Republic of Germany, which provides quite astonishing data: if we look at poverty as a dynamic problem, only 1.7 per cent of the population in the entire area surveyed appears as permanently poor.

HARTMANN/TASCHWER: What should we do with the bottom segment?

SLOTERDIJK: The traditional left would have claimed that our moral attitude of direct solidarity should be enough to carry those who are cut off from the system. Today, even on the left, nobody dares to say we must go back to forms of direct solidarity. And that is wrong, because without regeneration of direct solidarity social coherence as a whole will be an illusion. In this sense, the *Spheres* project is also an attempt to treat the total sclerosis of left-wing discourse with therapy.

HARTMANN/TASCHWER: Is your spherology a left-wing project, then?

SLOTERDIJK: Definitely, to a great extent. It would be too hasty to read the way I move between various disciplines and traditions as an indicator of right-wing sympathies. The *Spheres* project examines where the sources of real acts of solidarity come from. I would like to use atmospheric analysis to help formulate a language of participation that the left has mistakenly vacated to traditionalists or right-wingers. People on the left will have to learn the ethics

[1] Gerhard Schröder (b. 1944) is a politician and a leading member of the German Social Democratic Party (SPD). He was Chancellor of Germany from 1998 to 2005.

of generosity. In any case, we have to find a completely new description for the ability of people who are not immediate neighbours to be mutually interdependent. It's impossible to achieve this with the tired old vocabularies of class struggle that wore out a long time ago.

HARTMANN/TASCHWER: Interdependence among strangers is a question posed by the new twenty-five-member European Union as well. Ten years ago you published a book with the title *Falls Europa erwacht* [*If Europe Awakes*].[2] Austria's Federal Chancellor quoted it just recently. Has Europe become more wide-awake in the meantime?

SLOTERDIJK: I really don't know if social systems can sleep and whether nations are collectives that can be woken up. But it is a fact that since the debacle of 1945 the Europeans have fallen victim to a lethargocracy, the rule of lethargy. Throughout all the hectic activity, paralysis has held sway almost everywhere. What we need now is for the Europeans to develop positive concepts from their achievements. In future, they should talk more self-confidently about their post-heroic and post-imperialist way of life and political style. There are signs that a new European self-affirmation is taking root, expressing those tendencies, and in that sense, perhaps, we can speak of awakening.

HARTMANN/TASCHWER: Is this possible awakening related to the present nightmares of the USA in Iraq?

SLOTERDIJK: Definitely. The Bush era has already had an irreversible historical effect. The Atlantic alliance of the Cold War era has collapsed under it. The Atlantic is seen as frontier waters again, and no longer as the new Mediterranean. Europe has a Western border again for the first time in many years.

HARTMANN/TASCHWER: What about the border to the East? I'm thinking of the European Union enlargement.

SLOTERDIJK: I seriously believe the EU enlargement on 2 May marks the end of the post-war era. August 1914 and May 2004 are key dates in the history seen as a whole. Europe is occupying its historically evolved borders once again. It has reached its territorial optimum – further expansion would probably be disastrous. We have decades ahead of consistent transfer benefits to support the new EU states. That will bring tensions, of course, but they will be very meaningful. We have seen that such injections of funds

[2] Peter Sloterdijk, *Falls Europa erwacht: Gedanken zum Programm einer Weltmacht am Ende des Zeitalters ihrer politischen Absence* (Frankfurt: Suhrkamp), 1994.

can function in relation to the Spanish or Irish economic miracles. Nobody knows whether the same thing can work with 40 million Poles and their national economy, which is very backward.

HARTMANN/TASCHWER: What are the prospects of Turkey joining the EU?

SLOTERDIJK: The answer is self-evident, considering the haphazard catch-up dynamic of the new EU states. With twenty-five members we shall never reach the requisite agreements on these issues in Brussels: why should the Poles, the Hungarians, the Czechs and the Lithuanians want to include voracious, unstable Turkey in the EU as long as they themselves need every euro available for distribution? But even if Turkey were allowed to join – which is practically impossible – it would be there as a second-class member because it would have to wait a long time before being allowed to enjoy subsidies from Brussels.

HARTMANN/TASCHWER: What will happen if the integration process fails?

SLOTERDIJK: Then vocal movements about disadvantage on the Carinthian model will spread across the whole of Europe.[3] In the case of the former East Germany a small, rather unpleasant neonationalist scene became vocal shortly after German reunification. We can expect something similar in the new EU member states as soon as the process of sorting out winners and losers is over. In five years people all over Europe will probably be talking continually about these angry provincials, and looking back nostalgically to the days when we regarded a dashing populist showman like Jörg Haider as a menace.

[3] This refers to the Austrian regionalist-nationalist movement led by the controversial politician Jörg Haider (1950–2008), Governor of the Austrian Federal State of Carinthia and leader of the Austrian Freedom Party (FPÖ).

# 14

# THERE ARE NO INDIVIDUALS

## *Interview with Sven Gächter**

GÄCHTER: Mr Sloterdijk, this is admittedly a frivolous hypothetical idea: suppose Anke Engelke invited you to her late-night show and asked you to give a reasonable synopsis of your new book, *Sphären III* [*Spheres III*], for the ordinary couch potato. How would you wriggle out of that?

SLOTERDIJK: The only frivolous thing seems to me the assumption that Ms Engelke would be in her job long enough to hit upon the idea.

GÄCHTER: Good. Now let's assume Harald Schmidt still moderated a late-night TV show. As a talk-show guest in the latter-day version of his show, with its appeal to the educated middle class, Peter Sloterdijk would be in good hands.

SLOTERDIJK: I have great respect for Harald Schmidt since the time he was a young cabaret artist back in Dusseldorf, when he larded his programmes with quotations from my book *Critique of Cynical Reason*.

GÄCHTER: Schmidt would be the perfect leading actor if the *Critique of Cynical Reason* were ever filmed.

SLOTERDIJK: Not many people in the German scene can make sense out of the intellectual plasma I described in *Critique of Cynical Reason*. I can think of two or three names at most: first of all, Bazon Brock, an entertainer and philosopher who can boast an authentic

* This interview between Peter Sloterdijk and Sven Gächter appeared under the title 'Es gibt lediglich Dividuen' ['There are Only Dividuals'], in *Weltwoche* magazine (14 July 2004). Available at: <http://www.weltwoche.ch/ausgaben/2004-29/artikel-2004-29-es-gibt-lediglic.html>.

Sven Gächter is editor-in-chief of the Austrian news magazine *Profil*.

oeuvre as a qualified trickster of the late twentieth century, if you like. The younger ones would include Christoph Schlingensief and Harald Schmidt, whom we just mentioned. After that we can forget the list because things get rather dull. The humour industry is flourishing but it lacks the necessary edge.

GÄCHTER: You still owe us the *Spheres* synopsis for people in a hurry or for beginners.

SLOTERDIJK: The foam theory I develop in *Spheres III* is useful for people who don't want anything to do with their neighbours but need a good explanation as to why they can't get rid of them. To put it another way: I am trying to give an answer to the riddles of simultaneity of very different life phenomena that are clustered in a tight space without having much to do with each other. Foam is a metaphor that helps to describe this great accumulation of human life forms – while avoiding the concept of 'society'.

GÄCHTER: It's a concept that belongs more to sociology than to philosophy. What worries you about this? Is it the descriptive vagueness? Or is 'society' too macro-theoretical for your approach?

SLOTERDIJK: I would prefer to use the term 'household' rather than 'society'. A household is a monadic factor with the potential for world-making at a single place. And a world naturally includes several co-players. Just as Robinson Crusoe had his Man Friday, the modern single has his or her media for simulating real communication. Today's single person is the successful version of the multiple personality that, regrettably, is usually described with a vocabulary strongly influenced by psychiatry. That doesn't seem justified to me, because many multiple personalities develop particular strengths precisely because of their elasticity, including that of not getting too bored with themselves. Anyway, according to my definition there are no individuals, there are only dividuals, which means parts of couples or of households, while a person who lives alone is generally someone who has learned through appropriate training to form a couple or a household with himself or herself.

GÄCHTER: A quotation from *Spheres III*: 'There is no doubt that philosophy as an ancient European form of thought and life is exhausted.' What is the connection between this sentence and your dictum of the death of Critical Theory?

SLOTERDIJK: There is no direct connection. Critical Theory is dead for other reasons than exhaustion of philosophy as a form of life. Critical Theory is dead because it is no longer able convincingly to carry out its mission as Germany's civil theology. Even if it's true that modern societies need something like a framework that can be used for civil theology, Critical Theory alone can't offer that any longer. If it still tries to, it becomes suspect as a sect, and that is exactly what we have seen for a long time now.

GÄCHTER: Does the rejection you have received from protagonists of Critical Theory such as Jürgen Habermas, sometimes in a very public way, stem from your refusal to join that 'sect'?

SLOTERDIJK: When it comes to members of a sect we can always presume one thing – a highly developed instinct for compatibility. I have always said that if we have to be creatures bound to sects, I would rather belong to a more entertaining sect.

GÄCHTER: Could we describe your *Spheres* project as a universalist theory of thought that is spatially modelled?

SLOTERDIJK: Yes, although I define 'spaces' not in the sense of physics but of a resonance community. Intervals exist between people that can be filled or bridged communicatively and, in a certain way, morally. My spheres theory concerns the moral intervals between people, starting with the basic assumption that, to begin with, all living beings can only exist within the closed confines of their immune system. In future we will probably have to make much greater use of the terminology of general immunology in order to reach an understanding of what people could have in common with each other at all. I reject the term 'society' because it assumes far too boldly that people build up common immune systems in the same way in all situations and at all times. This implies that 'society' is constituted as a bloc of immune systems and leads to false unification. All the old social immunologies were mainly controlled by means of a logic of belonging. Today, however, the outlines of a new, totally different social immunology are visible. They clearly tend towards individual immunology, that is, to world formation and self-protection at a local level. I think network theory and foam theory are more realistic than old-fashioned 'sociology'. Continuing to talk about 'society' today is a form of conceptual pretension.

GÄCHTER: Isn't your spheres theory ultimately the attempt to cushion the existential-philosophical shock by bedding it in foam, so to speak?

SLOTERDIJK: The existential philosophers have greatly overexaggerated homelessness. In fact, people sit in their apartments with their delusions and cushion themselves as best they can. Living means continuously updating the immune system – and that is precisely what foam theory can help to show more clearly than before.

GÄCHTER: If we grant the media the function of a control system, that is, an immune system in a way, they have functioned extremely well recently. The widespread publication of photos of torture at Abu Ghraib prison in Baghdad provoked unprecedented concern worldwide, more than all the pictures from the Balkan War,

Rwanda or various suicide-bomber attacks. Why? Because people never expected the Americans to do something like that?

SLOTERDIJK: Since the first Gulf War, the Americans have changed the rules of warfare by starting to manipulate pictures from the war. What used to be called *theatrum belli* is identified today by a mental field: all the generals in the age of the American wars start from the assumption there are always two wars in one, and two superimposed battlefields, with the battlefield of images playing an increasingly bigger role. The American generals of the image are required to wipe everything that could publicly damage the morale of the American troops or the reputation of the USA.

GÄCHTER: That plan failed spectacularly in the recent case of the torture pictures from Baghdad. Anyway, it's not about wartime pictures but post-war pictures.

SLOTERDIJK: Yes, but the scene of the pictures, the *theatrum belli* of the imagination, can no longer be clearly separated from material war events. The war of images has now become the actual, perpetual war. Realpolitik today must be constructed in the area of ideas, of fantasy. This is why the factions from the Pentagon and Hollywood, which have worked entirely separately so far, have converged through events during the Bush administration. The torture videos, in turn, were partly the revenge of auteur film on the Pentagon/Hollywood complex: a naïve, amateurish production that follows its own laws – and its own conscience. As for torture, traditionally an area of discretion behind closed doors, it has now entered the age of images – 'Sex, Torture and Videotape'.

GÄCHTER: What is remarkable is that the torturers themselves are now part of the production, especially shooting star Lynndie England, the grim US reservist.

SLOTERDIJK: Exactly. Lynndie England, the illegitimate sister of Monica Lewinsky as it were, has become world famous overnight like an amateur porn star. In other words, it doesn't matter whether you flirt with the president or the enemy, under present media conditions you have similar shooting star potential.

GÄCHTER: Producer, accomplice or victim of the picture war?

SLOTERDIJK: First-hand reporting is losing importance in relation to the reporting on the reporting. According to the modern logic of the mass media, only reports that have already been made can document that anything at all has happened that is worth looking at twice. From this perspective, in functional terms the media world is moving ever closer to the stock exchange where, as we know, securities that are already high are especially popular. The same applies to pictures, and shocking pictures in particular: if they are already getting good bids this will tend to continue. In my life as a viewer of pictures, I have seen few photos with such high aesthetic ambitions and such a macabre sense of the amateur aesthetics of horror as those from Abu Ghraib.

GÄCHTER: The photo of the Iraqi prisoner with the three-cornered cap on his head, the black cowl and the hands attached to cables probably has its place in the iconography of cruelty. But why was the effect of those particular torture pictures so devastating? What do you think?

SLOTERDIJK: The world had probably waited for those pictures. Anybody who wasn't totally wallowing in self-hypnotized solidarity with the Americans realized quite early on that the ostensible motives advanced for the Iraq War were a strange and unique case. You could guess that the war was a construct designed according to a particular logic of action whose beginnings preceded George W. Bush taking up office – I nearly said, 'seizing power' in the way Hitler did. The global public knows we are dealing with a distorted picture of the United States at the moment. The effect of the torture pictures fits into this scenario: they confirm the partly mindless, partly articulated background awareness that this war has involved a great deception.

GÄCHTER: In barely two and a half years the Bush administration has managed to create unprecedented atmospheric damage. Do you see this as a fleeting episode or a historical break, in the sense that the damage will not be reparable for a long time?

SLOTERDIJK: The Americans are in the position today of the Europeans in the High Middle Ages: that of the corrupt Crusader. The idea of the Crusades in the twelfth and thirteenth centuries was one of the most powerfully motivating ideas ever. It was discharged in a series of bloody wars. In the end they were not very successful, but they did result in Jerusalem being captured by the Christians for a while. The Europeans were granted the satisfaction of feeling like liberators and owners of the 'most important place in the world' – the Holy Sepulchre. The burial place of Our Lord was the 'ground zero' of the Middle Ages. Incidentally, Hegel dated the secret core idea of the European, the idea of religiously enlightened spirit, back to disappointment with the Crusades: the spirit that tried to possess the absolute stood before the empty grave and realized there was really nothing inside, and God could no longer be sought in the form of external things, of materiality. This is what paved the way that led from the internalization of mysticism to the Reformation, and finally to modern subject philosophy. Hegel saw the disillusionment about Jerusalem as constitutive for the character of the West.

GÄCHTER: Do you mean the new hasn't reached the Americans

yet, that they are reviving the crusade idea the Europeans long since abandoned, and their 'Jerusalem disillusionment' is yet to come?

SLOTERDIJK: We are dealing with a rascals' crusade that may possibly evoke earlier experiences in Europe's collective memory. But we don't have to descend into the historical subconscious – the facts of the present situation speak for themselves. A rhetoric of salvation that combines themes from the Old and the New Testament is being used to justify an extremely shabby and, perhaps even worse, a profoundly dilettantish version of so-called global politics.

GÄCHTER: Dilettantism is probably the most cutting insult towards a practitioner of realpolitik like Donald Rumsfeld.

SLOTERDIJK: The concept of realpolitik was introduced in the late nineteenth century to establish professionalism in the craft of politics ...

GÄCHTER: You are referring to Bismarck ...

SLOTERDIJK: Who, in every critical situation, first asked his advisers to present around twelve alternatives that he studied carefully before choosing the most appropriate one. Realpolitik according to Bismarck means emancipating ourselves, for reasons that lie in the nature of the case, from the imperative of common-sense morality. By contrast, Donald Rumsfeld, Paul Wolfowitz and their neo-conservative think tanks have succeeded in placing professionalism completely at the service of dilettantism. They assemble everything from the fields of military technology, media manipulation, administration and law that helps to give their basic dilettantish position a veneer of competence.

GÄCHTER: But where does the principle of dilettantism come from? Those people are by no means stupid in the accepted sense. Even George W. Bush can't be as stupid as people like to portray him.

SLOTERDIJK: The core of dilettantism is the feeling of being chosen: that you don't stand on stage because you are able to do something, but because you believe you have a vision that justifies everything. The vision is the working hypothesis of the chosen person. This seems all the more absurd in the case of the USA because the Bush administration didn't come to power due to their vision but through a more or less obvious electoral fraud, which was amateurish at the time. The Bush government took office under premises that were democratically very ambiguous and in reality impossible, and that had already caused serious moral damage to the system. And it continued like that.

# 15

# CONFUSED PEOPLE SPREAD CONFUSION

*Interview with Matthias Matussek**

MATUSSEK: Mr Sloterdijk, the last essay in your new book that completes your major three-volume work, *Sphären* [*Spheres*], contains the provocative thesis that our society is 'beyond need'. In the light of the new discussion about poverty, aren't you afraid of getting attacked for this?

SLOTERDIJK: At worst, by over-zealous spokespersons for federations. In fact, I am making a therapeutic proposal to the public: let's examine the mechanisms that cause one of the materially and mentally richest nations of all time to sink into a state of permanent grumpiness and agitation. Let's use the break in pampering that the present recession has brought to investigate distortions in consciousness in this civilization when the pressure is off.

MATUSSEK: Many intellectuals at the moment pride themselves on being economic experts, and debate about safeguarding prosperity and returns. Do you think it's wrong to prioritize economic issues?

SLOTERDIJK: Caring about material affairs is definitely not an unimportant matter for human beings. We live in a politico-economic system that plausibly promises affluence to four fifths of the population.

MATUSSEK: Which is unprecedented in human history.

SLOTERDIJK: The present pampering culture no longer

* This interview between Peter Sloterdijk and Matthias Matussek appeared under the title 'Verwirrte geben Verwirrung Weiter', in *Der Spiegel* magazine 35 (2004): 122–5.

Matthias Matussek is an author and a journalist at *Der Spiegel*.

concerns just a tiny aristocratic group but the majority of the population. In anthropological terms, this is a world novelty. But one of the business secrets of this culture seems to be that we shouldn't talk about this unprecedented collective luxury. Instead, fictitious news about shortages has to be published all the time. Incidentally, warnings about shortages used to be something for intellectuals, but federation officers have taken over from them now.

MATUSSEK: Despite the present demonstrations, recent system critique has been from the top downwards – numerous entrepreneurs who don't agree with the nation, with society and with politicians sit in Sabine Christiansen's talk show and moan.[1]

SLOTERDIJK: Talking of the media system, *Spheres III* also tells us about that. The media system exploits the entertainment value of complaining in the comfort sphere.

MATUSSEK: At one time you annoyed the cultural press with your books or with an essay lecture about cloning. Today you moderate the TV programme *Das philosophische Quartett* [*The Philosophical Quartet*] in the position of a 'national moderator', as you once put it. Where do you see your role in the present discussion?

SLOTERDIJK: For two decades I fought quite a last-ditch battle after saying in my first book that enlightenment works by cheering people up. Some people wanted to set me up as the fool who doesn't recognize the gravity of the situation. Meanwhile, many people have realized that in everything we do, we have to begin with the atmospheric facts. We can't live in one-sided negativity all the time. In this respect we could use a bit of emission control for the intellectual climate.

MATUSSEK: The philosopher as expert for the positive approach?

SLOTERDIJK: As long as the media business lives from moaning and meta-moaning there is no danger of the positive approach gaining ground.

MATUSSEK: Critics pour cold water on everything by nature. It's part of their profession.

SLOTERDIJK: But we should never forget that German criticism represents a late form of German idealism. In the latter, the soul is part of the base while the economy belongs to the superstructure. It follows that we are surrounded here in Germany by noble

[1] Television personality Sabine Christiansen (b. 1957) was moderator of Germany's most famous political talk show on ARD, the first German public TV channel, from 1998 to 2007.

depreciators who are convinced that one has to address the feeble base. People run things down because they themselves belong to the good. Being a German critic means being able to give an admonitory sermon off the cuff.

MATUSSEK: Does it worry you that Germany, the economic giant, is stumbling, and our European neighbours are watching with a mixture of concern and *schadenfreude*?

SLOTERDIJK: Actually, I'm relieved that people treat us with totally normal malice. It shows that the people from countries all around us have got used to their previously frightening neighbours. In the past, during the phase of German resocialization, it was thought better not to offend the former delinquents. People watched more or less nervously to see what would become of the bad child of the international family. Now we Germans, the notorious outliers of history, have finally been brought into the main field.

MATUSSEK: Do you mean the country has become normalized in the crisis?

SLOTERDIJK: Whatever the case, because the Germans have dropped down from the top, they have stopped being students of democracy with special needs that require the school psychologists to be called in constantly. Even the vigilant admonishers who wanted to attribute recidivist tendencies and murderers' genes to the Germans are finding it difficult now in many respects. No nation can be more ordinary than the Germans today.

MATUSSEK: In the 1980s, you described prevailing conditions as 'unhappily enlightened' – and contrasted that with cheerful, subversive protest. Today the left wing is in the doldrums. What happened to the great urge for change?

SLOTERDIJK: We shouldn't exaggerate in retrospect. At the time that my *Critique of Critical Reason* appeared in 1983, the radical left had been largely occupied with tragicomic repetition of scenarios from the 1930s. From 1967 until the Baader-Meinhof crisis of 1977, we acted out the People's Front and bravely prevented the rise of Hitler.[2] All the same, we had a script – even if it was half a century behind the times. Today, however, we don't have a repertoire for the left, whether moderate or radical. The age group

[2] Andreas Baader (1943–77) and Ulrike Meinhof (1934–76) were the leaders of the Red Army Fraction (RAF), an extreme left-wing political group formed in 1968 that was responsible for violent attacks in West Germany. Meinhof hanged herself in her prison cell in 1976. The 1977 'crisis' refers to the violent political unrest in many West German cities after Baader and three other imprisoned members of the group were found hanged in their cells in October 1977.

at the helm now is the most confused generation in German intellectual history.

MATUSSEK: The generation of 1968 has reached the top of society. Is that a lamentable situation?

SLOTERDIJK: The confused generation can only spread confusion. It does that successfully.

MATUSSEK: Isn't Schröder introducing reforms right now that the ruling CDU [Christian Democratic Union] should really have carried through in the 1980s?

SLOTERDIJK: Maybe we should realize that for nearly twenty-five years the German party system has been offering voters the choice between four varieties of social democracy: the unity party of prosperity spreads across the whole so-called political spectrum.

MATUSSEK: The former German Chancellor Helmut Kohl was the first to understand that, by turning his politics towards social democracy. His era was marked by the lucky accident of German unification – and everything that wasn't dealt with.

SLOTERDIJK: Kohl remains the undisputed lord of German lethargy. He led the Germans to the end of history. He turned the promise of post-history, general lethargy with a high level of affluence, into reality, with visible success. Things have become decidedly more uncomfortable since slimmer men have been in government. We are even being threatened with history starting all over again.

MATUSSEK: The new men are getting fatter again as well.

SLOTERDIJK: Nobody can beat Kohl on the scales. But now the new uncomfortable types have arrived and want to put the German lethargocracy back into competition with the best in the world. No wonder the great majority says, predictably: 'Wait, that's not what we signed up for! We haven't trained for the top!' That's why so many journalists and sociologists seriously consider German football as the oracle of the nation. On the football pitch we can see that simply praising ourselves isn't always enough to get by.

MATUSSEK: It seems poverty is being officially tolerated for the first time in Germany – this was previously unheard-of in Germany's centrist society of consensus.

SLOTERDIJK: Agenda 2010[3] contains nothing that Kohl shouldn't have already introduced twenty years ago. Now his successor has to take over the other side's operations. That is the usual SPD [Social Democratic Party] tragedy, by the way. As for the new

[3] Agenda 2010 was a reform programme for the German welfare system and labour relations. It was launched in 2003 by the Social Democrat/Green Party coalition led by the German Chancellor Gerhard Schröder.

visibility of poverty, it is related to the disappearance of the special German climate after 1945. Back then, when the whole country consisted of losers, the socio-psychological grip on the whole thing was much tighter than it is today. The post-war reconstruction was a collective effort. By now, being a loser is seen more as an individual issue again.

MATUSSEK: Is the thesis of the completed reconstruction actually right? Berlin, for example, has not been recreated at all, and is a city of construction sites, strips overgrown with weeds, and wasteland, which local politicians are actually selling as a prime opportunity.

SLOTERDIJK: It's always devastating when politicians talk like gallery owners. People in the special Berlin biotope have had half a century's practice at being kettled as an attraction. After the border opened, along with all the impressive new buildings there was constant competition over the memorials that were supposed to make historical remembrance impressive as well.

MATUSSEK: Remorse, made in Germany.

SLOTERDIJK: German remorse used to be a brand-name article in the moral markets of the world. Meanwhile it is only rarely in demand.

MATUSSEK: What is much more visible is German self-confidence, at least in foreign policy, which has even taken the liberty of resisting American messianic ideology.

SLOTERDIJK: I made a lot of enemies before the Iraq War started by saying that Schröder's vote against the US-British policy represented the voice of free and reasonable Europe – against the opportunists in the South, in the East, and in the German Parliament.

MATUSSEK: Is that the new German role, perhaps even a German identity: to push on with Europe as a kind of self-dissolution in the European project?

SLOTERDIJK: Europe's nation-states, including Germany, do not have to liquidate themselves. But they should remember their great common script: this is the home of the anti-miserabilism project, which should bring humankind as a whole, or a large part of it, into a worldwide community of comfort. Let's note that behind human rights are always rights to comfort that are wrongly described merely as 'material interests'.

MATUSSEK: Isn't that a rather harsh de-mystification of noble human rights?

SLOTERDIJK: Not at all. Human rights begin with the right to a lawyer; in the first place, they protect those who aren't able to speak for themselves yet. Once people can speak for themselves, they immediately start making material demands. This is an unavoidable sequence. It's impossible to imagine a majority that is full of human rights down to the tips of their toes but remains as poor as beggars. People who say and mean human rights are also affirming the trend towards opening up access to the affluence zone.

MATUSSEK: Is the new Federal German President on the right track in announcing that 'The nation needs the courage to change'?

SLOTERDIJK: He's humming the right theme tune. However, even the best speeches about courage and rolling up our sleeves are fundamentally flawed. If our new president has a good relationship to courage then he has to do something courageous, maybe pardon somebody unexpectedly or visit a proscribed country. Just urging courage on its own would be too German.

MATUSSEK: What can a German President do in this context?

SLOTERDIJK: He has to stay on the beaten track. The fact is, people in the affluence zone only accept changes that give them the security of knowing things will generally stay the same as they were. Comfort systems are controlled by tautologies. If, for example, Günter Netzer[4] comments after a bad football match: 'We have been watching a bad match', a light goes on all over the country because we have all seen the same thing. He probably says 'A seriously bad match' to boost his intellectual status.

MATUSSEK: He says what everybody wants to hear.

SLOTERDIJK: He says what everybody has seen. Right now he holds the highest informal national office – that of chief tautologist. Only he can speak with authority and call a bad match a really bad match. Right now the country's highest office is shared – Günter Netzer occupies one half and the German President the other. The latter holds the prerogative of saying that we can win anyway.

MATUSSEK: Mr Sloterdijk, thank you for this interview.

[4] Günter Netzer is a famous ex-football player from the German national team who later became a TV football commentator.

# 16

# GERMANS WANT TO BE COMPELLED

## Theory for the Year's End

### *Interview with Ulf Poschardt**

POSCHARDT: The year 2004 is coming to an end. What did the philosopher see in it?

SLOTERDIJK: To start with, three deaths in the autumn that may form a constellation. First, the death of Jacques Derrida: the last of the greats of our discipline. A distant colleague, but still present like a friend or a conscience. When we heard the news of his death from Paris during the Frankfurt Book Fair there was a hushed silence at the Suhrkamp stand, as if time had stood still. A few weeks later, the macabre death agony of Yasser Arafat began. He lay brain dead in a French military hospital, a living corpse, but was not allowed to be officially dead. As a head of state he had to remain in office while the jockeying for positions and millions took place over his near-corpse. This recalls the medieval legend of El Cid, whose dead body was tied to a horse's back to lead his troop into battle. The question is, on which horse's back Arafat's corpse sat during those days.

The third death happened several days earlier: the murder of a moderately talented but famous film director, slaughtered on the street in public view in a way that showed this was not just an execution but an excommunication of a man consigned to the animals for slaughter. The letter claiming responsibility was less a sign of terror than of enraged violated faith.

* This interview between Peter Sloterdijk and Ulf Poschardt appeared under the title 'Deutsche wollen müssen' ['Germans want to be compelled'], in the *Welt am Sonntag* (12 December 2004).

Ulf Poschardt is a journalist and author.

POSCHARDT: What do those three deaths have in common?

SLOTERDIJK: They form a kind of thanatological colloquium because they express something about exemplary deaths in our time. The philosopher Derrida died after a long, very consciously organized farewell to the scourge of postmodern humankind, cancer – an evil that has not yielded to any enlightenment or deconstruction. Yasser Arafat died as an icon and zombie, and Theo van Gogh as a victim of fanaticism because he tried to apply Voltaire's battle cry against the repressive Church – *écrasez l'infame!* – to Islam.

POSCHARDT: Which death did you think about most?

SLOTERDIJK: On the personal level, Derrida, of course, but nothing can compare to Arafat's end as an emblem of the state of the world. He died as the enemy of countless people, as a repository for the curses of millions, however much he was a votive image, a repository of hope, for many others. In ethnological terms he was a Nail Man, like one of those Congolese fetishes in which curses are hammered with nails. He was the perfect Fetish Man of the last quarter-century.

POSCHARDT: In the end he was merely his wife's puppet. Is that a neat punchline against the latent disrespect of women in Islam?

SLOTERDIJK: The woman's revenge occurred when she married him. Nietzsche used to say, 'A married philosopher belongs in a comedy.' Where does a married terrorist belong? Someone like that only fits into the chilling satire of the Middle East. Arafat was, incidentally, the only statesman of recent times who secretly bore the name 'terrorist' as an honorary title. Nobody else has done that since Churchill.

POSCHARDT: Churchill?

SLOTERDIJK: Of course. He described himself as a terrorist when he gave the order for the bomb warfare against Germany. In those days the history of the word 'terrorism' was more open than it is now, and since Churchill usually knew what he was doing he identified clearly with his methods.

POSCHARDT: Didn't the word 'terrorist' exist earlier?

SLOTERDIJK: Indeed, modern terror has a long history dating back to the Jacobins' use of the guillotine. In nineteenth-century Italy an anarchist who planted bombs was called a *dinamitario* – a beautiful job description, totally hardware oriented. Today's concept of terror, however, is very zeitgeisty, that is, it focuses on software and is designed for aesthetic effect. Churchill's admission shows that the word's history had not yet been decided. If terror is the means of conquering Hitler, one should admit it and wear the title of terrorist like a medal. Churchill did that. Arafat had his own particular ideas about that.

POSCHARDT: But in this sense terror would always be a means or an aspect of politics. In the sense of the defence capability of a constitutional state, it is part of its monopoly of power.

SLOTERDIJK: That's quite right. Politics is always a mode in which the state organizes how it appears to the people. The lofty state has to administer the terror it evokes itself. It is responsible for the aura that surrounds it as the 'coldest monster', to quote Nietzsche again. That means it not only has to keep its symbols of sovereignty intact, but also to manage the epiphanies of its violent core – think of the military parades in France on 14 July. Carl Schmitt wrote that 'The sovereign is the person who decides on the state of emergency.' Such a situation occurs when the latent means of terror are transformed into actually existing ones. In other words, the sovereign is the person who has the possibility of making convincing threats.

POSCHARDT: Would that make the democratic politician a kind of castrated terrorist?

SLOTERDIJK: Democracy means not having a need for terror any more. The careers of Castro and Arafat, but also of Menachim Begin, show the trajectory from terror to legality. The title of castrated terrorist suits figures like Castro and Arafat very well, although it is more about pacification than about castration.

POSCHARDT: Was Arafat a supremely skilful Machiavellian?

SLOTERDIJK: He was already head of the PLO in 1972, at the time of the attack on the Olympic village in Munich in which several Israeli athletes died. Back then he already showed his talent as a media politician, because anyone who successfully disrupts the Olympic Games becomes a global star. In November 1974, Arafat spoke to the UNO assembly in New York, scoring an enormous prestige victory for the PLO. The Munich drama was also the beginning of the hot phase of the alliance between terror and the media – that was the zero hour of terror as a media event. This has no connection any longer with the terror of the French Revolution that Hegel examined, and that was partly legitimated, or with the conservative nihilists who made regular attacks on the Czars. As we know, the author of *The Phenomenology of Mind* described the Jacobin murders as the frenzy of abstract subjectivity that wipes away everything obstructing freedom.

POSCHARDT: Did that shock Hegel the Swabian?

SLOTERDIJK: I don't think so. Hegel was cold-blooded, or he understood everything, which is the same thing. He saw terror as the price for a learning process modern people had to go through before they could live as citizens in a constitutional state. The terror of pure conscience is a stage in the curriculum that leads to the modern state: terror is the way that the spirit of freedom, which is simply abstract, first learns about its own state and learns to appreciate the indispensability of the law. This stage is a necessary experience because bourgeois society and its state only become consolidated in the post-terrorist stage. Expressed in educational terms, we could say that terror is an episode in the preparatory period for humankind's high-school certificate.

POSCHARDT: Do constitutional states react so vigorously to terror because they recognize their own previous existence in it?

SLOTERDIJK: Perhaps. They recognize in terrorism what they have dispensed with. But the present terror is basically very romantic. It is conceived as a hero cult and its aim is to found a new community through inflammatory theatrical acts of violence.

POSCHARDT: What about Bin Laden? The al-Qaeda fighters of September 11 were mostly fellow Saudis.

SLOTERDIJK: Bin Laden is an activist of the third dream. He places an Islamist dream alongside the American dream and the Saudi dream.

POSCHARDT: What dreams do the Saudis have?

SLOTERDIJK: Next to the Americans with their religion of success, the ruling Saudi cliques are the greatest escapists of our time. Because their money never runs out, they can live in an absolute dream world in which they are free to move through the centuries like sleepwalkers. They escape from the present to the past and then return again. At one moment they are in the seventh century riding through the desert with Mohammed, their minds full of plans; then they are in the eighteenth and nineteenth centuries and flirt with Wahhabi asceticism; and then they plunge into the twenty-first century and get high on the goods of the liberal world. They can endlessly afford that Arabo-Disney lifestyle feeling and can arrange themselves in a total virtual reality.

POSCHARDT: Does Bin Laden have anything in common with those Disney Arabs?

SLOTERDIJK: He is a creation of Saudi escapism, but a renegade from it at the same time. His goal is to destroy the most bizarre alliance in world history, the entente cordiale between the USA and Saudi Arabia. This alliance binds the world's two great escapist powers together in a kind of synchronized sleepwalking. We shouldn't forget that in its own way the USA is also a purely escapist nation. From the perspective of the Old World, the reason is obvious. The majority of the country's population consists of people who fled from miserable circumstances to make a new start elsewhere. The country itself is founded on the flight to happiness. Basically, the people are refugees from poverty in their home country, people who think they are escaping, whether from bad to better or from good to fantastic. But the dependence on oil means the American way of life is tied to the Gulf region, which forms an ironic bond between the earth's two great escapist extremes. The Saudi and the American dream mutually support each other. Such countries inevitably create their corresponding dream factories. The Arabs have also reached their own stage of myth creation and are beginning to give themselves a poetic image. They are inventing themselves as agents of a great history. The air is full of fairy tales and imperial epics – including the epic hostilities essential for any great story. The young men become soaked in a heroic fairy-tale paranoia that requires them to fight the nearby enemy at home and the faraway enemy across the Atlantic.

What makes Bin Laden so interesting is that he torpedoes the magical sense of fellowship between the two escapist powers. He has understood that dream factories can only be fought with the aid of alternative dream factories. Citizens of a genuine escapist power are no longer interested in resistances of yesterday. Escapism is the model for movement by which people can live away from resistance. If there are still obstacles left to face, it is only because the old evil followed you to your new home. You fled from the Old World and left all your old troubles behind and now what you left has caught up with you. The best thing would be to eliminate the evil at its own source.

POSCHARDT: Then the story of America's creation is based first of all on the flight of Europeans to a desired place that turns out successfully. It starts on the East Coast and flees further westwards until it reaches the Pacific coast. That is where Hollywood arose, where the escape was dematerialized and continued in imagination.

SLOTERDIJK: In fact, going West is fundamental for the entire modern age: from Europe across the Atlantic and further from the East Coast to the West Coast. But that was not the end of the great escapist drift by a long way. The escape energies accumulated at the Pacific wall and rose upwards. California emerged as the first land of 'get high, go easy, get rich, get famous'. Everything has the same dynamic, the same flight into the easy, magnificent, glorified life. People always want to get away from the old powers of depression. Still, the Americans sense that something is creeping up behind us that we can't get rid of completely. Persecutory forces are at work, pursuing us into the heartland of evasion. Many of those who are fleeing are tired and at risk of giving up the race. Is it coincidence that the USA is the paradise of psychotropic drugs – and the hell of overweight people? The scales tell them they don't look fit for escape.

POSCHARDT: From that perspective, would nation-building, the idea of exporting democracy – by armed force, if necessary – also be a consequence of that escapism?

SLOTERDIJK: Nation-building is the attempt to sedate possible pursuers on the spot.

POSCHARDT: Do you believe that?

SLOTERDIJK: Of course not. Not because I don't trust the Americans and don't wish them success in what they do. On the contrary, one wishes the agenda as such the best of luck. But, as Europeans, we know a few things that dampen our confidence in political engineering. Nation-building isn't a stupid concept in itself. We could use it to sum up a good part of what has happened in Europe since Napoleon. Above all, he characterized French world politics in the offensive phase after the revolution of 1789. The French democratic messianic ideology that Napoleon embodied is absolutely comparable to the America of today, and its consequences make us think. It took 150 years after Napoleon's death to get rid of the last detritus of his politics.

POSCHARDT: Can you give an example?

SLOTERDIJK: Let's consider Spain and Germany, both objects of Napoleonic nation-building. In Spain the effects lasted until the death of Franco in 1975. In 1808, Napoleon stood outside Madrid with an army of three hundred thousand men, as a liberator and herald of human rights, of course. All at once the miserable Spanish could participate in the achievements of the French Revolution, the abolition of aristocratic privileges, the end of exploitation of the people by a parasitical clergy. The conquerors didn't utter a single wrong word. What happened then? The downtrodden Spanish peasants, the poorest of the poor, ganged up together and picked out young men from the liberators' army and, full of hate, massacred them. We are reminded of this story today every time we say the word 'guerrilla'. After that, Spain needed nearly 170 years to find its own path to democracy. In Germany things weren't much better, because anti-French emotions led to the ideas of the German national movement splitting off from the ideas of the Enlightenment – with consequences that could be observed in 1945. Briefly, the Europeans know, or should know, what to think about import exemptions and import democracies. At best we get dictatorships in democratic clothing with a substructure of a market economy.

POSCHARDT: That sounds as if it would apply to us Germans as well.

SLOTERDIJK: At a distance, the Wilhelmine Empire probably seemed to be a construct like that. The Federal Republic of Germany, however, was fortunate and bypassed the usual emotional backlash against the liberator. But this is a historical peculiarity that the present propaganda mongers of nation-building mistakenly hold up as a model. We can't derive anything at all from the German case. The world in the twenty-first century will most probably become a form of global authoritarian capitalism. With the war on terror and the Islamists' jihad romanticism, war capitalism is already palpably close. The circumstances are such that there will soon be attempts to increase non-democracy.

POSCHARDT: Is it the task of intellectuals to remind democracy of its own roots?

SLOTERDIJK: In principle, yes, but the intellectuals themselves don't really know any longer where the roots lie.

POSCHARDT: That leads to the question: who are we Germans? Cosiness is more important to us than freedom. We would rather live nice and warm in a little shack than freezing in huge rooms. We are like Oblomov, the nineteenth-century Russian hero who spends his life on the sofa.

SLOTERDIJK: I think the Russian association leads to the issue itself, for modern Germans are actually much more Russian than they imagine. We resemble the romantic cliché of Russians from nineteenth-century literature. They probably slipped into us by a kind of soul migration during the Cold War. However, the Germans are cosy in a completely different way than their Eastern cousins. They stay away from the precipice; their cosiness remains compatible with work. German motivation is a reliable constant as long as it goes along with a strong imperative, because Germans don't want to get involved voluntarily. They want to be compelled.

POSCHARDT: They first have to hit the rock bottom of necessity.

SLOTERDIJK: If the rock bottom has spoken to them, they're capable of anything.

POSCHARDT: Where are we now? Have we hit rock bottom or are we still going down further?

SLOTERDIJK: I think the country's own success mechanisms are in such good shape that we can't fall much further. The German export economy, German science, the German legal system, the German social system, all of that is firmly established in positive routines that keep going even when a few individuals dig their heels in.

POSCHARDT: And what about freedom?

SLOTERDIJK: By now, most goals for freedom are defined apolitically or post-politically.

POSCHARDT: Strange things happen in Germany: People work illegally and complain there are no jobs. They moan about the collapse of the inner cities and go shopping in malls outside the city.

They complain about jobs migrating away and save money by going shopping in Poland. Are many Germans incapable of understanding their own actions and the consequences?

SLOTERDIJK: Most people are not particularly good at grasping if-then relationships – I wouldn't restrict that to Germans. In our case we have the added factor of the general infantilizing tendency of the social climate. The drug subculture offers the paradigm for the radical separation of one's own behaviour and awareness of consequences, and the open consumer society has more in common with this subculture than it realizes. Drug consumers have learned to ignore the consequences of their addiction, whether physical or moral. Their own ruin doesn't bother them: just watch how you cope with my self-destruction! 'You' means the legendary unreal collective of the Others that is to blame for everything and responsible for everything. This collective contains the so-called 'society', the biggest of all vague addresses. It is the perfect imaginary recipient for passing on blame that can't be addressed. I actually think our beloved homeland consists to a large extent of people who practise the art of passing things on. We blame our bad mood on the conjuncture; we pass on our own consumer behaviour to the desolation of the inner cities.

POSCHARDT: What can politics do in that case? Isn't it, in fact, the motive force of this infantilization?

SLOTERDIJK: Social policy is an enterprise for eliminating the serious case. It should and must promise that nobody will go under, and that is how it manages to prevent the experience of total scarcity. That is very right and human, but it has the unintended effect of making things progressively unreal. In the unreal climate, antecedent clauses no longer reach their consecutive clauses, and logical and practical connections become random: 2 x 2 only equals 4 in poor countries.

POSCHARDT: Can politics organize mathematics lessons again?

SLOTERDIJK: No, it can't. That would mean putting mathematics above the human right to cosiness. Politics can't dictate the logic of hardship. The state can't even balance its budget because the unreal imperative is stronger than financial reasoning. It was easier for the German state after 1945 when it had a poor population that didn't have to be taught the basic concepts of hardship. The state found it easy to deal with the population and to key into its basic resilience to pursue its projects. That is unimaginable today after a fifty-year-long intensive course in consumerism. Today's state could certainly do with its citizens having a tougher mentality for coping with economy measures or building successful new enterprises. It can't achieve either of these things under its own steam as long as its clientele is operating on a completely different dynamic. As a result, it is condemned to maintaining a climate of well-tempered unreality. The mood resembles people in a moderately affluent family who give their children the assurance that however they behave they won't fall out of the family nest. Middle-class children today are so well cushioned that they can do what they want without having serious worries about being downgraded. We won't even mention the offspring of the new upper class, who have far less stress. This puts today's state in a very difficult situation because it simply can't do what it was able to do previously with its members. Above all, it can't give any orders – and it isn't allowed to act as a fitness coach. Usually the state has the characteristics of a coach in the sense that it determines for which kind of contests and for which kind of stress the different population groups have to be trained, and at which arenas they should appear. Today the state, with the President as its mouthpiece, can only advise citizens to do more themselves on their own initiative. This is dreadfully similar to the famous double-bind command: 'Damn it all, be spontaneous at long last!' Present-day politics reminds me of the strategy of health insurance companies in the 1970s, when jogging paths were constructed in the woods on the city outskirts to allow the few people who wanted to do something healthy to let the general community off the hook by keeping themselves fit.

POSCHARDT: The way society is separating into different layers is having dire consequences. The performance elite has to work more and more, and is ridiculed for doing so. The gap between rich and poor is widening – and is supposed to be closed by redistribution. People evidently think any kind of differentiation is always a result of injustice.

SLOTERDIJK: Perhaps we should take a look at Niklas Luhmann's writings, for example, the important essay 'Am Anfang war kein Unrecht' ['In the Beginning there was No Injustice'][2]. But what happens today goes beyond questions of the sense of justice. People think they are feeling a psychological disintegration that goes deeper than a normal class divide. It is connected to the fact that key personnel with a sixty- to eighty-hour week are barely able to understand how those less heavily occupied experience reality.

POSCHARDT: Where does the hatred against the elites stem from?

[2] Niklas Luhmann, 'Am Anfang war kein Unrecht', *Gesellschaftsstruktur und Semantik: Studien zur Wissenssoziologie*, vol. 3. (Frankfurt: Suhrkamp Verlag), 1989, pp. 11–65.

SLOTERDIJK: To understand that, aside from the timeless psychology of resentment, it is useful to look back at the historical semantics. Sometimes the history of words is great politics in itself. At the beginning of the modern hatred of elites we find the anti-aristocratic sentiments among the plebeian layer in the French Revolution. At that time, citizens and plebs began with a common understanding that the conventional treatment of the people by a parasitic aristocracy and a clergy in the same mould couldn't go on. This verdict was put into practice in 1789. From then on, people in Europe used the word 'exploitation' until 1917, and in some regions until 1968, whenever they wanted to interpret widely disparate income relations. The term was unambiguous for the period before 1789: the aristocracy and its clerical counterpart really existed and appropriated the French nation's surplus product to lead their lordly life without doing anything themselves – and, moreover, there was a hyper-parasitic royal court that made the stupid mistake of showing off its extravagance to the nation. A situation like that creates – to put it mildly – various kinds of intolerance, and those fitted the description of bourgeois morality. In that regime, proletarians and citizens defined themselves quite logically as the exploited and the old ruling class as exploiters. When the citizens and proletariat mutually disentangled themselves after the revolution the exploiter title was passed on to entrepreneurs, and along with a grain of truth this involved a misnomer with serious and widespread effects. Now 200 years have passed and we still haven't really understood that a completely new figure has appeared on the stage of world history, that of the rich person who works, often more than anybody else. This type has still not found its rightful place in the collective wisdom and linguistic vocabulary of contemporary culture. The reason, perhaps, is that it was God's last thought. It is so improbable that even with the best will we only understand it reluctantly. To be rich, but to do more than anybody else: for many people, if not the majority, this still seems totally absurd. Nonetheless, quantitively and qualitatively, it is an impressive phenomenon. Without the working rich there would be no modern welfare state. The ominous high earners who constitute barely 10 per cent of the population generate more than 50 per cent of the national tax revenue.

POSCHARDT: The personal responsibility of the socially weak is still a taboo subject for discussion.

SLOTERDIJK: I don't believe in taboos, only in difficult topics. The most difficult topic is that a large number of poorer people are absolutely not exploited; they are people who nobody has deprived of anything, but who have consciously not used their opportunities, mainly because they probably found no incentives to rise above their situation. Of course, many people are in need through no fault of their own, and we help them, as we obviously must. But given the present facts, we can talk about a changed perspective even on the left wing. It is no longer a question of starting from accusations of exploitation and corresponding class solidarity, but of going back to seemingly old-fashioned concepts like empathy and shared responsibility for the weaker members of society.

POSCHARDT: Compassionate conservatives – a success model of the Republicans in the USA.

SLOTERDIJK: The European way will be different because we don't appreciate the political exploitation of religious feeling. But let me say a word about the situation of exploitation: the 'exploitation of man by man', to recall the Count of Saint-Simon's phrase, has largely been shifted to the exploitation of nature by human beings. We live in a situation where even the poorest believe they have the right to a share in this new exploitation of nature. Your earlier mention of the cosy, warm cabin fits this trend perfectly. High room temperatures today are almost always a theft from nature or, more precisely, from the history of the earth. We forget too easily that fossil energy carriers, the real benign geniuses of our time, have done more for the transformation of human living conditions in the past 200 years than all the cultural factors together. We have to think about this provocative statement to understand the extent to which most people today live from unfinanced ideas. We say 'culture', and have no idea where it comes from.

POSCHARDT: Let's look at the problem of roots. Who is conservative today? Who is progressive? The trade unions or the middle-class parties? Or have these terms become obsolete?

SLOTERDIJK: The trade unions are doubtless the crux of today's conservatism – compared to them, parties like the German Christian Social Union (CSU) are pure soviets. But there is no cultural success without conservatives.

POSCHARDT: And the Christian Democratic Party (CDU)?

SLOTERDIJK: Like every major party, it contains both elements, the preserving and the progressive. The old form of social democracy was another wonderfully conservative institute, populated by achievement conservatives. In contrast to that, the Schröder line of the new Social Democratic Party (SPD) expresses how the party's present internal learning processes work. We can generally say that unrest always arises from learning, and people can and must learn only when they are in power. The SPD's malaise comes from the fact that it contains a few people who really want to govern. If the party didn't have such people it could declare itself satisfied with cosy illusionary opposition, and spare itself the trouble of learning for today's world. As we have said, we only learn after leaving the safe reservation of irresponsibility.

POSCHARDT: The will to freedom is gaining a voice in the East of Europe and in the mosques of fundamentalism. Are we learning from the Ukrainians what we should be, and from the Islamists in Germany what we shouldn't be?

SLOTERDIJK: Two frontiers are becoming discernible – not frontiers of geopolitics but of political mentalities. The one is defined by hate and resentment, both in vehement, almost incurable forms, and the other by idealization and anticipation of rescue. Two of the strongest affects that humans are capable of are working right now on the frontiers of Europe. The Europeans have every reason to see this as an incredible opportunity. These facts should make us realize the real situation of Europe. Without exception, Europe's leading nations are the constructs that followed humbled empires. If we look at the history of mentalities in the past fifty years, we recognize the transitional pathologies of the vanished world powers. But those phenomena have had their day, and that is why a new European affirmation is emerging. In this situation we must narrate the European myth again, in such a way that the people listening to the story understand that it is about something magnificent, something we are proud to be part of. This presupposes that we demand our most beautiful myth back from the Americans, who took it with them over the ocean.

POSCHARDT: Which myth?

SLOTERDIJK: The story of the refugee Aeneas as told by Virgil. Anyone who hears it immediately understands where Europe is located: Europe is a place on the map of hope where defeated people have a second chance. What used to characterize the verve of American escapism must now become the core of European consciousness. The story begins, inevitably, with the burning of Troy, from which Aeneas, the greatest loser of all, flees with his father on his back and the Penates in his bags, to embark on a second attempt at life in Italy – and you know how the story goes on.

I think we should make this initial, non-imperial opening section of the *Aeneid* the founding myth of present-day Europe, and finally stop repeating those meaningless, lascivious stories of the bull and the maiden. Our main narrative says very clearly that Europe is a country where vanquished people can find their feet again. The Americans hijacked the story with their brilliant, unerring instinct, and the Europeans will have to get it back, whether they want to or not. Otherwise they will become boring collective nationalists and will be unable to solve the problem of the countless new citizens without whom they can't survive. We are looking for a new formula for European hospitality and integration, and Virgil delivered it in advance.

POSCHARDT: What will happen to the Americans if we take away their myth?

SLOTERDIJK: The Americans are putting their own dream at risk without the Europeans having to take anything away from them. They give the impression of being psychologically and politically blocked, and seem defenceless against the spirit of revenge that has gripped them. They can't get over the fact that people don't love them as they think they deserve. No good can come of this narcissistic touchiness. The Europeans may be lethargic but they have enormous potential, especially with the unique relationship between a culture of freedom and *savoir-vivre*. That is something that only exists in this particular way in the Old World. Europe is a big matrix of the art of living. I have just returned from Korea, very impressed by the country, which is experiencing something like the German economic miracle of the 1960s and 1970s on today's technological level. It is a country intoxicated with performance. You notice there that a collective capitalism exists in East Asia that is hugely different from our very individualized lifestyle. This brings us back to our European culture. I told myself we should be grateful for every minute we are able to live in this part of the world – unless our modernizers destroy culture and education with their disastrous economism. The danger signals are clear to see.

POSCHARDT: Has gratitude got lost with freedom? Have we lost the feeling that we should count ourselves lucky?

SLOTERDIJK: '*Sich glücklich schätzen*' ['Count yourself lucky'] – isn't that one of the most beautiful expressions in the German language? I suspect you may be the first person for years to use it in a meaningful context again. It is a fantastic, suggestive phrase, basically very un-German. The best German for identifying a very un-German feeling.

POSCHARDT: We say people 'shrink away' from happiness. That describes a very typically German type of movement, I think.

SLOTERDIJK: I wonder whether it isn't actually part of the mood in Western culture as a whole. Coaching is on offer everywhere to teach us to present our own life in the light of discrimination we have suffered. People think they make more of an impression if they portray themselves as victims of an attack. We are constantly filling out invisible forms for compensation and submitting them to an obscure authority. I think this illustrates the Germans' well-known tendency to complain. Although the feature pages in the German press have picked up the complaining habit, 'complaining' isn't the right word because it actually belongs to a musical category or a biblical one, if we think of the threnodic prophet Jeremiah. What we are talking about has no relation to the musical mode of *lamento*. In fact, our complaining involves filling out misery forms. If we sign and stamp them, we can be sure we will get something for it from somewhere.

POSCHARDT: That sounds more like filling in an order form, whereas the de facto lament is enough in itself.

SLOTERDIJK: Shakespeare says somewhere: 'I will not praise that purposes not to sell.'[3] In our case the analogy should be: 'Who would complain if he couldn't fill in a form?'

[2] Sloterdijk's original German quote, '*Wer würde preisen, wenn er nicht verkaufen wollte*?', could be a paraphrased reference to William Shakespeare, Sonnet XXI. Or perhaps Sloterdijk is thinking of the proverb 'He praises who wishes to sell.'

# 17

# COMPARATISTS OF HAPPINESS

*Interview with Manfred Keuler and Paul Pantel**

PANTEL: Mr Sloterdijk, we have done interviews on the topic of work and unemployment, and poverty and wealth, with economic and social experts and with futurists and literary figures. They include, for example, Peter Glotz, Alexander Kluge and Hans-Olaf Henkel – all rather independent people from a variety of disciplines. The interviewees do not meet in person, only through their statements in the minds of readers who will then, ideally, continue the conversation themselves. To round off the interview series we would like to have the topic reviewed from a philosophical standpoint. We thought of you because there are exciting connections with our kinds of questions in your new book, *Sphären III. Schäume* [*Spheres III. Foam*], notably in the chapter titled 'Stimulus and Pampering. A Critique of Pure Mood'.

SLOTERDIJK: It sounds like a sort of 'colloquium of the absent'. If you are naming names, Glotz has persistently asked the fundamental questions from the left-wing perspective about the production of social relations through work, and about the division and redistribution of the results. Kluge, too, has never tired of investigating the cunning of reason in its more or less microscopic form – not the very grand type of divine reason, but the cunning of

* This interview between Peter Sloterdijk, Manfred Keuler and Paul Pantel appeared under the title 'Komparatisten des Glücks. Über Mangelfunktionen, Reichtumsmärchen und die Politik der Großzügigkeit', in Manfred Keuler and Paul Pantel (eds), *Absturz oder Neubeginn. Arbeitswelt in der Globalisierung: Interviews mit Hans-Olaf Henkel, Peter Glotz, Oona Horx-Strathern, Frithjof Bergmann, Rolf Hochhuth, Alexander Kluge und Peter Sloterdijk* (Munich: GIB Verlag), 2004, pp. 66–75.

ordinary people and their life strategies. He augments the Marxist concept of the base in an extraordinary way, making the whole social underground swarm with cunning Odysseus figures.

The gender issue comes into play here as well, because the German word *List* [cunning] is not just grammatically feminine. As far as Henkel is concerned, I see him generally as an edgy figure whose position is influenced by a degree of anarchism, as he starts with the entrepreneur and not with the bourgeois. Incidentally, our problem in the Federal Republic is actually the return of the bourgeois, of the person of private means, of the unproductive glutton as a mass event, a phenomenon we are seeing everywhere, including in the form of small savers and people who play the stock exchange. We have to take this class of apolitical gold diggers seriously. They include all the people who worship the economic utopia of the modern age and accept being dominated by a dangerous and irresistible fairy-tale theme, the dream of income without performance. I would gladly discuss this topic in an interview with Alexander Kluge: to what extent so-called society represents a collective for telling fairy tales whose key economic fairy tale is Fortunatus'[1] dream of a free income personally handed out to you by the goddess Fortuna or her modern successor, the lottery fairy. Lucky wins like these are supposed to be a shortcut by magical methods on the long road from wishing to success to great freedom: 'I woke up this morning and discovered I was rich!'

PANTEL: But that's really a subject for the popular press – in fact, we're miles away from that!

SLOTERDIJK: Quite the opposite! At the level of dreams – and dreams are something very real – we have never been in the grip of these fairy-tale themes as much as we are now. Looking at the subject superficially, the collective as such (or whatever we want to call 'society') is suffering at present from all the experiences related to the production of the feeling of shortage. But we shouldn't forget for a moment that shortage is an interpreted feeling. We shouldn't forget that today we live in the richest society of all time, and are tyrannized by the feeling of shortages more than almost any other group ever before. This is investigated far too rarely. Today's pervading feelings of shortage are generated, hallucinated and organized feelings of shortage, created in a kind of social

[1] *Fortunatus* is a German folk tale that was popular in the sixteenth century, about a legendary hero who lived on money from the never-empty purse of the goddess Fortuna. The story first appeared in the *Volksbuch*, a book of folk tales from 1509.

democratic-neoconservative dream factory of shortage. The main agents in this 'Hollywood of poverty' are the media, trade unions, employers' associations, health insurance bureaucrats and creative artists – in other words, everybody involved in evoking and interpreting collective feelings of wealth and poverty. They are busy all the time agitating us with a new genre of poverty films. Almost all our contemporaries, whether they publish or not, are riding on this roundabout of shortage theory while the real dropouts, the hard core of the Tuscany faction, so to speak, or the people who simply stayed on in Crete, or never came home from their holiday in Spain, take care not to intervene in such topics. Only a few well-known interventionists who commute between the *dolce vita* and the misery at home get flown in from Italy now and then to give finger-wagging lectures in Germany. Whereas people used to talk about a *jeunesse dorée*, today we could talk about a *critique dorée*, a type of golden criticism expressed by the spokespeople for federations for the wealthy.

PANTEL: If reality looks so different from the general assumption, that is, if there is much less scarcity than most people think – and, indeed, you have written that the 'major event of the 20th century consisted in the affluent society breaking out of the reality definitions of the ontology of poverty' – why does this major event get so little attention?

SLOTERDIJK: Because the standpoint from which we can see what really happened and will happen is not very easy to find. We can probably get to it only through psychological training that helps to remove us from the permanent agitation about shortage and its interpreters. In the past, people went to India for a year, perhaps, or to other parts of the world where they could observe authentic conditions of shortage. Incidentally, at the moment there are very active groups in Europe trying to articulate specifically European responsibility for Africa. I think that makes sense, partly because we can only re-establish criteria for ourselves by understanding the real contrast. The collective feeling of loss of criteria is especially typical for Germany. There is an all-pervasive climate in this country of false self-congratulation and false complaints, with the two systems meshing smoothly. People say, 'Maybe things aren't that bad here, but still, the conditions are incomparably awful.'

PANTEL: Yet the German Institute for Economic Research has just published a 'poverty report'. It says that one German person in eight lives below the poverty line, which is defined as 'less than 60 per cent of the average income'. Compared with many people in India or Africa, they are doing well, of course. They don't have to suffer hunger. But they are badly off in relation to the majority in

Germany. In other words, poverty and shortage can be defined in very different ways.

SLOTERDIJK: Certainly; and the relativity of this definition is exactly what we systematically obscure in our styles of speech. As I have said, we are usually only reminded of our own affluence when we are faced directly with absolute poverty. But I think we have to try to find the criterion again inside our system and, in fact, in the place where we live. We can't advise everybody to be dropouts just to get an outside view of their own world. We can't expect everybody to see their living conditions as if they came from Mars. People are always embedded in their own habits and things they take for granted, and feel naturally entitled to be naïve. But we can find a starting point for becoming properly aware of the situation even under those conditions – for *Dasein* inevitably means self-comparison as well. Thanks to the modern media, we have all become comparatists of good and bad luck. The existential comparative study has become completely natural to us. Human beings always tend to look on the brighter side and then on the darker side, and then try to capture the middle – unless they have a reason for seeing themselves as an exception and having the right to be happier than others, or they have a reason for being more closely tied to the darker side than usual, for example, if they belong to a religion of redemption which internalizes the figure of the Samaritan, or if they believe in a religion of socialist solidarity. We saw something like that in the worker-priest movement in twentieth-century Catholicism: young men from prosperous families discarded their cassocks and moved into working-class districts to share the lives of the poorest and more oppressed. Except for such extremists, average people are comparatists who commute in the middle between misfortune and good fortune.

PANTEL: But we have 5 million unemployed in Germany. Surely you wouldn't go to them and say, 'You're not that badly off compared to a carpet maker in Bangladesh, so be satisfied with your lot!' Isn't it a matter of unemployed people changing their perspective on their own situation, and the new viewpoint giving them opportunities for a different life?

SLOTERDIJK: That's an old debate. Carl Friedrich von Weizsäcker[2] said more than a quarter of a century ago that the way we interpret unemployment is a result of our inability to see an achievement in a positive light. And we are really talking about an

[2] Carl Friedrich von Weizsäcker (1912–2007) was a German physicist and philosopher.

achievement if we manage to reduce work. The fairy-tale theme of abolition of work has existed as long as work itself. Note that I'm not talking about the abolition of the active life!

Hard work, in the sense of *labor improbus*, as the Romans called it, drudgery, slogging, the physical alienation caused by humans being used as machines alongside horses and oxen for ploughing: across the millennia, that has been the dark spot on the *conditio humana*. Modern civilization, with its machine culture and modern forms of division of labour, has almost wholly emancipated itself from that. The only people who flex their muscles nowadays are body artists, or sports people as they are called. If muscles are flexed at all, this is done under the banner of acrobatics or artistry, simply because sport, if practised at a specific level, is done for show, just like a work of art. Sports people are actors doing body performance.

PANTEL: Why haven't we managed to interpret and use the free time gained through machine culture, that is, 'unemployment in the positive sense', in a different way, both in terms of society and the individual? On the contrary, as you say, there is the 'terror of unemployment that is expressed as having-nothing-to-do'. Why isn't there a more sensible solution?

SLOTERDIJK: There is no solution because the unemployed are seen as deficient entities. The jobless do not see themselves as liberated from work; their unemployment doesn't make them lords, but slaves, recipients of alms, bereft, basically like sick patients, in fact. Unemployment, as we interpret it, is a sociopathic situation in which people are deprived of the most important aspect of their human dignity as seen in economic terms. They are deprived of the satisfaction of ensuring their survival themselves on the basis of their own work. The unemployed are really in an unenviable situation, surrounded by a culture that defines autonomous life as wage-dependent. If the job is lacking, everything seems to be lacking.

Incidentally, you can find the toughest statements on this topic very early on, from Hannah Arendt. In her book, *The Human Condition*, she propounded a radical and snobbish interpretation of unemployment. It is a very ambitious, very nostalgic and rather difficult theory of humans as active living beings. What she describes as the *vita activa* is an attempt to say that humans know the world by three methods of casting off their shackles: action, work and labour. I can't go into detail here, but the main point is easy to explain: if the modern age tends towards eliminating action, which means politics, and towards transferring work to machines, for the great majority of people that leaves only working as the main purpose of life. And if a working society, which is essentially a philistine society, runs out of work, a human remnant is created, a political cave dweller without art, without education and finally without a job. That is Hannah Arendt's conclusion from the 1950s: modern 'society' as a conglomerate of tragic philistines. We have had half a century to watch this prophetic formula of the working society that runs out of work becoming concrete reality. But I believe we are at a turning point today. The difference between not having work and having work, between the unemployed and others, is becoming increasingly blurred, due to the phenomenon of the so-called leisure society in which people are increasingly working in part-time jobs or in a shorter working week, and large numbers of people are condemned to seeing leisure as an immense asset. (For the moment I'm ignoring the high-achievement class for whom a seventy- or eighty-hour week is typical.) This raises the question of which means those people use to structure their luxuriant free time.

PANTEL: To repeat the basic question: what is responsible for the unemployed being seen as 'deficient entities'? What is the mechanism, the principle, the force – what are the people, the interests behind this idea? Or is it simply lack of ideas?

SLOTERDIJK: I don't really believe it is ideas that are lacking. There is a lack of attitudes. We have enough ideas, but the attitudes with which we could pursue those ideas resolutely are not available. We have a kind of Sunday socialism that can be trotted out for rhetorical quotation now and again, but not an ideology of solidarity that functions on weekdays as well. We are familiar with a Sunday-type relationship to asceticism and a weekday consumerism. We are familiar with a sentimental state of emergency in which we show solidarity with people in acute distress (remember the events of the Elbe floods),[3] but we don't have a principled attitude to sharing or inclusion.

In addition, there is definitely the conviction inherited from Calvinism, a conviction more widespread in countries such as the United Kingdom and the USA than in Germany, that everybody gets the destiny he or she deserves. This implies that an active redistribution policy in the sense of eliminating severe poverty would be interfering with God's work.

PANTEL: But don't you think economic interests or forces exist that say that nothing should change, that the wage-labour principle

[3] Sloterdijk is referring to the enormous nationwide support for the regions devastated by exceptional flooding of the River Elbe in central Germany in 2002.

should be maintained, otherwise the system would fall apart completely, and we don't want that.

SLOTERDIJK: The argument has a grain of truth in it. We shouldn't forget that modern society, the system as a whole, has gone through a change of emphasis from a paternalist state that was capable of being strict to a maternalist state doomed to pampering. This touches on the great socio-psychological adventure of the twentieth century: the maternalization of the state system. It is embodied in the system of solidarity funds that, as we know, can only run on the basis of wage labour plus compulsory levy. This reveals the postmodern social nexus: everybody is involved in pampering everybody. It will obviously lead to paradoxes in the second or third generation at the latest. This is why there is presently a mood of public withdrawal of solidarity. We realize that the people now paying contributions can't be supported any longer by those coming up behind. We are realizing that the social contract always had elements of a chain-letter problem – which is despised and prohibited in other areas of life, of course. This insurance chain letter runs through the generations; the later we take our place in the recipients' line the more certain we are to be losers. That's one reason why we won't be able to abandon the principle of wage labour for a long time to come. The relationship between wage labour and social security contributions will remain the nerve of social linkage for the foreseeable future. This would apply even if we adopted the Swiss system of a total levy of social security contributions in which freelance professions, civil servants, employers and workers were all treated the same way and everybody paid for each other and for everything. All the same, it is an interesting alternative to the models so far. Firstly, it would lead to a strong reduction in contributions at the same time as an increase in insurance fund holdings. It's an inspiring model, but I really don't know if it is applicable to Germany and how it can be calculated in the long term.

PANTEL: What does pampering by the 'nanny state', the 'other mother' [*Allomutter*], as you call it, do to individuals? How does it change them? Does it raise them to be juvenile and to lack independence?

SLOTERDIJK: That description goes too far. Looking at today's young people, we can see immediately that they are not really dependent; they are demanding. And they take offence exceptionally easily. They also give up very easily, with a sour attitude that there's enough for all the other wretches, but they are the ones who get too little. This outlook produces the German weather, the country's regular grey. All the same, it's possible to carry on dreaming the dream of the land flowing with milk and honey. I note that the fairy-tale motif of the modern age that we have already mentioned, the popular dream of income without performance, has reached the stock exchange now. The famous 'securities' express nothing but the idea that people can easily get an income with venture capital defined as a risk premium. It's a field day for Fortunatus and idlers. However, this idea of risk is absent from the typical get-rich fairy tales of the modern age. The poor child in the 'Star Money' story by the Brothers Grimm is suddenly rewarded for being a good lad – all he has to do is to stand on the spot where gold rains down and lift up his shirt. Fortunatus, the honest German, is rewarded for getting lost in the right woods at the right moment to meet the virgin of luck, who tells him, 'I offer you six choices and you are free to choose one. Do you want wisdom, strength, righteousness, moderation – the classical virtues – or would you prefer health or riches?' Fortunatus, whose story was first written down in the *Volksbuch* from 1509 and has since been retold countless times, is important for the history of ideas because he was the first, when offered these options, to declare: 'Leave me in peace with your noble virtues, I want riches!' He was granted his wish in the form of a magic purse that, when he opened it, contained forty gold pieces in the currency of whichever country he was in. It was a perfect anticipation of the euro, in fact. It is worth noting that the owner of the purse didn't have to ask how the money got there. Fortunatus, the economic good-for-nothing, enjoyed the privilege of not having to ask any questions. He didn't have to be interested in the origin of wealth. He didn't have to refer to production or the tax system. He opened the magic purse and found what he was looking for. The fantasy of lasting abundance is situated directly at the level of fairy-tale themes and the dynamics of wishes, and declared valid – and that's it. In short, it economizes on thinking about production. This savings programme for thinking creates a type of person that doesn't have to deal with declining production any longer.

This is one reason, by the way, why the Marxist producer-person has a greater dimension of complexity than today's consumer. Today's affluent people tend to be located at the consumer end and don't know the answer to the question of whether they earn what they earn. They don't know how wealth is really created and they don't want to know any more either, because, as the last humans, they are equally indifferent to production and reproduction. It is true that people today know more about products – Marx would probably collapse if he were given a menu in a hotel that required him to choose between the ten kinds of dressing that come with salad nowadays. But don't worry; he would learn quickly, just as today's consumers learn to cope with the abundant options. Those well versed in shopping lore today can distinguish between Prada and not-Prada at a glance. That doesn't alter the fact that they are one dimension worse off than people who have learned how to ask the question in the classical tradition of political economy: where does value come from? That question has vanished from collective consciousness – the magicians have outstripped the producers.

PANTEL: The 'demanding young people' you just mentioned want – rightly – to share in the 'wealth'. But many people, or the majority, don't want wealth handed to them as a gift; they're quite prepared to work for it. Isn't it a tragedy for young people that they lack opportunities?

SLOTERDIJK: Which opportunities are lacking? Well, mostly those that guarantee security from the start. Young people have always had the freedom to define themselves as entrepreneurs. But we shouldn't forget that freedom is an attribute inherent to the individual! It can't be detached from the individual, and it can't be generalized in the abstract. And if for every person who makes use of creative freedom there are ninety-nine who don't, that doesn't contradict the promise of freedom.

PANTEL: The French Christian philosopher Simone Weil – you cite her in your work – believed that accepting the law that it is essential to work to stay alive is the most perfect act of obedience a person can perform, comparable only to acceptance of death. How is it possible that people sometimes give more thought to buying a DVD player than choosing a profession?

SLOTERDIJK: I cited that statement because it is exaggerated and outdated. It seems to me Simone Weil was postulating a metaphysics of the proletariat as if the heavy burden of life and the alienated grind were eternal constants. But this fails to understand the major event of the twentieth century, the victory over the workload. The labour-saving forces of modern technology have fundamentally changed the *conditio humana*. We are no longer beasts of burden; the era of heavy work is over, and so is the era of servitude. Simone Weil didn't consider relief from the load. Instead, she anachronistically composed a Christian metaphysics of the worker and misguidedly sanctified the 'voluntary daily death of factory work' as if Christ were standing at the workbench until the end of the world. These ideas are certainly noble, but they are confused and, above all, out of date. Automation, relief from the workload, social security – she didn't consider any of that. Nowadays we have workers who tend to be overweight and are under-challenged. They have a large amount of surplus leisure time and ponder how to conceal their unproductiveness. Astonishingly big unfilled gaps are still to be found at the core of so-called productive labour. Consider how the working day was constructed in real existing socialism: in the morning people had to be at work on time, and after that they did whatever they wanted to. Even in the Western working world there are huge segments in which the situation is similar, not just in the public service sector. In general, we can say that work is always tied to a factor of pretending to work, including the pretence of productivity, utility and indispensability. Such pretences, incidentally, are part of every product our economic system brings to the market, because every product is aimed at persuading buyers to take it, although it is clear that it is the sellers who always get the better deal – precisely because of the successful illusion of utility. Given this, the young people who think seriously when buying a digital camera or a DVD player are the men and women of the moment. They are showing they have learned one thing: as customers they don't want to be taken for idiots, at least not for total idiots. In the first place, a product is always a proposal for exploitation that the producer makes to the customers: 'Buy me! I'm using you a little, it's true, but just between us, I'm always getting the better deal.' That's what the products would say if they could be honest. In this context, let me quote Walter Benjamin, who imagined products as a whole talking the language of whores. When a potential customer goes past, the product whispers to him: 'Come on, little fellow, I'll give you a blow job!' – at which the poor customer grabs the offer. The customer probably realizes that we'll have to wait until the coming of the Messiah to escape from the system of unequal exchange.

PANTEL: You have written that the Biedermeier period[4] was the last time that the defenders of past events fell for the illusion that one could safely escape from the disintegrating force of progress. If we consider globalization as progress, do you think we are living in a postmodern Biedermeier era?

SLOTERDIJK: Definitely. Seen from a socio-psychological angle, globalization, wherever it has been successful, or rather, where it can look back on a long accumulation of means of comfort, has given rise to a paradoxical human type: the dissatisfied satisfied person. And that is precisely the Biedermeier person, and *eo ipso* the person of the present in the metropolises of comfortable life. Nietzsche once criticized the writer and former theologian David Friedrich Strauss as a regular *satisfait*. The term is useful because

[4] The Biedermeier era in Germany covers the years between the Congress of Vienna in 1815 and the European revolutions of 1848, a period of middle-class expansion associated with specific styles of interior decor, art and literature.

today's Germans are essentially *satisfaits*, but actually dissatisfied *satisfaits*. They are dissatisfied with their own satisfaction because they sense that they live below the standards of their own lives to some extent. Existentially they are under-challenged and over-challenged at the same time. That is the socio-psychological result of the successful establishment of the comfort system in the Western or Westernized world. Incidentally, we can only get closer to the exact meaning of the term 'globalization' in this context: in principle it describes exclusively the great sphere of comfort in which the Western welfare states and the nouveau riche from the young capitalist countries live. Everybody knows that this sphere is surrounded by a desolate outer zone, planetary suburbia.

Using the term 'globalization' as if it were an inclusive global system or even a global society can cause dreadful confusion. I suggest restricting the term 'globalization' to the history of production of the great comfort system to which probably not more than a quarter of humankind belongs. Beside it is a huge periphery whose inhabitants have no chance of ever getting in, and a semi-periphery consisting of people within reach of entry to the comfort system, perhaps not in the present generation but in the next one or the one after. Interestingly, these are the zones with the highest dynamic of ambition. We can see this at the moment with the new EU member states: typically for semi-peripheral countries, they display genuine dynamics of ambition comparable to those that today's '*satisfait* Europeans' experienced from the 1950s on, in the happy days of the optimal relationship between appetite and the possibilities of satisfying it. People had great ambition, they knew they only had to work hard for a while and then they could start placing their orders. Those were golden times; they will not return.

PANTEL: You say we should have a positive attitude towards people showing their own prosperity openly, but there must be something else as well. We can see it in the USA, where wealth is quite closely tied to the duty to be charitable, the willingness to give something away. Is that an ideal for you? Should we demand it more insistently from European businesses as well? Do we have an under-developed attitude to generosity?

SLOTERDIJK: Absolutely! But by its nature we can't demand generosity; at most we should encourage it. I think this is the biggest socio-psychological mission of the next generation. We too have to work to prepare a climate of public generosity in which people aren't always waiting for the state. We are waiting for a practice of generosity by quite normal heroes, who are convinced they have something to spare and think it is normal to give more than the tax office takes from them. They would be people whose self-esteem demands they give away a great deal – beyond the highest taxation rate. In addition, it is high time to ensure, by further developing the law on foundations and donations, that an increasingly bigger share of redistribution funds becomes intelligent money. Taxes, in fact, are stupid, blind, anonymous money, no man's money. Gigantic sums flow into the coffers of some minister or administrator or other, and are poured out over rightful and wrongful recipients in more or less transparent but indiscriminate ways. Foundation money, on the other hand, would have the power to transform these sums into intelligent money because they would be paid as precise allocations to a specific address. Nebulous aid would become clever investment. Intelligent use of money – that's the categorical imperative of redistribution, and it is chronically contravened in the existing system. We must develop a mood of public generosity so that it's not just the wealthy who reach the position of being compelled to say, 'We already gave! We're not giving anything!' Everybody should be able to say, 'We already gave but we can still give more.' That would be the key to a kind of redistribution converted from duty and compulsion to voluntariness and generosity. Of course, this is only possible if there is a kind of euphoria of affluence, and it is impossible for that to develop in the general climate of fictitious stories about scarcity. That is the subject of the third chapter of *Spheres III*, in which I talk about stimulation and pampering. Some stuffy reviewers have interpreted it as a conservative rejection of the classical welfare state. In fact, it is a reflection on how we can outdo the welfare state through the community of the generous.

PANTEL: You argue that it is particularly important to protect fragile things. In connection with what we have discussed here, what would be worthy of protection?

SLOTERDIJK: This concerns two opposite extremes: the first, and most fragile, is the dyad, that is, the area of interpersonal relations, paradigmatically embodied in the mother–child relationship. In our society it is generally well protected. It is extraordinarily well embedded in our legal system, and we could regard its guarantee of maternalization without borders as the last father function of the state. We shouldn't forget that, in evolutionary terms, the father is the one who protects the mother–child sphere. This original pact between the male and the female world must be reproduced in the appropriate form, even in the modern world. The most fragile thing in every known society is the mother–child sphere. It is the utopian centre of the collective and at the same time it is its centre of heat, the anthropogenous radiation field per se. When that is violated, human lives go round; large numbers of mad and degenerate people start appearing and the 'society' collapses from within.

The second most fragile thing is, of course, the great totality itself, which is constructed like foam. That is what I try to show in *Spheres III*. If we want an adequate description of the system of cohabitation, we shouldn't continue talking about a 'steel-hard shell', as Max Weber did, but about fragile constructs. The images of hardness are outdated; we finally have to change metaphors. Medieval cities added an outer wall that was removed at the beginning of the modern era because it was dysfunctional. The big comfortable hothouse in which we people in the West live today no longer has city walls. It is incredibly open, with soft borders, which is why it constantly has to be prepared for harm without losing its essential serenity, which is its working atmosphere. Now, however, a factor that we hardly noticed before comes into play. The great vulnerability of modern foam goes together with an astonishing elasticity, which ensures that destruction, losses, fallen buildings and collapsed passages are replaced within a very short time. The real lesson of September 11, 2001, is that shortly after the disaster we were told that something new would be built quickly on the same spot. That is the crucial information we receive from 9/11.

The hysterical military reaction that was called the 'war on terror' was politically opportunist and systemically confusing. The real story lies in the process as a whole: if a building like that collapses, we immediately build a better one. If Daniel Libeskind has his way, the new one will be even taller than its predecessor. In other words, we shouldn't underestimate the elasticity of the system! Fragility, and the impossibility of perfect protection, are consistent features of modern comfort foams. But because 'society' is actually not monolithic, because social aggregates are formations constructed from the bottom upwards out of single cells and foam bubbles, they have enormous elasticity. The false semantics of combating terror suggest lofty images of the entire system collapsing. Nothing could be further from the truth. When two big foam bubbles burst, the whole system may continue vibrating for a while, but a rupture like that has astonishingly little effect on the remaining cells. Elasticity is the primary feature of the foamy system. If we want to talk about the hothouse system of affluence, we must talk about two things: first, fragility, and, second, elasticity. It remains to investigate whether catastrophism and the tendency to inflate the new terrorism with fantastic over-interpretations merely represent the flip side of the common tendency towards fictional narratives about shortages.

# 18

# IMAGE AND PERSPECTIVE

## An Experiment in Atmospheric Seeing

*Interview with Tim Otto Roth**

ROTH: Mr Sloterdijk, I would like to talk to you about your experience in dealing with images. I would also like to stray a little to look at the subject of imachination – a neologism I use to describe the alliance between *imago* and *machina*. Let's speculate about possible spherological implications of the interplay of human imagination and the machine. What role do images play in your professional environment?

SLOTERDIJK: We can divide philosophers into the kind that are involved in expelling images from thought, and those who believe that thought as such is dependent on images, metaphors and figures. Obviously, I see myself as part of the latter group, although so far it has only occupied a minority position and has been partly ignored in the academic establishment. It is easy to forget that the foundation of the general concept of the image, whether as icon or as *eidos*, belongs to the field of early philosophy. Philosophers can claim to have been the original image theoreticians in the sense of having discovered the images as images in the first place, and taking them seriously. To understand this, we have to remember a rare fact: before philosophy emerged, the Greeks, and everybody else, had a way of seeing that was dominated by the absolutism of the natural perspective. To put it very broadly, the eye looks outwards into the situation and finds a holistically composed continuum of

* This conversation between Peter Sloterdijk and Tim Otto Roth appeared under the title 'Bild und Anblick: Versuch über atmosphärisches Sehen' (15 February 2005). Available at: <http://www.imachination.net/next100/reactive/sloterdijk/index.htm>.

Tim Otto Roth lives and works in Oppenau and Cologne.

visual presences. We don't perceive the sums of these presences as images that can be isolated, but as aspects of the 'condition' or the 'surroundings' as a whole, of what we traditionally call 'nature' or, more recently, 'environment'.

Philosophy is now coming to grips with analysis of this total environment, always in relation to the first sciences, geometry, arithmetic and semantics. Philosophers can really claim to have been the first to develop something like a tracker that can project sections into the holistically structured continuum of visible conditions. If you like, philosophers have invented eidetic cutting machines with which we can cut shapes out of the rolled-out dough of the present and give definitive explanations: this is the shape of a horse; this is the shape of a person; this is the shape of a star; this is the shape of a righteous man. The original process of seeing images is brought round to itself in philosophy. 'Image' in this context doesn't yet mean a segment of the world in a frame, but the outline of a thing that, by virtue of its contours, gives itself its own frame in a way. It is not just by chance that the 'ideas' Plato discovered are closely related on a linguistic level to the Greek word for the concrete, that is, the outlines of beings, alias *eidoi*, defined in terms of species. This is why we talk about 'ideas', or eidetic constants. The word *eidos* means the stabilized expectation of seeing in relation to a thing. The eidetic original image and contour image corresponds to the cut-out shape with which we cut recognizable forms out of reality. In other words, in the history of things that are visible generally, we can identify Plato as the founding father of the image principle.

Behind Plato's discovery, incidentally, is an experience that put the Greeks ahead of other peoples of their time – the experience of the written alphabet, a graphic image that conveys information about a phonetic reality. A person who can read writing trains the ability to select similarities from the mass of dissimilarities. If we write down the name of a thing, obviously the name doesn't resemble the thing at all. But the name of the thing raises the idea of the thing that resembles the thing. Writing turns out to be a tool for visualizing ideas by phonetic representation. In this sense, philosophy made the practice of writing possible in the first place. That led to the most momentous innovation of European intellectual history: Greek cursive writing that included the vowels allowed people to understand texts almost without reference to their context. This, in turn, created a revolutionary figure – a reader who could read a book on his own. He was followed by the researcher, the historian and the autodidact. A mental process of image-making evolved through the culture of reading, and connected up over the centuries with visual and real image-making – particularly in artistic professions. In this respect, philosophers, writers and illustrators belong together.

ROTH: In your *Spheres* trilogy you repeatedly refer to an image that was already shaped in antiquity: the sphere. In all three volumes of the work, *Bubbles*, *Globes* and *Foam*, you describe people as atmospherically sensitive political animals whose being-in-the-world hinges on the effort to live in something well-rounded. Your trilogy contains a remarkable number of illustrations for a philosophical project. Some of the illustrations you use are mimetic or illustrative. But most of the images don't directly relate to passages in the text. What function do pictures have in your trilogy?

SLOTERDIJK: The images in *Spheres* aren't generally used as illustrations but as autonomous visual presences. Of course, there are instances when they only act as evidence or examples, especially in the second volume. When I talk of globes or macrospheres in that book it makes sense to show those kinds of objects. The resonance between image and text is very close and figurative there, and in such cases the tension between the two levels tends towards zero. Usually, however, the images I have chosen are not simple optical additions to the written text. Where they work as intended, their nature is largely evocative. What these images evoke is not duplication of the text's content, but idiosyncratic extensions of the text into the realm of imagination. The image sequences in my books express that my text as a whole is not written on the traditional white pages of the old European book – even if the *Spheres* book may look like any other book. That would be a wrong conclusion. I may seem to be a conventional author satisfied with the monologic, the one-track logic of philosophical discourse. Such monologues are written black on white. Yet the white of the book page in *Spheres* is actually a reference to the grey of the monitor. My claim is that the monitor is radically different from the good old white page of a book, particularly because of its enlarged functional capacity, which never remains at the point of what is put into it. Somehow the printed page always cites the inscriptions chiselled in stone on ancient monuments. Roman Antiqua, the prototype for European letterpress culture, is an elegantly constructed monumental script. This made it especially appropriate for conveying TRUTH. Everything changes the moment we switch into the realm of digital monitors. Today's average computer offers such a comprehensive font program that writers will not be able to use all of it in their whole life. This makes authors into graphic designers who have to create their own scriptural image. The script itself becomes a fashion medium and a matter for the user to define. We no longer use the old, elegant European monumental script to express truth.

The given forms of the new technology condemn us to a new form of freedom. Authorial freedom today means doing our own graphic design. The relationship between text and footnote, text and quotation, and text and image also changes in the same realm of the monitor. The way I insert images into the text expresses that I am already working in the electronic white cube that faces me as a flat screen. For this reason, the composition of *Spheres* can rather be compared to an installation. The images are placed in the book like exhibits in an installation. Because they are usually rather crazy in relation to the text, they induce a slightly trance-like effect. They address the reader's brain on a different wavelength than the text.

ROTH: In relation to the monitor, on the visual level the second and third images in your first volume, *Bubbles*, struck me immediately. In terms of media, those photographs of the Sun's surface and of a galaxy from the SOHO and Hubble satellites create a contrast to the other illustrations. Do you see a difference between these digital photographs and other, more classical pictorial examples such as drawings, paintings, photographs or pictures of archaeological objects?

SLOTERDIJK: A very great difference, actually, although the eye can't recognize it at first. But the hermeneutic apparatus attached to the eye registers the difference easily. I wanted to suggest just now that the images as images only constitute a subset in the history and amount of what is visible. Taken by itself, the visible – the realm of views – is an immense reservoir structured as a surprise space for acts of seeing. Whatever else I do as a visual being, I navigate in this space. Let's assume I am a prehistoric man looking at the horizon: the leopard wasn't there a minute ago, and now it's standing in front of me. Its presence changes the meaning of my situation. By nature I am incapable of ignoring the leopard's presence. To me, its presence means the coming-to-visibility of a formerly invisible being. The point is that in this case the new visibility is something that appears of its own accord and forces me to react. The sight of the leopard that is present signifies danger. By contrast, if I only see its image it would be an all-clear signal – it would even suggest to me I were capable of manipulating the leopard. The modern age's relations of seeing are structured totally differently from a world in which leopards appear at the camp. In the first place they depend on a major event called 'research'. It was, above all, Heidegger in his later work who made it clear what that meant. Research is a measure for organized clearing away of hidden things, which is the same as saying that things that were not yet within the range of visibility are brought into visibility, indeed, more or less violently. Artists and natural scientists are allies in the major offensive against concealment. We could say we live in a kind of mine where the extraction of new visibilities is done. In recent decades the ordinary collieries in Germany were closed due to unprofitability but the mines that exploit the *lethe,* the 'shelter of being',[1] concealment, are working to full capacity more than ever. Their production exceeds anything known beforehand. Think of the new pictures of the earth from space taken with cameras on board satellites: they offer one of the most popular and most spectacular contributions to the attack of research on the realm of hidden things.

Paradoxically, before the modern age, the earth as a whole was the epitome of a shrouded object – it was the underlying factor no natural view could comprehend. Today it seems have the least secrets of anything. If I understand correctly what you mean by the hybrid word 'imachination', the term says that mechanical optics revolutionizes our relationships of seeing, and indicates how it does this. As soon as we discarded the term 'revolution', because it is the wrong description for a process that should have been understood much more technically and precisely, we were confronted with an alternative expression for the basic events of our epoch, namely, unfolding. Taking this metaphor literally is enough to get to the heart of the matter. Something that was concealed up until now, that was self-enclosed, enfolded and not illuminated, is dismantled and manipulated to form an enlarged surface – the folded object is unfolded, bringing the former interior to the surface until the light falls on it. This formal representation of the general procedure of rendering visible touches on the modus operandi of enlightenment in general. Enlighteners negate the conventional boundaries between light surfaces and dark interiors and bring formerly hidden things to light. That's why I say we are not living so much in a revolution as in a process of folding outward, an 'outfolding'. I even made the suggestion in my *Spheres* book to drop the term 'revolution' and replace it with 'explication'. Making a revolution is more an episodic political gesture that is important in specific situations, for example, when it is necessary to clear repressive secretive persons out of the way – monarchs and other manipulators of the Arcanum. They are regarded, with some justification, as figures that block the way to the basic work of the modern age, which consists, as we have said, in continuing to explain things further.

[1] A reference to Heidegger: 'Der Tod birgt als der Schrein des Nichts das *Gebirg des Seins*' ['As the shrine of the Nothing death is the shelter of Being'], in Martin Heidegger, *Bremer und Freiburger Vorträge*, ed. Petra Jaeger (Frankfurt: Vittorio Klostermann), 2005, p. 18.

ROTH: I have a suspicion in relation to this outfolding. You describe the machinists' statement about the human body as encapsulated in La Mettrie's dictum, 'Voilà une machine bien éclairée',[2] in two ways, the first time as a blow for liberation and the second time as a loss of spheres. Meanwhile, haven't we had to realize that the body is still a very mysterious machine, not least because of the complexity that genomics has revealed on the very lowest cellular level?

SLOTERDIJK: That is the irony of research: by discovering complexity it generates another mystery. Maybe there is a law that says the mass of enigmas stays constant.

ROTH: Wouldn't you say this enigmatic characteristic gives the human self-image a kind of spherical quality?

SLOTERDIJK: We could look at it like that. As we have noted, the euphoric movement of revelation ranging from the anatomists of the sixteenth century to the physicists and mechanics of the nineteenth and twentieth centuries followed the goal of making visible everything that was previously unseen – up to the sonic vibrations that were visually depicted in the nineteenth century by means of cumbersome phonographs on carbon paper made with the aid of a swan's quill. Then, on the threshold of the twentieth century, came X-rays, a fantastic tool for satisfying the desire for transparency. Recently the trails of atoms were visualized in the cloud chamber – and this kind of research is still continuing. All these contributions to making visible things that were formerly invisible begin, in substance, with the early anatomists' intervention into the interior of the human body, and with the European captains and geographers sailing out into the oceans. We have to understand that the internal and external cartography express the same cognitive attitude. They can both be used to extend the field of view and operations.

Anatomical and geographical maps also have an important common characteristic: they make the attractive qualities of the body, its aura, disappear – not the cultural and metaphorical qualities that Walter Benjamin spoke of, but the energetic and real aura, the delicate casing in which bodies swim. Remember that 'atmosphere' in Greek simply means 'vapour ball', and all living bodies live in specific vapour balls that can't be easily represented. To emphasize it, *Dasein* means having an atmosphere. Our whole image policy until now has been based on stripping the body of

[2] Julien Offray de la Mettrie (1709–51) was a French philosopher and physician best known for his work *L'homme machine* (*The Machine Man*), 1747. Sloterdijk is referring to his famous dictum, 'Here is a well-enlightened machine!'

its atmosphere. Removing the atmosphere makes it possible in the first place to unfold the body and expose levels of visibility that never existed in that form, and could never exist. The cost of pushing through the surface is that we have to imagine the delicate shell is gone. We can see this particularly clearly from conventional maps. For centuries, they have produced a picture of the world without a climate because they could always depict only a terrain without any atmosphere. The geographer's eye looks down on the site from above, as if there were no air and no clouds overhead. True, we can use graphical symbols to denote special fauna, flora and ground formations, and political colours to signify that Polish is spoken in the green and Czech in the yellow country, but that doesn't change anything about the primary finding: the geographical atmosphere is always deprived of atmosphere. The atmosphere was always the big loser in all traditional pictorial processes, starting with the maps colonialists made in the sixteenth, seventeenth and eighteenth centuries, and ending with the present-day magnetic resonance system. What these processes visibly present to us is a body segment without the auratic shell. Meanwhile, everything that can't be treated with this type of technique gets lost. Still, we shouldn't claim that auratic or atmospheric quantities had no advocates in theory at all. I would like to remind you that in his construction of the cosmos, Plato took care – you can read about this in *Timaios* – to give the world body a soul, the world soul, in fact, that not only pervades it from all sides but also surrounds it like a shell. We could see this as an admission of the atmospheric imperative, as if Plato had wanted to express that even the largest body, the cosmos, cannot do without its shell. The situational relationships between body and soul have to be precisely established. The body should be in the soul, not the soul in the body – and the Platonic world body fulfils this condition. If it were not the case, we would land up directly in a metaphysics of death, as the soul would then regard itself as the body's prisoner and would have to imagine post-mortal liberation. This position is unfortunately fairly widespread in the history of ideas – as a result of false readings of Platonic motifs. But in Plato's work itself the world soul pervades the whole cosmos in such a way that it also shines over and beyond the edge, like an aura or a corona. The body swims in its atmospheric surplus. We should take note of that, because we are now going to discuss the drama in progress in today's pictorial worlds. There are many indications that the reduction in the atmospheric sphere is being increasingly reversed. Due to a wide variety of motives, the shells that were formerly made to vanish are reappearing from extremely diverse technological and psychological sources. What was once an expendable surplus in traditional cartography is resurfacing as an issue of personal rights and becoming respected as an entity to be explicitly represented. I think this is a very important, joyful moment in the history of visibility: what was previously invisible, the atmospheric sphere, has come so far today that we make it the subject of very explicit visualization and theatrical presentation.

It is meteorology, a field whose significance is not easy to imagine, that furnishes the paradigm for this. Around 200 years ago, in Goethe's time, people first began the great discussion about air, the discussion that has kept humankind in suspense ever since. Goethe himself, incidentally, was very interested in the morphology of clouds. For some decades now, thanks to satellite optics, we have had a completely new form of illustrated weather news on television. Indeed, this media genre merits a discussion of its own at some point. The daily report on the climatic situation represents one of the most extensive forms of theatrical presentation of the realm of the invisible ever seen in human history. It is significant that weather forecasts have the best audience figures almost everywhere that television is watched. Despite their guaranteed banality, they are the only successful programmes right across the board. There are obvious conclusions to be drawn from this. Contemporary culture has developed to the extent that people recognize current climatic conditions as a political issue. Anybody talking about the weather is talking about the general issues of the day. Everybody knows, *nostra res agitur*. If there is a report on the Chancellor's speech, or a train crash, the conversation at the table carries on as normal. When the weather report begins, silence reigns and people watch and listen – here is the real issue. Looking up at the sky ourselves is not enough any more. We want official confirmation before we believe what we see with our own eyes. We want to see from above how the cloud formation is bearing down on us. The new development is that deep down we have become strategists for judging the macro weather situation. A demand for a new outlook has grown up. I consider it momentous, and interpret it as a symptom of an all-embracing twilight of the atmospheres. It all points to the fact that the age of reductionism is dying out. Iconic primitivism is putting an end to itself. By now, images are omnipresent but their rebellious presence doesn't automatically mean dictatorship. Images today are much less dominant than they used to be, for two main reasons: first, there is a broad division of powers in the image space that prevents individual icons from taking power; and, second, the law of complexity increasingly applies to images as well as other things. Conventional over-simplifications have reached a dead end.

ROTH: However, I see the twilight of the spheres more in the area of image production. I think *imachination* is covertly about a change in pictorial policy. Given the complex image production process, nobody today can still claim that they alone have an overview of this technical production process and can see the consequences in this highly specialized process. This is the question: isn't it much more a matter of image production having become a communicative act, with a chain of image-processing from the mathematician up to post-production workers working together on images – in other words, communication as the technical Communion song in the machine?

SLOTERDIJK: That is certainly the case. But I think we should no longer ask the question about the collective fabrication of images as we did in 1960 or 1970, when suspicion as a form of thought had become all the rage once again. I admit I am increasingly irritated by the neo-Marxist attitude of methodical paranoia that was dominant back then, and which slides so easily into existential paranoia. The conventional logic of distrust, that heavy legacy of the failed French Revolution, is out of date today, particularly because the specialized process you just highlighted has its own laws that even an evil lord couldn't control. The Romans had a proverb: *Caesar non super grammaticos* – the emperor may command everything, but not the rules of grammar. This is less clear in relation to the rules of production of images, but the same tendency applies. Of course, in terms of media policy, there are notable, sometimes dangerous clusters of power. Still, we can't ignore the fact that even a media mogul can't change the syntax and grammar of imagery at will. The visual world as a whole is still a polycentric field that can't be controlled from a single centre. The figure of the malignant lord is more of an illusion than a verifiable experience.

ROTH: My question was actually in a different direction. Vilém Flusser[3] claimed that it is not the politicians who govern today, but the computer scientists who write the programs. I'm not happy with this assertion because it presupposes that the people who program have an overview of the whole process. I tend to think that the self-image of the image producer has changed. When Peter Galison[4] quotes a physicist who specializes in elementary particles as saying, 'The experimenter is not a single person, but a composite,'

[3] Vilém Flusser (1920–91) was a Czech-born philosopher, writer and journalist who later specialized in media studies.

[4] Peter Galison is a historian of the history of science and a professor at Harvard University.

I think this corresponds in a sense to your concept of atmospheric realities.

SLOTERDIJK: That may well be. But the fact that today's image-makers are teams mastering sophisticated techniques is one reason that an exaggerated theory of suspicion can't take us any further. Paranoia sees only a small segment of the world. Of course we know that atmospheres can be poisoned, and we also know that the lie holds sway sometimes. Nonetheless, teamwork, high-tech and complex actor networks are increasingly limiting the parameters of fraud and the corresponding suspicion. Rather, we are doomed more and more to trust under complex conditions, which means that whatever we do ourselves must presuppose that other parts of the system are functioning. In a universe of justified mistrust, we would be compelled to react to Galison's thesis with panic. It would mean everyone is busy faking and lying. But I think mistrust can only be partially justified, and in most things it is better to work with trust. When I hear the experimenters themselves are now only elements in a complex situation that is watching itself, I feel I can relax. It means that things are operating generally in the right way, within the scope of what is normal and possible. If that weren't the case we would be in a state of constant fear. We would have to be suspicious about everything, and rattle the bars of the matrix, shouting 'I want to get out!', like the imprisoned souls in the world dungeon in the Gnostic legend. In modern terms, it would mean Luddism and the curse on the sciences. But as soon as the reality of the atmospheric factor becomes explicit we have an instrument for moderating the transition from suspicion to trust. This can involve a Leninist remnant: 'Trust is good; control is better' – and why not? Trust is the result of secure expectations, and control is one securing mode among others. But it doesn't have the last word. Lenin is only one voice in the conflict between the basic moods of suspicion and trust.

ROTH: Aren't you talking about a blind Gehlen-type trust that takes the form of simply abandoning trust? I meant a completely different kind of consciousness that doesn't actually fulfil this function of relief in Gehlen's sense.[5]

SLOTERDIJK: We shouldn't underestimate Gehlen's great economic discovery, which he called 'relief'. Without it we wouldn't be able to cope with the simplest situation. If you don't want to go mad from obsessive total control you always have to start from an atmosphere of original trust. Nobody can spend a long time asking

[5] Arnold Gehlen (1904–76) was a German philosopher, sociologist and anthropologist and a leading proponent of philosophical anthropology.

whether the air in a room is breathable or not. We simply have to start from the assumption that it is breathable and see how far we get. This basic diagnosis, that we are condemned to trust, can be confirmed in many different ways. We can see a persistent connection with the emergence of the atmospheric sphere. Oddly enough, we only become aware of the atmosphere through its destruction. It is the environment of original trust, but we usually only realize that when it is destroyed by deliberate attacks. In that case, ideas about protecting the atmosphere have to become concrete. When we have grasped how vulnerable the subtle, atmospheric premises of life are, we will be in a position to achieve the right configuration of trust and caution. Remembrance of the worst things benefits the most fragile. We know what happened in Auschwitz, we know what happened at Hiroshima – those were mass killings perpetrated by forcibly placing people in unlivable environments. Atmospherocide is the typical modern form of a war of extermination. Today, precisely because of everything that has happened, we have to combine trust with alarm systems. In other words, humans are dependent more than ever on cohabitation with machines.

ROTH: But this cohabitation is not about an individual person, and not about the classical 'I and the world' relation. That would be too easy. We are dealing with many subjects that are amalgamated via machines into a great complex.

SLOTERDIJK: It would be better to call those subjects 'agents'. Of course, right now we don't want to talk about their ontological characteristics or their epistemological privileges. As Schopenhauer said, 'That which *knows all things* and is *known* by none is the *subject*.' That's far too pathetic as a construct in the context of our practical concerns. We're thinking more in terms of agents who are competent with regard to their actions and statements. From such a perspective the world seems to be populated by the kind of active figures that can't do anything but react to each other with statements and actions. This immediately begs the question: which role do the images produced by the agents play in the attempt to coordinate their operations?

ROTH: The status of imagery has changed in the huge scientific image complexes. It is no longer about the conventional fixed visual concept, but about the image as a medium of communication. This performative entity is perpetually moving. Because its way of being is still in data form, the entity tends towards intangibility. Boundaries between media, such as those between text and image, dissolve. The machine is constituted from this process of individual subjects and becomes an amalgam.

SLOTERDIJK: I think Deleuze[6] had a similar idea when he introduced the new ontological figure of 'assemblage'. Such *agencements* are initially quite indifferent to the human–object difference. They form dynamic units beyond humans, machines and the environment. Bruno Latour's[7] sociology of epistemological fields also assumes precisely such larger units. The researcher is no longer privileged in relation to the environment, the laboratory in which he is presently sitting, the computer he is writing with or the apparatus he serves. He appears as an agent among agents. In agent ensembles of this kind, it turns out that the human–object opposition does not continue any further. But what certainly does continue further is any contribution that helps us to understand the communicative fluid better – and this brings us back to the dimension of atmospherology, the study of atmospheres. There is fairly strong resonance between the atmospheres theory and the theory of agent ensembles. The first seems closer to humans; the second rather remote from humans. Both together give a more realistic picture of the hyper-complex situation.

ROTH: One final question: what is your favourite picture at home?

SLOTERDIJK: I don't think I have a favourite picture at home. But I do have a favourite view. You see, I can't get away from the difference between image and view. I used to appreciate the aesthetics of pure art. Now I'm becoming something of a nature aesthete and have come to the conclusion that I often prefer views to pictures. That's not very unusual: Bazon Brock[8] once remarked that he would rather see a bosom than a black square, and I admit I generally feel the same way. I read Brock's statement as a plea for the view. For example, what I love most of all is the view of my library, especially in the evening when I come home late. Usually I leave the light on to get the feeling I'm being waited for. I like the sense of being surrounded by good spirits, many thousands of silent advisers who offer me their services and leave me in peace otherwise.

[6] Gilles Deleuze (1925–95) was an influential twentieth-century French philosopher who worked in the field of pure philosophy and history of philosophy and in many other disciplines, including anthropology, geology and psychoanalysis.

[7] Bruno Latour (b. 1947) is a French philosopher, anthropologist and sociologist of science, and one of the main developers of actor-network theory.

[8] Bazon Brock is a German artist, art critic and theorist, specializing in multimedia studies. He is a professor emeritus at universities in Hamburg, Vienna and Wuppertal.

# 19

# ON PROGRESS

## The Holy Fire of Dissatisfaction

### *Interview with M. Walid Nakschbandi**

NAKSCHBANDI: Mr Sloterdijk, the proverb says: 'Progress sits in the saddle and rides humankind.' Has progress got human beings under control now?

SLOTERDIJK: People who are crazy about horses may like that proverb, but we should beware of skewed images. Progress is about moving forward, not about control. Still, it's good to start in an offbeat way. It is true that the disastrous concept of progress has become rather like a modern form of holiness. We find references to progressive things all over the place, including the decorations on banknotes and the logos of major companies. It's almost as if the curious word 'progress' represented a universal concept of movement, and without it the world's modernists would lose their sense of direction. Not many expressions of that type exist. The only concept that would be equally powerful in terms of generality and importance is, perhaps, circulation, the cycle. The traditional awe of cyclical processes – beginning with the self-reflection of God and going right up to recycling of ecological waste – relates to the metaphysical thesis that the good and the cyclic are ultimately the same thing.

* This interview between Peter Sloterdijk and M. Walid Nakschbandi appeared under the title 'Das heilige Feuer der Unzufriedenheit: Peter Sloterdijk über den Fortschritt', in Utz Claassen and Jürgen Hogrefe (eds), *Das neue Denken – Das Neue denken* (Göttingen: Steidl Verlag), 2005, pp. 69–77.

M. Walid Nakschbandi is a journalist, television producer and manager of the Georg von Holtzbrinck Publishing Group.

NAKSCHBANDI: So it was a nicely rounded issue to begin with. But then something got in the way?

SLOTERDIJK: You could say that. From the nineteenth century on, the bourgeois world began trying to find the good in the line. That is a remarkable process because the line didn't have a high reputation in traditional geometry. In the past, people had always seen linear processes as final movements, movements that could wear down and basically lead nowhere except to decay. Circular processes, however, lead back to themselves, and that qualifies them for the good infinity. The greatest break made by the modern era is that human beings conceived an absolute movement of a new type that constantly moved upwards from a less valuable to a more valuable state. That means something like upgrading of being as a whole. It is a rather heretical idea because if we assume God created the world, such a process is pure sacrilege. After all, God can't have created anything except the best.

But why is it that we don't all feel we are under the curse of heresy? The answer is that since around the sixteenth century our society has been experiencing a mental shift that contemporary people still can't evaluate completely: the shift from a metaphysics of the complete world to a metaphysics of the incomplete world. This means we have shifted from the concept of creation, that is, of the finished work, to the concept of gradual development – from completed being to relative becoming. And that made us capable of participating in movements that go from the less good to the better without being suspected of blasphemy.

NAKSCHBANDI: How should we imagine that transformation?

SLOTERDIJK: Moving directly from God to the world, we seem to go from the very best to second best. This is how Plato classically articulated it in *Timaios*, his dialogue on natural philosophy. He said that because God is good, perfectly good in fact, anything he produced in his capacity as the world artisan or demiurge must be as excellent as possible within the limits of reality. That is, the work of a perfect author will be slightly less perfect than the author himself. But if the author has to be one degree better than his statement, the work of the best author remains the best possible. This means that the perfection of God implies that of the world, with the said limitation.

In other words, the deeper the insight of a philosopher, the more optimistic his manner of expression was. Optimism is the last word of classical philosophy because a long time ago thinking meant nothing but the celebration of being. The most appropriate form of being-celebration is superlative speech: we must only say the best about God and the world. This is the exact point at which we feel the break between antiquity and modernity most powerfully, because nobody today would be willing to celebrate everything in existence as the best, the highest, the cleverest, the most perfect, etc. Those superlatives are only possible in satire now. The modern world substitutes the rhetoric of superlatives with a comparatist one. Today, we always want to compare conditions so that the earlier come out worse and the later come out better. This puts us in contradiction to all the established theories in antiquity: when the ancients talked about changing conditions they nearly always told stories of decay. According to them, once, in the Golden Age, everything was perfect, and then the first deficits appeared. Finally, everything was rather bad and, in the end, quite devastating. The third deterioration brings us to the narrator's present day, the Iron Age in which humans are found. A narrative that follows a downward line like that could serve as a popular explanation for why people feel miserable: they are in bad shape because they are at the murky end of a decline from the perfect to the corrupt.

In the ancient world, however, there was also secret knowledge that taught its adepts to see the general unhappiness as only apparent. The real sages of the past thought they had discovered a secret reason to rejoice that released an inner reserve of happiness. According to them, a person who was unhappy with the world was only deceived by the semblance of unhappiness. This deep irony defines the relationship between the sage and the masses in the ancient world. The sage pretended to have discovered a deep-seated reason for happiness that normal unhappy people were not capable of perceiving. The sage alone saw the great cycles of order from an esoteric perspective, whereas profane people remained trapped without vision in their preoccupation with unhappiness.

That is exactly what has changed in the modern age. A great reversal of auspices has taken place, and it has been achieved by the powerful idea of progress we referred to earlier. We must admit, however, that we generally know only a very trite form of this. All the same, even we normal people make our comparisons in a semi-optimistic light because we are used to putting the less good together with the better. We remain as optimizing logicians or idealists who want to improve the world, and at the very least we try to improve things. Today, this logic still lies behind every pragmatic programme we have to carry out. The duty to improve relates to all spheres of existence – the daily environment, machines, production processes, medicines, teaching methods, living conditions, etc. Consequently, what is essential for us is no longer the perfect archetype but a series of improvements. Plato's original images have been transformed into models that can be optimized. Models are blueprints for construction that aspire to further perfection.

NAKSCHBANDI: Give us an example.

SLOTERDIJK: Modern design is full of striking examples. Let's take a typical design object like a ballpoint pen. First it had to be invented: it began with a refill with a tiny ball at the top, and the whole thing was encased in a stabilizing sheath. The writing movement triggered the rotation of the ball, drawing the ink flow out of the refill. In a Platonic world, the original ballpoint pen would also be the ultimate ballpoint pen because nothing better could follow. Things look different from a modern perspective, and it is no surprise to us that the world is awash with thousands of variations of the ballpoint pen idea. Some of those variations can be more than mere modifications of the archetype, and sometimes represent genuine optimization or further development. Such improvements relate, for example, to the pen's 'click' mechanism, which is self-retractable in some models to prevent damage to our best suit even if we forget to shut off the refill. Or the pen may be made more comfortable to hold, or the ink flow improved, etc. Countless luxury and cheap versions of the ballpoint pen have been developed and customers can choose from a price range of 20 cents to €20,000. Immense design energy is being expended on this all the time. A product that was invented years ago is rethought over and over again as thoroughly as if it were supposed to be reinvented.

Does it really make sense to talk about progress in this context? The ballpoint is a good example of how it is impossible to repeat the initial progress, that is, the conceptual and technical leap that happened when that type of pen was first invented, with the whole impact of the first-time-ever. It is impossible really to invent the object a second time. On the other hand, the basic idea can be varied ingeniously and endlessly – and that's usually enough to give us the feeling that the horizon is open. We attach importance to the fact that micro-optimizations always remain possible. Perhaps that is the actual stance of progress.

All optimizing tendencies in individual developments have a culmination area like an estuary, of course. I would argue that today, in a large number of areas of technical and social evolution, for example, we are already in the culmination area of primary innovations. Many inventions from the past are approaching their final saturation phase. Where the models have largely been perfected, things come to a standstill that can only be superseded aesthetically – think of the automobile industry, with a product that has certainly been thought through to the end in most respects. Additional micro-innovations such as the retractable outside mirror can be accumulated and hailed as a revolution, but we all know there can't be any real improvement beyond the 'very good' marker.

Let me make it clear: at most, the points I have just made are a prelude to what I want to say on the topic of progress and innovation from a philosophical perspective. By now we should have realized that the concept of progress is a naïve metaphor of movement that was only partially useful in the initial stages of industrial society. The idea of progress was a useful, nearly indispensable pilot metaphor for the transitional period because it helped those who made the transition to believe they were going in the right direction with their progressive vehicle. Conservatives, incidentally, never shared this belief and mocked the concept of progress from the very beginning.

NAKSCHBANDI: Who are those conservatives?

SLOTERDIJK: Conservatives include, for example, anti-modernists, religious fundamentalists, devotees of classical metaphysics and owners of choice libraries and wine cellars. In other words, everyone who adheres to the metaphysics of perfection and believes more in decline than in progress. In addition, there are the moral conservatives who are convinced that human beings are bad and should be controlled rather than let free.

NAKSCHBANDI: In your opinion, how does the breathlessness related to the concept of progress occur? Why are we never satisfied with what we have?

SLOTERDIJK: For centuries, we have only cultivated the movement of setting off and have neglected the culture of arriving. To use a river metaphor: we are strong at rising, but rather clumsy at debouching. We only rarely allow ourselves to regress into the feeling of completion, and that isn't enough to develop a culture of debouchment. Everybody knows the related scenes. When several progressive gentlemen sit together in a really excellent haute cuisine restaurant for a few moments, they forget progress and realize that now is the time for perfection. They praise what is on their plates so lavishly that we understand: those people are not setting off; they have arrived. Otherwise, we avoid being at our destination almost everywhere. We live in an automatic mode of setting off as a matter of habit.

The few people today who admit to having arrived, the rare people who enjoy things, the people in the river estuary, may be heralds of a future civilization. We don't understand such people very well yet because they don't seem to feel the holy fire of dissatisfaction any longer, the fire from which progress originated. I think this will change in a matter of decades. By the beginning of the twenty-first century our experiences with the world's dynamics of innovation have become so complex that the language of progress alone isn't adequate for expressing our experiences any more. That is why we should place the rhetoric of debouchment beside the usual rhetoric of progress. Sooner or later people will understand that standstill at the highest level is an extremely valuable asset, although at first it may infuriate some entrepreneurs condemned to being dynamic. But even they are not completely immune to the subversive realization that in some respects, perhaps the most important ones, they have long since reached their goal.

NAKSCHBANDI: Is the state of having arrived a state of happiness?

SLOTERDIJK: It reminds me of Thomas Hobbes' famous metaphor about life as a race. He said that constantly being overtaken is misery, while constantly overtaking others is felicity. For those standing in the culmination area, however, overtaking and being overtaken cease because such movements are only meaningful at the beginning of an optimization series and lose their purpose when the solution has been found. If people carry on after that, they have merely fallen into a habit.

But let me finish off the thought I started: I wanted to explain why I think the concept of progress is no longer right for expressing our experiences with modernization. We should replace it with two or three other concepts that correspond better to the meanings of the old concept of progress that are worth preserving. For the moment, I shall mention two such expressions: *relief* and *density*. The first term refers to the anthropologist Arnold Gehlen, and it is no exaggeration to say that, in my opinion, it represents the most important category of modern human science. It describes the basic direction of technical and social evolution in an astonishingly convincing way. Let's suppose a supporter of progress had to explain where the progressive journey is going. Generally, we would hear the trivial but accurate response that we are moving towards a state in which things will be better than ever for human beings. What does 'better' mean? This comparative contains practically everything that can be described by the term 'relief'. Where heavy weights once had to be carried, processes should be found to make things easier to handle. Of course, 'heavy' and 'light' are subjectively tinged expressions that don't mean the same thing to everyone. Yet everyone understands what we mean by relief from the burdens of life.

To explain this from the technical angle, I am fond of quoting the history of touch-operated appliances. These are the everyday objects that most clearly demonstrate the technical change from heavy to light actions. In an earlier technical phase, ordinary tools usually had handles – as we know, a handle is a designated contact point between the hand and the instrument. Such tools were body extensions or organ extensions in the sense described by Marshall McLuhan, that is, they were direct continuations of the arm and the hand in a harder material. An axe with a helve was used to split wood for burning in the kitchen stove. In the world of tools with handles, actors still carried out most of the gestures useful for life with their own physical input – the angel of expulsion put it well when he spoke of the sweat of the brow without which one should not eat one's bread.[1]

Today we live in a world of touch-operated tools that are used completely differently – we press a button or flip a switch and the heat sources turn on by themselves. Another way to explain how technology brings relief is to point to the transition from gestures made with our whole hands to fingertip operations – a typical transition for the present appliance scene. Now we move the world with a contact pressure of 5 to 10 grams, almost as little as we needed in the past to place the pick-up arm of a record player in the groove. Maybe that's the most modest way to characterize the trend towards the technical way of handling reality, and the most dramatic at the same time. This is exactly where the concept of relief comes into play. Because it contains a description of a trend of transforming workers into users, it can borrow several meaningful aspects from the concept of progress, which has long since become too crude.

This is also where we should mention the history of analgesics. People today forget that up to the mid-nineteenth century surgical operations could not be performed without horribly maltreating the patient. The first effective anaesthetics came into use in the 1840s. If I remember rightly, the first successful operation under chloroform narcosis took place in a hospital in Massachusetts. One year later the new process had already become globalized. From then on the medicine sector in the Western world exploded, and surgery became a key focus of medicine. Doctors outdid priests in importance, not with the message 'We'll bring you enlightenment', but with the offer: 'We'll anaesthetize you if necessary. We'll relieve you of the burden of consciousness during operations, and while you are asleep we'll repair what has to be repaired.' That's what a progressive offer sounds like – and here 'progressive' is an exact synonym of 'bringing relief'. This was followed by an important change in religious semantics during the last century: if life gets easier the demand for

[1] The Bible, New International Version, Genesis 3:19: 'By the sweat of your brow you will eat your food until you return to the ground, since from it you were taken; for dust you are and to dust you will return.'

redemption declines, and themes related to fulfilment and realization become more important.

The concept of relief has a second merit – it raises the question of who pays the costs of the relief, for the relief of one person must, by its nature, create a heavier burden for another, assuming one also calculates as an anthropologist using the principle of constancy in relation to the weight of the world. Such calculations are to be disclosed and the shifts in pressure should be explained. If, for example, the majority of people in the Western world are no longer starving today, this is partly due to an unprecedented shifting of loads that occurred at the cost of farm animals. Mass animal farming has created an immense animal proletariat whose living conditions are scandalous, not only for conservatives.

NAKSCHBANDI: How is the concept of distribution of loads related to these transformations?

SLOTERDIJK: Distribution of the load is fundamental for the modern world because an intuitive and unconventional concept of justice depends on it. If we were to ask what real injustice is in the existential and non-juridical sense, a plausible answer could be: injustice means that some people have a very easy time and others a very hard time – and justice would describe the appropriate equalizing measures. In this context, the concepts of load and relief show an internal relation to the theme of justice. One reason why the modern social system is attractive is that the state functions within it as a general guarantor of equalization. The seriously underestimated phenomenon of the tax state that was transformed into the welfare state during the twentieth century is related to this. Many people today are only vaguely aware that the state share of the gross national product amounts to 50 per cent and above in Germany and many other West European countries. Hardly anybody can envisage what that means morally and psychologically. A good half of what the productive part of the population earns is absorbed by the fiscal authorities and put into a gigantic redistribution centrifuge, with the state and its servants not neglecting themselves, of course. In the year 2000, Germany's gross national product amounted to 2 billion dollars, with over half of that going as booty to the public sector. Modern forms of life can evidently only be guaranteed by the state's generalized kleptocracy. Just for once, we should look at things like this: if we looked at the welfare state's redistribution performance merely from the quantitative angle we would be shocked and awed. The whole picture becomes almost incredible if we take into account the mirror distortions in the prevailing rhetorical systems. In popular commentaries, the relief systems are often described as if redistribution occurred upwards and as if our state increasingly leaves its ordinary citizens to die of hunger.

This distortion of the picture of the immense capital flows rechannelled by the state is partly conditioned by the political system being lost for words – as it no longer has any possibility of expressing itself, it borrows its vocabulary mainly from the economy that is understandably doomed to reproduce dissatisfaction all the time. This borrowing is devastating for the state because a subsystem of modern society can't function if it doesn't cultivate its own values. Citizens see the speechless state as a pseudo-entrepreneur, always blathering on about innovation and reform, and why? Because it can't, it doesn't want to, and it dares not speak openly about its real business, the fiscal kleptocracy and its justification through redistribution.

A second dimension of the concept of progress that traditional rhetoric can't deal with adequately is the phenomenon of increasing density. A considerable part of what we have always called progress until now can be much better described as density. If we have the impression things are progressing in social terms, this is generally linked to an increase in density of transactions. Increased density means that in a particle system the number of possibilities of contact and collision increases. Consequently, in situations where progressive relationships dominate, the probability of collisions increases.

NAKSCHBANDI: It sounds dangerous …

SLOTERDIJK: It is really dangerous, and growing danger provides a precise criterion for the degree of progress of relationships. It is not very easy to explain such twists to people who have simply supported progress. They wanted progress and what they got is complexity. The concept of complexity is associated with the news that nothing at all is simple any more. The term 'density' helps us to grasp such effects: countless particles, countless institutions, countless enterprises, countless individuals are moving towards each other with growing intensity and are doing so in continually higher frequencies. The number of their contacts or collisions is growing exponentially. I read somewhere recently that 10 million emails per minute are sent all over the world, mostly in the industrialized zone. That figure makes 10 million traffic accidents per year, and the same number of private court cases, seem tame.

NAKSCHBANDI: What does this complexity mean for our lives in practical terms?

SLOTERDIJK: It means there is a growing need to simulate simplicity. The people who can master things well are the ones who can make complicated relationships simple. That is why mastery is the greatest asset modern individuals demand. The most popular simplification technique, as we know, is to ignore problems. Ignoring means seeing unsolved issues as resolved – that makes ignorance as a practical equivalent for superiority irresistible. Generally speaking, there's an immense need for techniques for dealing with complexity. Today the greatest market of all is open for people who can offer effective simplifications. Of course, this is closely linked to relief.

Complexity increases the burden for problem-solvers and this, in turn, gives a new boost to relief techniques. This connection is the core of the so-called 'knowledge society'. Knowledge that really interests us is always empowering knowledge that makes complexity amenable to handling. 'Amenable to handling' means things are processed so that we can make a profitable decision on the computer with our fingertips.

The concept of density also helps to explain why, despite the tremendous relief in which our life is embedded, we have the impression that things aren't getting easier, but on balance more difficult. For all the undeniable 'progress', why isn't the world more transparent and more user-friendly? The increasing complexity is really unreasonable – and people will rebel against it sooner or later if they have expected something else. The most embittered critics of progress are disillusioned believers in progress. But if we start from a false concept, can we really complain when we realize it doesn't work? Aren't we responsible ourselves for the disappointment that comes from choosing the confusing word 'progress' to guide us? If we don't want to fall into a semantic trap, we should drop the term 'progress'. We realize that we're caught in such a trap partly because we become aware that using specific words puts us into defensive situations and depressive states. In that case it is better to look for a different kind of language.

NAKSCHBANDI: Can Western culture learn something about these questions from other cultures?

SLOTERDIJK: Most people in the Western world assume that the rest of the world has to learn from them, and not vice versa. In fact, we could learn a great deal from non-Western cultures: a different attitude to happiness, to death, to simple, elementary things. I think it is a serious symptom that in our society the simple things are being reintroduced as a second-order luxury. Though it may sound odd, there is a kind of homesickness for poverty and it is actually for the elementary things that may be associated with poorer circumstances. Our society displays a surfeit of wealth and of the multiple options we constantly have to think about. That's why many Western people now are interested in the lifestyle of cultures that are on the verge of the transition to affluence. However, I think it is doubtful that we can really learn from this. In the end, learning something from other people means wanting an exchange with them and seeing them as a model. Western interests usually don't go that far. Westerners are more likely to want something the others have in addition to their own advantages.

# 20

# A TEAM OF HERMAPHRODITES

*Interview with Dirk Kurbjuweit and Lothar Gorris**

KURBJUWEIT/GORRIS: Mr Sloterdijk, how are you watching the football World Cup championship – as a fan or as a philosopher?[1]

SLOTERDIJK: I am actually more interested in the archaeology of masculinity. Football matches are atavistic; they are experimental anthropological designs. For thousands of years, male human beings have tried to answer the question: what do we do with hunters nobody needs any more? In anthropological terms, men are constructed to take part in hunting. But hunters have undergone a huge sedation programme for nearly 7,000 years, since the beginning of arable farming. The higher the religion, the stronger the attempt was to convince the inner hunter that it is basically shameful to be a man, and that men as men will never partake of salvation.

KURBJUWEIT/GORRIS: Unless they play football and substitute the hunt for game animals with the hunt for goals?

SLOTERDIJK: That's right. Hardly any other game so clearly imitates our ancient proto-artillerist feelings of successful hunting. When we have completely paralysed the inner hunter and killed him off, we reach the inevitable conclusion that the stupidest thing in the world is how footballers react after scoring a goal. It is a

* This interview between Peter Sloterdijk, Dirk Kurbjuweit and Lothar Gorris appeared under the title 'Ein Team von Hermaphroditen', in *Der Spiegel* news magazine (3 June 2006): 70ff.

At the time of the interview Dirk Kurbjuweit was a journalist at *Der Spiegel*, and Lothar Gorris was a departmental head at *Der Spiegel*.

[1] The interview took place shortly before the World Cup football championship held in Germany from 9 June to 9 July 2006.

really obscene sight. The remarkable goal-shot orgasms the football players put on for the paying spectators are enough to make a female porn actor feel ashamed by comparison. But as soon as we stop murdering our inner hunter and let those ancient hunting feelings come out, we immediately feel what those players on the pitch are dealing with. The oldest human feelings of success are being played out again, the act of hitting a hunting target with a ballistic object, a target that tries to protect itself by every possible means. I think this is the point to introduce the concept of 'deep play'. It describes the kind of games that enthral everybody.

KURBJUWEIT/GORRIS: In other words, the prehistoric man within the man of today is mostly redundant, and only useful for playing games. Are women better off?

SLOTERDIJK: Women were originally gatherers and we need them more than ever today because a gatherer is only one step away from becoming a consumer. In this respect, women are much more compatible with capitalism than men. The female consumer still shows us traces of the quiet, triumphal satisfaction of the gatherer bringing something home in her basket. This has led to that mysterious universal female object, the handbag. A man without a spear or a ball is acceptable, but a woman without a handbag – that's against nature.

KURBJUWEIT/GORRIS: Does football excite you personally?

SLOTERDIJK: I found a passable relationship to football at the second attempt. But to become a normal human being I had to make a digression by way of anthropology. As an anthropologist I can allow myself to be human, so to speak. The basic characteristics of a human involve being willing to go crazy with other people to some extent. I allow myself to do that now and then in my old age.

KURBJUWEIT/GORRIS: Have you bought a Goleo?[2]

SLOTERDIJK: I'm not the type for mascots.

KURBJUWEIT/GORRIS: Do you sing along with the national anthem?

SLOTERDIJK: I'm physiologically incapable of that. Sometimes I watch the players during the anthem and see how they purse their lips, only moving them slightly. Some lapse into a deep German silence. That's what I would probably do. I usually like singing, but only in an artistic form. Singing national anthems is not part of my basic education.

KURBJUWEIT/GORRIS: The 'national team' is one of the

[2] Goleo was a stuffed animal toy that became a media mascot of the 2006 Football World Cup in Germany.

few terms that allows us to use the word 'nation'. What does the national team represent for us Germans in particular?

SLOTERDIJK: First, it means the same as it does for every other modern nation that appoints its team to represent it. This results in representational rituals that the majority of the population want to participate in. We Germans are a special case in this respect – as in most others – because of our history. After 1918 and the Versailles Treaty, if not before, we became a wounded collective, and in need of revenge in some respects. After 1945, on the other hand, we became a collective that is afraid of our own revenge impulses and blanks them out. We are a bizarre group that can only experience internal cohesion in the regret mode.

KURBJUWEIT/GORRIS: You have written that nations are communities of excitability. What can arouse a nation more than the World Cup in its own country? Lots of people still get queasy at the idea of Germany being excited.

SLOTERDIJK: Of course. If you have experienced collective excitement as 'demonic territory', to quote Thomas Mann, you are wary of everything that stimulates people. We have been like people who have burnt their fingers since the time we realized that collective arousal could actually be a product of specific political orchestration.

Such emotional liturgies are created by defined rules and, by nature, can be instrumentalized. The Saturday entertainment and the will to war are psychologically related. Enthusiasm proves to be a phenomenon that can be misused. That means we shouldn't just see the German tendency to caution as a neurosis. It should be enough to point out that caution can also be morally misused. If, as a German, you have ever watched the English celebrate and sing anthems, you might automatically think fascism had made a diversion to the British Isles. We Germans have a teacher inside us that would like to propose a sobering-up programme made in Germany for other nations as well.

KURBJUWEIT/GORRIS: Excitement in Germany quickly gets ugly, as the controversy about Jürgen Klinsmann showed.[3] Why aren't we able to trust the national coach and his team?

SLOTERDIJK: Trust is not a German option. We know what Lenin said: 'Trust is good. Control is better.' The Germans reinterpret that as: 'Trust is good. Grumbling is better.' Our dear fellow citizens are incredibly keen to be disparaging. That's why the

[3] Former football player Jürgen Klinsmann was manager of the German national team for the 2006 World Cup championship.

position of national coach in this country is even more uncomfortable than in other countries. But it's generally true that the national coach resembles a hunting-group leader and his successes affect the mood of the collective.

KURBJUWEIT/GORRIS: Do we grumble our last heroes into the ground?

SLOTERDIJK: We have no more heroes anyway. We've replaced them with stars.

KURBJUWEIT/GORRIS: What distinguishes the star from the hero?

SLOTERDIJK: The hero dies early and the star outlives himself. That formulation gives us an overview of the field. Both are actually destined for an early end – the hero on the battlefield where he falls and the star through his return to civilian life, which is equivalent to being released from service, and is consequently like a symbolic death. An early death wouldn't be a bad thing for most sports people because they almost all become unpleasant after their careers. Even the most interesting athletes turn into dimwits if they carry on as sports functionaries. For the rest of their lives they do nothing but contradict the reasons why they became famous. They start brilliantly – and end in self-demolition. Achilles escaped that because he had a real showdown.

KURBJUWEIT/GORRIS: It's hard to detect the hunter in David Beckham or Ronaldinho, the stars of modern football.

SLOTERDIJK: Stars today have to live in a state of permanent over-exposure. They enjoy a passive privilege in relation to attention: they are seen very often – and almost never see themselves. The answer to that is to become a model. The players who cope best with their roles as stars are those like Beckham who deliberately transfer to the fashion world. Somebody like that shows that the player has understood his own de-heroizing. It follows that it's better to appear as a hermaphrodite than a male hero nowadays. The soccer models are following an evolutionary trend that has been observable since the 1960s: the trend towards hermaphrodization. This is a long-term movement in which men disarm and are discovered as clientele for cosmetic products.

KURBJUWEIT/GORRIS: Is the German national football team a team of hermaphrodites?

SLOTERDIJK: In principle, yes, although Klinsmann is resisting this. I think he didn't throw Kuranyi out for his weak performance but because he was angry that he needed half an hour to shave his little beard. That's an anti-hermaphroditic vote by Klinsmann, an anti-model protest.

KURBJUWEIT/GORRIS: Your colleague, the Berlin

philosopher Gunter Gebauer, says: the game with the feet has always been a mute protest against scholarly culture.

SLOTERDIJK: I agree with that. One of the most fascinating questions of recent cultural history for me was this: why have we always regarded the Renaissance from the fifteenth to the nineteenth centuries only as the return of the literature and arts of antiquity? Any child knows that there was already a fascinating mass culture in antiquity, that of the original sports. But our classical Renaissance only recapitulated the things that catered to the pleasures of the upper class. There was a long delay until the most fascinating figures of antiquity, the athletes, were reinstated again alongside the artists, philosophers and scientists. The athletes only reappeared a hundred years ago, and since then they have dominated the scene. Their reappearance brings people's thymotic impulses into full use once again. According to the basic psychological teachings of the ancient Greeks we not only have the *eros*, which makes us desire things, but also the *thymos*, which means our efforts to assert our own merits.

KURBJUWEIT/GORRIS: Do we show our merits today with skilful dribbling?

SLOTERDIJK: Among other things. We have finally dared really to quote ancient mass culture – which means the production of new competitive games. That's why we have recently started building competition venues as in neo-antiquity – the Greek stadium and the Roman arena.

KURBJUWEIT/GORRIS: Why was the athlete rediscovered so late?

SLOTERDIJK: People probably felt it would be dangerous to play with that kind of energy. If the nation is allowed to gather in arenas it could easily become politically volatile. The new enclosures of mass culture were only erected when it became clear that those kinds of mass sporting events wouldn't develop into revolutions. Antiquity bequeathed a perfect archetype for that – the arena with its rising steps. If we look at the most modern stadiums such as the Allianz arena in Munich, we realize immediately: this is the Coliseum again.

KURBJUWEIT/GORRIS: In the modern arenas with their lounges and business areas, the sponsors and VIPs edge out the traditional fans.

SLOTERDIJK: This transformation follows a basic trend of developed capitalism: the transformation of the workers into players, into stock-exchange speculators. Typically, they are prepared to sever the link between performance and fee. We know approximately what wages are because they are connected to performance. But today, wages are no longer enough. People want bonuses. The demand for bonuses is the current form of anticipated profit. This society naturally meets up in the stadium as well. They are among their own kind there. The people on the pitch are best buddies with those in the lounge. Everybody knows that it's only about bonuses. We're only gradually beginning to understand how dangerous that is, because we're slowly being confronted with the demoralizing effects of the system. Incidentally, the postmodern stadium is a tough truth machine. Unlike in modern-day theatre, where only losers appear from the start and talk about their problems, getting more and more entangled, in the modern arena it's always only about the desire for the primal verdict: victory or defeat.

KURBJUWEIT/GORRIS: Football is an extreme example of globalization. In some Bundesliga clubs hardly any of the players are German. In the Champions League final, Arsenal London fielded two English players and Barcelona three Spanish ones.

SLOTERDIJK: That final showed the game of two world-class selections that simulate local clubs. In other words, the football club and its city are transformed into locations in the same way as the cities as such are transformed into locations. In the era of globalization – that is, since 1492 – hometown has become location.

KURBJUWEIT/GORRIS: If the Champions League is a contest of locations, what does that make the World Cup?

SLOTERDIJK: A restorative enterprise, actually. In a situation in which nations are swimming with the tide of post-nationalization, nations reposition themselves as nations for the sake of the championship. It is rather regressive.

KURBJUWEIT/GORRIS: Why?

SLOTERDIJK: National teams hardly exist in reality beyond championships. In championships something like national simulators are represented. They remind a population that it can also identify in a national sense if it wants to.

KURBJUWEIT/GORRIS: Does it work?

SLOTERDIJK: It works very well, because people's sense of participation is chronically under-used otherwise. We don't live in a world that addresses needs for participation. On the contrary, people always belong to themselves, and at best to their own future. For good measure we have a few relationships or, as people so aptly say, we're linked up. But linked-up people are in a post-national situation anyway. People generally don't want to be owned by the community any more. Civilization is moving towards dissolving communities, and for good reason: because self-confident individuals find it increasingly hard to tolerate permanent pestering by groups they belong to. We don't want to be representatives of our own tribe, or to have to represent our country abroad. All the same, there are situations in which we identify on a national basis again for a few hours.

KURBJUWEIT/GORRIS: If the national factor is shown in the national team, wouldn't it be logical to add a question to the form for new immigrants, such as: 'Who played for Germany in the 1974 World Cup final?' Wouldn't it prove how much somebody is interested in this country?

SLOTERDIJK: Why not? In turn, the person questioned would also have to be given the possibility of proving with the converse answer that he or she belongs here. Up until now, the bad Germans were the good Germans – we should allow foreigners to be the same as well. Immigrants should have the freedom to say, 'I'm a bad patriot, that's why I fit in here. I can do without the gang of Beckenbauer and Co.[4] I think the sport is idiotic and I'd prefer us to lose. That gives me the right to be a member of this nation.'

KURBJUWEIT/GORRIS: But should immigrants know about the miracle of Bern?

SLOTERDIJK: There could be a question like: 'What bores you most?' If somebody puts a cross by the miracle of Bern, he or she would be a case for the alien police department. Anybody who doubts the miracle of Bern is suspected of being associated with a terrorist organization.

KURBJUWEIT/GORRIS: How do you explain the hysterical glorification that the 1954 soccer world championship title unleashed here in Germany?

SLOTERDIJK: It is mainly related to the intellectualization of football. For as long as research on mass culture has existed, popular culture as a whole has been idealized. This research was, and still is, a refuge for those who survived neo-Marxism and looked for new fields of work after its demise. The topic of soccer provided a way to remain true to the interests of the proletariat. All it required was to formulate upscale interpretations of trivial events.

KURBJUWEIT/GORRIS: What do you remember of those events in 1954?

SLOTERDIJK: I was a child in Munich at the time. One day my mother, who wasn't interested in football at all, took me by the hand, and we rushed off to Prinzregentenstrasse, the place where the German team appeared to the fans after winning in Bern. That's how I saw Fritz Walter with the cup. When my mother started

[4] Franz Beckenbauer, a former German football player and national German team manager, is regarded as one of the greatest living football players.

saying she wanted to leave, I felt something had upset her. Perhaps it reminded her of the days in the Nazi German Girls' League when they were supposed to feel proud of the state. In every other respect she was the most apolitical person I have ever met. Of course, I didn't understand anything at all. I only noticed all the grown-ups behaving very strangely and being enthusiastic for a reason that was completely obscure to me.

KURBJUWEIT/GORRIS: Were you more aware of the World Cup championship in 1974?

SLOTERDIJK: In those days people used to say, 'What do I care about the Vietnam War if I have orgasm problems?' You could say that about almost anything, including soccer dramas.

KURBJUWEIT/GORRIS: You're probably never going to become a real fan.

SLOTERDIJK: I'm afraid not. The only thing about football that really impresses me deeply is the ability of young players to fall over and get up again. I find that inspiring.

KURBJUWEIT/GORRIS: You mean you want to see tough fouls?

SLOTERDIJK: No, I only want to see men getting up again. It seems to me like a declaration of anti-gravitation. We know what usually happens when people get older and heavier. Sometimes I fall off my bike, and the struggle to get back on my feet again is a cruel affront to my dignity. That's why I have great respect for players who get up quickly again after falling down. Those are moments when I'm completely emotionally involved. Falling down is part of the game, but it is the getting up again that makes it magnificent. That's why I don't like the new obligatory medical treatment on the pitch. An injured player who can still walk has to be carried on a stretcher. It's awful.

KURBJUWEIT/GORRIS: It doesn't fit in with the hunter, does it?

SLOTERDIJK: Players used to hobble off the pitch heroically on their own. Now they are carried off compulsorily, and I think it's a mistake.

KURBJUWEIT/GORRIS: Mr Sloterdijk, thank you for this interview.

# 21

# UNDER A BRIGHTER SKY

*Interview with Robert Misik**

MISIK: In a speech about the generation of 1968 you once said, 'We must risk more confusion to get more democracy.' Is confusion a productive force?

SLOTERDIJK: For over 200 years, every important revolutionary movement has been associated with productive confusion in some way. When things are moving forward the semantics is always murky to begin with. We live in interesting times today because the historical semantics of the left and the right that we have used as orientation for the past 200 years is dissolving in a sort of confusion.

MISIK: If confusion is productive, does that mean the systematic approach is unproductive?

SLOTERDIJK: Not in every respect. But you are right: if the world could be completely tidied up it would turn into a museum in which everything would have its allotted place according to specific organizational principles. Everything would have been pacified for the last time and would have achieved what Hegel called satisfaction – a kind of positive Philistinism.

MISIK: The theoretician is always someone who tidies up the world. In your last book you presented a new theory of globalization – its hallmark is not acceleration, but density. What is so interesting about density?

SLOTERDIJK: This refers back again to my colleague Hegel and

* This interview between Peter Sloterdijk and Robert Misik appeared under the title 'Unter einem helleren Himmel', in the *taz* newspaper (13 June 2006). Available at: <http://www.taz.de/1/archiv/?dig=2006/06/13/a0226>.

Robert Misik is an Austrian journalist and author.

his idea of the 'condition of the world'. Conditions of the world are connected with the perception of epochal changes. Take the period from 1492 to 1900 – from the discovery of America to the end of the colonial division of the world. Until 1900, Europe experienced an over-production of people for expansion. Before then, Europeans had experienced the world as a non-dense space. Afterwards the world was occupied. The only thing to do was to expand in mutual opposition. The age of world wars remains as the first monument to this density.

MISIK: Did that change people?

SLOTERDIJK: Feelings about life altered. Today's Europeans have largely understood that in a dense world the whole expansionist, heroic attitude aimed at conquest doesn't work any more. The result is a more cautious, more calculating, politer, more civilized type of person.

MISIK: Does that mean globalization is congestion?

SLOTERDIJK: Wherever we go, someone is ahead of us. The discoverer is the person who arrives first. His epoch ended with a race for the poles – in which even the Austrians were involved, by the way – that culminated in the conquest of Franz Joseph Land.

MISIK: Did people occupy ice floes as the colonial era came to an end?

SLOTERDIJK: That shows how important it was back then to be the first somewhere, even if it was only an island full of glaciers.

MISIK: Isn't the contemporary hero the entrepreneur who conquers markets?

SLOTERDIJK: Whereas the world as a whole is tending to adjust to the co-operator type, the entrepreneur is still oriented towards conquest and expansion. The result is ersatz continents created for expansion. This explains the incredible rush on the capital markets – they are today's colonies and Franz Joseph Lands. Space is already tight in the real economy. The law of mutual hindrance developed fully a long time ago. The imperial, expansive gesture only gets extra time on the capital markets.

MISIK: In your latest book you call this world 'the world interior of capital'.

SLOTERDIJK: People live in capitalism as if they were staying in a hothouse. This makes the assumption that there must be an exterior occur all the more spontaneously. The interesting thing to note here is that people paint this exterior just like another interior where they can have exciting experiences under pleasant conditions.

MISIK: Must experiences remain consumable?

SLOTERDIJK: They should be paid into the account of one's

own personality, which wants to be enriched, not to collect traumatizing experiences.

MISIK: You almost insist that for the world interior, there is also a world exterior. That is your response to Toni Negri and Michael Hardt, whose book *Empire* assumes a capitalist orbit without a centre, but without an outside either. What is the outside you are talking about?

SLOTERDIJK: Negri has a strategic interest in reclaiming the worlds of poverty and the non-comfort zones for the empire because that's where he finds recruits for his multitude, the people who are opposed, tomorrow's revolutionaries.

MISIK: He finds them inside as well.

SLOTERDIJK: The dream of the coalition of the internal with the external opposition is the sequel to the dream of the communist gathering. I have devoted a forthcoming new book to this idea; the title is *Zorn und Zeit* [*Rage and Time*]. In this book I show that the classical left operated as a rage bank in which everybody who knew that helpless anger was not enough could deposit their rage. Rage banks in the form of left-wing parties are needed to make the anger of the disadvantaged operate on the political level. That is why the principle of the left doesn't work any more today, because the left itself behaves more like part of the system of well-being and not as the agency for collecting and transforming rage.

MISIK: What exactly is the reason for this rage?

SLOTERDIJK: The welfare state's promise is that unemployment doesn't mean poverty but at worst the descent into the lower strata of the petty bourgeoisie under conditions that may be sad, but aren't miserable. The tension has grown since it has become clear that this guarantee can't be honoured. But first of all, those in the interior who have been excluded sink into depression. At the moment there is no language of rage, no historical perspective for moving from depression to pride.

MISIK: One reflex reaction to globalization is particularism. Is the resistance of the local region the opposing truth to globalization?

SLOTERDIJK: It applies at least for places that are not totally devastated, not completely turned into transit spaces, into places without a self – such as airports, hotels, etc. I distinguish between places without a self, the transit wastes – and the self without a place, that is, the groups deprived of territory, groups that people like to call nomads. In between are the middle zones where place and self are connected by shared cultivation. We can still see that very impressively in Central and Western Europe – pleasant, civilized communities where the arts of living are comfortably established. Incidentally, astonishing examples of cultivated activity emerge even in the area of transit life, particularly in upscale international hotel chains where numerous oases of luxury have been opened to offer a relatively good lifestyle for people who travel too much.

MISIK: Do you know people who are happy in places like that?

SLOTERDIJK: Well, happiness is a fleeting thing. Freud even suggested that evolution didn't plan it for *Homo sapiens*. Humans should be quite happy when they live in a state of ordinary unhappiness rather than neurotic misery.

MISIK: As regards your controversy with the Frankfurt School, you once remarked that it is mainly about contrasting moods. Whereas one always has to approach Critical Theory prepared to be depressed, you are more of a philosopher of good cheer. So how can you say humans are destined for unhappiness?

SLOTERDIJK: Critical Theory was once my theoretical homeland. It was influenced by the experience of the Holocaust, by the universal dehumanization. This gave rise to the experiences that characterized the generations of the first half of the twentieth century. Incidentally, the mood of French existentialism was not much lighter either. The years after 1968 tested how far such definitions are still valid – and revealed that they aren't really valid. At some point our changed experiences must be translated into a new attitude. That's why the left wing after 1968 appeared as the hedonist left. They were sure that human happiness was achieved by unchaining a person's own libido.

MISIK: At the end of the 1970s, you were a Sanyassin and spent some time living with the Bhagwan in Poona.

SLOTERDIJK: In my case, the Indian adventure was a product of that seventies atmosphere. Added to that was the conviction that a purely materialistic concept of revolution is not enough. In those days, we wanted to reverse base and superstructure and make the mental factor the central focus.

MISIK: There are metaphors for influences. Some people say: 'Once a Trotskyist, always a Trotskyist.' Can we also say: 'Once a Sanyassin, always a Sanyassin'?

SLOTERDIJK: Basically, yes. The experience of transposition that occurred then is irreversible. Having that experience made you immune to theories in which depression is always right. And you stop wanting to win the competition about who is the unhappiest person at all costs. You live under a brighter sky. What it means for me is that India has completely faded into the background, but the transposition I went through then still affects me today.

# 22

# MAKING THE EFFORT

## The Reader

*Interview with Torsten Casimir**

CASIMIR: In neurobiological terms, reading books is closely related to reading traces in tribal history, which dates back much further. What does it mean when a society increasingly dismantles these abilities?

SLOTERDIJK: We are seeing a transformation in the system of finding things. The old system of reading traces has been replaced several times: first, the farmer forced out the hunter; then urban humans forced out the farmers; and now the finders and looters are forcing out the urban reader in monitor space.

CASIMIR: In the past century, books still gave the urban reader deep insights into the world. Today we guard against depth and are often exonerated from the need to understand. Times are hard for books.

SLOTERDIJK: I think the crisis of the bourgeois personality is the main explanation for the crisis of the book. In the humanist age there was a hidden but very effective equivalence between the individual and the book. Being educated meant having the ability to write the novel of one's own life, or having done so. Educated people could present the sum of their experience in a literary form. But it means the people of the humanist age were people who had experiences in the first place. The basic idea is that people pay the

* This interview between Peter Sloterdijk and Torsten Casimir appeared under the title 'Ein Freund der Mühe: Der Leser', in the magazine *Börsenblatt des Deutschen Buchhandels*, 173/36 (2006): 10–13.

Torsten Casimir was editor-in-chief of *Börsenblatt* at the time of the interview.

high price of effort to turn their own life into art and thus become individuals to begin with.

CASIMIR: That sounds like sports.

SLOTERDIJK: In a way it is really about bringing sport into our existence. The idea of experience dates right back to the Greek concept of *paideia*, which concerns the translation of athleticism into the world of letters. Humans are taken in hand in the sense of athletics and made into all-round athletes of competence in writing. That works on the basis of a connection between pride and resilience. The Greek athletes, and the Greek teachers, had a term for this: *ponos*. Just as philosophers were called 'friends of wisdom', athletes were called 'friends of effort'. In other words, the idea of the educated person is a form of glorification of suffering based on athleticism.

CASIMIR: But nobody today likes putting effort into things.

SLOTERDIJK: What we are seeing, above all in the computer world today, is the incursion of untrained people into culture. With computers, lack of fitness can pose as fitness, or inability as ability. This brings enormous relaxation and pampering. The modern situation is characterized by the idea of education disappearing because nobody nowadays is prepared to pay the toll costs for education, that is, to suffer for experience.

CASIMIR: People suffer all the same. The strain of remaining stupid – is that a topic you share with Odo Marquard?[1]

SLOTERDIJK: People today suffer from all kind of things, but not from education. They suffer, for instance, from not getting a job any more. But they aren't prepared to go through the education system to get the qualifications they would need for a job. They prefer downloading. The word means that people in search of experience no longer go to the source of knowledge but let knowledge come to them – the same way you order a pizza for home delivery.

CASIMIR: You are rather sceptical yourself in relation to overdoing educational efforts. But your advice is about being economical with the little lights we call intelligence.

SLOTERDIJK: That's certainly true. We should note the change of metaphors: from the sun of enlightenment to the little control lamps of electronic systems. We don't illuminate our lives with the floodlight of truth any more. We choose to rely on numerous little control lamps of everyday cleverness.

[1] Odo Marquard (1928–2015) was a conservative German philosopher known for his work on philosophical anthropology and finiteness.

CASIMIR: Less light. Does that mean another big project for relief?

SLOTERDIJK: Absolutely! On the other hand, there's a new form of education that I call hyper-alphabetization, which involves learning reading and writing all over again, as it were. The first time we did it as school pupils; the second time we do it as typographers. The fact is, with computers the ancient *Homo orthographicus* is overlaid by a new *Homo typographicus* that not only learns reading and writing but also acts as a designer of his or her symbolic image. This shows that the computer is certainly not a rejection of the Gutenberg tradition but quite the opposite, its enhancement. Nowadays everybody in the Western world learns reading, writing, printing and design.

CASIMIR: Is this a higher form of media competence?

SLOTERDIJK: Of course. And that is one reason why we can definitely welcome the computer into a meaningful educational alliance with Gutenberg culture. The point is to re-combine media alliances intelligently. You can rot your brain very quickly with television, but no law dictates that. You can regress at the computer but nothing is forcing you to do that.

CASIMIR: Conservation-minded people would like to defend the good old book against the new, technically superior media. You have also remarked somewhat ironically that books are better than other media for killing flies. Is that enough?

SLOTERDIJK: It would be quite mistaken merely to defend the old media with irony. Many colleagues I have discussed this with have told me that while they approached the new media with open arms, they are far more sceptical today about what electronic media can achieve in terms of preserving knowledge. These techniques are proving much more fragile than was previously thought. The book, however, is a medium that simply leaves you in peace for the first 100 years. It stands the test as the reliable bearer of what is entrusted to it.

CASIMIR: Another line of defence is that books have to be technologically updated as e-books. Is that a future prospect?

SLOTERDIJK: These are all ideas that may possibly work on the basis of data storage capacity, which has become terribly cheap. In the past, successful data storage media, such as marble tablets and paper, were the most rare and precious commodities. Today, data storage space is second only to Sahara Desert sand as the world's cheapest and most plentiful commodity. That leads to an incredible inflation – and to universal conservation of things not worth conserving. We will have to live in that entropy in the future. The printed book will easily outlive its electronic rivals.

CASIMIR: But won't the book itself become entropic? I'm thinking of the flood of new things every year. How can we reliably decide on all the things we don't have to read?

SLOTERDIJK: In the past, critics used to do that for us. They did the pre-selection. Criticism of that kind no longer exists today. Now each reader and each cultural agent has to be his or her own search engine. There's no way to avoid this. We live in the age of hyper-publicity and over-documentation. That is the result of our endless luxury of storage space. Every petit bourgeois today can document his or her life better than Louis XIV could. Far too much is conserved. But this evokes a sort of terminator in us that goes on a shooting spree with a weapon of ignorance and liquidates everything he can't use immediately.

CASIMIR: It's a beautiful mission. But it results in us terminators missing a great deal.

SLOTERDIJK: We know that, whatever the circumstances, the great majority tends to leave aside the best, even if it is accessible. For example, there are intellectuals who haven't read *Moby Dick*, perhaps the best book ever printed. That's very strange, isn't it? Most people live in the calm conviction that there is something more important than the best.

CASIMIR: We probably shouldn't disturb that at all …

SLOTERDIJK (laughing): There's nothing to disturb.

CASIMIR: You are an admirer of Jean Paul, who says books are nothing but 'thick letters to friends'. Yet trying to have an effect on one's reader-friends only works if they are people who at least partly obey the text. Still, obedience to the text is vanishing rapidly.

SLOTERDIJK: Universal literacy has a side effect. The moment the art of reading and writing becomes a basic democratic technique and loses its special hierarchical and sacral function, we begin to see something like the secularization of written things and, in time, profanation as well. But even after profanation, a kind of difference persists between the author and the reader. As long as that difference is felt clearly at a psychic level, the book has enough eroticism and authority to be able to create a gap in relation to the reader. This effect, that the author pre-empts the reader as it were, gives the book a head start. That is its opportunity, and will continue to be.

CASIMIR: What about friendship?

SLOTERDIJK: When Jean Paul said books are thick letters to friends, he was using a metaphor that expresses the transformation of the book from an authoritarian to an amicable medium. Bourgeois reading culture lives on the basis of this transformation, and the result is what generates pleasure in books in the first place.

CASIMIR: The author Florian Illies claims that city-dwellers are developing a rampant yearning for the countryside: being offline for a while, slowing down – the ideal conditions for thick books. Is the desire for reading having a comeback in Germany now?

SLOTERDIJK: You're talking to somebody who has just produced a book trilogy of 2,400 pages. One doesn't do that totally naively, but very likely with something in mind. Among other things, I wanted to suggest that this project is just as important as an existential sabbatical. People who really want to read my *Spheres* project as a totality won't be able to do it without taking unpaid leave. And it looks as if people are actually prepared to do that, otherwise the first volume, *Sphären I*, wouldn't have sold 20,000 copies in Germany. There are fast books that act like injections. But there are also books that are something like a long holiday.

# 23

# THUS SPOKE SLOTERDIJK

*Interview with Res Strehle**

STREHLE: My compliments, Peter Sloterdijk: your world history of rage and resentment is a winner.

SLOTERDIJK: It began with my intuition that these topics contained a huge store of hidden insights. As soon as that intuition was confirmed, the book wrote itself. Rage is like Nietzsche's *Abgrund*: the longer you stare into it the more steadily it will stare back at you.

STREHLE: Your book shifts the focus away from Freud's Eros, which explains a great deal but leaves big blank patches, to *thymos*, an ancient Greek term that means pride as the source of positive energies.

SLOTERDIJK: We certainly live in an era of changing perspectives. The stage is revolving, not least in the field of psychology where a great paradigm shift from psychoanalysis to neurobiology is happening. In its own way, my interest in the thymotic pole of the human psyche expresses a great change in feeling about the present period. Many people feel they are witnessing a world crisis. In some periods we simply carry on living in a straight line. But at other times it seems that we are actually seeing the wheel of the world turning. Many people today can feel how the scene around them has changed. The time of naïve triumph over socialist rivals has ended everywhere in the liberal capitalist world order.

STREHLE: You talk about rage collecting, and you interpret

* This interview between Peter Sloterdijk and Res Strehle appeared under the title 'Also sprach Sloterdijk', in *Das Magazin*, the weekly supplement of the Swiss daily *Tages-Anzeiger* (4–10 November 2006): 46–55.

Res Strehle is a Swiss journalist and was editor-in-chief of the *Tages-Anzeiger* (Zurich) at the time of the interview.

political and religious movements as savings banks and rage banks where investors can deposit their grievances. This also creates a changed perspective on political parties, which you describe as 'collection points of dissidence'.

SLOTERDIJK: Rather disappointingly, hardly any reviews of my book so far have mentioned its logical centre. *Rage and Time* basically presents a general theory of collections. The ancient agrarian empires were already totally dominated by the theme of hoarding because the granaries were the places that housed the secret of royal power in the early theocracies, or regimes ruled by god-kings. Collections of weapons, jewellery, money and gold augmented this wealth. Works of art in museums, knowledge in academies, universities and libraries, and religious salvation in the treasure house of the Church show that a great variety of non-monetary goods could be collected. I'm adding a dimension to this list that we haven't paid enough attention to so far: rage. Some emotions seem only fleeting; in fact they are definitely collectible – as shown most of all by religious feelings. If we ask what happens when rage is collected and conserved, we discover a new view of modern political parties and movements. We understand more about their character and function if we describe them as emotion collection points that manage the investments of the small rage owner.

STREHLE: You write that Catholicism and communism knew very well how to collect rage. Capitalism was not bad at it either. Early on, the classical economist Joseph Schumpeter described the dynamic of capitalism as creative destruction.

SLOTERDIJK: The spirit of capitalism is the spirit of reinvestment. That means people shouldn't simply own their treasure quietly and enjoy its presence. Real capitalists must be able to let go of the treasure. We could also describe this as modernization of greed: modern owners really own their property when they send it off on a journey of valorization, if necessary in the form of floating capital that has to go around the world and return with a mighty plus on the home account – provided it doesn't get dashed to pieces on a reef, always a risk. The modern spirit of realization demands that every potential should upgrade itself, which means that rage can also look forward to more cheerful times. If God is dead he is out of the picture as a collector, absorber and preserver of rage – but what should be done with protest potential? If there is no reward in the nether world, how can there be compensation for suffering, without which the notion of a sophisticated concept of justice can't exist? In this situation we can expect a new page to be turned in the book of the history of ideas. On this page will be written in letters of blood: 'World history is the world's Last Judgement.'

STREHLE: Political Islam seems to be at the start of a new chapter just now. Is it engaged in writing world history in letters of blood, as you say?

SLOTERDIJK: It incorporates the hallmarks of the two previous collection points for revenge, the Catholic-metaphysical and the communist-activist. It shares the idea of post-mortal punishment with Catholicism because it rightly portrays Allah as a wrathful lord. The philosopher of religion Jacob Taubes commented ironically on the resonance between leader and followers in monotheism: 'As is the Lord, so is the common man.' He was saying that if we know Jehovah, the Jews shouldn't be a surprise to us. The same applies to Christians and Muslims in their appropriate context. Islamism, however, has much in common with communism because both ideologies involve presentation of projects for political salvation. When it comes to salvation of the whole world, expansionism is on the agenda. Nobody knows where this will stop. Perhaps, like present-day Catholicism, in the long term it will be content for the world to stay permanently divided into Islam and non-Islam.

STREHLE: Do you mean political Islam doesn't want to expand?

SLOTERDIJK: Well, in the twentieth century the Islamic hemisphere first had to come to terms with its own growth. When we talk about Islam today we're always talking about an unprecedented population explosion. In the 1960s and 1970s we started discussing the new demographically conditioned world hunger problem, but we tended to overlook the fact that alongside the fertility of people living in poverty there was also a direct, offensive campaign for procreation. The Muslim population increased eightfold, from 150 million people in 1900 to 1.2 billion in the year 2000. This was partly due to massive bio-political control that uses aggressive growth in national populations as a political means. If Islam had remained demographically where it was in 1900 we would hardly talk about it today. But meanwhile the population bomb has exploded. The young men who will bring trouble in the coming years have all been born already. The older ones among them recently left their mark during the riots over the Mohammed cartoons. We saw angry young men in their twenties on the streets. Millions upon millions will join them in the coming years.

STREHLE: Without any real perspective?

SLOTERDIJK: They are doing what anybody in their situation would do. They grab the first opportunity to play a role on some kind of stage – regardless of whether it is the local stage or a dream world stage. We must take their performances seriously. What we are seeing is rage in its purest form, as raw material. This is the expression of generalized anger against a world that is completely and utterly divided up and occupied, and in which nobody can assign young people a place of their own. Nothing enrages people more than the idea of being superfluous, whereas they enter the stage with the idea of playing an important role. The sharpest lines of conflict occur when the demand for importance meets the threat of being superfluous.

*(The telephone rings. 'Hello? Yes, of course, I'll be delighted to see you again after forty years. It has really been a long time. Well, see you then.')*

STREHLE: It sounds like a school class reunion.

SLOTERDIJK: Yes, it is.

STREHLE: As a philosopher, can you still make yourself understood to your old schoolmates?

SLOTERDIJK: Yes, of course. Incidentally, the graduation year of 1966 was a very good year at Wittelsbacher Gymnasium in Munich. Everybody, without exception, has achieved something. We were the greatest possible contrast to today's young people who feel the pressures of career and anxiety about making a living early on. If I can generalize, all that was very remote from our feelings. Many of us vowed solemnly and faithfully never to do alienated work. Nobody wanted to let the 'system' buy out his dissidence. Many young people today complain that no one guarantees them a job for life. Nothing in recent years has alienated me as much as the confused rebellion of young people in France in March 2006 against the proposed law for a more flexible first job contract that was designed to reduce employers' reluctance to hire new employees. The protestors' revolt exposed their real dream of having total security from the very start. For an old veteran of the 1968 movement, that is obscene. But we were probably naïve. For some reason we were convinced nothing negative could happen to us. In those days dissidence was the surest way to success. People who disturbed the peace, if they did it right, could rely on being recognized as extremely useful members of society sooner or later.

STREHLE: Many people today are afraid of being losers. When it happens they explode with crazed anger, like the frenzied killers from the white lower-middle class in the USA who go on shooting sprees in schools or shopping malls. Is this anger comparable with that of Islamist attackers, who often choose their victims in a similarly random way?

SLOTERDIJK: No, I'm sure it's something completely different. The berserk gunmen from the white middle class are usually just children who vent their injured feelings on the collective in a destructive, individualistic way. The American assassins are psychologically very different from the Muslim activists. They follow a different script from the Islamist warrior assassins who only function when and because their collective gives them support.

STREHLE: Do you see the response to this threat, the 'war against terror', as a rational strategy, or was it collective punishment at the time? In the end it didn't shrink from torture, illicit killing, secret prisons and saturation bombing.

SLOTERDIJK: I'm convinced that our anti-terrorism policy is fundamentally wrong. Instead of giving the enemy a chance to identify themselves openly it makes them guilty from the very start. What's more, it subjects them to the methods of waging war in a post-heroic fashion, in which battles are no longer fought, but instead the enemy is eliminated from a position of boundless superiority. That style of fighting suits societies with low biological reproductivity because on our side nowadays we have no sons to squander. But this makes waging war very similar to pest control. Instead, we should be doing everything possible to break out of this asymmetry which is insulting to people's dignity – for example, by supporting the building of Islamic parties in Europe in which respectable forms of dissidence and representation of interests can be developed. That would be the best and most convincing response to terror – interrupting the spiral of reciprocal degradation and encouraging eye contact instead of a contest of scorn.

STREHLE: What role do the media play in these conflicts?

SLOTERDIJK: We should never forget that acts of terror like September 11 or the explosions in Atocha Station in Madrid are closely related to the Western entertainment industry. They operate in the field of our familiar horror clichés – the present terror is the translation of widespread fear-and-pleasure games from the cinema screen to the TV monitor. Real terror operates according to the game rules of a politicized snuff movie: real corpses, total entertainment. Evidence shows that terror profits from a monstrous reward system that follows the basic principle, 'Threaten us and you'll supply us with our most important topic.' As soon as something like that happens, all the channels of the Western world broadcast the message. The audience in the Middle East would have to be blind and deaf not to understand the invitation. Any attack from that quarter is rewarded with an orgy of attention.

STREHLE: You're very sceptical about the role of the media and you demand that every journalist decide whether he or she wants to be an agent of enlightenment or a player in the incitement system.

SLOTERDIJK: A thought experiment could be useful here. As soon as there is news about terror, journalists have to be clearly aware of their complicity in terror. Should they simply pass on the immediate feeling of shock, or even enhance it in certain circumstances? Or should they decide to play down the news – for example, by putting it in quarantine? That was an excellent old European method of fighting the plague. Perhaps the media plague is more dangerous than the bacterial one because it can create chaos in the motivation system of a whole civilization. The real point is not to reward serious crimes with excessive attention. That inevitably encourages repetition. Regrettably, the complicity between the media world and the terror scene has been so well harmonized for so long that we have to speak of genuine collusion and effective co-dependency – that's how drug therapy describes the intermeshing between addiction and dealing or the alliances among addicts. At some point we have to say openly: you, the journalists, are the dealers in this game.

STREHLE: If you were an editor-in-chief, would you refuse the deal?

SLOTERDIJK: There are two options: Either you create a grand coalition of abstainers that goes on strike against the pressure to spread terror – or you denounce yourself for rabble-rousing.

STREHLE: But the media could also function as a way of letting off steam.

SLOTERDIJK: If emotions weren't rational to some extent we wouldn't have them at all. That also makes sense in terms of evolutionary biology: if nature equipped us with some impulse or other it must involve a fitness benefit. It follows that pride and rage belong to the human make-up just as eroticism does. Evolution wouldn't have produced people capable of rage if that emotion were only senseless ballast. In fact, it is an important derivative of stress, and stress is the biological interpretation of acute danger, which means it is vital for survival. Normally a living being reacts to real present danger by fleeing or attacking. Both reactions require a high degree of energy, and that's exactly what the stress reaction provides. The early heroic poems describe great stress like a divine gift – or like inspired enthusiasm that seems to flow into the soul from outside.

STREHLE: And things get dangerous when that rage is collected and frozen into resentment?

SLOTERDIJK: Quite right. When people's need for validation is rejected they start feeling enraged. If they are prevented from expressing the rage, it is stored up. Since the nineteenth century that has been called resentment. Dostoevsky and Nietzsche started a new chapter in the study of the human soul with their investigations into the denigrated, insulted and revengeful person. They were thymotic psychologists, like their successor, Alfred Adler. On a diversion via Kojève and Lacan, he left deep, hidden traces in French psychoanalysis. We can still get drunk on the ambiguity of the word *désir*.

Oddly enough, it describes two completely different things: first, erotic desire in terms of the Freudian libido, and, second, the desire for recognition described by Hegel.

STREHLE: At the end of your book you suggest psychological systems for healing injuries. Which direction should they take?

SLOTERDIJK: Modern civilization has already achieved a certain amount in this field. The possibility of a meritocracy controlled by money, as facilitated by the market economy, has done much to detoxify social relationships. When someone achieves something, others realize it as long as the achievements can be shown visibly. The Greeks created four theatrical arenas of ambition where gifted people could distinguish themselves: the agora as the stage for political debate, and the theatre, the stadium and the academy for debating scientific opinions. Willing and able people flourished in these arenas. Today, these forums are all fully functioning again. We can't imagine any more how badly the old aristocratic society was psycho-dynamically screwed up. For centuries, social existence mainly consisted of absurd fights about privilege. People fought with family trees, rival illusions of nobility took the field against each other, and arguments about precedence were fought out in a space completely empty of achievement – hollow dreams of potency without a beginning or an end. The Europeans lost more than a thousand years with that kind of nonsense – we have to state that clearly once and for all.

STREHLE: In your book you go a step further and propose a sort of code of behaviour for world society.

SLOTERDIJK: Be careful. I would never go that far. I say that a behaviour code for the world must first be ground in the mills of the present debate between cultures. Incidentally, this culture clash would still be taking place even if Huntington hadn't predicted it.[1] It's in the nature of things. Friction exists between the West and the Far East as well as the Middle East. The game rules for coexistence of 8–10 billion human beings are being discovered in the process. Of course, this only works if the unavoidable conflicts between the great players don't get too destructive. Then again, it is also not enough if a few omniscient experts in international law and some fervent Protestants meet in Washington to dictate the necessary measures and wait for the others to join in. Rage remains a basic force but it won't continue collecting in the forms of the nineteenth and twentieth centuries, when it developed into communism and

[1] See Samuel P. Huntington, *The Clash of Civilizations and the Remaking of World Order* (New York: Simon & Schuster), 1996.

fascism. It has largely retreated into individual ambitions, and vents on the broadest front in mass culture. That's why we always have to understand the function of mass culture for letting off steam and as a form of popular therapy.

STREHLE: Are you talking about computer games, for instance?

SLOTERDIJK: They are important too. Every individualist and collective form of mass culture can function to contain rage and let off steam. The only thing that doesn't play a role any more is what some intellectuals still dream about: a new communism, a new World Bank of rage. The requisite possibilities of collection are lacking for this. A second wave of communism is less likely than a giant meteorite hitting the earth's surface in the next thousand years.

STREHLE: When you mention conflict on the Asian–Western border, are you thinking of North Korea's atom bomb?

SLOTERDIJK: No, North Korea is a very different problem. The country is a singular phenomenon and perhaps simply a brief episode in history. I'm convinced the Chinese will put an end to that irritating situation sooner or later. If the North Koreans really go crazy the Chinese will invade. We don't have to lift a finger. The Western world's hysterical reaction to the Korean threat seems rather absurd to me. The USA is too far away and beyond reach of any existing North Korean long-range missiles. Eastern Europe might be reachable – but for what?

STREHLE: Isn't that more of a mythological horror image – a madman with a bomb?

SLOTERDIJK: A great deal of our politics still plays out in the cinema and in thrillers. Frankenstein appeared on the scene nearly 200 years ago, and since then the role is there to be filled in the mass imagination. No mass culture without horror. Real figures can also act in these scripts because the amusement system all around us has largely erased the difference between real and fictitious horror. We are constantly going back and forth through the revolving door from the horror genre to real terror. We could also say Washington and Hollywood have become too similar to each other. We must hope that one day people will be better able to distinguish again between real threats and fictitious ones.

STREHLE: Are Iran's nuclear development plans a real threat? After the Iraq debacle, international sabre rattling won't work in that case any more.

SLOTERDIJK: Iran is evidently not letting itself be intimidated.

STREHLE: Do you see this as a danger?

SLOTERDIJK: Nuclear weapons are our invention. It is in the nature of things that others imitate us in the most risky aspects of our civilization. It is part of the risks of our 'way of life' that an Iranian driver comes driving down our lane towards us in the wrong direction. As we know, drivers going in the wrong direction are always convinced everybody else is driving in the wrong lane. This view is very widespread in the Middle East at the moment: the West is driving on the wrong side and they are on the right side.

STREHLE: It's a matter of perception.

SLOTERDIJK: More than that – it's a war about perception. To put it cautiously: the probability that something good will come out of an Iranian atom bomb isn't very great. But the probability of it causing much harm isn't that great either. So far all the nuclear powers have taken responsibility for their own weapons very seriously. Our experience up to now shows that anybody with nuclear weapons becomes part of the deterrent system. The only ones who have really used the bomb are the Americans. That's why they tend to believe more than anyone else that other countries could repeat their lack of control and actually use the transcendent weapon. The mad enemy – that is, the actor who gets away with everything – is the personification of one's own question.

STREHLE: And do you see the much-talked-about use of nuclear weapons by terrorists as an illusion?

SLOTERDIJK: The really annoying thing about terror is that it distracts us from much more important problems.

STREHLE: From questions of social development? From the destruction of the ecological system?

SLOTERDIJK: Naturally, in Europe the question of social development is taking a new form again. Inequalities have grown dramatically. In the Middle East, however, the question of social development is posed as a demographic question and therefore as the risk of civil war. Enormous psycho-political explosive material has collected there, and it is mostly religiously coded. In addition, in the coming fifty years humankind must make the transition to an economy based on post-fossil energy. Environmental problems are becoming more acute every year. There is a whole slew of such top-list priorities.

STREHLE: You conclude your book with a moral appeal: we should learn to see ourselves with others' eyes.

SLOTERDIJK: That isn't a moral appeal; it's a totally normal intellectual attitude. Seeing yourself from the outside is a modus vivendi that requires a degree of asceticism. Asceticism means, purely and simply, exercising to achieve fitness. That's what gives the expression a relation to morality. It is an obvious lesson: we have to keep fit for everything to come. We are facing a period of tremendous friction. We can't simply wish away the coming conflicts. Marx once said that the point is not to make the real contradictions disappear, but to create a form within which they can move.

# 24

# FATHERS SHOULD BE KEPT OUT OF BROTHELS AND PUBS

*Interview with Jan Feddersen and Susanne Lang**

FEDDERSEN/LANG: Mr Sloterdijk, what has put you in a rage this year?

SLOTERDIJK: I'm not sure – I'm not easily provoked. What I remember is the student protests in France against the introduction of the new contract for first-time employment. It was designed to give more scope to employers so as to overcome their reluctance to hire new employees. Absurdly, the workers affected saw this as an attack on their presumed basic right to employment for life from the first working day onwards. Their opposition was completely illusory, as if they wanted to demand top jobs for all.

FEDDERSEN/LANG: But isn't idealism typical for a student movement?

SLOTERDIJK: We should distinguish between illusionism and idealism. The attitude of younger people has changed. I come from a generation that grew up under totally different conditions. At the time of my school-leaving examination in 1966 nobody dreamed of making compromises with the world of permanent employment. Our motto was, 'You'll never get my labour power.'

FEDDERSEN/LANG: But that only applied to left-wing activists, not to the people they wanted to champion, the workers.

SLOTERDIJK: It's true that a bohemian student scene evolved

* This interview between Peter Sloterdijk and Jan Feddersen and Susanne Lang appeared under the title 'Väter weg von Puff und Kneipe', in the daily *taz* newspaper (23 December 2006). Available at: <http://www.taz.de/1/archiv/?dig=2006/12/23/a0209>.

At the time of the interview Jan Feddersen was a journalist and editor at the Berlin *taz*, and Susanne Lang was an editor at the *taz*.

in the early 1970s, during the period of so-called full employment. This bohemian group from the 1968 movement produced a political surplus that created fantastic opportunities. We're still living from that today. The recent protests in France, however, showed that young people have become almost overwhelmingly petit bourgeois.

FEDDERSEN/LANG: Because the young want to work rather than revolutionize?

SLOTERDIJK: Because they let the logic of the consumer world define their wishes. In life stories in the past, youth played the role of a psychosocial moratorium where people in a state of indecision, or even confusion, were tolerated and protected. There was always the assumption that they would make the best use of this in their careers later on. Nowadays eighteen-year-olds take to the streets and demand the right to a permanent job for life!

FEDDERSEN/LANG: In France young people in the *banlieus* took to the streets as well, and set fire to cars. Are they the real angry ones in our society?

SLOTERDIJK: No. Both protests are primarily mimetic movements that mimic a kind of rage the actors themselves don't always feel. France has a rich popular tradition of outrage.

FEDDERSEN/LANG: We're pretty good at that in Germany too, aren't we?

SLOTERDIJK: Yes, but it has less of an impact here. The atmosphere in France is more rigid, and that leads to a dialectic of stagnation and explosion. Things are more fluid in Germany, which is why today, unlike in the 1980s, protest doesn't have a broad basis any longer.

FEDDERSEN/LANG: Are you referring particularly to the time when the Green Party was very vocal?

SLOTERDIJK: Anyone who wants to understand the Greens should realize that post-1945 Germany has achieved something extraordinary in the production of loser attitudes. In Germany, thymotic culture, which is based on self-affirmation and pride, was reduced to a stump. What remained of self-affirmative behaviour had to be expressed in terms of moralism. The Greens led the way in this – some of them were veritable Jacobins.

FEDDERSEN/LANG: This means the Greens as a party acted as a good rage bank, as you explain in your new essay, *Rage and Time*. Are they still playing that role?

SLOTERDIJK: The function of the political party as an institution, not just the Green Party, has fundamentally changed today. From a historical perspective, parties were never just organs for expressing interests, but were collection points for emotions as well. They had the task of organizing collection of hopes, illusions, wishes and rage. They used various combinations to address different segments of the public at different times. People who looked for national symbols to give them satisfaction took up position on the right wing. Others who identified with symbols of material progress, of developing justice and of the welfare state, assembled on the left wing. Finally, the liberals provided a meeting ground for people who pinned their hopes mostly on the advance of different kinds of freedom in the modern state. Interestingly, the middle-class parties acted as collection points for militant satisfaction.

FEDDERSEN/LANG: What does that involve?

SLOTERDIJK: The middle class is the class that turns its own satisfaction into defiance. How do we explain that? Modern society popularizes the possibility of comparison. That's why there is asymmetrical growth between the reasons for being satisfied and the reasons for being dissatisfied. As soon as the means of satisfaction become more widespread, the means of comparison grow as well. We all compare ourselves with each other, with the result that we see people all around us who are ahead of us, and that seems unfair. This is how countless people who are objectively winners in terms of modernization and progress subjectively see themselves as protestors.

FEDDERSEN/LANG: That explains why we live in a German world. Do luxury and satisfaction lead to fear of social decline?

SLOTERDIJK: This question neatly points up the paradox of that wasted freedom. Dissatisfaction with luxury indicates that people don't have an organ for calculating probabilities. We are oriented to facts on the one hand, and to hopes and expectations on the other, but we don't have an internal mechanism for dealing with probability. This is why we can't evaluate the unimaginable improbability of our own lifestyle. The only people who can do that are people who come from outside or who move between a culture of poverty and a culture of wealth.

FEDDERSEN/LANG: In terms of political parties, does this mean that today they are advocates of the improbable?

SLOTERDIJK: I see them as service providers in the market of political illusions. Their pact with improbability is fateful and obsessive. Of course, the people who get elected are the ones who correspond most closely to the voters' expectations. But expectations of that kind all tend towards increasing improbability. The general product that each party must offer today, without exception, is the plausible illusion that the party's politics will optimize its clientele's lifestyles.

FEDDERSEN/LANG: Yet most politicians have stopped

pointing to any kind of optimization – they promise the status quo, in a very alarmist way, in fact.

SLOTERDIJK: Guaranteeing the status quo means a great deal in a situation where liberalism has been emptied of meaning. In a situation where most ideologists have long since resorted to threats that things will get worse again, assurances that things will stay the same are nearly gospels. We must realize that in the political arena the forces that threaten have always wrestled with the forces that make promises. At present the threatening forces have the upper hand, which is why the two most suggestive topics for threats, international competition and terrorism, have such powerful connotations here in Germany. People would much rather hear beautiful promises, and by now they are happy when they aren't threatened too often. And the same people were assertively making demands not long ago!

FEDDERSEN/LANG: In other words, the myth of the general strike has no validity any more?

SLOTERDIJK: Even less so in Germany than in other countries. The left wing was powerful as long as its threats remained credible. At that time, when communism appeared as the real existing alternative, the Western workers' parties didn't have to do much to demonstrate to the employers' side that social peace had its price, even in Germany. Those times are over. Today the left wing is threatened, not threatening. Strategists define the threat as armed advice. Today people on the left are disarmed and confused.

FEDDERSEN/LANG: If the left wing isn't holding any trump cards, does that mean it's superfluous?

SLOTERDIJK: In the last third of the twentieth century the whole of politics in the Western world imploded into the centre. At the same time the communist system imploded in Eastern Europe. Resentment has become increasingly diffuse since then. That is the hallmark of the post-communist situation: the left wing has stopped functioning as the collection point for rage. What is it supposed to canvass with now? I think it must shift its focus away from revenge campaigns and towards civilization campaigns. From fighting to learning.

FEDDERSEN/LANG: We understand immediately what you mean by 'revenge campaigns' – but what might left-wing civilization projects look like?

SLOTERDIJK: For instance, one could focus on the differences between religions. Why has Islam become so prominent in the post-communist situation? Because its activists have made an impression as potentially threatening factors. In my book I examined the question of whether Islam will succeed in becoming the third collection of rage after Catholicism and communism, and my answer is 'No'.

FEDDERSEN/LANG: Why won't it succeed?

SLOTERDIJK: Its assumptions are too regional. You can't collect the resentment of jobless German or Polish people in an Islamic context. Of course, you can oppose modernity and you can retreat into Islam and build a stable existence there, but it can't be constructed into a movement coming from the centre of modernization. It can't promise a better modern age. That's what communism succeeded in doing for a while.

FEDDERSEN/LANG: But to what extent are the differences of religions a project of the left?

SLOTERDIJK: If there is a world war today, it takes the form of a clash of monotheisms. Those antagonisms have to be civilized.

FEDDERSEN/LANG: That doesn't sound really new. But hardly anyone is able to define exactly how that civilizing process should happen. What do you suggest?

SLOTERDIJK: For example, civilizing by reshaping religion through art. Thomas Mann gave an example of how this could happen in his fictional trilogy *Joseph and His Brothers*. The book shows how, thanks to contact with a foreign religion, the exclusive and bigoted form of monotheism was transformed into an inclusive religion based on art.

FEDDERSEN/LANG: Could the left adopt that?

SLOTERDIJK: Not directly. First of all, this lesson concerns the parties in the conflict that have dogmas and positions, that manage a truth fund. But the post-communist left wing could tag on immediately afterward provided they have a sense that conflicts, friction and confrontation can be productive. Today, struggles are still the significant learning situations. We shouldn't yield to any illusions. Today, even more than in Hegel's times, humankind is condemned to auto-didacticism as a matter of life and death. War is the main school and anybody who doesn't fight doesn't learn either. No neutral teachers are available. The struggle itself must generate the rules, which go beyond the struggle.

FEDDERSEN/LANG: Do you mean class struggle?

SLOTERDIJK: Well, good old class struggle was based on a precarious fantasy of victory: the proletariat had to gain complete control over the production process and that would end the antagonism with capital. The Russian Revolution showed where that led: to genocide against the bourgeoisie perpetrated by the noble hangmen, the professional revolutionaries who appear as advocates of the proletariat. Today, we have moved away from that type of advocacy and prefer the idea of self-organization at grassroots level. Perhaps the model of advocacy or tribuneship could still make sense in periods of mass misery. Now we are working with networking constructs and the assumption of self-organized units.

FEDDERSEN/LANG: Are you sure this applies to all left-wing tendencies?

SLOTERDIJK: It certainly applies to the alternative rainbow culture. Maybe palaeo-Stalinists and old Maoist Party cadre wouldn't feel at home in that diverse scene, but who cares? In *Empire*, Negri tried to combine palaeo-left and new left approaches, without convincing results. He just renamed the masses as the multitude and created a new fetish – the rainbow as the alternative proletariat.

FEDDERSEN/LANG: Multitude as the formula for excuses?

SLOTERDIJK: I would look at it differently. First, Negri is only doing what left-wing radicals chronically do. He is continuing the quest for the subject of the revolution. But two ideas are hampering him: first, the subject is not one, but many. He can live with that for the moment. In addition, it turns out that revolution is an obsolete concept because the process of capital and the empire are always more revolutionary than their opponents. On this point, too, Negri acts as if he could live with this knowledge, but in fact it cancels out his position. He has to be content with the appearance of keeping up with the times by updating Marx's hymn to the revolutionary power of the bourgeois class.

FEDDERSEN/LANG: There is a slight hitch: the bourgeoisie didn't and doesn't want to make a revolution.

SLOTERDIJK: In fact, they did – because there are two types of revolution, the erotic revolution of the bourgeoisie, which is driven by greed, and the thymotic revolution of the poor, which only functions if it continues to be driven by pride. Marx had his reasons for celebrating the revolution of greed very vigorously and simultaneously claiming it was not enough. For the left-wing revolution is made not in the name of greed, but of pride and its two moral derivatives, rage and outrage. The goal of such a revolution was to provide the denigrated and insulted with dignity as subjects. Those are movements of empowerment, and the leitmotif of the proletarian *thymos* runs through them: dignity through labour! Dignity through struggle! But as soon as the left wing becomes, in turn, a greed party, as is happening everywhere in Germany, it implodes and becomes part of the total centre.

FEDDERSEN/LANG: That would bring us back to student protests and burning cars in the *banlieus*. In the end is it really about future opportunities, about demands for work?

SLOTERDIJK: I'm not sure. If we rely on the protagonists' descriptions, in the *banlieus* it was mostly about a form of rioting as fun in the context of a dreadful lack of social prospects. Thanks to copycat contagion, the TV pictures launched a wave of violent games – car burning with the aid of a popular issue of Molotov cocktails, with 1,500 scenes of fires in one night.

FEDDERSEN/LANG: Is it about attention-getting for the offended?

SLOTERDIJK: Yes, but not in the sense of demands for dignity because that would involve a project requiring long-term patience. It was more about immediate gratification for a spectacle of vandalism. This is a case where the modern media are guilty of alliances with the worst tendencies. It is always the most disgusting actions that get rewarded with the biggest attention bonuses.

FEDDERSEN/LANG: What should a civilized left wing do to change this system of incentives?

SLOTERDIJK: The only solution would be to integrate the marginalized people into a meaningful process of economic ownership.

FEDDERSEN/LANG: In other words, jobs for all?

SLOTERDIJK: Yes, but not in the sense of permanent employment for life. We have to make fighters into entrepreneurs – it's the same energy. The effects of satisfaction come either when positions are available in the world of work or people create positions for themselves on a ladder of ambition.

FEDDERSEN/LANG: Do we have to get children off the street?

SLOTERDIJK: Of course, children should be kept off the street and fathers should be kept out of brothels and pubs. This is best done with extensive job creation schemes, and the economy of ownership is still the best way to create jobs.

FEDDERSEN/LANG: How do you want to tell that to the losers in this society? Support and demand, or something like that?

SLOTERDIJK: In structural terms, we only have three forms of existence: entrepreneur, worker and unemployed. An effective difference only exists among the unemployed: some become passive while the others become fighters. When resentment meets lust for battle, the activists easily slip into the proto-fascist position. Civil war also creates positions. To paraphrase a saying of Thomas Hobbes, not only war has given everything to every man but civil war has, as well. If we want to leave out these variants, the only thing left is the entrepreneurial alternative.

FEDDERSEN/LANG: You are presupposing something: sovereign subjects responsible for their own actions.

SLOTERDIJK: The main precondition is that we see unemployment neutrally. To begin with it is merely the expression of two highly desirable developments – first, that wage labour isn't the most important part of life any longer, and, second, that people are freed from jobs that are better done by machines. In this respect the reduction of work is good news. The left should have cultivated this viewpoint as its civilizing mission. The substitution of machines for men is something absolutely worth affirming, and so is the reduction of labour time by a third within 200 years, that is, by around 1,700 working hours per year. What we should develop is a strong cultural and educational concept for the people liberated from work, combined with the formation of free communities in which people can mutually stimulate and enrich each other, including outside the world of work.

FEDDERSEN/LANG: So you don't believe that monetary wealth leads to social peace?

SLOTERDIJK: It only satisfies those who have it. Capitalism operates on the premise that peace on earth comes when everybody is turned into a consumer. At most that is a dangerous half-truth. Part of the civilizing project is that we don't see people only as creatures at the feeding trough, but also as beings that want dignity.

FEDDERSEN/LANG: Is that where religion comes in again?

SLOTERDIJK: In the foreseeable future religions will continue to be part of the problem rather than the solution. If there were a world spirit it would probably be warning us that the civilizing way is the only one still open. In fact, two structural complexes stand facing each other on the great stage and they are totally out of balance internally. One is an over-eroticized West devastated by greed, and the other is an over-thymoticized Middle East devastated by resentment. Unless they are brought into balance again, global self-destruction is on the agenda on both sides.

FEDDERSEN/LANG: You don't sound really worried. Are you optimistic?

SLOTERDIJK: Yes, actually. But contrary to my initial feeling, I have learned to hope at the second attempt. If you have a fair amount of luck you can't keep on pushing pessimistic positions. In fact, there are also intellectual reasons for moderate optimism.

FEDDERSEN/LANG: What makes you optimistic?

SLOTERDIJK: Some of the thought constructs developed by Herder, Hegel and Whitehead can be reformulated to create resilient optimism about processes. In a dense world – and density is the main characteristic of our form of world – the autodidactic tension increases. We can see the side effects of actions catching up with us faster and faster. Where fate was, there will be feedback. Humankind is an infernal conscious-raising group whose members put so much pressure on each other that they will probably be able to work out a halfway liveable code of behaviour in the present century.

FEDDERSEN/LANG: Is that your version of the opposite of waiting for a new revolutionary leader?

SLOTERDIJK: 'Revolution' and 'leader' are compromised concepts. The model process I have in mind has more to do with a new version of Adam Smith's argument of the invisible hand. Although it seems very naïve, in reality it offers a complex idea in anticipation of cybernetics and chaos theory. If we set chaos theorists and cyberneticists to work on social evolution, after calculating all the obtainable variables they will conclude that, whatever the conditions, we can expect something better than the ultimate meltdown. Optimism as minimalism. With this information we can carry on working.

# 25

# THE ATHLETICS OF DYING

*Interview with René Scheu**

SCHEU: Mr Sloterdijk, are you afraid of death?

SLOTERDIJK: Yes, I am, and the reason is that I came close to it at a very early age. In a certain sense that is where I come from. If I didn't have any idea of death I would probably act like the French captain La Palisse whom Albert Camus refers to in *The Myth of Sisyphus*. This officer was renowned for his fearlessness, his thoughtlessness, in fact. The soldiers wrote a song celebrating this: 'A quarter of an hour before his death / he was still alive.' From a philosophical perspective, this highlights an interesting position: there is life over which death does not cast a shadow.

SCHEU: An unconscious life? Philosophers don't usually appreciate that.

SLOTERDIJK: Perhaps because modern philosophers are so fixated on existence and its mortality that they find it difficult to imagine life with a purely expansive dynamic. But even if they lack the ability to do so, it doesn't mean that type of life doesn't exist – a life without blockages, without reflection, without exaggerated self-absorption and, above all, without the engram of a near-death experience.

SCHEU: Did you have to confront the possibility of death early on?

SLOTERDIJK: You could say I began as a dead person. It was

* This interview between Peter Sloterdijk and René Scheu appeared under the title 'Die Athletik der Sterbens', in *Schweizer Monatshefte* 6 (2007): 34–9.

At the time of the interview René Scheu was editor-in-chief and publisher of the magazine *Schweizer Monat*.

a complicated birth. My parents were Rhesus-incompatible, and that's sufficient for starting off as a near-dead person. I developed severe jaundice immediately after I was born, which led people who saw me to comment that blue eyes look particularly good with yellow skin. To be honest, I didn't see it as an aesthetic privilege. From the first moment of my life I was already reminded of its end. When the beginning evokes the end it makes a starting point that colours everything.

SCHEU: In dark colours?

SLOTERDIJK: It was a dark beginning, but it was followed by brighter intervals that kept getting larger. These clearings have meant most to me as a philosopher. Incidentally, Emil Cioran used a similar trope in one of his darkest books, *The Trouble with Being Born*, where he says: 'We do not rush toward death,' but 'We flee the catastrophe of birth.'

SCHEU: You have spoken of the possibility of a life in which death casts no shadow. Isn't that merely the fantasy of a philosopher whose birth was a death agony?

SLOTERDIJK: We have to distinguish between death and dying. In the end, nobody can know death – anybody who knows it is already beyond all knowing. We simply observe its protocol, its attendant circumstances, at most the process of annihilation, from the internal perspective up to the critical boundary. Dying has a claustrophobic dimension that is difficult to overestimate. The Romantics suppressed it by always emphasizing the agoraphiliac dimensions of dying: everything becomes big, beautiful and open, you stand on a field of blooms in May, you have more space than you ever had and you fill it with your soul. The truth is, in the death agony, space becomes narrower; you have no place any more, either in this world or in this time. The feeling of a choking point like that is the most unbearable thing imaginable.

SCHEU: Is a life without relation to death really a life worth living? Or would it be something like the infinite extension of thoughtlessness?

SLOTERDIJK: It would be worth living – I use the conjunctive because I personally feel different about this. Yet I can definitely imagine a life like that. Making appreciation of life dependent on its inner relation to death is an old European quirk. Life also exists with its very own intensity and wakefulness, without morbidity and backlog, and without interest in what is beyond death, even without the need for reunion in the world beyond with loved ones who have died. If we look at our concept of life in relation to the Hindu hermeneutics of death, for example, we become startlingly aware of our dependence on our own history and culture. In the Hindu concept, the wish is to be delivered from life and released from the wheel of rebirth. In Western culture, by contrast, dreams of reunion are a major source of thanatological fantasies. By the way, it seems to me that in constructing ideas of the world beyond, the fear of negative encounters has been just as powerful as the positive dimension ...

SCHEU: We want to live forever but are afraid to meet really nasty people in the hereafter ...

SLOTERDIJK: Then let's rather live forever on earth. That would be the conclusion of a thanatological explanation of the will to life. The fear of meeting people we hate in the nether world has roused some people's hopes that there is absolutely no hereafter. People never give up hoping that heaven may be a labyrinth in which the inhabitants lose their way. That reminds me of a popular joke. St Peter is taking a new arrival around heaven and shows him the different sections: the Jews here, the Muslims there, and the Hindus on the other side. At the end of the tour, he points to a grim-faced group behind a wall and says, 'Hush, those are the Catholics. They think they're alone here.'

SCHEU: We can see something like the birth of real life from the spirit of consciousness of death, not only in Western philosophy but also in our popular fantasies – look at Hollywood. Which cultural influences do you think are responsible for this?

SLOTERDIJK: A strong heroic-athletic pathos developed in Greek culture and extended to all areas of life. Since then life has meant being in good form and our greatest hope is a chance to die at our peak. That is the hidden message of the *Iliad.* The two strongest warriors on the plain of Troy, Hector and Achilles, depart this life at the right moment. They both escape an existence after their best form.

SCHEU: In Christianity, however, people achieve their triumph not in the perfect timing of death but in God, the guarantor of the triumph over death.

SLOTERDIJK: Our modern consciousness of death is indeed a secular relic of the Catholic *memento mori* culture. If you will allow me a brief digression into philosophical history about an author who combined both the Greek and Christian legacies ...

SCHEU: Go ahead ...

SLOTERDIJK: It is interesting that Martin Heidegger, who was a former acolyte, was at his least Catholic at the time when he spoke most about death. This radical communion with oneself, death not only as one's own possibility but superlatively enhanced as the 'most deeply personal possibility', as the possibility of impossibility, to some extent as the anticipation of the Last Judgement in one's own soul, was also fascinating for the Protestants of the 1920s. As a result they believed – wrongly – that Heidegger was their man. Heidegger's idea culminated in something extremely un-Christian: the heroic appropriation of one's own death. In Christianity, on the other hand, death was celebrated as casting off the trappings of life, as relinquishing any form of property rights. Heidegger made dying into a borderline case of skill, an appropriation of expropriation. This leads, of course, to a heroic attitude that fitted the general political situation of military nationalism between the two world wars.

SCHEU: But the Christian attitude towards death seems more ambiguous to me than you have depicted it so far. Christianity heroized death as well.

SLOTERDIJK: That's quite correct. In the accounts of Matthew, Mark and Luke, the Messiah dies on the cross in a pose of extreme self-sacrifice, and the expropriation he suffers is emphasized with great clarity, whereas, strangely enough, in the Gospel according to St John, there is an athletic conclusion in the phrase the Redeemer uttered on the cross: 'It is finished.' This statement is typical of the Hellenization of Christianity. The man on the cross becomes like an athlete who raises his arms at the moment he crosses the finishing line. (*At this point Sloterdijk fetches the* Novum Testamentum Graece et Latine *and checks the relevant text.*) '*Tetelestai*', '*consummatum est*': it sounds as if Jesus is summing up his own dying performance at the moment he arrives at his goal.

SCHEU: To be able to die, the facility of death – are you saying that the techniques you call 'anthropotechnics' in your books, the techniques of self-domestication of humans, are ultimately directed towards overcoming death? Thanks to genetic engineering, will death soon become an option: the only people who must die are those who want to?

SLOTERDIJK: Modern technology undoubtedly has an inner teleology. If we want to understand it, we have to go beyond the usual perception of technology as an extension of our bodily organs. Organ extensions are also dream or fantasy extensions. There is nothing in the results of technology that was not previously contained in metaphysics; and there is nothing in metaphysics that was not previously contained in magic. In other words, there is a line from magic to technology, and we have to ask what the magical and the bio-technological disposition of consciousness have in common.

SCHEU: And what would be the answer?

SLOTERDIJK: Probably that we can see magical thought expressed in the most up-to-date technologies. Magical thought starts from the assumption that there is no natural death. Death is always the result of an occult scandal …

SCHEU: Scandal?

SLOTERDIJK: Something evil, a dirty trick, manipulation. Death is a result of external machinations that can be attributed to evil actors. People wouldn't die if there weren't somebody who meant harm to them. From this perspective, the naturalization of death is a remarkable achievement of higher metaphysics. It understands nature as a neutral force for order that is powerful enough to put even death in its place. Incidentally, any modern neurotic person would agree with the magical idea that there is no natural death. He knows that unfortunately he is living under one roof with his murderer – his own body. The lung, that old devil! I know exactly what it's planning. It will murder me one day – but it shouldn't think I'm going to give up smoking just to please it! Or the prostate, the projected time bomb in the male body that could have been invented by the nastiest feminists. The domestication of death is the greatest cultural achievement of metaphysical thought. It has taken over from the original paranoia. Today this function has been delegated to medicine.

SCHEU: The first human being will be cloned some time in the near future. Do you see a danger in human genetics?

SLOTERDIJK: Keep calm. The domesticating forces that were constructed around these technologies are so great that it would be absurd to assume some crazy despot could seize control of the world using an army of biological robots.

SCHEU: When humans interfere with their genetic make-up it can sometimes have irreversible consequences. For example, they could decide on specific characteristics that would deprive them of their natural openness.

SLOTERDIJK: Agreed. But we have long since been familiar with this problem in another form. It is good old alienation. To a great extent, human living conditions are nothing more than large-scale attacks on the openness of the world. The traditional victims of these attacks are farmers and proletarians – or, at least, that is how critical social theory has portrayed these groups. For thousands of years, they have been deprived of the possibility of living up to their real potential. In short, that humans undercut other humans is a historical finding that has troubled class societies from way back when.

SCHEU: That sounds as if you believe in a classless society in which everybody can achieve his or her potential.

SLOTERDIJK: No. The only reason I don't believe in that is because many people reject openness. This is what all those who criticized exploitation in the name of justice refused to see. If people choose alienation they shouldn't be forced into liberation.

SCHEU: Does that mean there will be two kinds of people in

the future: those who are for openness and those who vote for bio-technological alienation?

SLOTERDIJK: That's possible, but I don't think that's the decisive question. I would like to refer to the issue of a life liberated by death in its present bio-technological form. In other words, the discussion about the gene for longevity. The first big fraud case in the still young history of human bio-technology concerned precisely this object. The Korean researcher Hwang Woo-suk was supposed to have achieved sensational findings related to this gene. A whole battalion of scientists in California worked on the decoding of the longevity gene, which people obviously believed to exist. The technology prophet Ray Kurzweil described the present as the moment just before the breakthrough to immortality. The idea was: keep going, just don't slack. The slogan was: 'Live long enough to live forever!' Now let's assume a scenario in which all human beings can soon live for 150 or 200 years. We would have exactly the situation we discussed earlier. Death would no longer be a natural end. Instead, it would always be left to the discretion of individuals themselves or an external agent. Where there was once death, there will be murder or suicide. Stone Age logic turns out to be right.

SCHEU: Would you describe these techno-biological imaginings as naïve but not reprehensible?

SLOTERDIJK: The childishness of the belief in a very long life, what we call eternal life, is rather touching. But we Europeans have ourselves to blame. We should never have let the people who later became Americans go. It was clear that they moved away to be able to dream in peace somewhere else. Now we have to deal with their flights of fancy.

SCHEU: You argue in your books for collaboration between humans and technology. You say there is nothing a priori wrong with people acquiring technical equipment and engaging in biological optimization and digital networking.

SLOTERDIJK: My technicism, or support for technology, is part of my blueprint for General Immunology. It mainly concerns what I call the 'incubator system'. We must look at human history as a series of attempts to optimize the human incubator. After all, we have been incubator creatures since the earliest times. That is why *Homo sapiens* was made into a hybrid from the beginning. Humans first became the exceptional beings they are as part of a long, unconscious self-breeding sequence, and this experiment has always taken place in an incubator facilitated by the use of tools. Today we are slowly realizing this – and it would be naïve, if not reactionary, to refuse to acknowledge it.

SCHEU: What once occurred unconsciously is now coming close to conscious manipulation.

SLOTERDIJK: That's right. That's why I think there should be an absolute ban on fraudulent claims in relation to human biotechnology. Only what can be done with high precision is ethically responsible. But if people could really be trusted to do what they must be able to do, for example, to eliminate certain dreadful forms of inherited pathologies, they wouldn't be infringing any human rights. There is no human obligation to be ill! I would strongly advocate a second Hippocratic oath. Doctors should pledge not only to benefit health as such but also to benefit the conditions of the possibility of health. Anyone infringing this, by neglecting research, for instance, would be guilty of denial of assistance.

SCHEU: You have made yourself very unpopular in Germany with statements like that.

SLOTERDIJK: In this country people are quick to label you as an ogre. Fortunately, the Swiss have a more pragmatic attitude.

# 26

# DO YOUR DUTY TO ENJOY!

## *Interview with Christoph Bopp**

BOPP: Professor Sloterdijk, how do philosophers express themselves nowadays? I remember reading the word 'explication' somewhere, but I think you're not an analytical philosopher concerned with the meaning of words. What defines a philosophical author now?

SLOTERDIJK: You're starting right at the beginning with questions that should be left until the end! The rules say you should start by asking things like: what do you think about the fact that autumn is coming? Or: what is your relationship to Switzerland? But you want to know fundamental things immediately and if I gave the right answers you would only be able to respond with enlightened silence.

BOPP: Let's avoid that. However, a journalist can hope for indulgence if he starts head on. Given the scope of your work, he is certainly at risk of asking about things he should really have known. And if you pose the question of the author's self-image you can be fairly sure that it has already been answered, at least indirectly.

SLOTERDIJK: So how does the author see himself? Seeing oneself as an author is a statement with its own implications. Most people can't or don't want to claim authorship. I can only do it myself by looking back at a life trajectory marked by around thirty occasions on which my books first entered the public arena. With a

* This interview between Peter Sloterdijk and Christoph Bopp appeared under the title 'Der neue Kategorische Imperativ: "Erfülle deine Genießerpflicht!"', in <litart.twoday.net/files/Peter-Sloterdijk-/>

Christoph Bopp is a Swiss journalist.

long track record like that you can hardly deny you are an author – even if your career was affected by a trend that ran through the cultural superstructure in the 1970s. At that time people used to talk seriously about a sad event called the 'death of the author'.

BOPP: Well, by now the subject is already dead philosophically as well.

SLOTERDIJK: Its wretched end is part of the same wave of declarations of death. Yet the subject is still around, haunting, very much alive, just like the ghostly 'author'. Take my own specific case: how can a dead man write thirty books? At which desk could he have done that?

BOPP: Anyway, you coined the phrase 'thinker on stage' for Nietzsche.

SLOTERDIJK: That expression contains part of my author theory. I described Nietzsche as a thinker who not only performed like an actor on stage but actually also saw his psyche as a stage on which rival 'artistic drives' duelled with each other. He offered his own self to these drives as a *theatrum belli* and let the conflicting energies fight each other. This is an image I was able to adapt for household use. We shouldn't envisage the author as a river flowing calmly and untroubled from source to estuary. True, there are states of fluidity, but the clashes are more important for production. The author is actually a moderator of the partial energies at work inside him, and his writing oversees the collisions.

BOPP: Does he describe them like an accident reporter?

SLOTERDIJK: He looks into his inner self and reports which corpses are lying on the street again today.

BOPP: In your book, *Rage and Time*, whose title alludes to Heidegger's *Being and Time*, you casually remarked that Heidegger was not the kind of author who – to quote Nietzsche again – would have been able to deal with such 'dangerous truths'. Do you mean Heidegger would have sidestepped such clashes or avoided them?

SLOTERDIJK: To avert any possible misunderstanding: Heidegger made an enormous contribution to contemporary philosophy. I was a follower of Critical Theory, however, and that means I was only able to concentrate on Heidegger after my return from India, after 1980. He had previously been regarded as a non-person in our circles and was buried under an obscure taboo. That's why I only discovered later what he had to offer – for example, a very inspiring theory of moods [*Stimmungen*]. This involves pre-logical shades of *Dasein* that precede all individual cognitions. Such gains in the scope of philosophical discourse are significant because they help to correct the over-exaggerated rationalism of tradition. They allow philosophy to connect up with a large variety of life experiences that were previously inaccessible to philosophical discourse.

BOPP: But aren't you very critical of Heidegger in *Rage and Time*?

SLOTERDIJK: Yes, I try to show that the founding of historical time – in fact, 'historicity' is one of the pathos-imbued words Heidegger used in his youth and middle period – didn't occur in the way he imagined it. We do not receive either a 'call of Being' or a 'call of care'. Instead, great history arises through the memory of injustice and the process of resentment. When the sediment of unprocessed and unrequited experience of suffering forms in human memories, a history-making mechanism goes into motion, a sort of 'causality of fate', as the early observers of tragic events described it. The effect is that the consequences of an evil deed reappear at a later time in another place.

BOPP: The timespan stretches from the suffered and remembered injustice to its retribution.

SLOTERDIJK: That's right. We can't comprehend the original process of the founding of time at all without investigating those feelings of setback and the transactions for reparation. At this point a gap opens up in Heidegger's studies, and I tried to close it in *Rage and Time*. In doing so, I couldn't avoid moving Heidegger closer to Nietzsche again. The latter broached the major moral topic of the epoch in the twentieth century with his theory of resentments. But aside from Max Scheler's contributions,[1] there was hardly any advance in the area of resentment analysis after Nietzsche's great intervention. It was high time to take a new approach to the phenomenon in the light of our experiences with the gigantic conflicts in the twentieth century. If we don't show how resentment could become the primary historical power in it, the whole epoch remains obscure.

BOPP: That seems to me not just a type of analysis, but also a totally different perspective on history. It means no longer looking at it as development, as an unfolding process. We can't explain any more how something became but, rather, in retrospect, we can see stages and events happen that become realized to some extent and become, in turn, the seeds for further realizations.

SLOTERDIJK: We should be mindful here of the synergy between involuntary and voluntary memory. The phenomenon of

[1] Max Scheler (1874–1928) was a German philosopher, psychologist, sociologist and anthropologist. He is known as the founder of philosophical anthropology.

resentment itself is composed of moments of voluntary and involuntary memory. Europeans were able to observe this recently in the remarkable process of the break-up of Yugoslavia. At that time Milošević preached the myth of lordly defeat to the Serbs. In his infamous speech at the Gazemistan memorial on the 600th anniversary of the Battle of Kosovo in 1389, he said that the more the Serbs had lost back then, the more they had won since. That was a sort of admission of failure of all histories fuelled by resentment: 'We' – whoever he actually meant by that, but in any case 'a collective of chosen losers' –

BOPP: 'We' have entered history ...

SLOTERDIJK: I have speculatively deduced far-reaching consequences from those kinds of 'entries'. I proposed describing the historical collective that is generally called 'peoples' or, more recently, 'nations', as groups processing resentment that put themselves under stress by remembrance of collectively experienced traumata. For most people, those traumata are something inherited from far away, something they could certainly not have suffered themselves. As an individual, I can't remember humiliation inflicted 600 years ago, but somehow I acquire joint ownership of this trauma.

BOPP: Identities that already carry the seed of violence within them to some extent....

SLOTERDIJK: After the Second World War the Germans showed in an exemplary fashion that there is an alternative way out of humiliation. They have worked on their trauma so intensively that they have completely broken out of the repetition compulsion. In the truest sense of the expression, they have become a different nation.

BOPP: You spoke earlier of 'ownership of a trauma', and you also work with economic metaphors in *Rage and Time*. The book features 'rage banks' where people can deposit their savings. That makes rage into 'capital' that can be invested. And investments are made to increase the capital. But if we talk about 'banks' there have to be 'bankers' who manage the resentment capital. Who would these 'historical subjects' be? Great figures? Lenin or Hitler?

SLOTERDIJK: Most of all, it is the political parties that use the function of resentment banks. The best way to describe the differences between parties is this: the more they move towards the edge of the spectrum, the more we can justly suspect them of making deposits in the collection of 'dirty energies'. In this context, what distinguishes the extreme left and the extreme right is that the left takes up the dirty energies to refine them whereas the right expresses them more or less unfiltered. The political pathologist's findings show that the left tends to dream and be hypocritical while the right tends to brawl and stink. That doesn't say anything about the criminal energies at work on both sides. Historical experience reveals that, in the twentieth century, for every murder in the name of race there were two or three murders in the name of class.

BOPP: Can you explain once again how this bank scheme functions?

SLOTERDIJK: To begin with, not only money can be accumulated but also affects such as rage. Moreover, knowledge or art collections have functions analogous to capitalism. Similarly, the Church collects the treasures of salvation. We can always talk of capital when values are accumulated at a collection point to be transferred from the form of treasures to the form of capital. A treasure lies passively on a pile, as in Scrooge McDuck's storehouse, or in the legendary gold cellars under Bahnhofstrasse in Zurich. Capital, on the other hand, is always travelling, always on investment tours.

BOPP: Does this imply that knowledge, too, is not inherently 'value free'?

SLOTERDIJK: As research it is structured in the form of knowledge capital. Accumulated knowledge is used as capital to create more knowledge.

BOPP: The crises are the essence of capitalism.

SLOTERDIJK: Valorization crises can also be seen in the non-monetary banking system. Knowledge loses value when what Thomas Kuhn called a 'paradigm shift' occurs, when new basic assumptions for the organization of realizations are established. In art history the crisis appears as a modernization boost that leads to a new relationship between the existing and the new. I am trying to show that an accumulation process and the related capital formation have also existed in the area of political affects. Above all, the classical internationalist left has positioned itself as the 'world bank of rage'. It has tried to operate a kind of emancipatory politics on a transnational scale with the outrage assets and rage assets of millions of small owners.

BOPP: With the promise that ordinary people will also have a share in the privileges of the rich.

SLOTERDIJK: Bank transactions are not the only context in which we can talk about yields and dividends. Interest should also accrue when the rage and anger account is in credit. That occurs when appropriate political practice leads customers' deposits to be converted into enhanced self-esteem. If my outrage credit is deposited in an efficiently managed rage bank, which means a party that works determinedly towards its goals, I am not just abstractly participating in an enterprise to improve the world, I also become part of a project that I am proud of and that improves my affective position. My rage is transformed into enhanced self-esteem. Unfortunately, the left-wing parties have often failed to achieve this. Then the clients withdraw their deposits. They either become apolitical or take their savings to a right-wing bank, which then practises direct revenge politics and chooses the uncensored form of expressing rage. The right-wing bank directors appear relatively uncensored as rowdies, populists, provocateurs and rabble-rousers, drawing in the frustrated voters and rabble sympathizers. At any rate, a person who identifies with the party boss's rabble-rousing gets gratification very directly. My rage will no longer be idealistically ennobled but at least I will be able to express it openly as part of my life. It's obvious that such scenarios must end in disappointment. For every slap in the face the populist gives he gets one and a half slaps back – a classic loss-making business. Generally speaking, the problem of political parties seen as rage banks is the mismanagement of affects. That can go as far as open investment fraud.

BOPP: Could you give an example?

SLOTERDIJK: From the perspective of the philosophy of history, the biggest emotional fraud in twentieth-century history occurred in August 1914. This triggered the implosion of left-wing internationalism, following which the parliamentary left in Germany and elsewhere granted the war credits, falling into step with the policy of waging nationalist warfare. This meant that the left wing's transnational and progressively invested emotional credit was misused for a nationalist-imperialist war. The left-wing system has basically never recovered from that disaster. It also partly explains the pathological radicalization that occurred in Russia after 1917 and the daydreaming on the extreme flanks of politics.

BOPP: The thymotic impulses seem to have died down to some extent in Western Europe today. We have accepted that the capitalist system satisfies our needs adequately and we can safely leave it to shape the future. There are still conflicts now and then, but they are ritualized and occur periodically between labour unions and the state. Labour-union bosses have to be credible and convince their clientele that they have fought and haven't let themselves be cheated.

SLOTERDIJK: But these negotiating rituals are much more important than people generally think because they are about a thymotic yield. Conflicts between social partners are never just about percentages. Wrangling for recognition and satisfying frustrated expectations is always important as well.

BOPP: We really have it so good. After all, we've got everything. Everything is always available. Consumerism instead of communism. . . . *(A woman's voice over the loudspeaker says, 'Would you like breakfast? We're happy to serve you.')*

SLOTERDIJK: There's the answer to your question! A voice from above tells you your needs. That's consumerism personified. For sure you would like breakfast? Yes? Then it's your damned duty to enjoy it. And if you can't enjoy it, our job is to show you ways and possibilities to enjoy things anyway. This is the new categorical imperative: do your duty to enjoy!

BOPP: Can this imperative be generalized?

SLOTERDIJK: Absolutely. All it needs is for us to recognize that we are being called on to metabolize. There's not much to object to in that. People used to see it as a mortal curse that human beings – as metabolic beings – are bound to the material sphere. The spirit, however, knows no hunger and is driven at most by a longing to see the higher things. Today, things are shown in reverse. Now you are supposed to forget everything that could release you from needs. Avoid the temptation of not needing anything at all costs. Don't get the idea you can cheat your way out of the permanent cycle of consumption. Your body has to do its consumer duty.

BOPP: Only the body?

SLOTERDIJK: No, the senses were also recruited for duty a long time ago. The eye is on image duty day and night. The ear is on music and sound duty and, since the wellness wave started rolling, the skin is permanently on feeling duty as well. The modern angel of prosperity floats above everything. It no longer says, 'Fear not!' as it did to the shepherds way back then, but instead, 'Enjoy it!'

BOPP: Is it a monotheistic angel?

[Peter Sloterdijk's latest book has the title *Gottes Eifer: Vom Kampf der drei Monotheismen.*[2]]

SLOTERDIJK: Consumerism is a kind of behaviour with a high capacity for anthropological connectivity. I suspect that all cultures that have involved a high degree of superego formation can veer towards consumerism relatively easily. People who are used to thinking in terms of service and performance can extend these principles to consumption as well. First you achieve something, and then you can afford something.

BOPP: But isn't the capitalist the ascetic and the aristocrat the epicure?

[2] English edition: Peter Sloterdijk, *God's Zeal: The Battle of the Three Monotheisms* (Cambridge: Polity), 2009.

SLOTERDIJK: That was Max Weber's opinion, but his view was one-sided. At the very least, capitalism was driven just as much by the luxury of the epicurean classes. We still get instructive illustrations of this today: a psycho-historical phenomenon has spread in Africa and the Arabian oil states – an overabundance of epicurean uselessness. Overnight, the pride of Arabian manhood was swamped with unexpected wealth, and this created the oil sheikhs, the newcomers to extreme consumerism who can be compared with the Russian nouveau riche that emerged recently. These people have never had work experience. This shows how easily consumerism penetrates into the psyche: people are evidently beings attuned to luxury by nature. Accession to wealth is possible from all sides. Whether Shintoist, Calvinist, Catholic or animist – people react very similarly once they get rich: they finally feel understood and accepted!

BOPP: Is luxury capable of globalization? Could it bring eternal peace?

SLOTERDIJK: That is psychologically and economically impossible. Part of the nature of luxury is that it creates strong paradoxes. Satisfaction with life can never be derived from net luxury. It lives chiefly from comparison: most people would gladly do without absolute advantages as long as they are relatively better off than others. Not everybody can take first place. This paradox is insurmountable, and no kind of egalitarianism can get around it. There will always be a group of people that are more 'equal' than all the others.

# 27

# EVEN A GOD CAN'T SAVE US

## *Interview with Julia Encke**

ENCKE: Mr Sloterdijk, why must we change our life?

SLOTERDIJK: The global crisis dictates change. We must change our life decisively because otherwise we are participating in an economic and ecological programme of self-annihilation. In the ancient history of humankind there also were stern authorities, gods, gurus and teachers who troubled their followers with enormous demands. Nowadays, we have to deal with an ungodly goddess called 'crisis' who demands that we evolve new forms of life. Human groups usually have a long-term project, a will to continued existence. But that project of permanence is completely incompatible with the present modus vivendi. Incredible things are happening in this context.

ENCKE: What exactly do you mean?

SLOTERDIJK: For example, the state has reached such a peak of helplessness that it is openly considering whether to give its citizens money to go shopping. Unbelievable! We have to be publicly reminded to maintain at all costs the level of extravagance we once achieved. I can still remember how Edmund Stoiber[1] told the people of Munich during an earlier crisis, 'Go on, give your wife a fur coat

* This conversation between Peter Sloterdijk and Julia Encke appeared under the title 'Uns hilft kein Gott' ['No God will Help Us'], in the *Frankfurter Allgemeine Sonntagszeitung* (22 March 2009): 21.

At the time of the interview Julia Encke was a member of the *FAZ* newspaper's editorial team in Berlin.

[1] The southern German politician Edmund Stoiber was Minister President of the Federal State of Bavaria from 1993 to 2007 and head of the German Christian Democratic Party from 1999 to 2007.

now!' The reason was that Rieger Pelze, a leading fur goods store in Munich, had a financial crisis, and Minister President Stoiber, who was a stalwart supporter of the Bavarian system of nepotism and a personal friend of the firm, thought almost like an old comrade from 1968 that 'the personal is political'. The present procedures for rescuing the extravagant society aren't any less incredible. Overnight we have been catapulted into a giant seminar on economics and anthropology where people reflect on how global and real expenditure can continue.

ENCKE: Who is supposed to change their life? Do you really mean everybody? Or do you mean a specific 'elite'?

SLOTERDIJK: My book makes the first ever attempt at a literal interpretation of the generic subtitle of Nietzsche's *Zarathustra*: 'A Book for Everyone and No One'. It is 'for no one' because the elites to whom the book could be addressed do not exist yet. At the same time, it is 'for everyone' because a new selection process has begun which will determine who lets the crisis speak to them. Humankind will divide, and is already dividing as we watch, into those who carry on as always and those who are prepared to make changes.

ENCKE: Let's take an example: Peer Steinbrück.[2] What should he change?

SLOTERDIJK: The first thing he has to understand is that his mission can't be to secure jobs on board the *Titanic*. He should study icebergs a little more carefully. Jobs on board the *Titanic* only existed as long as the ship was afloat. Incidentally, nobody would gladly step into Steinbrück's shoes. He is in a position whose occupants are bound to become unhappy. He knows better than anybody else that the right things can't be financed.

ENCKE: What is your advice to him?

SLOTERDIJK: To reflect that, from now on, everything that lacks a sufficient vision for the future will be seen one day as a contribution to the collision with the ultimate iceberg. He has to persuade himself and his colleagues all over the world to create joint advisory boards that make politics capable of pursuing clear long-term projects again. Politics has to be emancipated from election-period panic.

ENCKE: What can I do personally as a journalist?

SLOTERDIJK: You can react against the pressure to talk about irrelevant things. Journalists are called up to the distraction front

[2] The politician Peer Steinbrück was Federal German Minister of Finance from 2005 to 2009 and deputy head of the German Social Democratic Party in the same period.

every day. Austria has just gone through an astonishingly short 'Fritzl week' and we can't thank the Austrian justice system enough for succeeding in closing the trial in three and a half days with a succinct judgement.[3]

ENCKE: You mean you're actually not complaining about Austria!

SLOTERDIJK: That's unusual for me. But the Austrian authorities have spared the rest of the world endless debates, and not least themselves. You can imagine what our press in Germany would have done in tandem with our justice system – we would have been treated to a festival of unnecessary news for months. The story would have been exploited to a much greater extent as legal drama and scandal journalism, with a full demonstration of the parasitic function of the press: to distract from the important issues, which has long since become its major function.

ENCKE: How do you see yourself? As a coach for improving the world, or as a postmodern guru?

SLOTERDIJK: Well, philosophers are persons with a strong monologue. On the one hand, there is somebody inside them who shares the common human confusion about the state of the world today. On the other hand, a part of their personality claims they have learned something and can give advice. The latter figure, who sits with me in the consultant's seat, may have become a little more imposing at the moment. I have listened in to the world situation and related my present perceptions to the general knowledge about the evolution of high cultures in the past 3,000 years. This produces some urgent messages.

ENCKE: Not everybody wants to hear those urgent messages. In your book you accuse intellectuals of summarily dismissing people who give serious warnings as pompous idiots. You say that hardly anybody wants to face up to the extent of the threat. Do you think these people are cynics or are they simply too naïve?

SLOTERDIJK: In the present case there isn't a complete alternative between cynical and naïve. Twenty-five years ago, when I wrote *Critique of Cynical Reason*, I tried to squeeze the whole typology of the intellectual field into these two alternatives: either people are naïve, in which case they are too close to the problems, or they are cynical, which means they are too indifferent to the problems.

[3] Sloterdijk is referring to the case of Josef Fritzl, a man from Amstetten in Austria who imprisoned one of his daughters for twenty-four years and repeatedly raped her. She bore seven children by him. The crime was discovered in 2008.

Today we need a third position. I'm talking about people who are neither cynical nor naïve.

ENCKE: You mean people who deconstruct everything to keep the world at bay?

SLOTERDIJK: Deconstructivism has become plausible partly because modernism has produced too many embarrassingly naïve forms of world salvation. The social catastrophes of the twentieth century stemmed from ideologies formulated by certain semi-visionary people who solved the mystery of the world with grand prophetic gestures. Whether private property or subversive Judaism was blamed for all evils – the deconstructive attitude was always justified in opposition to seductive, primitive formulas.

ENCKE: But that isn't enough any more?

SLOTERDIJK: Richard Rorty[4] once described his colleagues in the philosophical and humanities departments somewhat bitterly as 'detached cosmopolitan spectators'. What he meant is: you talk about the crisis as if it were an opera production. At most we stand on the periphery looking at the catastrophes through opera glasses, without understanding that many disasters that occur today not only contain their own inherent harmful aspect, but also have a signifying quality for our future.

ENCKE: What do you mean by a 'signifying quality'?

SLOTERDIJK: Hans Jonas and Carl Friedrich von Weizsäcker had already raised the issue of 'warning catastrophes' back in the 1980s.[5] They meant that humankind receives warnings from the real world that have to be decoded and translated into the behaviour of individuals and institutions. That's exactly what people who are satisfied with the role of detached cosmopolitan theatregoers can't do.

ENCKE: Don't we also use an opera glass for protection? If people are really confronted with that degree of real threat, it can make them incapable of acting, and can drive them to suicide in extreme cases. People are creatures that need protection.

SLOTERDIJK: For 3,000 years the avant-garde of humankind has lived in this situation: that they see something overpowering and the intelligentsia shivers. It seems to me the concept of 'God' was one of the strongest protective shields. For an aeon, humans

[4] Richard Rorty (1931–2007) was an American philosopher and comparatist.

[5] Hans Jonas (1903–93) was a German-born American philosopher who was a professor at the New School for Social Research in New York City. Carl Friedrich von Weizsäcker (1912–2007) was a German physicist, philosopher and expert on peace studies.

retreated behind it to defend themselves from the monster. Anyone who saw the outer side of the shield would be frozen to a pillar of salt. Remember the shield of Perseus with the terrifying head of the gorgon as its centrepiece. But the hero is on the inner side of the shield and turns the terror outwards. This image is a very good description of the situation of the intelligentsia when it tries to protect itself in close combat with reality.

ENCKE: Do you mean we must shake off false security and live more dangerously?

SLOTERDIJK: Above all, we should think more consciously about danger. What lies ahead is a kind of gorgon-like enlightenment. We must decide to build a global immune system that opens up a common survival perspective. We have to work now on a protective shield for the earth, for humankind and for its technological environment. That will require global ecological management. I call this co-immunism.

ENCKE: As at other points in your book, this is a wordplay on communism. Is *You Must Change Your Life* a left-wing manifesto?

SLOTERDIJK: I am not envisaging a neo-communist project. Communism, as we know, tried to be a religion of conquest, like an atheist Islam, and to pull all industrialized nations into its orbit in an aggressive expansionist movement. What did the communists really want? To seize political power so as to institute extreme educational dictatorships for immature populations. You have been warned against repetition. The movement postulated in my book doesn't aim at forced conversion. We have to achieve everything voluntarily on the basis of good advice – or 'assisted willingness', if you like. That's why I talk throughout the book about the life of practice and about shaping oneself by self-improvement.

ENCKE: You have a fairly positive image of human beings.

SLOTERDIJK: I start from a strong ontological thesis: intelligence exists. This leads to a strong ethical thesis: there is a positive correlation between intelligence and the will to self-preservation. Since Adorno, we have known that this correlation can be questioned – that was the most promising idea of older Critical Theory. It started from the observation that intelligence can go in the wrong direction and confuse self-destruction with self-preservation. That is one of the unforgettable lessons of the twentieth century. What is on the agenda now is an affirmative theory of global co-immunity. It is the foundation of, and orientation for, the many and varied practices of shared survival.

ENCKE: Have you designed a utopia?

SLOTERDIJK: If you called this utopian it would make my hair stand on end! If you were right, I would belong to the tradition of mad men who wanted to make the world better. On the contrary, I thought I had demonstrated pragmatism, though admittedly with a dash of prophetic agitation.

# 28

# A PLUG FOR HIGHER ENERGIES

## *Interview with Mateo Kries**

KRIES: Mr Sloterdijk, the title of your book, *Du mußt Dein Leben ändern* [*You Must Change Your Life*] refers to Rainer Maria Rilke, a contemporary of Steiner. You preface the book with a quotation from Nietzsche that also made a great impact on Steiner, in which Nietzsche advocated the practising existence. Is your interest in Steiner connected with the life-reform movements at the beginning of the twentieth century?

SLOTERDIJK: Life reform was the major topic in the period around 1900. It was the alternative to the concept of revolution that had structured people's consciousness of the possibility of transforming the world since 1789. It put the idea of non-political or supra-political transformation on the agenda. Life reformers such as Nietzsche and Steiner held the common view that it was pointless to carry on repeating political phrases and founding a new party in the back room of a pub. They thought it was much more important to rebuild one's whole life from the smallest elements, as it were. They posed the question: how can we maintain human existence in a vertical tension that still does justice to the human being as a metaphysical animal? How can we create a pull from above, although the ladder on which people climb up can't be leaned against anything up there any more, because the other side no longer exists? The

* This interview between Peter Sloterdijk and Mateo Kries appeared under the title 'Ein Stecker für höhere Energien', in *Die Welt* newspaper (25 October 2011); available at: <http://www.welt.de/print/die_welt/kultur/article13679318/Ein-Stecker- fuer-die-hoeheren-Energien.html>.

At the time of the interview Mateo Kries was chief curator at the Vitra Design Museum in Weil am Rhein.

twentieth century ended with the recognition that the revolutionaries were wrong and the life reformers right. Meanwhile, fear of the gurutocracy, rule by gurus, has receded to some extent and today people are more willing to see Steiner as a quite normal genius rather than a guru.

KRIES: Still, we have to realize that Steiner vanished off the map from his death in 1925 to the end of the twentieth century, and was dismissed as a spiritual crank. Anthroposophy became fossilized, and that led to the whole movement being isolated. Steiner was associated with Kandinsky and Jawlensky, but in the succeeding decades his students only developed his radical aesthetics in minor ways. Wasn't there some justification for the criticism of Steiner and anthroposophy?

SLOTERDIJK: The few followers of anthroposophy I knew in the 1960s to 1970s made an unpleasant impression. They went around as if they were imitating an angel who was practising how to stride like a human. Moreover, pop culture had long since made its mark on us, and the anthroposophists were still talking about their eurhythmics. In those days anthroposophy followers were out of pace with their surrounding culture, but they are catching up now. We have new grounds for asking what makes the movement relevant to the present day. One possible answer is that on a broad level we were no longer able to agree with the answers given by classical and contemporary philosophy to the question of the character of subjectivity. To some extent, Steiner made it possible to access human subjectivity in an upward direction. He found the plug for accessing higher energies that were normally banned from the conversations of middle-class society. That can't fail to have consequences because it creates intellectual dissonance. Think of Gottfried Benn's dictum: 'In Germany philosophers who aren't linguistically capable of expressing their world view tend to be called seers.'

KRIES: The concept of the seer is appropriate because Steiner actually demanded that people should try to imagine seeing abstract-philosophical associations in pictures 'before their eyes'. He made the famous blackboard drawings during his lectures.

SLOTERDIJK: In a sense, those blackboard drawings are the precursors of PowerPoint presentations. When he was speaking Steiner relied on the idea embracing him at the right moment – a theme that can be traced back to the heights of German idealism. Fichte, for example, made it unmistakably clear in his instructions to his students that the lecturer has to be open to the flash of illumination that may come while he is speaking. The concept of the medium is central for understanding the Steiner phenomenon. It partly explains the fascination that still emanates from his work and personality today. People are increasingly realizing that a definition of mediality based solely on machines and apparatuses is not enough. We have to return to the concept of the medium established in the nineteenth century, which is intricately interwoven with ghost sightings.

KRIES: How does that relate to Steiner in a modern-day context?

SLOTERDIJK: Personal mediums are people with antennae. Hugo Ball, a co-founder of Dadaism who experienced a spiritual change after 1918, wrote in an important essay at the time that the whole world had become a medium. Steiner had already realized that two decades earlier. His life curve ended at the moment when the process of the masses becoming the medium with the aid of popular broadcasting began. The first radio test broadcasts took place in 1923. Steiner died in 1925. By 1930, probably one in five of all German households owned a radio receiver. A new form of social synthesis via the ear emerged. Steiner had put out his antennae much more sensitively than everybody else who had been engaging in what has been called 'discourse' since Michel Foucault founded discourse theory. 'Discourse' literally means running to and fro, but not receiving live at the moment.

KRIES: Looking at Steiner in those major historical contexts, his death also coincided with the end of the earlier phase of modernism, the phase that was charged with expressionism. This was followed by the triumph of rationalism from the second half of the twentieth century on, and in the post-war period there was a pervasive longing for a middle-class mainstream in which there was no place for Steiner anyway. Artists like Sigmar Polke, who said, 'Higher beings commanded: paint the top right-hand corner black!' were loners. It is only today that the social constellations seem to offer the conditions again for Polke's oeuvre, with all its ramifications, to be located within the intellectual history of the modern age, and not as the work of a weird outsider.[1] Why do you think it took so long?

SLOTERDIJK: It may be due to another factor that co-determined the cycles of readability of Steiner's work. I'm thinking of a theme that Helmut Lethen[2] had already put on the agenda of the humanities twenty-five years ago: the 'Birth of the Cool' in the 1920s from the perspective of the history of ideas. In the 1920s, there was a cold snap in the intellectual sphere with quite a different impact from

[1] Sigmar Polke (1941–2010) was a German painter and photographer known for his work in postmodernist realism.

[2] Helmut Lethen is a Germanist and cultural scholar. He is director of the International Research Centre for Cultural Studies in Vienna.

that which Paul Valéry meant, for example, when he remarked with rather paternalistic Cartesian overtones that good intellect is 'dry'. From the 1920s on, the motto was 'Good intellect is cold'. If we extrapolate this position as a constant factor at work in the background character of twentieth-century culture, it is clear why a system like Steiner's has always risked being marginalized. After all, in many ways it is the epitome of uncoolness. Coolness will have nothing to do with improving life and the world. As soon as a do-gooder enters the room, the coolness enthusiasts leave.

KRIES: Has that changed today?

SLOTERDIJK: Today's zeitgeist allows more scope to specific forms of uncoolness again. Many years ago I read Nietzsche's *Zarathustra* with my American students. I was afraid it would be too full of pathos for them. But they simply read the whole thing right through like a rap. They didn't find it at all bombastic and overblown. They had no trouble reading Nietzsche's extreme flights of rhapsodic style, which are difficult for people educated in old Europe, straight off the page.

KRIES: Your view may be confirmed if we look at particular tendencies in fashion today. In periods of almost overwhelming progress, the things that are really fashionable are those that look rather uncool and contradict the accelerated tempo – at the moment, heavy horn-rimmed glasses and knitted ties. But there are also other parallels to the present. Think of the many objects and buildings with a polygonal and crystalline form, like certain designs by Steiner's circle. At first these designs even seem to draw aesthetic inspiration from the molecular world, yet their heaviness and occasional clumsiness are reminiscent of the yearning for stability and solidity in an increasingly fast-moving age. Paul Virilio interpreted Steiner's Goetheanum in the sense of his own bunker thesis as a space for protection against the temptations and risks of accelerated modernism. As decelerated architecture, so to speak. Do you agree?

SLOTERDIJK: In the first place I understand houses as immune systems in spatial form. On this definition we can ask what happens if the form really follows the function. What is the way to build when the immunitary imperative is at the beginning of a spatial creation? A house would then be envisaged beginning with its most intimate rooms and not with the splendid entrance hall. Good architects conceive the house starting from the bedrooms, whereas the modernists, who have brought the cold trend of the modern age into the home, have come up with weird proposals such as folding the bed up against the wall in the daytime.

KRIES: Steiner, on the other hand, designed a bed for his Haus

Duldeck that looks like a gigantic ocean steamer. It almost seems to swallow you with its curves and bumps ...

SLOTERDIJK: One of the key words for understanding some of the more recent architectural tendencies is a word borrowed from English sociology, 'embedding'. Given the ubiquitous, rampant tendency towards being mobile and dis-embedding, people are getting interested in foundational or embedding situations again. Embedding means that humans, as beings sensitive to spheres, want to understand space as space for immersion.

KRIES: The immersion always includes immersion in an endless intellectual cosmos. Steiner once said that if we could pull a human heart inside out we would get a universe. This can be applied to Steiner's architecture and design. His interiors are the reverse of his intellectual cosmos. And to refer back to your image, he wanted to listen in to that cosmos. Is that, perhaps, one of the intersection points for Steiner's artistic creations and his philosophical works?

SLOTERDIJK: In his case the two things are inextricably interwoven. Steiner created a kind of antenna anthropology that we can't simply do without any more, even if we have to rewrite every phrase of this doctrine. Since the dawn of the modern age, people actually have been listening in to the ether and want to know what is to be done. Martin Buber wrote in his book *Mystische Zeugnisse aller Zeiten und Völker*, published in 1906/07 – and this is very typical for the reception situation of early modernism – 'We listen to our innermost selves – and do not know which sea we hear murmuring.'[3] Steiner had begun with a much more precise reception at that time. He spoke as if being dictated to, and apparently heard in the ether a mandate to attempt life reform that put people of our era on a new track. Now, 100 years later, after the twentieth century – a lost century from a spiritual perspective – we are standing on the same spot again.

Today, the phrase 'You must change your life' is no longer interpreted only in terms of Buddhism, Christianity or Stoicism, or in Nietzsche's sense, but as a mission to develop a form of life that makes human coexistence on this endangered planet possible. If you tune your antennae more finely you can hear this on all sides. Large numbers of people feel this very clearly, and Steiner is an ideal transmitter for this unavoidable message. He was important, and remains so, because he was one of the people who put out antennae even before the birth of radio.

[3] Martin Buber, *Mystical Confessions: The Heart of Mysticism*, ed. Paul Mendes-Flor (New York: Syracuse University Press), 1996.

# 29

# MORTGAGING THE AIR

## The Financial Crisis

*Conversation with Gabor Steingart and Torsten Riecke**

STEINGART/RIECKE: Let's start with the biggest question of all, the debt question: who is mainly responsible for the present mess in Europe? Is it the finance market systems impelled by greed, as you once put it, or the politicians dependent on their own promises? Or is it the citizens themselves, who always want more than they are prepared to pay for?

SLOTERDIJK: It may sound odd – and your question expresses it wonderfully – but today we are coming back from modern debts to classical ones. The question is: who is to blame for the debts? This implies there are obviously two ways people can be tied to a guilty past. The modern way is through debts. Financial debts are rather like sins we can be forgiven for by redeeming them ourselves – whereas moral debt has to be forgiven by others.

STEINGART/RIECKE: But it seems we can't redeem our debts any more; we can only hope for forgiveness.

SLOTERDIJK: The old cloven hoof of religion has reappeared in the concept of debt in modern finance – from the moment, in fact, that the debts grew so big that the idea of redeeming them lost all credibility. The debt mechanism can work as long as there are

* This interview between Peter Sloterdijk, Gabor Steingart and Torsten Riecke appeared under the title 'Die Staaten verpfänden die Luft und Banken atmen tief durch' ['The Countries Pledge Air and Banks Take Deep Breaths'], in *Handelsblatt* magazine (17 December 2011).

Gabor Steingart is a German journalist and author. He was editor-in-chief of *Handelsblatt* from 2010 to 2012.

Torsten Riecke is a journalist and was head of the Opinion and Analysis section of *Handelsblatt* at the time of this interview.

people who seriously believe that a debtor is in a position (a) to pay off the whole loan amount, and (b) to pay the extra charge in the form of interest. Anybody who can credit something like that can become a creditor.

STEINGART/RIECKE: What you describe was the basis of economic behaviour in transactions in the past 200 years.

SLOTERDIJK: Much longer! A good example occurred in the sixteenth century: the wealthy tradesman Jakob Fugger had the Tyrolean prince give him the country's silver mines as security, whereas a bungling relative from another branch of the family, Fugger vom Reh, accepted the city of Lüttich [Liège] as a deposit – but realized one morning that a city can't be a deposit because it can't be seized in foreclosure. To have trust you need to be smart about security.

STEINGART/RIECKE: But hasn't the connection between guilt and debts been lost because in modern economic theory debts can't be considered as guilt any more? Aren't they regarded as investments, and isn't it therefore seen as a kind of basic right for present generations to help themselves to the putative treasures of future generations? The Americans call that a stimulus package. Nobody in modern credit capitalism thinks about redeeming debts any more.

SLOTERDIJK: Basically it's a matter of cultivating a pathological relationship to the past. Crimes or sins are pathological – they bind perpetrators to what has happened by foreshadowing the suffering that will ensue later. Their crimes will catch up with them. The long arm of guilt that stretches out from the past to grab people in the present is represented mainly by credit in modern society. Credit, in turn, has to be tied to two stabilizing factors: first, the deposit, and, second, a state that guarantees foreclosure.

STEINGART/RIECKE: On that argument the cuckoo, not the German eagle, should represent the state.

SLOTERDIJK: It would generally be helpful if we talked less about a federal chancellor and more about a federal bailiff. The real semantic or juridical-moral centre of the body politic is located where legal enforcement is guaranteed. For a community that relies mainly on a credit-driven economy, the mechanism that assures credit by enforcement is the ultimate moral criterion. In other words, before we expect justice from the state we should be clear that the state, as guarantor of legal enforcement, has long since been at the heart of specifically modern transactions.

STEINGART/RIECKE: In Greece the creditors have realized that they have lent more than they can impound. Evidently they are not very smart about collateral either. For them it is like a replay of the Hans Fugger situation.

SLOTERDIJK: We are reaching the point again where states are going to experience what happened to Fugger vom Reh. As we know, he dropped out of economic history, whereas the family line represented by Jakob the Wealthy prospered – due to collateral smartness. And that's exactly what is missing today. Governments mortgage the air over their national territory and banks take deep breaths. This may lead to a European-wide disorientation of historical dimensions, possibly comparable with the massive moral-economic meltdown of 1922/23, the period of hyperinflation.

STEINGART/RIECKE: Since that period the Germans have been more traumatized than other nations, and even more deeply after the second hyperinflation after the end of the Second World War. Is this moral way of reflecting on the crisis typically German?

SLOTERDIJK: I would say that the German language is delightfully German in this respect – it delivers these ideas to our doorstep. We shouldn't criticize it for one of its merits, that of making it easy to understand connections that might otherwise remain obscure. Saying the words 'debt' and 'guilt' in English doesn't clarify anything, and that particular play on words doesn't work at all in the Romance languages. But if we consider the issue, we come to the same conclusions all round because it is always the knots that were tied in the past that bind the present to the past.

STEINGART/RIECKE: What you are saying is a curious way to provoke the people who coined the slogan 'Occupy Wall Street'. They say, 'Occupy' or, even better, 'Expropriate the creditors!' You argue back: 'Creditors have a right to demand repayment of the debts on their books.' Is the protest against the banks simply a big mistake?

SLOTERDIJK: First of all, the debtor is always the guilty party, the party that owes something. Given this, it would be good to set up a lawyer's office that specializes in reclaiming debts opposite every bank branch, to make the connection clear to people coming out of the bank with loans. The probability that a borrower will get into debt in the sense of owing both interest and the capital sum is constantly increasing. This makes us suspect the seriousness of the borrower's intentions. Our confidence erodes fastest when the really big players turn out to be the most unscrupulous because they never seriously considered repaying the loans.

STEINGART/RIECKE: Do you mean the United States?

SLOTERDIJK: The Americans illustrate this very well: they have long since stopped thinking how to repay the national debt. Of course they talk about saving, but in today's parlance that means reducing new borrowing. My grandmother interpreted the concept of saving very differently in her day.

STEINGART/RIECKE: Do you mean the concept has become distorted?

SLOTERDIJK: Saving used to mean putting something aside. Today's finance ministers use the word to applaud themselves when they make fewer new debts.

STEINGART/RIECKE: In other words, the banks stand acquitted?

SLOTERDIJK: Be careful! The banks as banks aren't responsible for every mistake. First of all, for a society driven by money, honest belief in repayment is indispensable.

STEINGART/RIECKE: We could say that just an illusion of repayment would be worth a great deal. But even that is unreal in the case of Greece, as well as Japan and the USA.

SLOTERDIJK: Repayment illusion is a lovely name for a moral construct protected by the state – provided the state itself remains credible as a debtor. That is hardly the case today.

STEINGART/RIECKE: The illusion is fed by the fact that the debts are continually recycled. All the debtor nations pay their debts every few months with new debts.

SLOTERDIJK: That's an idea Dante himself couldn't have come up with. We should add a fourth part to his *Divine Comedy*. As we know, Dante conceived Purgatory as the purification system for venial – let's say, redeemable – sins. They would be marked on the sinners' brows with seven 'P's – even in the hell of purification everything important must be in writing. After every stage, one 'P' (for *peccatum*) would be erased, until the former sinner would stand there with a clear brow. No one in medieval times could imagine that charges from the past could be restructured. But that is exactly what would happen in the annexe to Purgatory. The drawback is that one would never get away completely from the past again and there would be no chance of being accepted into the sphere of heavenly joys.

STEINGART/RIECKE: Ludwig Erhard[1] said that moderation was an integral part of the social market economy. Have we forgotten that?

SLOTERDIJK: Most people let their income determine their level of moderation. True, you can artificially boost your income with private credit, but income is the determining factor, and for the majority of people it is modest enough to ensure they don't build castles in the air.

[1] Ludwig Erhard (1897–1977) was a conservative German politician, Minister of Economics and architect of the 1960s 'economic miracle' in West Germany. He was Chancellor of the Federal Republic of Germany from 1963 to 1966.

STEINGART/RIECKE: The citizen, the ego, stays within limits. But the state, the 'we', isn't able to?

SLOTERDIJK: One thing we should not forget in this situation: the first half of the twentieth century was marked by so-called 'system competition'. We had real existing socialism on the doorstep, that is, the communist command economy. The situation created enormous psycho-political pressure, especially here in Germany. It inspired the general social democratization of the West. In other words, comrade Stalin gave us the gift of the welfare state. But that competition had definitively ended even before the implosion of the Soviet Union. Margaret Thatcher knew what she was doing when she held out for over a year in the battle with the British miners.

STEINGART/RIECKE: But communism was still alive in her time.

SLOTERDIJK: It still existed as a system but no longer as a source of inspiration or a pervasive threat. By 1975, if not before, people had recognized that communism was a paper tiger, an empty threat. Back then, there were authors who seriously said: 'Now is the moment to try out real existing capitalism for the first time.' Until then, there had never been pure capitalism. Instead there had been a mixed system, let's say a worldwide relatively successful semi-socialism that had developed out of the systemic alternatives of social democracy versus Leninism. The removal of pressure from the Soviet Bloc engendered the neoliberal phase that is coming to an end today.

STEINGART/RIECKE: Going back to your concept of semi-socialism: have we possibly gone too far with system convergence? Socialism, as we know, was completely run down. The machines were worn out; the people, intellectual and spiritual life, and the buildings as well. But we in the West – contrary to what the left wing often claims – didn't take from the rich and give to the poor; we took from creditors. Semi-socialism allied with the banks and got loans in the night to impress voters the following day. Haven't we simply relocated the wear and tear in the future?

SLOTERDIJK: To a great extent, national debt is an indicator of a structural deficit of socialism in the community coffers. What can't be obtained in the form of taxation is borrowed from irresponsible creditors. The social deficit expresses that precisely in the scale of national debt. In the era of flourishing Rhine capitalism in Germany,[2] the level of national debt was low because

[2] 'Rhine capitalism' (sometimes called 'social capitalism') denotes the economic policies in Germany and other European countries in the 1980s at

semi-socialism functioned better under conservative governments. Ludwig Erhard's social market economy rewrote this concept so resonantly that even conservatives liked it. In reality we have long been living in a fiscally organized semi-socialism integrated by the mass media and based on an interest-driven economy that many people call capitalism.

STEINGART/RIECKE: Do you mean it was not the 'invisible hand of the market' but the invisible hand of Stalin that gave us the social market economy?

SLOTERDIJK: Stalin's hand certainly played a major role, and trade-union positions were much stronger at that time as well. Most of all, we had a completely different basic psycho-political situation back then: Almost everybody believed in ceaseless improvement. The real historical breach came at the moment when people in our part of the world found themselves looking not at a clear horizon but at a horizon that was cloudy, even menacing. In psycho-political terms that is the primary fact in the present-day West. In the past we could cultivate luxury pessimism: just remember the dying forests. In tune with that luxury pessimism we also had a hysterical, over-exaggerated attitude to the atomic threat. Nowadays realistic pessimism has the upper hand.

STEINGART/RIECKE: How do we get out of this mess of debt again? The neoliberal approach is politically discredited, and people are starting to believe in the strong state again. Are the left-wingers correct after all, as Frank Schirrmacher, editor of the *Frankfurter Allgemeine Zeitung*, has said?

SLOTERDIJK: Unfortunately, the left can't be right because they haven't introduced any new ideas into the debate. They only repeat washed-out slogans: 'You must take it by violence from those who have.'

STEINGART/RIECKE: The left responds to the debt question unambiguously by saying the banks are to blame – they have pumped us full of the debt drug like a dealer.

SLOTERDIJK: That's like the cigarette smoker who gets a tumour and claims damages from Marlboro.

STEINGART/RIECKE: But who is supposed to liberate the state from the misery it created itself? In the end, doesn't the money have to come from the rich?

SLOTERDIJK: That is the obvious conclusion. The money is there. The wealth is enormous. Nonetheless, from a psycho-political

---

the time of the 'neo-American' economics advocated by Margaret Thatcher and Ronald Reagan.

perspective, we have been cheering on the wrong side for centuries. We have seen redistribution as something that can be achieved either by murderous violence, as in Leninism, or by moderately gentle fiscal force as in the Western system. But that was done without reckoning with the citizens.

STEINGART/RIECKE: Will the rich give their money voluntarily?

SLOTERDIJK: You know, taxes are a wonderful instrument for testing the donor capability of different population strata. We have 40 million working people in employment in Germany. Around 16 million are exempt from direct taxes because of their low incomes. They are also not heavily involved in the VAT system because they spend a large part of their income on food, which has a VAT rate of only 7 per cent. It is nonsense to say, as we hear so often in the tax debate, that everybody pays the same amount of VAT. If we look at this pseudo-truth in detail we can see, of course, that the same people who top the list for paying VAT pay the lion's share of income tax.

STEINGART/RIECKE: That is because some people can't distinguish between absolute and relative, and judge things on the basis of relative tax rates. The rates are relatively high for small incomes and the yield from them is low in absolute terms.

SLOTERDIJK: The so-called taxation experts don't use their brains, which would tell them that the people who are more involved in the income-tax sphere because of their higher degree of consumption naturally also account for the greater part of the VAT returns, even if it's true that VAT affects everybody. But the new idea is self-evident: on one hand we have a society with a very high level of private wealth and, on the other hand, massive public debt. The rich city of Bremen is a good example, because it is the German city with the biggest public debt. What are the results? A child could work it out.

STEINGART/RIECKE: Do you want to hit the wallets of left-wing professors in Bremen?

SLOTERDIJK: We must call on the strong with their strength, that's right. But it shouldn't be done any longer by using the method of confiscatory taxation. We finally have to restructure the whole sphere of public finance to become a matter of honour. In psycho-political terms this is a very ambitious manoeuvre, something that can easily take a hundred years. But we have to be clear about the historical dimensions of the problem. We believed that the problem of nobility was resolved from the time a large number of aristocrats had their heads chopped off in the French Revolution. But it is not resolved. The result of the French Revolution shouldn't be that the national population gets the right to behave like the mob. On the contrary, the common people should be raised to the rank of the aristocracy. I think we haven't fully realized the superior kind of psycho-political tendencies of the French Revolution – whereas the liberation of the mob has been largely successful.

STEINGART/RIECKE: Do we have the aristocratic idea innately as human beings?

SLOTERDIJK: The only people who have shown that public spirit can support the state in a casual way are the Swiss. To paraphrase O. W. Fischer in the film *Helden*:[3] 'No aristocratic title is more beautiful than the simple Swiss address, "Herr".'

STEINGART/RIECKE: Haven't the modern Greeks taught us that the rich don't pay voluntarily? In a way, Greece is living out the model of an abstinent country that demands taxes but doesn't collect them.

SLOTERDIJK: The idea of the state hasn't caught on at all in Greece. I get annoyed whenever people say Greece is the cradle of democracy. The real Greece is a psycho-political ruin in which 400 years of Turkish occupation left a residue of resignation, privatism, wisecrack attitudes and remoteness from the state. It reminds me of what Joseph de Maistre said about the Turks in Greece. (Incidentally, they had enough time to become Europeans while they remained on European soil for 400 years. But what happened? The Greeks became orientalized; they failed to Westernize the Turks – if they ever tried to. In those times, however, they didn't know about the fairy story of the cradle of democracy.) Remember De Maistre's verdict on the Turks of that time: they remained Tartars camping on European soil.

STEINGART/RIECKE: Where is the cradle of democracy? In Paris?

SLOTERDIJK: More likely in Rome. Initially it wasn't a question of democracy as a form of popular rule, it was more about the *res publica*, which is about having an open space in which people feel that the noblest thing anyone can do is to participate in shaping the body politic. And that was more to do with Roman philosophy of the state than the Greek heritage.

STEINGART/RIECKE: But how do we achieve the psycho-political change you are discussing and demanding, in which citizens give voluntarily, without the state collapsing?

[3] *Helden* was the German version of the film *Arms and the Man*, starring O. W. Fischer (1958). The film was adapted from the play of the same name by George Bernard Shaw.

SLOTERDIJK: There are two main possibilities: first, that human beings are asocial creatures by nature – as representatives of black anthropology from Thomas Hobbes to Adorno have told us – and only fear can force them into coexistence. Think of Schopenhauer: bourgeois society resembles a group of freezing porcupines that huddle together for warmth and can only hurt each other. These images are enough to substantiate the pessimism of black anthropology. But there is another track. If we consult the works of the 'moral sense' philosophers that gave rise to political economy, the works of the Scots, of Adam Smith and of Lord Shaftesbury, one of the most wonderful figures in European intellectual history, we get a completely different picture. Shaftesbury taught and practised an enthusiastic attitude to sociability.

STEINGART/RIECKE: Wilhelm Röpke, the author of *Jenseits von Angebot und Nachfrage*,[4] also had a view of humankind that regarded capitalists as more than just monsters and the state as more than merely an auxiliary machine.

SLOTERDIJK: Convivial philosophers assume that human beings are creatures that feel well in company. Human beings like seeing their reflection in the eyes of others and are full of empathetic virtues. The main thesis here is that concern is first nature to us and bourgeois coldness is only acquired with additional education through whole epochs of negative dressage. Philosophers then plump up the results into dark anthropological theories.

STEINGART/RIECKE: Because we have redacted empathy away.

SLOTERDIJK: Still, empathy is the basic given factor. Everything else is more of an acquired vice. I want briefly to point out one thing: people in a fiscal democracy in which there are still elements left over from absolutism are accustomed to being called on as donors anyway. They wouldn't suffer any more than they do now if we introduced a new official term for channelling public emotions, stating that from today, everything we pay into the communal coffers is not called 'taxes' but 'donations' from citizens. That they are now called donations doesn't alter their obligatory character. That was, by the way, the starting point taken for the almost totally ignorant debates on my theses that shocked the German cultural press two years ago. Many of the people who voiced their opinions had not read Marcel Mauss; it was he who pointed out that

[4] Wilhelm Röpke, *A Humane Economy: The Social Framework of the Free Market* (Chicago: Henry Regner), 1960.

donations involve a curious unity of duty and voluntariness.[5] His theory about the dual nature of donations contains everything one needs to know to see the plausibility of switching from confiscation to donation as the way to fill the communal coffers. Incidentally, Mauss was a socialist and he knew what he was talking about. The spontaneity of donations doesn't eliminate their obligatory character – that doesn't occur to a convinced étatist and fiscalist. An alternative interpretation of social relations can only emerge from the idea that the whole society functions in donor streams and will no longer be animated by the tax burden.

STEINGART/RIECKE: So far your ideas haven't found many supporters. Taking seems more blessed to us than giving.

SLOTERDIJK: The German Social Democrats have just discussed increasing taxation again at their party conference. What they didn't want to understand is that in recent years in America the initiative called 'The Giving Pledge' has begun turning billionaires into social democrats. Social democracy lives from the simple formula: 'half for the communal budget'. Warren Buffet's words rang in my ears because he and his fellow campaigners seem to be aware of precisely that figure. Apparently, the 50 per cent logic has found its place in the minds of American billionaires. Meanwhile, here in Germany all those flatfooted psychologists are lumbering around and still using the language of threats when tax increases are up for discussion.

STEINGART/RIECKE: Is Warren Buffett your hero rather than Sigmar Gabriel?[6]

SLOTERDIJK: I think Sigmar Gabriel is able to learn. My opinion is based on personal observation and a wise proverb from the Middle Ages: if God considers somebody for office, he equips him beforehand with the intellect appropriate to that office.

STEINGART/RIECKE: What does that poetic statement mean?

SLOTERDIJK: That office and intellect converge. Which is really not stupid, by the way. Most people laugh about it, but I think the contemporary word 'competence' expresses precisely this faith in the relation between office and intellect.

STEINGART/RIECKE: The SPD decided to increase taxation again. They only argued about how much they should take.

[5] Marcel Mauss (1872–1950) was a French sociologist, ethnologist and anthropologist. Sloterdijk is referring here to his theory of 'give and take'.

[6] Sigmar Gabriel, a leading German Social Democratic politician, held the post of Vice Chancellor and Minister for Economic Affairs and Energy in the centre-left coalition government that took office in Germany in 2013.

SLOTERDIJK: They are sticking to the old pattern of compulsory state-organized taking.

STEINGART/RIECKE: What actually distinguishes your donation from compulsory taxation? You cite Benjamin Franklin, who said that only two things are certain in life: death, and paying taxes. Isn't it a habit that has become second nature to us?

SLOTERDIJK: Absolutely. We shouldn't underestimate the depth of habit. When Franklin said only death and taxes are certain, he put those two phenomena into the same category of resignation. That means, in relation to these two things, we have become psychologically almost incapable of learning. Anybody who interferes with taxes should abandon hope, as in Dante's Hell. Mortality and the duty to pay taxes are handled in the same area of the brain. They are surrounded by the same feeling of inescapable fatalism.

STEINGART/RIECKE: But your flatfooted theologians object that they really need binding agreements because, after all, the welfare state has binding expenditure commitments.

SLOTERDIJK: Everything is binding in the alternative system as well. But the quality of the transaction as such will be experienced differently. People will finally be acknowledged in terms of their donor qualities – it would be an almost invisible but incredibly far-reaching psychological revolution if the people who really fill the communal coffers would be taken seriously as such for the first time. It is quite wrong that at the moment when I devote myself most to the system in general, the moment when I pay my taxes, I see myself pushed into the most passive and undignified role by the fiscal authorities.

STEINGART/RIECKE: In our system the donor is actually the debtor.

SLOTERDIJK: That is a psycho-political mistake that could explain modern democracy's failure. The étatists of all kinds don't take it seriously enough. They think the systems run forever on their own. Our whole world is founded on a fundamental psycho-political error because it doesn't sufficiently value the voluntary dimension in all the transactions between the state and its citizens.

STEINGART/RIECKE: But hasn't the liberalism of the Free Democratic Party fallen for the same friend–enemy pattern by inventing the hand that gives back in reciprocation for the hand that takes – that is, by reducing taxation? Isn't it the same stupid policy, only with different symptoms?

SLOTERDIJK: I don't know what those people really think. The motivations behind this kind of rhetoric are certainly related to pleasing their clientele. But the liberals, like everybody else, don't use the right tone to address their clientele's positive community consciousness. They behave as if they were merely a party trying to avoid taxation. We shouldn't forget, however, that the avoidance reflex stems from a false psycho-political development that goes back a very long way. Now it is becoming disastrous because it coincides with decades of the state pursuing terribly wrong fiscal policy.

STEINGART/RIECKE: Is that the origin of the present crisis?

SLOTERDIJK: The analysis of the origins should come before the crisis report: we have a huge crisis of trust that is also the credibility crisis of credit. It is gradually becoming impossible to take countries seriously as borrowers. The cannon is no longer the *ultima ratio* of states; instead, it is bankruptcy.

STEINGART/RIECKE: Yet the state has two things not granted to us private citizens: it can wage war, that is its first right, and it can print money. It is doing the latter now, to avoid bankruptcy, to be able to carry on. While we are sitting here, money that has not been earned is being put into circulation in Frankfurt, and the same goes for America. What do you think of that?

SLOTERDIJK: Twentieth-century economists hailed printing money as the lesser evil if it helped prevent recessions. As soon as recession was defined as the worst possible evil, inflation policy obviously became the lesser evil. This brings us back to social democracy. In the world-historical competition with Leninism it always presented itself as the party of the lesser evil.

STEINGART/RIECKE: But nowadays all social democrats and all conservatives are involved in the business of flooding the markets with money. Whatever our political differences, the advocates of monetary flooding make up the really grand coalition.

SLOTERDIJK: Maybe some financial genius will come along soon and show us that the United States' national debt can tend towards infinity without anything happening. It would be a new mathematics that the brain of old *Homo sapiens* isn't ready for.

STEINGART/RIECKE: But do you agree with the analysis that a recession would be the worst case?

SLOTERDIJK: I have another worst case in mind, that of complete general demoralization. That's what we're heading for.

STEINGART/RIECKE: Demoralization of society as a whole?

SLOTERDIJK: Collective demoralization is worse than a temporary recession can ever be. Recessions have the saving grace that they accustom people to exercising moderation again. I don't mean being moderate as in tightening one's belt, but practising moderation in terms of not losing one's sense of proportion. We have lived for decades in a spooky atmosphere with ambiguous messages constantly raining down on people and making them crazy. They are being told simultaneously to save money and waste it; they are supposed to take risks and do solid business, and they are supposed to speculate sky-high and keep both feet on the ground. In the end this completely wears people down. The same demoralizing effect likewise comes from the rapid growth of incomes without performance. This poisons young people because they start dreaming about pursuing pseudo careers. The whole thing has an ugly psychological name: the dream of excessive reward. Many people get up in the morning and want the highest premium right at the start. The inner millionaire has been awakened in everybody. However, he or she is simply not yet the same as the real, existing person.

STEINGART/RIECKE: But isn't the same attitude there at both ends – at one end the bank employees, who rely on their bonus and have the feeling they are owed something; and at the other end those who believe they are owed part of the national income without doing any kind of work for it?

SLOTERDIJK: The welfare system is indispensable, but it also spreads disinformation that leads to false attitudes. The Americans took a more courageous route in the Clinton era. They took the vague idea that society owes us support when we're in need and reworked it into the precise idea of welfare state credits with a time limit, which every citizen has a right to.

STEINGART/RIECKE: The programme was called 'Welfare to Work' ...

SLOTERDIJK: And it meant that every citizen going through a bad patch could rely on support. The side effect of this was a sharp reduction in the intentional propagation of poverty within the welfare system. Before then, after giving birth to her fourth child a woman could get a secure position in the welfare system, rather like a public servant.

STEINGART/RIECKE: Ronald Reagan actually spoke of the 'welfare queen' who strutted through the ghettos because she boasted an astonishingly high income.

SLOTERDIJK: This phenomenon is also related to the false psycho-political construction of our fiscal affairs. When money first enters the fiscal system it is just a factor to be used, without characteristics. It doesn't show the imprint of the donor group any longer. The recipient shouldn't be able to trace the donors' input at all. We used to call it 'state dough', neutralized money. This confuses the recipients because they can't feel the warm current reaching them in a material sense from the donor side. On the contrary, there is often a kind of recipient anger because the clients are annoyed, thinking it could easily be more. We don't know much about the real processes in the transfer.

STEINGART/RIECKE: That brings us back to the politicians

again. You talked about the need to create an employers' movement symbolically modelled on the workers' movement. What can that achieve?

SLOTERDIJK: An employers' movement is very meaningful if you use a metaphorical concept of the employer. Nowadays I would express it differently. We are looking at a new start in which each taxpayer is seen as a future sponsor. Only then will the community be on the right psycho-political track. Everybody who fills the national coffers has the right to the title of sponsor. Sponsoring, in any case, demonstrates an interesting analogy to the relationship between taxpayers and the tax state because it is based on the idea of service in return. This should also apply to the situation between the fiscal system and citizens in a democracy. At the time I first proposed this idea, it was interpreted as an argument in support of universal patronizing arrogance. It's actually about something very different, namely, that we should develop a universal sponsoring consciousness by which everybody who contributes to the communal economy should be recognized as a donor. In immensely big societies like ours, the currency of recognition is the psycho-political fluid that remains the only halfway reliable medium for democratic coherence.

STEINGART/RIECKE: Can you describe this in detail?

SLOTERDIJK: We can look back today on 3,000 years of high culture in which the coherence of the many was almost always created by phobocratic means: with the rule of fear, even in the churches. The great structures were integrated by fear of the Lord and consolidated with mechanisms of paranoid integration based on the idea of common enemies. We seem to have largely overcome all that. In present-day societies, which are primarily communities for shared concerns and entertainment, social coherence can't be achieved with purely phobocratic methods. Threats don't get us very far nowadays. From this perspective the Germans are amiable folk. For the past three or four years, they have been threatened daily with horror stories by climate theorists and tax or finance scaremongers. But what have the Germans done at Christmas time for the past three or four years? They have proved that people can't be bullied in relation to their feeling about life. They have broken one consumer record after another. This tells us something that has far-reaching significance.

STEINGART/RIECKE: There are evidently social tendencies for immunization against scaremongering.

SLOTERDIJK: Your profession is getting more difficult too, isn't it?

STEINGART/RIECKE: But we journalists are also working

in the field of the quest for meaning. After all, newspaper readers aren't only looking for shock and horror; they are looking for orientation as well. In this respect, we are all registering rising circulation and more website visits in this crisis, because people are looking for orientation and Mr Ackermann clearly can't provide it on his own.[7]

SLOTERDIJK: We are heading for a time when people will become aware of the experimental character of politics in general. More and more people are also starting to understand the experimental character of economic decisions at the highest level. That is very disturbing because there should be things that aren't experimented with. That's what the Pope says as well. But he's more concerned with sex and the family.

STEINGART/RIECKE: Are you thinking about the state and the rules of the game for society?

SLOTERDIJK: Yes. Sometimes I think if Montesquieu came back, he would have to say to himself: I didn't understand the distribution of powers properly. I only mentioned the judicative, the legislative and the executive, but I didn't take note of the speculative.

STEINGART/RIECKE: Habermas doesn't even try to look for the psycho-social level, but says we should remove these things from the jurisdiction of the nation-state. He says we need new European institutions. He acts as if he were the new constructor of an extra supranational level that is supposed to use new institutions to solve our problems in this area, which is actually more pre-democratic than democratic. He is building a new Europe for himself. What do you think of that?

SLOTERDIJK: Habermas has evidently not thought through some of the assumptions of his theses properly. The fundamental thrust of his ideas is quite plausible and has a certain appeal. But the basic analysis is missing, because what he doesn't see is that nation-states continue to exist today not only because of their sluggishness, their traditions and their cultural attributes. They remain alive and have a future because their system of solidarity continues to be organized on a national scale. That means nobody today is a national socialist, but everybody is a social nationalist. Now, and for the foreseeable future, we are living in real social nationalism because the great majority of generational contracts are still concluded in a national format, with the exception of an ongoing but rather marginal tendency towards integrating migrants into

[7] Swiss banker Josef Ackermann was chief executive officer of Deutsche Bank, Germany's biggest banking group, from 2006 to 2012.

national social budgets. However, we are still light years away from a supranational social state.

STEINGART/RIECKE: Wouldn't a European transfer union create something like that?

SLOTERDIJK: No. We would achieve that if all Europeans were to receive their pensions from Brussels – that's the way a united Europe would work. We can't construct it from the other end, from the parliaments and the commissions. The social nationalist reflex is already there, and we can say, 'Ubi bene, ibi patria'. I am at home where my retirement pension is guaranteed. The people who give me my homeland are those who calculate my pension. As long as that happens through the auspices of the good old Federal German Employment Agency or my public service pension scheme, I will keep my national ties and remain securely in the social insurance system. We could only think about the things Habermas is talking about if we could give that up. But, as always, he starts building from the top down.

STEINGART/RIECKE: Democracy appears too rarely in what constructivists are propagating now in terms of institutions and fiscal union – all the slogans all along the line from Habermas to Chancellor Merkel.[8] Not only do they fail to include the social insurance system, but the idea of democracy is also completely absent.

SLOTERDIJK: The very grand coalition of post-democrats that negotiates destinies in Europe has existed for a long time. Naturally it is a benevolent post-democracy, but of the kind that wants to force citizens to take part in all the procedures as always, only in this undignified form of compulsory fiscal behaviour that goes back to absolutism. In Habermas's scheme there would be more parliamentary business and more elections, but his Europe would basically be the same monster consisting of twenty-seven states operating compulsory taxation that already completely bewilders citizens, only with more symbolic superstructure. If Europeans had more pride it wouldn't be possible to keep playing this game with them. But as I have already pointed out, people have been trained for centuries in the deprivation of their dignity – the training of death and taxation – and that can't be shaken off quickly. If a free spirit like Benjamin Franklin mentioned both things in one breath, then it is easy to understand why a social democrat today can only speak

[8] Angela Merkel, a leading Conservative German politician and chairperson of the German Christian Democratic Party, served as Federal Chancellor of Germany from 2005.

fatalistically about the topic of taxes, with an added twist: we'll give fatalism a helping hand by increasing the highest tax rate.

STEINGART/RIECKE: So far we have talked a great deal about the state and its institutions. Could you please say something about capitalism and the money business: where do you think changes, changed thinking patterns and changed processes have to be implemented? Or is the state the main engine of events as a whole?

SLOTERDIJK: I think the state has made capital errors with its mad central-bank policy in the last twenty years, and now that people can see the results of those errors they want to correct them by repeating them on an even bigger scale. You only have to look fairly carefully at the effect of flooding the markets. The result is that most of that money – up to around 80 or 90 per cent – doesn't go into the real economy but into financial speculation. We are dealing with purely technical central-bank mistakes, which you can easily understand if you read Walter Bagehot's book *Lombard Street*, which is on my desk over there. It is the central bank errors that have opened the floodgates to speculation. That's why I don't believe a word of the greed psychology that is so fashionable right now. Of course people have the 'I want' reflex, particularly in the form of 'I want as well'. There is women's urge to collect, and men's expectation of booty, and in our hermaphroditic age these two acquisition reflexes constantly get mixed up with each other. But who has left easy money lying around where anybody passing by would have to be an idiot not to take it? In the end it is the central bankers who have made speculation possible.

STEINGART/RIECKE: Show us the way out of this stupid situation.

SLOTERDIJK: The possibility for the real economy to obtain credit has to be decoupled from the shady, speculative world of commercial banks, funds and other institutions. In other words, if the state really wants to function usefully as a lender of last resort, in emergencies it should offer short cuts for genuine credit-seekers in the economy instead of throwing eight-tenths of smart money at speculators at low interest rates. A short cut of that kind between the highest-level bank and the real economy must be tried out, and there are clever institution designers around who understand such things. That would be a simple measure to restrain the financial market branch, which has become too powerful, to its limits within the system.

STEINGART/RIECKE: We began by acquitting the bankers as creditors. When it comes to guilt, are we going further now and saying that the central bankers are guilty?

SLOTERDIJK: Given the premise that the basic mistake has

already been made, many banks have acted correctly – but, as we know, 'There is no right life in a false life.'[9] Besides, the banking sector had its black sheep who are guilty above and beyond their role in that wicked game. Countless players have capitalized endlessly on the structural errors of the finance system and have created a beautiful inflation of assets that was not easily visible to the general consumer public. But ordinary people must have the impression that the rich are getting richer all the time, and the poor poorer. That is only partially true because in hidden inflation the noted assets of the rich get bigger, but the bogus values can hardly be translated into market prices. This is clearly demonstrated by the derelict houses in the USA and Spain that can't be sold.

STEINGART/RIECKE: What have you learned about our present system from the book on your desk – Bagehot's classic *Lombard Street* – which was first published in 1874?

SLOTERDIJK: This book probably marks the first appearance of the idea that is falsely applied everywhere today: I mean the suggestion that the world's central banks rapidly flood with money when recession threatens. Bagehot knew how bad a recession could be. He recommended avoiding shortage crises and suggested resorting to risky methods instead. He certainly couldn't imagine that markets would be flooded for decades, as practised regularly by Greenspan and Co.

STEINGART/RIECKE: But that would mean you see the crisis as the result of the state's failure. Yet you still have a mild view of Ms Merkel. Why?

SLOTERDIJK: True, I have a rather milder view of her at the moment. She is the premier essayist in the state nowadays. In that capacity, we can't joke about her at all because she is really toiling away there at the head of the body politic. In any case, she already deserves the Nobel Prize for economics for her opposition to Euro Bonds, although she is surrounded by social populists right across Europe who would gladly have carried on playing their deadly game.

STEINGART/RIECKE: Does she get too little support from economics as an academic discipline?

SLOTERDIJK: Economic science seems to me to be a discipline that has lost its basic principles. The whole faculty is in a dreadful state. One increasingly gets the feeling that the theories as such are fiction that is trying to become reality and can't be linked to any

9 Sloterdijk is referring to Adorno's famous dictum, reproduced in Theodor Adorno, *Minima Moralia* (New York: Verso Books), 1978.

external standard. This is not a new observation for a theorist of cognition. Niklas Luhmann[10] had already stated twenty years ago that good theory is like a panel flight above closed cloud cover. Visual flight is only for amateurs; the clear view down to the ground is always harmful for social scientists because they let their subjectivity and sentimentality influence them.

STEINGART/RIECKE: We live in a period of permanent stress tests for our citizens. Right now, we are waiting for some parting words of comfort from the philosopher.

SLOTERDIJK: I have discovered a first-class comforter.

STEINGART/RIECKE: A whisky?

SLOTERDIJK: One of the most beautiful proverbs I have come across in a long time. It comes from Piet Klocke. Do you know him?

STEINGART/RIECKE: Yes, of course.

SLOTERDIJK: He's the fantastic cabaret artist . . .

STEINGART/RIECKE: The one who sounds like Mr Rürup?[11]

SLOTERDIJK: He has discovered that most sentences don't have to be spoken right to the end. He just runs on immediately into the next sentence. Well, I think we can pass on a proverb from Piet Klocke to people in need of comfort. It goes like this: 'However big the chaos, there's always a tiny spark of hopelessness in it somewhere.'

STEINGART/RIECKE: Mr Sloterdijk, thank you for this interview.

[10] Niklas Luhmann (1927–98) was an influential German sociologist and social theorist.

[11] Bert Rürup is a German economist and former chairman of the German Council of Economic Experts. He was a leading consultant on the reform of the German pension and social welfare system from 2002 to 2009.

# 30

# IS THERE A WAY OUT OF THE CRISIS OF WESTERN CULTURE?

*Interview with Peter Sloterdijk and Slavoj Žižek**

LE MONDE: For the first time in the history of the Western world, the future has run into a crisis. And the new generations don't think they'll have better lives than their predecessors. Lack of interest in politics, the economic crisis and retreat into the identity of our origins: how can we describe the moment in time we are presently living through? Can we call it a crisis of culture?

SLOTERDIJK: What do we mean by using the term 'Western culture' for the culture we have lived in since the seventeenth century? In my opinion we are talking about a form of world based on the idea that the age of the cult of the past is over. The pre-eminence of the past has been destroyed. Western people invented an unprecedented life form founded on anticipating the future. This means we live in a world that is more and more strongly 'futurized'. Consequently, I believe that at a deep level the meaning of our 'being-in-the-world' embraces futurism, and this is the fundamental feature of the way we exist. The pre-eminence of the future dates back to the epoch at the beginning of the Renaissance in which the West invented the new art of making promises. I mean the time at which credit intruded into the life of Europeans. In antiquity and the Middle Ages credit hardly played a role because it was managed

* This conversation between Peter Sloterdijk and Slavoj Žižek appeared under the title 'Comment sortir de la crise de la civilisation occidentale?', in *Le Monde* (28 May 2011). Available at: <http://colblog.blog.lemonde.fr/2011/05/28/peter-sloterdijk-slavoj-zizek-comment-sortir-de-la-crise-de-la-civilisation-occidentale/>.

Slavoj Žižek is a philosopher, cultural critic and performer.

The interviewer for *Le Monde* was Nicolas Truong.

by usurers who were condemned by the Church. The usurer directly blocked the future of anybody who had to repay credit. Modern loans, by contrast, loans with moderate interest, opened up a future. For the first time, promises of repayment could be fulfilled or honoured. The crisis of culture involves this: we have reached an epoch in which credit is increasingly blocked from offering a sustainable future because nowadays people take out loans to repay other loans. In other words, 'creditism' has entered its final crisis. People have amassed so many debts that the promise of repayment that underpins the credibility of our construction of the world is no longer viable. The seriousness of the promise vanishes in the mists. If you ask Americans how they imagine the debts amassed by the US federal government will be repaid, their response will undoubtedly be: 'Nobody knows.' And I think this not-knowing is the hard core of our crisis. Nobody on earth knows how the collective debt should be repaid. The future of our culture has run up against a wall of debt.

ŽIŽEK: I completely agree with the idea of a crisis of 'futurism' and of the logic of loans. Let's take the so-called 'sub-prime' economic crisis of 2008: everybody knew it was impossible to repay those mortgage loans but everybody behaved as if they were able to do so. In my psychoanalytic jargon I call this fetishist denial: 'I know it's impossible but I'm going to try anyway....' People are well aware they can't do it but in practice they act as if they actually could. All the same, I would rather use the term 'future' to describe what Peter Sloterdijk calls 'creditism'. The word 'future' seems more open to me, incidentally. The expression, 'no future' is pessimistic, but the word 'future' is more optimistic. I'm not trying to revive Marxist communism, which actually resembles immense creditism. To describe our economic and political, ideological and intellectual situation, I can only quote what is probably an apocryphal story. It's about a telegram exchange between the German and the Austrian general staff in the First World War. The Germans sent the Austrians a telegram with the words, 'The situation here on the front is serious but not disastrous.' To which the Austrians replied, 'Our situation here is disastrous but not serious'! And that's exactly what is disastrous: people can't pay their debts but in a sense they don't take it seriously. Beyond that wall of debts the present epoch is approaching a kind of zero point. First, the massive economic crisis forces us not to stay on the same politico-economic track any longer. Second, as we can see in China, capitalism will not be naturally tied to parliamentary democracy in the future. Third, the bio-genetic revolution is forcing us to find a different kind of bio-politics. As for the social divisions in the world as a whole, they create the conditions for unparalleled explosions and popular uprisings . . .

LE MONDE: Multicultural capitalism or social individualism, global nationalism or global nomadism – the failure of Europe, the retreat into identities based on origins – the collective is also immersed in a crisis. How can the idea of communality be given new meaning today?

ŽIŽEK: Even if we must reject the naïve communitarianism, the homogenization of cultures and the kind of multiculturalism that has become the ideology of the new spirit of capitalism, we must still make the different cultures and the individual persons enter into dialogue with each other. On the level of the individual we need a new logic of discretion, of distance or even of not-knowing. Coexistence in a tight space has become a total reality, which means we are dealing with a need that is vital for life, a crucial point.

On the collective level we must really find a different way to articulate communality. Multiculturalism is completely wrong as a response to the problem, on the one hand because it is a kind of unprofessed racism that respects the identity of the other but imprisons him or her in terms of their particular characteristics. It's a kind of neo-colonialism that reverses classical colonialism by 'respecting' communities, but from the perspective of its universal stance. On the other hand, multicultural tolerance is a decoy that de-politicizes public debate and diverts social questions towards race issues and economic questions towards ethnic issues. This attitude of the postmodern left wing is intrinsically estranged from the world in many respects. Buddhism, for example, can serve and legitimate an extreme form of militarism. In the period between 1930 and 1940, the entire institution of Zen Buddhism not only supported but also legitimated the hegemony of Japanese imperialism. I like using the word 'communism', particularly to provoke upper-class types, but the questions I am asking actually relate to 'communal' properties such as biogenetics and ecology.

SLOTERDIJK: We have to rediscover the real problems of our times. The memory of communism and of the great tragic experience of twentieth-century politics warns us that there are no dogmatic and automatic ideological solutions. The problem of the twenty-first century is that of coexistence in a 'humankind' that has become a physical reality. It is no longer a matter of the 'abstract universalism' of the Enlightenment but of the real universality of an enormous collective that is starting to become a real-life community of circulation with greater opportunities for continual encounters and clashes.

We have become like particles of a gas under pressure. The

question nowadays concerns social ties within an oversized society, and I think the legacy of the so-called religions is important because they represent the first attempts at meta-national or meta-ethnic syntheses. The Buddhist sangha was a spaceship in which deserters from all ethnic backgrounds could take refuge. We could use a similar description for Christianity, which is a kind of social synthesis that transcends the dynamic of closed ethnicities and the subdivisions of class societies. The dialogue of religion in our times is nothing but reformatting of the problem of 'communism'. The assembly held in Chicago in 1893, the World's Parliament of Religions, was a particular way to pose questions for our times with the aid of these fragments, these representatives of unknown origin of the human family members who had lost touch with each other after they left Africa . . . In the age of assembly, human beings have to restructure and reformat everything they previously thought about the bond of coexistence of a humankind without boundaries. That is why I use the term 'co-immunism'.

All the social federations of history, from primal hordes to world empires are, in fact, structures of co-immunity. The choice of this concept recalls the communist legacy. In my analysis, communism goes back to Rousseau and his idea of the 'religion of man'. This is a constitutive term, a sort of communitarianism on a global scale. This exaggerated homogenization inevitably had terrible consequences – but they were probably unavoidable errors. Although we know more today, the problem still oppresses us. We can't escape this situation. The goddess, or divine being, that appears on the last pages of my book is the crisis: it is the only instance that has enough authority to make us change our lives.[1] Our starting point is a shattering, evident truth: we can't go on like this.

ŽIŽEK: I'm less interested in looking for 'co-immunism' than in reviving the idea of true communism. But I assure you, it is more about Kafka's than Stalin's communism, more about the communism of Erik Satie than that of Lenin. In his last short story, 'Josephine the Singer or The Mouse Folk', Kafka sketched the utopia of an egalitarian society, a world in which artists like the singer Josephine, whose singing draws big crowds and fascinates and astonishes them, are celebrated and showered with compliments but without gaining any material benefits from this. It is a picture of a society of recognition that maintains ritual and revives community festivities but without hierarchy or herd behaviour.

[1] Peter Sloterdijk, *You Must Change Your Life*, trans. Wieland Hoban (Cambridge: Polity), 2013, p. 444.

The same applies to Erik Satie. Everything about Satie, the famous composer of the *Gymnopédies* who declared he was composing 'wallpaper music', music for an environment or background, seems removed from politics. Yet Satie was a member of the Communist Party. Far from writing propaganda songs, he gave auditory expression to a kind of collective intimacy, the exact opposite of elevator music. That is what my idea of communism consists of.

LE MONDE: Peter Sloterdijk, your solution for getting out of this crisis is to reactivate the practice of individual spiritual exercises – whereas you, Slavoj Žižek, insist on political, collective mobilization and on reactivating the emancipatory power of Christianity. Why is there such a divergence?

SLOTERDIJK: My proposal simply calls for introducing pragmatism into the study of so-called religions. This pragmatic dimension forces you to look more closely at what religious people do, namely, internal and external practices that we can describe as exercises that build a personality structure. What I describe as the chief subject of philosophy and psychology is the system of a series of exercises that form the personality. And some of these exercise series that make up the personality can be described as religious. But what does that mean? We make spiritual movements to communicate with an invisible partner. These are absolutely concrete things that can be described. There is nothing mysterious in this. I think that so far the concept of a 'system of exercises' is a thousand times more effective and useful than the term 'religion', which relates back to the state bigotry of the Romans. We shouldn't forget that the Romans reserved use of the terms 'religion', 'piety' or 'loyalty to the faith' for the Roman legions stationed in the Rhine Valley and lots of other places. The greatest privilege for a legion was to be awarded the designation *pia fidelis* because it expressed special loyalty to the Emperor in Rome. I think Europeans have simply forgotten what *religio* means. The literal meaning of the word is 'care'. Cicero provided its correct etymology: 'to read' – *legere*, *religere*, which means, to make a careful study of the protocol that regulates communication with higher beings. In other words, it concerns a specific kind of care or, in my terminology, a training code. This is why I believe the 'religious return' can only be effective when it leads to the practice of intensive exercises. By contrast, our 'new religious people' are mostly lazy dreamers. But in the twentieth century, sport gained precedence in Western culture. It is not religion that has returned, but sport, after being nearly forgotten for 1,500 years. Not fideism, but athleticism came to the fore. At the dawn of the twentieth century, Pierre de Coubertin wanted to create a religion of muscles. Although he failed to found a religion, he triumphed as the creator of a new system of exercises.

ŽIŽEK: Early on, the Russian avant-garde artists saw sport as a totality of physical practices. The Soviet director Sergey Eisenstein (1898–1948) wrote a very fine text about the Jesuit Ignatius von Loyola (1491–1556), who was concerned with forgetting God, or at least was somebody who established specific spiritual exercises. My thesis of the return of Christianity is very paradoxical: I believe one can only really feel like an atheist via Christianity. If you look at the great atheist movements of the twentieth century, in reality we are dealing with quite a different logic, namely that of theological 'creditism'. The Danish physicist Niels Bohr (1885–1962), one of the founders of quantum mechanics, had a visit from a friend at his weekend cottage. The friend hesitated to go through the door of the house because of a horseshoe nailed there – in Central Europe this is a superstitious custom to stop evil spirits from entering. Niels Bohr's friend said to him: 'You're a leading scientist. How can you obey that kind of popular superstition?' To which Bohr replied, 'I don't believe in it at all!' 'So why do you leave the horseshoe there?' his friend insisted. And Niels Bohr gave the following beautiful answer: 'Somebody told me it works even if you don't believe in it!' That would be a very good picture of our present ideology. I think the death of Christ on the cross means the death of God and that he is no longer the Great Other who holds the strings. The only possibility of being a believer after the death of Christ is to be part of collective egalitarian relationships. Christianity can be seen as a religion that accompanies the ruling order, or as a religion that says 'No' and helps people to oppose that order. I think Christianity and Marxism have to combat jointly the surge of new kinds of spirituality and capitalist herd behaviour. I represent a religion without God, a communism without masters.

SLOTERDIJK: Let's suppose we landed at the closing session of the Council of Nicaea and during the assembly one of the archbishops asked: should we put our brother Slavoj Žižek on the Index? I think the great majority would vote for an anathema because he is committing what the elders called a 'heresy'. Slavoj Žižek takes a selective position with regard to the whole truth: heresy means selection. And in this particular case, selection involves omitting the sequel to the Bible story that tells of the resurrection after the death of Christ. If you leave out the resurrection you forget the main issue, because the message of Christianity is that death is no threat to us any more. The worldwide success of Christianity is based not only on the message of universal love but, above all, on the neutralization of the threats with which death weighs on every conscience. Without ignoring pagan phobocracy: all empires are founded on the power of fear. We can tell the story as Slavoj Žižek has done, but we have to add a second, liberating dimension: without a rupture with phobocracy, the rule of fear, there is no freedom, either Christian or atheist. Otherwise we are only exchanging masters: Jupiter or Christ, there's no difference at all as long as the two divine beings remain phobocratic powers. Regrettably, Christianity has become the most terrible phobocracy in the whole history of religion, especially through Augustine, who created a veritable fear reactor with his theory of predestination. Fortunately, the philosophy of the Enlightenment deactivated it. Christian phobocracy even persisted in the communist adventure, in the form of state terrorism. And the story isn't over yet. Muslim phobocracy is not willing to stop. We have to reconstruct the emancipatory dimensions of an enlightened Christianity for everyone looking for a way out of the concentration camp world of classical phobocrats. And I will gladly accept an atheist reconstruction on condition that the emphasis is on eliminating the phobocratic elements of ancient paganism.

LE MONDE: The historical moment we are presently living through seems to be characterized by rage. The sense of outrage peaked in the slogan of the Arab revolutions, 'Get out!', or the democratic protests in Spain. If we can believe Slavoj Žižek, then you, Peter Sloterdijk, are too severe towards the social movements you regard as originating from resentment.

SLOTERDIJK: You have to distinguish between rage and resentment. In my opinion there is a whole spectrum of emotions that belong to the realm of *thymos*, that is, to the realm of pride. There is a kind of fundamental, irreducible pride that resides in the very depths of our being. Joviality, a benevolent view of everything that exists, can be expressed on this thymotic spectrum. Here, the psychological field is never clouded over. If we descend a few steps on the ladder of values we come to self-pride. If we go down further we come to humiliation of this pride, which provokes rage. If the rage cannot be expressed and is condemned to waiting to be expressed later and elsewhere, this leads to resentment, and so the process goes on, ending up with destructive hate that really wants to annihilate the object that caused the humiliation. Let's not forget that, according to Aristotle, good rage is the feeling that accompanies the desire for justice. Justice that knows no rage remains a helpless movement. The socialist tendencies of the nineteenth and twentieth centuries created collection points of collective rage. That was doubtless something very right and very important. Tragically, however, too many people and too many organizations of the traditional left slid into resentment. This creates the urgent need to think about and imagine a new left beyond resentments.

ŽIŽEK: What satisfies the conscious mind in resentment is related more to the fact that we harm other people and destroy the obstacle than with benefiting ourselves. We Slovenians are like that by nature. You know the legend in which an angel appears to a farmer and asks him, 'Do you want me to give you a cow? But watch out, I'll also give your neighbour two cows!' And the Slovenian farmer says, 'Of course not!' Yet for me, resentment is never really the attitude of the poor. It is rather the attitude of poor lords – Nietzsche analysed that very well. It is the morality of 'slaves'. Only he was wrong in relation to the social standpoint: it is not about real slaves but about the slaves that Beaumarchais' Figaro wants to substitute for the masters. I think capitalism contains a very specific combination of the thymotic aspect and the erotic aspect. Capitalist eroticism, in comparison with bad thymotics, which creates resentment, is totally mediated: 'I want to have that, not for myself but so that somebody else doesn't get it.' I agree with Peter Sloterdijk: basically the biggest difficulty lies in the question of how to conceive and describe the act of giving beyond exchange and beyond resentment. I'm rather pessimistic about that. People are corrupt; they can't be changed. Sometimes it's possible, depending on the circumstances. You know the totalitarian formula: 'You love mankind in the abstract but you hate real people.' Well, in this respect I'm totalitarian – I love humankind but I often find real people weak, wicked and cowardly. I deeply and utterly deplore all that human stupidity.

I don't actually believe in the reality of the spiritual exercises Peter Sloterdijk proposes. I'm too pessimistic for that. I would like to add a social heterotopia to those sporting-type practices of self-discipline. That's why I wrote the final chapter of *Living in the End Times*[2] in which I sketch out a utopian space of communism by referring to works that make what we could call collective intimacy visible and audible. I'm also inspired by certain science-fiction films in which chaotic heroes and neurotic types form real collectives. Individual life stories can guide us as well. It is often forgotten that Victor Kravchenko (1905–66), the Soviet sport medallist who criticized Stalinist terror very early on in his book, *I Chose Freedom*, and who was shamefully attacked by pro-Soviet intellectuals, wrote a sequel with the title, *I Chose Justice*, during the struggle to construct a more equitable agricultural production system in Bolivia. We should follow and encourage the new Kravchenkos who are now appearing everywhere, from South America to the Mediterranean coast.

SLOTERDIJK: I think you are a victim of the psycho-political

[2] Slavoj Žižek, *Living in the End Times* (London: Verso Books), 2010.

evolution of the East European states. Everyone in Russia, for example, is carrying the load of a whole century of political and personal catastrophes on their shoulders. The tragedy of communism still affects the peoples of Eastern Europe and they can't get away from it. All of that creates a spiral of autogenous despair. Although I'm a pessimist by nature, life has refuted my original pessimism. You could call me an optimist who achieved optimism at the second attempt. In this respect, I think, we are quite close because we began from radically different starting points and have had parallel biographies in some senses, reading the same books along the way.

LE MONDE: To sum up, a word about the affair of Dominique Strauss-Kahn.[3] Is this a case of a simple moral lapse or a symptom of a more important malaise?

SLOTERDIJK: We can't dismiss the possibility that it is about a matter of global importance that goes beyond an ordinary everyday event. Maybe Dominique Strauss-Kahn is innocent. But the story shows that over-exaggerating the power of an individual can create a kind of religion of the powerful that I describe as sexual pantheism. We thought the age of the Sun King was finally over. But strangely enough, the twenty-first century is multiplying these power people in thousands. They imagine all the objects of their desire can be penetrated by their aura.

ŽIŽEK: The only interesting aspect of the DSK affair is the rumour that his friends are said to have approached members of the family of the victim, Nafissatou Diallo, in Guinea, and offered an exorbitant sum of money if she withdrew her accusation. If this is true, what a dilemma! Should one choose dignity, or the money that can rescue a family by giving it the possibility of living in prosperity? That would perfectly sum up the real moral perversion of our times.

[3] Dominique Strauss-Kahn (known as DSK), a leading French politician and former head of the International Monetary Fund, was charged with rape of a hotel employee in New York in 2011. He was later acquitted but remained permanently disgraced by sex scandals.

# 31

# QUESTIONS OF FATE

## A Novel About Thought

*Conversation with Ulrich Raulff**

### I. Karlsruhe Conversation

RAULFF: Mr Sloterdijk, some time ago I read a report in the *Frankfurter Allgemeine Zeitung* about the public discussion you had with Heiner Geißler[1] at the beginning of March 2010 on the occasion of his eightieth birthday. According to the report, you brought the term 'fate' into the discussion twice. That struck me as interesting. First, you are quoted as saying that Luhmann's concept of 'differentiation' of subsystems is the coolest possible reference to the power of fate: complex social systems unavoidably follow the legitimacy of self-referential functioning. Second, you put forward the argument that the West's involvement in Afghanistan proves that the modern world doesn't escape the tragic. The word 'fate' appeared in this context as well. What does it mean? To what extent are you talking about something else apart from military failure or lack of political strategy?

* This interview between Peter Sloterdijk and Ulrich Raulff appeared under the title 'Schicksalsfragen: Ein Roman vom Denken', in *Marbacher Magazin, Ausstellungskatalog Schicksal: Sieben mal sieben unhintergehbare Dinge* (Marbach am Neckar: Deutsche Schillergesellschaft, No. 135), 2011, pp. 14–72.

Ulrich Raulff has been director of the German Academy for Language and Literature in Marbach am Neckar since 2004.

[1] Heiner Geißler is a German politician and member of the Christian Democratic Party (CDU). He was a government minister for youth, health and the family in the 1980s and was later involved in critical movements on social policy and globalization.

SLOTERDIJK: I used Afghanistan in my argument as a topical example of all the situations in which people are doomed to make mistakes whatever they do. Even modern people are forced to experience that sometimes we can only choose between mistakes, mishaps and great misfortunes because there is no right and simple behaviour at that particular moment. As regards the situation in Afghanistan, I explained in the discussion with Heiner Geißler that Western politicians currently have the choice of two evils: if the Western troops stay in the country, the authorities that are responsible alienate their own populations because they still don't really understand what their soldiers are doing there after all these years. Dead soldiers are continually being repatriated, yet there is no recognizable military success. As a result this policy is very unpopular. But if we withdraw from Afghanistan we will be abandoning the country to forces that are likely to do the worst for their own people and the world in general. In short, we can only choose between two evils. In this context I think we should use the concept of the tragic once again, beyond its everyday meaning. Interestingly, ordinary speech today defines more or less everything that used to be called fatal as tragic, particularly the deadly accident. For us, the accident is the authority that governs the tragic or the fatal – both terms express that people today are occasionally overwhelmed, as they have always been, by the feeling that they are ruled by the force of horror. Accidents and catastrophes are opportunist factors that confirm their mastery now and then by hitting out blindly. People are helplessly confused then, because as modern subjects they like to think they have protected themselves technically and politically against bad luck. Suddenly all the trappings of competence we have built up against the blows of fate seem useless, and from one moment to the next people sink back into a state of almost archaic helplessness. The word 'helpless' touches on the ancient starting point of the Enlightenment: for enlightenment, as it took shape for the first time in ancient Sophism, is primarily a prophylactic of helplessness. There is a concept in Greek Sophism that is hardly discussed in contemporary philosophy, although it expresses one of the most important ideas of ancient ethics: the concept of *amechanía*, which is usually translated as 'helplessness'. It literally describes the lack of *mechané*, which means the cunning or the device or the machine we can use to get out of a situation of existential difficulties …

RAULFF: To thwart the procedure, so to speak …

SLOTERDIJK: Exactly, because *amechanía* describes the situation in which human beings are denied just what the Greeks believed made them wholly human, that is, the ability to retaliate against attacks, being equipped with options for action or, as we would say today, being in full control of their agency. As soon as people sink into *amechanía*, they land in a situation that just doesn't seem appropriate for human beings. Ancient Sophism thought more profoundly on this point than the academy. According to Sophism, the meaning of all training, both spiritual and physical, is that people react against the extreme situation of *amechanía* so that they can become real experts – experts of existence in general and beings that find the right words in particular. Whenever people talked about *paideia*, and later, education, they had to remember that these concepts had their starting point in a very elementary concept of existential competence. The legacy of Sophism became part of Stoical ethics that wanted to develop human beings as creatures that would never be helpless. This ethics is based on the postulate that humans should always be able to do something, even in situations in which the only possible thing they can do is to remain calm and composed.

RAULFF: That describes a level that goes deeper than the inability to use our own understanding without someone else's guidance, the condition our famous Enlightenment sought to change. Helplessness describes a level below that, complete incapacity to act . . .

SLOTERDIJK: True, helplessness is one dimension beyond normal legal immaturity. Our understanding of legal immaturity involves the idea, of course, that the ward needs a legal guardian who is equipped with the means to avoid helplessness. The ideal of the relationship between the ward and the guardian would naturally be to encourage the former to reach the state of independence. A bond like that is already prefigured in the ancient rejection of *amechanía*. It is also the basis of the initial relationship between teacher and pupil. The Greeks already had a concept of humans as beings that should know how to help themselves. The old Sophists were not at a loss when it came to answering the question about the character of human beings: for them, humans were the creatures directed by an indestructible 'I-can' whatever the circumstances. A living being of that kind, which had Aristotle, and therefore language, and Sophism, and therefore the art of retaliation and improvisation, pitted his competence against external powers in the same way as the helmsman defies the storm with his experience. It is no coincidence that Plato, who was very close to Sophist thought despite being polemically opposed to Sophism, liked choosing examples that presented people as experts. For instance, the architect who knows how to build a house so that people aren't compelled to spend their lives in the terrible condition of homelessness, or the helmsman, *kybernetes*, who ensures that we reach our destination even in heavy seas.

In short, the anti-*mechanía* attitude runs through the entire Greek enlightenment and culminates in the teachings of the Stoic stance. If you read the relevant letters of Seneca, you can see he had a highly developed sense for philosophizing in the face of emergencies. Emergencies are situations in which regression into helplessness seems nearly inevitable. In the age of Emperor Nero, the Roman Stoics' awareness of emergencies was attuned to the most extreme situation that could happen to people of that time, the situation of the gladiator in the arena waiting for the final blow from his victorious opponent. In Seneca's letters, the battle of life and death in the arena replaced sea voyages as the model for emergencies. In the arena the losing fighter directly faces the agent of death who will kill him. There is only one way he can prove his ability to stand up to that: by showing he has learned to fall with dignity. It is right and fitting for a player on the stage of Being to cut a good figure until the last moment. This *savoir mourir* is no longer Socratic. Seneca derived a new picture of human existence from the gladiator role: *Sine missione nascimur*, he wrote in one of his letters, as if he wanted to introduce a kind of arena fatalism. In the Coliseum of life, the fight always has to be to the death. We should be aware that the *missio* meant the sign of remission, the upturned thumb with which the audience in the arena could grant life to a brave loser. In *sine missione* fights the rules disallowed this option and the gladiators had to strike the deadly blow. When Seneca says we are born *sine missione*, it means that as mortals we are always compelled to go to the final end. From his perspective, it follows that we only have one way left to prove our worth, to prove the strength we have gained from wisdom, and that is still to be standing when everybody else has fallen to the ground, literally and metaphorically. The act of standing upright becomes the final evidence for the lack of helplessness that we, the brave gladiators of the cosmos, should aim for. We could go as far as to link the concept of substance to the upright position of the stoical finalist. If Heidegger had not despised Latin philosophy he would have gained something from it for his enframing theory.

RAULFF: But what does fate mean in this situation? Is it the general situation in life of constantly being in a fight *sine missione*, or does the term only apply to the final constellation?

SLOTERDIJK: Fate is both things: the series of tests and the endgame. The power of fate is already evident in the arena complex. People standing below in the sand track have a clear view of their situation because of the architecture: complete immanence, the closed scene with no exit, and the lascivious crowd in the rows that wants its spectacle. The situation is the message. The building expresses fatality with spectators. If I am a gladiator, I feel how my existence down there is absolutely exposed. The others in the rows enjoy the privilege of being in the audience. They can hide among the masses and keep their backs covered. The fighter is visible all the time from all around; he is held out into the final risk – there is no place he can retreat to, nowhere to lean on, nowhere to rest. At most he achieves a postponement if he wins out this time, but if he doesn't fall in today's games, then he will fall in the next or the one after. If he leaves the arena standing, he is excused from the next fight – that is what it means to live on reprieve. The second volume of my *Spheres* trilogy contains a digression with the title 'Dying Later in the Amphitheater: On Postponement, the Roman Way', in which I relate Derrida's concept of *différance*, which means both difference and postponement, to the arena idea of Stoic fatalism.

For the Romans, the games were a didactic medium for presenting people with the fundamental truth of existence in the empire. Life in a tight time situation like that means nothing but the attempt to die later – later than your antagonist of today, as late as possible. Most of all it means being unable to hide when dying. In the arena, imperial fatalism comes into its own, affecting the mob as well as Caesar, the gladiator as well as the pupil of philosophy. The universe itself is the arena, and nobody is granted the *missio*, the reprieve. Given these conditions, the Stoic tries all his life to memorize the mnemonic phrase that he doesn't need to be discharged from the lost skirmish anyway because basically all fates are good. After all, as humans we are merely local functions of the cosmos; every death happens at the right time and place. If this sounds rather exaggerated, you should consider that ancient philosophy is nothing more and nothing less than the attempt to overwrite the tremendous improbability of this cosmic-harmonic doctrine. As in all great teachings of faith, the point is to profess the incredible as if it were the surest thing of all. Ancient philosophy and Christianity are very close on this point. For our ancestors, clear fatalism in the sense of faith in the things that are securely anchored in every destiny served to hold back the annihilating darkness in the life of the few and the many.

RAULFF: You began by saying that the accident has replaced the tragic event for us. Seen from the aesthetic perspective of the tragic, accidents acquire a degree of worthiness. They represent the lofty in the scenes of everyday life. The situations you have described now with reference to ancient philosophy always display an aesthetic component. In each case – and I am struck by this generally in relation to the concept of fate – there is somebody looking on, whether in Greek theatre or the Roman arena. An observer always appears who watches the others trying to cope with their lot, whether they triumph over it, stand there and accept it, or fall quickly. How does this observer belong to the function field of the concept of fate? Does fate really need an observer who watches from the safety of the shore, as suggested in the existential metaphor of the 'shipwreck with spectator'?

SLOTERDIJK: The Lucretian spectator on the safe shore takes part in the general theorizing about life that occurs in classical antiquity. Phenomenology began as observation of fatal events. Since the time that theory has existed in the world, there is, in fact, always somebody who watches from a relatively secure position as fate overtakes others. This applies first of all to the gods of the ancients who permanently enjoyed the world play, watching without suffering, and equally to the Greek theatregoer – not to mention the audiences at the Roman circus. In fact, theory begins with tragedy, which is quite a lot older than philosophy. The Greeks learned the act of watching everything in the form of tragedy. The dramatists seldom used the explicit concept of fate in their plays, but they didn't need the general term because the tragic form per se provided a vehicle for observing fates. The 'goats' songs', or tragedies, presented the heroes' dilemmas by showing the audience the conflicts, traps and complications that can lead to human life coming to an end. They used observation of fate as a cathartic mechanism – indeed, in line with Aristotelian theory, they wanted to chasten the spectators through *phobos* and *eleos*, that is, through awe and lamentation or, as it used to be translated with less pathos, through 'fear' and 'empathy'. This presupposes that the observers are not primarily reflective but begin as empathetic spectators who put themselves in the shoes of the unfortunate hero without completely identifying with him. The origin of tragedy is a ritual of empathy. In the theatre the collective soul is affectively synchronized; this is how the individual is made fit for the *polis*. Cultural theorists would say that Dionysian theatre with its annual productions was an apparatus for strengthening the memo-active fitness of Athens. At that time one could only be a good Athenian by starting to wail with the other spectators at the same point in the play – we can detect a faint echo of this humanizing parallel occurrence of affects in Goethe's 'awe is the best of man'. By the same token, reliable members of the *polis* were recognizable because they laughed together with the others at the right moment.

RAULFF: We have now considered various situations in our investigations into the concept of fate. Afghanistan provides an example of the dilemma of acting in a situation in which we have to choose between evils of equal or different dimensions, evils of unequal speed, different effects and different temporalities. You briefly mentioned *amechanía*, the situation of helplessness when action is no longer possible at all. Finally, you referred to the mishap or accident that occurs suddenly and destroys the normal pattern of life. It seems there is a regular repertoire of situations that constitute our knowledge of the fateful or tragic.

SLOTERDIJK: Such basic situations and the latent or manifest consciousness of them are part of the field kit of the drama of humankind. This equipment for dealing with fate was first assembled by the ancient poets and philosophers in the form of theatrical performances, or as myths and collections of proverbs, and finally also in the first manifestations of philosophy. These were the provisions the people of the emergent high cultures had available for dealing with their journey through life. The diverse types of wisdom always come together at one point: all the versions of ancient consultation about fate converge in the warning that humans should never succumb to hubris. Anyone who allows himself to be tempted by arrogance, who feels much too secure in his thick skin, in his high-handedness, in his phallic cockiness, calls down disaster. This brings us back to the spectator problem again, because if the gods generally behave like unaffected, eternally laughing spectators of the world theatre, there is still a scene they don't watch without intervening in the game, and that is the spectacle of human hubris. If this appears the gods don't keep calm; they intervene and destroy the cocky people. The gods invented the pathos of distance and they don't appreciate it when people want to be too similar to them. On the other hand, modesty doesn't offer adequate security against the inauspicious. To quote Epicurus' famous proverb: 'People can insure against most things but when it comes to death we all live in a city without walls.' The ancients' awareness of mortality assumed that lack of walls signified the last word on the *conditio humana*. Death means the end of capability, and compulsion gets its chance. And the word 'must', the idea of compulsion, includes the incredible gravitational force of invincible natural laws as the ancients experienced them.

Death and necessity – an inseparable couple in the ontology of the ancients. Given this, we can understand the enormity of the philosophical turning point represented by Socrates' death scene. It was the beginning of the triumphal progress of the extraordinary idea that even death was something that should be translated from 'compulsion' into 'capability' – Greek on the example of Socrates, and Roman on the model of the gladiators who took the death-blow without a grimace. This idea had already begun seeping into the lives of private individuals in middle antiquity and became epidemic in late antiquity. The last thing someone struck down by the final blow should do is fall off the sofa quietly, without a whimper; instead he should be able to elect to face death like an athlete faces his opponent.

The philosophical idea of death as an athletic event soon made its entry into the early Christian martyr scene and flourished later in the monastic culture of the Middle Ages. Thomas von Celano's biography of St Francis contains a passage describing how Francis, when he felt his end nearing, performed a wrestling ritual: he undressed completely – a daring gesture, because his brother monks had not yet had an opportunity to verify whether he bore the gaping wound of Christ in his side – and lay down on the ground in the position of an ancient fighter in the *palaestra* to fight the last wrestling match with his opponent. At this juncture the author of the vita used the formulaic expression *nudus cum nudo*, a naked man with a naked man, well aware that for the monks' ancient predecessors the Latin word *nudus*, the Greek *gymnos*, meaning the naked man, was simply the wrestler anointed with oil. In his death pantomime Francis mentioned the Greek comportment of the gymnasts, the naked fighters who prepared for the *agon*. We should read this as an indication that the Greek and Roman translation of animalist compulsion into human skill in relation to the last things had conquered the inner core of Christian monasticism. Even *in extremis*, those perfect practitioners of faith were expected to retain an element of skill and endurance – the monks in the early monasteries of Byzantine Christianity who described themselves as the athletes of Christ had reason for doing so. The resistance to *amechanía* is also clearly noticeable here. This may have been partly due to the fact that, if we follow St John's account of the events of Golgotha, the crucified Christ created an athletic *topos* for himself. In the story of Jesus, the hanging on the cross was to be understood not only as a simple execution but more as the fulfilment of a mission.

RAULFF: And as withstanding a test.

SLOTERDIJK: A test in the sense of the Roman theatre of cruelty. St John, the Greek, goes so far with his depiction of the athleticization of Christ that he attributes to him the last word *tetélestai*, an Agonist word that Luther translated as 'It is finished.' It should actually be, 'It is achieved.' In English it would be 'Mission accomplished.' The word unites the fulfilment of the prophecy and the fulfilment of the supreme stint of heroic passivity. It makes Christ into a Hercules who adds a new deed, the greatest of all, to his heroic *ponoi*. It would be impossible to imagine Christianity, especially in its medieval version, without the additional bolstering given by the art of suffering the death agony.

Being compelled to die is occasionally transformed into having the ability to die, even to the point of willingness to die, specifically in the mysticism of the late Middle Ages that tried to stretch the extreme form of ability to be passive to the point where it became willingness-to-be-nothing. The mystic is the person who keeps calm when God takes the place of the ego. He is an athlete of being-extinguished. In his case the abolition of fate has achieved its goal long before any enlightenment.

RAULFF: Do you find traces of this in modern philosophy? Let's say, in the philosophy of the last 100 or 150 years?

SLOTERDIJK: They are definitely there, even if only marginally. Think of Schopenhauer and what came after.

RAULFF: Yet it is characteristic of the modern age that the concept of fate returned in it and should actually play an important role again. Recently I came upon a remark by Lucian Hölscher that around the mid-nineteenth century a big cold current of religious thought affected Western philosophy, and this was the beginning of the revival of the concept of fate.

SLOTERDIJK: That is probably the right perspective. The eighteenth century apparently issued the final condemnation of fate. At that time the process of enlightenment entered its decisive phase, and thinking in terms of fate seemed to be finished forever. The Enlightenment held the opinion that people have no destinies, they make history. Leibniz, for instance, turned up his nose at what he called 'destin à la turque'.

RAULFF: Turkish fatalism …

SLOTERDIJK: That scornful epithet stayed in circulation until Schopenhauer. It describes people in ontological slavery who don't stand on their own two feet because they submit to the powers of fate. People who think like that don't learn the upright gait that was so important to the protagonists of the Enlightenment. Fatalists remain incapable of discovering the forces released by one's own enterprises. The European Enlightenment is firmly based on the idea that human emancipation only gets moving through anti-fatalism. To quote Ulrich Sonnemann's neat phrase, all enlightenment is an enterprise for 'sabotaging fate'.[2] This formulation has potential because it talks of sabotage as if fate in the twentieth century resembled a power station run by reactionaries that the revolutionary had attacked with a bomb. For anti-fatalists from Voltaire

[2] Ulrich Sonnemann (1912–93) was a German philosopher, psychologist and political writer on the fringes of the Frankfurt School and Critical Theory.

to Kant, the concept of fate was not philosophical and should no longer be part of the vocabulary of world wisdom. The strong ego of the Enlightenment intended to get along in future without fate. It wanted to break the hegemony of chains of events and ultimately dissolve fate in self-made history. That was the beginning of the long process of overstrained subjectivity, which is approximately identical with the history of more recent philosophy. We are grateful to Odo Marquard[3] for the classical representation of the complications in which the new, apparently unauthorized history-making subject of the Enlightenment inevitably got entangled when venturing into major politics. The protagonists of enlightenment involuntarily saw their optimism about progress, their exuberant project-making and their energetic historical planning culminating in the human ego being immensely overloaded. They had to recognize that history is the field where things turn out differently than we imagine. From that time on, people have needed apologies – Marquard called this the art of not having been there.

Along with the apologies, excuses also became fashionable, usually in the form of explanations of one's own failure because of what was described from that time on as 'the forces of reaction'. In the first place, all of this was not a reason for despair, but a theme for reflection. The discovery that progress was non-linear led to reflection on the relationship of human energy to non-human drives that have an impact on the world. This much was clear: the post-Titanic ego, due to its relative weakness, which had become obvious, had to tackle the question of finding superhuman allies to support its exuberant plans. From the start, there were only two potential partners with whom it would be possible to form an alliance to realize the *opus magnum* – nature and history. As a result, late- and post-Enlightenment philosophy indulged in alliance fantasies in both directions. It waxed delirious about unions with nature on the one hand and history on the other. Those who sought an alliance with nature became romantics: what the human subject failed to achieve of its own accord could be promoted instead in the same spirit by a benevolent allied nature. This motif has profoundly influenced European thought for 200 years. The key point here is how nature cooperated with human interests as an artist and a healer, as a source of wealth and as Schelling's striving towards the light. In the twentieth century it was Ernst Bloch who went furthest in exploring the pathetic implications of this position. From

[3] Odo Marquard (1928–2015) was a German philosopher who specialized in contemporary Western philosophy and philosophical anthropology.

this perspective, nature has a priori a sort of two-thirds majority in all our goodwill enterprises, and if we let its progressive aspects become truly effective it would be dreadfully bad luck if the project of the Enlightenment didn't achieve its goal. My point is that, from the mid-nineteenth century on, this serene concept of nature as an alliance clouded over. After that, the triumph of darker elements and unpleasant themes such as nature as a competitive struggle, as unfathomable cruelty, as deliberate fermenting of blind force and suchlike came to the fore.

The inspiring discoveries of Schopenhauer and Darwin worked in the same direction. Finally, to a great extent nature no longer played the role of the major alliance partner of the Enlightenment. We looked into the heart of darkness and murmured, 'the horror, the horror'. This created the impression that only anti-naturalist thinking could take us further. Then the slogan changed from 'forward to culture' to 'back to nature'. On the other hand, after the relative failure of revolutions, weak human beings had their eye on 'History' as their strong partner, History with a capital 'H' and in the lofty singular. History is the goddess who knows what is going to happen to the world. If she joined in the Enlightenment we could trustingly follow her progress through times and spaces. This concept of history carried traces of older meanings, from the Stoics' *pronoia* to the *providentia* of the Christian doctrine of salvation and the philosophical process myths of the Neoplatonists whose echo we can still hear in the works of Comenius, Hegel and Schelling. In this alliance, too, the weak humane person could link up with a strong basis of support with the power of Being on its side. This achieved by itself what mere planning and fiddling around by human beings couldn't manage. From our perspective this aspect is naturally more interesting because the hypostatization, the attribution of real identity to history, was accompanied by the general cultural picture in which fate could re-enter the scene. In fact, the moment that history and fate amalgamate – initially with moderately enlightening intentions – is the moment for second-order fatalism. For the individual, this means he or she can be sure of doing the right thing as soon as they think of their mortal life as occurring within the endless flow of history. Then they see themselves as tools of historical movement and as junior partners in a superior, meaningful event. This metaphysics of cooperation with the global coming-into-being provided a pattern of thought and feeling in the nineteenth and twentieth centuries that released enormous creative (as well as criminal) forces among revolutionaries, reformists, therapists and artists. But just as the concept of nature clouded over with time, the concept of history became much darker as time went on. Although everybody who lived in the twentieth century involuntarily felt that the world would somehow go on, they began to doubt the meaningfulness of movement. In the end, many people only felt the great movement going on and on like a maelstrom, a whirlpool pulling them into the depths. That is the moment when the concept of fate could return with overtones of early antiquity – similarly to the Greek *moira* or *ananke*, the goddess of fate who was surrounded in earlier times by dark and mysterious hints that she was older and more powerful than the Olympic gods.

RAULFF: But the concept of fate often reappears in the modern age as the name for a remarkable deed by which a great figure wrests free of blind forces. Fate, or destiny, comes to mean the sudden blow that tears the fateful fabric, the act with major consequences ... The key word here is 'sudden'. All at once the old fabric is torn. Nietzsche: 'I am a destiny ...'

SLOTERDIJK: When I lecture about the eternal return, I have to explain 'why I am a destiny' ...

RAULFF: This also applies to the theoreticians of decision: for them fate is the abrupt act that tears the fabric of the past.

SLOTERDIJK: In my opinion, decisionism and the philosophy of the deed are subversive products of classical Enlightenment historicism. For decisionists, there is a sharp remainder of human history-making in the form of disastrous epoch-making. This happens through sudden decisions with which the great agent prepares to ride the wave of the world as it moves onward. This is the moment for the distinction Nietzsche introduced between active and passive nihilism. Without this, it is nearly impossible to understand the path of ideas in the twentieth century. In both forms nihilism is the inevitable reverse side of historicism. It has to take the upper hand as soon as we abandon the classical assumption that all epochs are equally close to God. Then comes the idea that history is what ultimately leads to nothing. In principle there are only the two positions Nietzsche described with his distinction between passive and active nihilism. First, people let themselves drift along ...

RAULFF: Nirvana ...

SLOTERDIJK: Nirvana, fun, drugs. The drug world is significant in this context because it not only expresses disinterest in history, but also disinterest in being-in-the-world as such. In *La condition humaine*, the French novelist André Malraux described an old Chinese man – I think it was the father of one of the young revolutionaries at the centre of the novel – who chose to let the world drown in unreality. Malraux used extreme irony in his depiction of the opium dealer, who had once been a sociologist at Peking University, because from this person's perspective even the most serious thing people could achieve at that time on the world stage – revolution – became blurred in the meaninglessness of the world as a whole. What a terrible world that was, the China of the late 1920s as seen through the eyes of this French novelist: the fathers dreaming away their lives in an opium haze while their sons imagine they will achieve self-fulfilment in murders for the future. Clearly, Malraux could only have presented the figure of the man on the opium couch on the basis of Nietzsche's theory of passive nihilism. At the same time he highlighted the instability of revolutionary struggle because it could only mean nihilism in action. Just as weighing out opium implies fleeing from reality, the revolutionary actions of the Shanghai activists in 1927 imply fleeing beyond reality. This is best illustrated in the two most powerful scenes from *La Condition humaine*: right at the beginning, when the young fighter Chen commits his first murder in a kind of active trance and discovers the surrealism of killing, and then again towards the end of the novel with the self-sacrifice of Comrade Katov, who gives away his only cyanide capsule, which is supposed to guarantee him quick death in an emergency, to two young Chinese comrades to allow them to end their own lives in the last night before the execution. He himself accepts being burned alive by Kuomintang soldiers the following morning in the boiler of the locomotive. This shows active nihilist ethics at the most extreme end. Malraux was one of the key witnesses of the twentieth century because he understood early on that communist commitment was identical with active nihilism.

Incidentally, we could ask ourselves whether Carl Schmitt[4] wasn't also arguing the line of active nihilism, and whether his superimposed Catholicism wasn't just a mask for nihilism, with decisionist trimmings in this case. Precisely because everything leads to nothing, he pictured the great designers of society being called upon to make decisions with fatal consequences. The horrible jurist Schmitt thought that people who postponed the inevitable end of the world should have a free hand. Schmitt granted licence to major perpetrators to take superhuman risks – such as Hitler when he launched the Second World War. In retrospect we would be right to say that, all in all, active nihilism with its posture of a fresh start emerging out of abrupt decision, and its faith at rock bottom, and the great rupture, was a disappointment, a self-hypnotic swindle. The truth is that nothing old ended and nothing new began. Anyone who wants to

[4] Carl Schmitt (1888–1985) was a conservative German theorist who specialized in legal, constitutional and political theory. His support for the Nazi regime made him a controversial figure.

keep on living always has to connect to the previous state and carry on from there in some direction or other.

RAULFF: Isn't it more that historical thought always hovers between an attitude of loving breaches and hating them? By all appearances we are currently in a phase that is afraid of breaches, although as you rightly say we always need both and should take both into account. Passive nihilism spreads until active nihilism intervenes. Then it destroys the passive and devours it with a strong project. Commentators have observed, incidentally, how nihilism as a figure of thought was used in the courtroom in Nuremberg to explain and excuse criminal actions, for example, in relation to the trials of the *Einsatzgruppen*, the mobile SS killing squads. To exonerate the accused, European nihilism was presented as a global chain of guilt with the catastrophic German deeds as only part of that, and the guilty actions of individuals in turn only as a microscopic fragment of the fateful whole. Just imagine, such arguments even extended to the defence strategies of the lawyers at Nuremberg.

SLOTERDIJK: Regrettably, Heidegger made a special contribution to this field. His works represent a dubious peak in the indirect apologetics for lapses of the twentieth century and their exaltation to decrees of fate.

RAULFF: Prepared in terms of the structure of care …

SLOTERDIJK: Heidegger's early work had already presaged the turn to thinking in concepts of 'fate', using the basic existential structure of care. To begin with, we should note the method of thinking: it is not that I care, but that care is sent to me and takes me into service. In the works of his middle and later periods, Heidegger attached the concept of fate generally to the occurrences of civilization that we know as technology. In this context, we hear disastrous statements such as that the industrialized landscape and mass production of dead people in concentration camps stem from the same….

RAULFF: … 'process logic' …

SLOTERDIJK: … and arise from the same fateful objectification and misuse of everything by production and presentation, that is, the unstoppable rush of self-empowering framing subjectivity. We still don't know what to make of these statements. They abrogate the possibility of being guilty of anything at all. We can see something slightly comparable in the neurological hype that nothing and nobody can resist at the present time. In fact, it opens the way for a renewed attempt to popularize fatalism as naturalism, in this case as neuro-fatalism. The art of not having been the guilty person remains as topical as it was in the period of the first setbacks in the Enlightenment project. From this perspective, Marquard actually provided the key to the moral ecological system of the modern age: as soon as the human capacity to act explosively increases, a demand for irresponsibility begins. Everybody talks about responsibility, but in reality most people have a stake in effacing the possibility of making perpetrators responsible for their actions.

RAULFF: This is what Marquard described as 'refatalization'. In this respect a concept like fate, or whatever is offered as an alternative, always has an exonerating function, not only individually but also on the level of the species.

SLOTERDIJK: Nietzsche invented the most powerful image of the global dilemma for which one needs and seeks relief when he described man as a being hanging on the back of a tiger in dreams. In that situation we think twice about whether to wake up the passenger. Nobody has practised getting off the tiger's back. Some progressive moralists today are coming round to the idea that the tiger doesn't exist at all. According to them, we have been standing on firm ground all the time, responsible for ourselves from top to toe. For them, there is no dark underbelly that empowers and sometimes devours us. By contrast, authors such as Heidegger or Friedrich Georg Jünger[5] focused on the monstrous in their considerations on the modern world, the former with his theory of frames that concerns a super-tiger called technology, and the latter in the form of a meditation about the titanic quality of modern civilizations. Since then, there has been an almost never-ending discussion about the weirdness that lies at the roots of the enterprises of modernity. Thinking like that makes us imagine ourselves as insects in the scaly skin of a dragon. Dreamers on a tiger's back or gnats on the scales of a monster – those are the images that have shaped being-in-the-world after the collapse of the perpetrator illusion following the French Revolution, and after the implosion of the Napoleon bubble.

RAULFF: In this case refatalization seems to be not only giving relief but also oppressive.

SLOTERDIJK: First, the key word 'relief' is the best word for this situation. To understand that we have to go back to the era following the French Revolution and the Napoleonic Wars. After the heroic period, losers stood around everywhere looking for excuses. Fate was just the right thing. Napoleon was exiled to a remote Atlantic island, the heroes were pensioned off, history stagnated and a strong demand for non-responsibility hung in the air. People

[5] Friedrich Georg Jünger (1898–1977) was a German poet, author and essayist in cultural criticism.

had meant well but things turned out differently. In *Les Misérables*, Victor Hugo portrayed a sad figure who created a paltry business out of the memories of great days – the sergeant from Waterloo, a veteran who earned a living from saying he had been there. That was the beginning of the memorial industry, which is now an integral part of the exonerated life of the modern age: somebody once called it 'mobility on a stationary basis' and this is still the most profound statement about our way of being. Kierkegaard memorably described the experience of the calm after the storm that was history in his little-known essay, *A Literary Review*. It is here, incidentally, that we find the first instance of insulting the audience in modern philosophy, which seems to have inspired the Man chapter of Heidegger's *Being and Time*. In this essay Kierkegaard discovered a new kind of monster, gigantic in its lack of character – the modern public, in fact, whose formation brought the art of not having been there to its present stage. Heidegger would later describe this public as follows: 'Everyone is the other and no one is himself.' Its fate was to have arrived too late for the real history.

RAULFF: The epigones ... Immermann[6] ... All the deeds that would have been worth doing are already written down in the history books, and all the works it would have been worth writing are already in the libraries.

SLOTERDIJK: To pursue the point even further, it means that history had already come to a standstill at Waterloo. The first concise post-historic era occurred in the years 1815 to 1818, during the occupation by the Belle Alliance victors when France slumped into political catatonia – an episode that has been erased from or, more precisely, never entered French memory. The country regained its status as a sovereign nation with the Bourbon restoration of 1818 to 1830, but the cost was standstill, political and ideological regression, and bitterly warring rival parties splintering into chaos. The post-historical mood became chronic under the rigid Bourbons. You just have to look at the pompous, overblown portraits of Louis XVIII in French heraldic ermine to realize that post-history and simulation belong together. The French were the first to learn that people can fake entire epochs. At that period the best one could do was to write medieval novels or memoirs beyond the grave. This is just what Walter Scott and Chateaubriand, the great masters of ersatz history and ersatz life, did. Given this constellation, we can understand the hunger for fate. Along with post-historical paralysis

[6] Karl Leberecht Immermann (1796–1840) was a German novelist, dramatist and poet famous for his contemporary criticism.

comes nostalgia for turbulent times with all their blood and pomp. Incidentally, one topic of recent literature on Heidegger and Co. is 'yearning for harshness and severity', which is a rather good characterization of the heroic disposition of the young conservative spirits of the early twentieth century. The formulation aptly fits the post-Napoleonic age. It describes the nostalgia for the days when the French lived on victory reports. This nostalgia is still alive today. Among current politicians, Dominique de Villepin is the one who most clearly embodies the epic-heroic view of history.

RAULFF: This resembles the Bainville tradition that brought royalism into the twentieth century via the digression of the *Action française*.

SLOTERDIJK: De Villepin, who is a Gaullist and a lyrical Bonapartist, wrote quite an interesting book about Napoleon's hundred days. The book reveals an intensely nostalgic picture of the author's view of France in its best period – heroic and grand, although unfortunate in the end. It gives an idea of the role the author would like to play in his lofty nation.

RAULFF: Typical historical-mythological French thinking, astonishing for a modern-day politician.

SLOTERDIJK: It has something of the drama of the gifted child from the right wing who concocts a story with plumed helmets and clinking swords. Anyway, we're familiar with similar exercises on German soil as well. Here, as in France, the point of such exercises is to postulate an inspired new start after a significant military defeat, or after it feels as if history has come to an end. We can also trace this pattern of the end and a new beginning of the world drama in post-war periods in detail, by looking at the case of the young Heidegger. His lecture in the winter semester of 1929–30 on the fundamental concepts of metaphysics included the magnificent treatment of boredom, in which Heidegger described the world of 1929 as if it were conclusively over. He asked: 'What is our actual condition?' and answered: 'Our condition is such that nothing moves us deeply any more.' Our own epoch leaves us empty. That is the Freiburg variation of the theorem of the end of history. Its end is shown in our emptiness that proves the absence of the essential in our existence. Of course, Heidegger only followed this train of thought with a strategic intention because he believed being immersed in extreme boredom would lead to a dialectical reversal into its opposite, the greatest state of tension. He wanted to compel the rebirth of history out of the spirit of being left in a state of emptiness. According to Heidegger, profound boredom is the most philosophical of moods: in it, we experience the difficulty of an existence in which being is abandoned. In the state of ultimate boredom of having-nothing-else-to-do, Being will experience even when it is in absent mode. Only once we have penetrated into it totally can we feel, first remotely, then increasingly clearly, the returning call of temporalized Being that commissions a new chapter of history: 'The event needs you!' That sounds like a tempting call to join the first loud political movement that comes along ...

RAULFF: Which naturally promises the direct way out of the absence of fate.

SLOTERDIJK: Naturally, because it bursts on to the scene with brute force to kick-start history, which is at a standstill. From this perspective, in Heidegger's work it could also have been the communists whose revolutionary historicism would have suited his onto historical approach well. But its options did not correspond to Heidegger's profile, which was closer to the national Bolshevik revolt, Niekisch and his consorts. In the days of national revolution, the concept of fate in its most massive form became important again. Great history, in Heidegger's opinion, is sent. Indeed, it is sent by the noblest sender, Being. But as the sending Being transmits itself via existence, it needs people who are sent: they will be the rare people who are simultaneously moved and resolute. The only other example we have of this concerns the Christian Apostles, who promulgate an unconditional message. When being moved and being resolute occur together, it creates an action through a medium, an acted action, so to speak, that makes history by following the call of Being and reinforcing it with its own calls. In terms of form, it is like the model of the eternal love story between human beings and God. Such stories regularly start with the subject that has been left empty wanting to be emotionally moved. The unbelievers who want to believe think that once really moved, we would rush ahead with good reason and would finally know what had to be done. My deed should move me in such a way that I can do it. For most people, the reality is precisely the other way round: anyone who follows the tendency to rush ahead thinks up the emotion to match.

RAULFF: The person in the grip of emotion thus stands on both sides of the passivity–activity relationship. This causes an enormous reinforcement, a dramatization of existence. Being emotionally moved involves immersion or submissiveness. As the former female bishop would say, we lie even deeper in God's hands. On the other hand, the resoluteness creates an ascension ...

SLOTERDIJK: I have been thinking about such figures of mediatory subjectivity for decades. I always come back to a short, lucid essay titled *The Difference Between a Genius and an Apostle*, that Kierkegaard wrote in 1848 as part of his polemic against the

Danish pastor Adler.[7] This short essay with its strong inner dimension is something like the Magna Carta of a spiritual media theory. We should read it every two or three years to hone our analytical tools. In an extremely compact style, Kierkegaard described two diametrically opposite modes of communication, that of the genius and that of the apostle. Genius-type communication is based on self-expression; it corresponds to the aesthetic mode of being-in-the-world. As Kierkegaard says, it stems from the humorous self-sufficiency of the genius. The genius has done enough if he or she manifests the interior world in highly artistic work without caring whether the world around is following him or her. Genius needs no authority. The public's admiration is ample compensation for what it is missing at the level of communicating the truth. The apostle is an entirely different story: this is a person with an absolute teleology because he or she is motivated by an unconditional in-order-to, an unavoidable task. Apostles submit to a call from above and gain authority insofar as they invoke that call. This creates a performative loop: St Paul can only invoke the fact that God called him, but he can't provide external evidence of this, of course. He can only affirm it in the act of speaking himself: 'Paul, a servant of Christ' – he has to repeat it endlessly, and by repeating it he is putting his existence at the service of the mission that mobilizes and makes use of him. In submitting to the absolute goal he lays claim to a mandate. This is the key concept here. It seems to me the question of mandate was Heidegger's major problem until the very end. He knew that authority and destiny belong together somehow. He cherished the hope of authority for his message but he sought it outside the Christian succession in a philosophical line of succession, as if the vocation and authorization for his profession were also based on a kind of apostolic chain that was inaugurated and actualized by Being itself. If that were not the case, Being would not be Time, and the temporal succession of ideas would not be a true event but a mere sequence of self-dissolving paradigms. The Greek beginning is enormously important for Heidegger because it was there that the transmission chain began – although jamming transmitters have dominated since Plato. Being as Time also sends out its followers as if they should go out to the whole world and baptize people in the name of the basic concepts of metaphysics: world – finiteness – solitude. People sent out like that live in the ecstasy of being ambassadors set marching by Being itself. And Heidegger wanted to be regarded as an

[7] Søren Kierkegaard, *The Present Age*, and *Of the Difference Between a Genius and an Apostle* (New York: Harper & Row), 1962.

absolute person set marching by the grace of the shrouded absolute sender.

RAULFF: He wanted to be a *homme fatal* himself.

SLOTERDIJK: In fact, he realized that he would only gain authority if he reinsured himself with the supreme sender. That is the reason why he was religious as well, and this distinguishes him from the nihilists. Resolute nihilists leave the sender behind them and declare themselves as the *force majeure*. A Gnosticizing spirit like Heidegger, who took a Protestant stance in his early works and a Catholic stance in his later works, always knew he must have Being backing him because Being shared the function of absolute sender authority with the God of the New Testament. Heidegger's work has undertones of the Gnostic view in the sense that he sees the function of God not in creating but in being the sender. His God was not the one that created the Sun, Moon and Earth, but the one who sent indications to the dark world on how salvation could be conceived. The only knowledge that counts in this approach is knowledge of salvation – and here salvation means collecting from the dispersal. Incidentally, an arrangement like this corresponds to the dream of absolute authorship: it reflects the will to move on from the phase of experimenting with talent to the level of communicating truth. That is the author fantasy par excellence, and it can't be fulfilled simply by being a genius. A depressed genius can have endless fun but still commit suicide in the end. The simple genius doesn't achieve transformation into a messenger. Messengers do not belong to themselves and should never desert the flag.

RAULFF: Are you thinking of David Foster Wallace?

SLOTERDIJK: Yes, of course. In his case, the Kierkegaard-type humorous self-sufficiency of the genius was not enough; his depressive constitution got in the way. As far as Heidegger is concerned, he was light years away from such complications because he …

RAULFF: … always felt he was in good hands.

SLOTERDIJK: He seems to have been constantly surrounded by a supportive environment.

RAULFF: He felt structurally protected in something or other, maybe in language, or the destiny of being, or the landscape. He always gives the impression of being sure that there is a sustaining power.

SLOTERDIJK: I think I know better now where he derived that from. For several years I have visited the Black Forest regularly, in the region between Sankt Blasien and Todtnauberg. It is a strange area. If you spend time there peacefully looking at the farmhouses and you start responding to their charming effect, something stirs inside you. Those Black Forest houses have an archetypal aura of security. We must imagine what it means for the people living in such a house that the roof takes up three-quarters of the house's volume. It stands out so far that it seems to enclose the whole of the rest of the building. Like henhouses that seem to cluck contentedly ...

RAULFF: The epitome of being protected ...

SLOTERDIJK: Protected to the highest degree, as safe and secure as on the seventh day of creation. Some houses are so beautiful that you just want to stand there and say, 'Perfect.'

RAULFF: The hat – to shelter something with your hat – to protect, or to shepherd – Shepherd of Being ... these motifs play a pre-eminent role in the late Heidegger.

SLOTERDIJK: The same goes for the mountain range, hiding, seclusion. All this is directly there in those cocooning houses. Even if you don't go up to the loft the whole year round, you live with its presence. It is the prototype of the mountain range under which a protected existence evolves. The effect is very touching. In this case the house becomes a living-tool – and if living and thinking belong together, the house there is a thinking-tool and a world-tool in one. By staying in Heidegger's region I have gained access to some ideas of his that you can't get simply by reading them. Incidentally, you don't find any traces of this at Heidegger's notorious hut, which is only a humble lean-to, a green-painted shack.

RAULFF: I am pleased that this digression on the sensitivities of the later Heidegger has helped us towards a more positive definition of the concept we are discussing. So far, we have described the topic mostly in negative modes such as compensation, exoneration, excuses, pre-emptive confrontation, etc. I have been meaning to ask you the whole time: can't you also envisage a legitimate, positive way of using this concept? Do you think it still has a halfway meaningful field of application in the present day?

SLOTERDIJK: Are you still talking about fate?

RAULFF: Yes, indeed; I'm sticking to it quite obsessively ...

SLOTERDIJK: Well, the concept remains meaningful, although today it is used in a narrower sense than in ancient times. The Fates have laid down their shears – they probably had to hand them in at hand-luggage control. The Moirai, the ananke, fate, kismet – we can't revive all that. It is time for a reformatted, weaker, more modest concept of fate. It's no secret how we will get it: it will appear for us in the third act of the drama of the history of ideas that began in Europe in the seventeenth century. We have already referred to this. In the first act, fate is swallowed up by the rational version of Being. In Spinoza's work the world appears as a *gesamtkunstwerk* composed of causalities. That suspended fate in natural laws, after which fate could retire peacefully because everything happens through good imperatives anyway. The necessary and sufficient conditions arrange things between themselves. Fatalism vanishes in universal causality and can then dissolve temporarily into the optimism of the philosophy of praxis. To quote a classical warning against superstitious belief in astrology, 'In your breast are the stars of your fate.'[8] The age of the pathos of self-determination has come, and we just don't need heteronomous powers of fate any more. But it won't stay like that for long. After the first naïve wave of practice has crashed, the second phase will start. We are being overwhelmed by the evidence of old and new kinds of heteronomy currently overtaking the anti-fatalism of the Enlightenment. Neo-fatalist concepts have taken over since it became clear that things are going to turn out differently than we imagined. Counter-enlightenment tendencies are celebrating a return match. Oswald Spengler almost believed that deeper minds would always feel attracted to the concept of fate. Even the largest growing organisms on earth, the high cultures, are subject to fate in the form of morphological necessity. The cultures are winding down like plant life or thousand-year-old musical boxes, and our life is synchronized with them. A good part of our latter-day literature on fate is written in this tone. It processes the darkness in our conditions of existence affirmatively – from Goethe's *Primal Words, Orphic* to Nietzsche's *amor fati* to the *retour du tragique*. The last motif has been a topic for French authors such as Jean-Marie Domenach, from a Catholic perspective, and Michel Maffesoli, from the standpoint of postmodern pluralism.[9] A while ago we entered the third phase, in which we are just as remote from the Promethean rationalism of the Enlightenment as we are from the coy irrationalism of the counter-Enlightenment. This is the basic position from which to get a clear overall view of the field. We are at the end of the parable of fate: the Enlightenment neutralization of the concept and its irrationalist revival are followed by post-Enlightenment clarification.

RAULFF: There were occasional objections to this, of course. You have already mentioned Marquard, who used the term 'fate' to protest against the technocratic enlightenment's crazy notion that anything is feasible, and Koselleck does something similar as well.[10]

[8] 'In thy breast are the stars of thy fate.' (Friedrich Schiller, *The Piccolomini*, Act II, Scene VI.)

[9] Jean-Marie Domenach (1922–97) was a French journalist and writer with a Catholic perspective whose influential book, *Le retour de la tragique*, appeared in 1963. Michel Maffesoli is a French sociologist specializing in postmodernity and the presence of the imaginary in everyday life.

[10] Reinhard Koselleck (1923–2006) was a leading twentieth-century German historian.

SLOTERDIJK: In my opinion, both of them belong to the category of *Abklärung*, 'clarification'. The great master in this field was, of course, Niklas Luhmann. I was referring to him when I claimed, in the discussion with Heiner Geißler we mentioned at the beginning of this interview, that the most profound *incognito* of the idea of fate or destiny in the modern age is the concept of 'differentiation of subsystems' that Luhmann used. Maybe he would object, but it seems to me it was a meaningful statement. When Luhmann speaks of differentiation it sounds almost as if he were telling us *ex officio*: 'Not only books, but also systems, have their destinies.' The destiny of social systems is that, from a specific degree of complexity onwards, they differentiate functionally of their own accord. We notice this partly from the fact that they become obscure in terms of common sense. As soon as a system has become differentiated you can't apply everyday reasoning to it any longer because it has become autonomous and self-referential. Expert reason and everyday reason are estranged from each other. The expert has the task of explaining to the layperson that things in differentiated subsystems function as they function and it can't be any different even when, and precisely when, it seems absurd to common sense. We can also describe this as follows: when they are differentiated, social systems reach the level at which the people who are the targets of sociological enlightenment are required to understand that society has no logical centre and doesn't produce any true self. Society has no God spots, as it were, where it can look into its own interior. Sociology, too, is only useful to the extent that it understands that it doesn't really understand its subject ...

RAULFF: Does this mean Luhmann is also on the side of the post-Enlightenment?

SLOTERDIJK: I would call Luhmann the third member of the group of clarifiers next to Koselleck and Marquard. What they all share is the objective irony with which they view the results of historical activism. Clarification is always post-optimistic.

RAULFF: In his day Marquard, in particular, represented the position of objection to the social-technological ideology that was still in its original happy state in the 1970s. In other words, he opposed the belief in the feasibility and predictability of everything.

SLOTERDIJK: The concept of fate has needed modernizing from the time we could no longer bring on the kind of crude heavy weaponry of history and ontology that was typical in the nineteenth century. The semantic content of the recycled concept of fate can be dispersed rather more finely now. To give one example of a nuance in meaning that has become detached from the complex of discourses on fatality, let me mention the concept of the irreversible as it has developed in thermodynamics and process theory. Whereas human history represents the realm of second chances and of things happening 'once again', the sphere of physical processes is defined by unrepeatability and irreversibility. Another example is the concept of inviolability: this expression has had a notable career in theological circles in recent decades. In using it, we are repeating a gesture we have known since the Romantic period: omnipotence of the subject – no thanks! Anyone who says 'inviolable' nowadays is thinking of the 'mortal coil' in the theological sense that can't be shuffled off by any clarification, or by any technological relief.

RAULFF: Theologians are not the only people who talk like that. There are similar cases among aestheticians and phenomenologists: Gumbrecht with his repeated emphasis on the epiphanic presence, Karl Heinz Bohrer with his focus on the aesthetic moment – those are also expressions of inviolability.[11] They relate to instances that can't be planned and produced, moments of an emotional presence that either appear on their own or withdraw without our being able to protest about it.

SLOTERDIJK: By the way, both Gumbrecht and Bohrer refer to the strongest instance of 'fate' in modern German poetry. In Rilke's eighth *Duino Elegy*, we hear the sigh: 'This is what fate means: to be opposite / and to be that and nothing else, opposite, forever.' Towards the end of the poem comes the question: 'Who has turned us round like this, so that / whatever we do, we always have the aspect / of one who leaves?' The poet's lament relates to the fact that for us, as humans in general and individuals of the modern age in particular, unlike for dumb animals, the world no longer represents pure openness. We have stacked up the space before us with projects. Fate is decided here through human beings' existential orthopaedics. It has failed so fundamentally that we will always be those who turned round, who go away, who are incapable of being present. It seems to me we encounter the concept of fate here in a soft, almost innocent version, because it designates a tragic dowry of civilization, not triumphal and not masochistic, but tinged with melancholy. Heidegger described something vaguely comparable when he spoke of the insanity that is inseparable from human beings' period of residence in the world. Going astray is ensconced in normal existence itself, which has always been in a kind of flight.

[11] Hans Ulrich Gumbrecht is a German-born American literary scholar and professor at Stanford University. Karl Heinz Bohrer is a German essayist and literary scholar.

Heidegger is almost saying: 'Being human is being away' – like the expression 'Let's get out of here!'

RAULFF: May I return to the other point again: is there a possibility for you to integrate the concept of fate into your own work? It seems to me you touched almost directly on the concept a couple of times in the development of your work, from the *Critique of Cynical Reason* to *Eurotaoism* and *You Must Change Your Life*, but you haven't adopted it personally, if I can put it like that; in a sense you have narrowly squeezed past it. All the same, I would like to ask whether fate might be a positive, interesting concept for you.

SLOTERDIJK: I would say the most interesting concepts are retired concepts.

RAULFF: Concepts in the retirement home for the history of concepts?

SLOTERDIJK: Their retirement is part of their charm. When their service is over, old concepts find a small part-time job now and then. This is how a new use of the concept of fate would appear to me. It has to be brought into play far more casually than in its heyday; it has to become almost feather-light. This reminds me of a passage in Nietzsche's work I often return to – the song 'Before Sunrise' from the third part of *Zarathustra*. The scenery is imposing: as we can expect from the prophet of the new world age, Zarathustra is already up at dawn, running across the mountains and engaging in dialogue with the heavens before the sun appears. This is where the decisive phrases come – wait, I have to find the place (*Sloterdijk leafs through the book*): 'Truly it is a blessing and not a blasphemy when I teach: "Above all things stands the heaven of chance, the heaven of innocence, the heaven of accident, the heaven of wantonness." "Von Ohngefähr" [Lord Chance] – that is the world's oldest nobility.'[12]

RAULFF: That is very beautiful.

SLOTERDIJK: 'Which I have given back to all things, I have released them from servitude under purpose.' At this point we have to interrupt and add a commentary on the metaphysical content of the formula 'servitude under purpose'. In its strongest form, the idea of fate was not an improvised home remedy for hypochondriacs on cloudy days – it was a world principle placed on a high ontological throne; it was the work of the good reason of all things. The philosophical concept of fate appeared at its most splendid in late antiquity in the form of the stoical Heimarmene, who represented

[12] Friedrich Nietzsche, *Thus Spake Zarathustra*, trans. R. J. Hollingdale (London: Penguin Books), 1961, pp. 186; 4,209ff.

something like the sweeping reason of the government of the universe – incidentally, in mythology, Heimarmene was known as the daughter of Ananke. Nietzsche rejected such fictitious ideas of a lofty premeditated necessity in the course of all things by letting chance off the leash:

> I have released them from servitude under purpose. I set this freedom and celestial cheerfulness over all things like an azure bell when I taught that no 'eternal will' acts over them and through them. I set this wantonness and this foolishness in place of that will when I taught: 'With all things one thing is impossible – rationality!' A *little* reason, to be sure, a seed of wisdom scattered from star to star – this leaven is mingled with all things: for the sake of foolishness is wisdom mingled with all things. A little wisdom is no doubt possible; but I have found this happy certainty in all things: that they prefer – to *dance* on the feet of chance.

These lines were written on the Independence Day of modern thought – and inevitably they deal with the emancipation of the coincidental. Nietzsche still employs the metaphysical language of thunder and lightning in some places, but on this subject he has already changed to contingency thought. This much remains today from good old fate: Luhmann's theorem of double contingency. A system in which everything could be different relates to an environment in which everything could also be different. But the fact it is actually the way it is involves a touch of fatefulness.

RAULFF: And would that be your answer as well?

SLOTERDIJK: In principle, yes, as long as it means the emancipation of the coincidental. I really like terms that are out of commission. Antiquated concepts contain riches you can discover by chance as if you were clearing out the attic. A word like 'fate' is an archive in itself. That reminds me of Gottfried Benn's remark: 'Words, words – nouns! They only need to open their wings and millennia drop off from their flight.'[13]

RAULFF: I think that's wonderful.

SLOTERDIJK: 'Fate' is the kind of word from whose flight the millennia drop off.

RAULFF: The concept in itself is a gigantic theory novel, a novel of thought. So far we have only unpacked a couple of expressions

[13] Gottfried Benn, 'Epilog und lyrisches ich', in *Gesammelte Werke*, vol. 4, ed. Dieter Wellershoff (Wiesbaden: Limes), 1968, p. 8.

and metaphors from the crate, but it is quite astonishing what that revealed.

SLOTERDIJK: We have indicated a few examples of mythical and terminological conceptions of the fateful in the Western tradition. Aside from this, we shouldn't forget that there is an independent oriental world of theory, namely the Indian, which has had a concept such as karma for 2,500 years. This covers much of what Eastern philosophers have experienced or devised on moral causality, long-term relations of culpability, coincidences of incarnation, and existential inequalities and their future compensations. India belongs to a world sphere that, seen as a whole, had a far lower level of technological and political freedom than the Western sphere. As soon as you open up to its culture you feel something of the dominant need there to react to prevailing conditions with far more soul, many more gods and much more asceticism.

RAULFF: Doesn't that also mean, with far more poetry?

SLOTERDIJK: It is true that the people of the Indian hemisphere were condemned to produce an interior world from very early times, just like the people of the bygone days when Europe was still called the Occident. In this state of the world, the way outward was largely blocked and the external facts were not very inspiring. Only enormous achievements of practice and recasting make the world and life bearable. To explain with an analogy, I am fond of recalling the ancient European tradition of constellations that modern people hardly know about any more – at most they know Ursa Major or Orion's Belt. In antiquity every halfway-educated person knew the forty-eight constellations like the back of their hand, and each of the constellations was associated with innumerable stories. The constellation-studded sky was evidence of how earlier people had vested the external world with excess matter from their inner world. In this state of the world the concept of fate assumes enormous importance because it simulates a kind of grammar for recasting good and bad fortune. A single star starts off being nothing but a meaningless point of light, part of a constellation, a cipher. This is how apparently meaningless coincidences are woven together in an ad hoc fabric of meaning. The concept of fate indicates the psychological work that will be necessary if people want to recast chance into something meaningful and liveable. Only well-insured people like us in the modern age have been able to emancipate themselves from chance. Only in technological culture can one travel with such light psychological baggage as we have grown accustomed to carrying. Most of the generations before us didn't have that kind of relief from burdens. They had to try to understand the world like a big carpet with a pattern that is too big to be recognizable, but they still wanted to believe absolutely in its existence. In its most human form, the idea of fate was the core element of the belief that we ourselves are threads and figures in a divine carpet-weaving workshop.

## II. Marbach Conversation

RAULFF: Mr Sloterdijk, to follow up and round off our first meeting of several months ago, today we should talk about some topics that we didn't mention last time. I am thinking mainly about the symbolism of fate in early modernism, especially Fortuna with all her attributes, each of which is extremely interesting in its own right . . .

SLOTERDIJK: And each of which would merit a large exhibition. Fortuna's classical attributes are the helm, the sail, the wheel that rises and falls, the cosmos sphere on which the goddess balances, the globe and its miniature versions, the ball and the lottery ball. Today, unfortunately, nobody gives a thought any more to the symbolic sources of the countless balls that we play with in present mass culture.

RAULFF: Except for Horst Bredekamp, who is interested in the ball games of the Medici . . .[14]

SLOTERDIJK: Yes, he is one of the few contemporary scholars of visual imagery to have examined these topics. But the whole theme of balls, globes and spheres has a miserable existence in the margin of the official attention system.

RAULFF: What is the reason for this? Is it perhaps because, despite Huizinga,[15] people haven't taken the game seriously in terms of its function for cultural creativity? Or is it that playing games has always been associated with a kind of vagueness? With an inherent shakiness?

SLOTERDIJK: I think you're right. For a very long period vagueness and shakiness were unpopular with theorists – they disliked them. One exception is Paul Valéry's work, where we can still see the morose, classical-rationalist type of character with a visceral abhorrence of anything approximate. On the other hand, we can only understand something about the twentieth-century

[14] Horst Bredekamp is a German art historian. Raulff is referring to his book: Horst Bredekamp, *Florentiner Fußball. Die Renaissance der Spiele. Calcio als Fest der Medici* (first published 1993; revised edition, Berlin: Wagenbach, 2001).

[15] Johan Huizinga (1872–1945) was a Dutch historian and cultural theorist who played a major role in developing modern cultural theory.

culture of rationality if we view it as constantly extending the zone of calculability. It is an enterprise to bring labile factors, all kinds of vagueness, enthusiasms and turbulences into the realm of exact thought. In the Europe of old, these unstable entities were treated as mythological forms; uncertainties were attributed to divine moods or predestination. But probability calculations began to appear in the seventeenth century, and since the twentieth century we have been able to apply chaos theory, fractals and algorithms to everything crooked, twisted and tattered.

We don't talk about Fortune nowadays, of course, but about risk. That presupposes a leap into a different discursive order. For an author like Petrarch it was still right and proper to survey the whole field of existential instability with a collection of exemplary stories or novellas about good and bad luck. Research tells us that his gigantic book *De remediis utriusque fortunae*[16] was one of the most frequently copied secular manuscripts of the pre-Gutenberg age. This shows, incidentally, that we can discern the beginning of modernity from the rise of the advice manual. Petrarch's work shows him as the first great master of literary life training. He was completely abreast of his times because in the dawning modern age he understood that he could particularly arouse interest in the role of a fortune therapist. His approach was still completely Stoical-Christian. He appealed to his readers with the message: if you have to live in this world in which moody Fortuna throws her balls – the bewildering goddess Fortuna, who sometimes pampers you and sometimes lets you drop – you should start by learning to respond with indifference to the balls she throws. The best way is to practise keeping an equal distance from her so as not to cling to good luck too much and not to lament bad luck too much.

RAULFF: What do latter-day advisers who have started talking about risk have in mind? What is their goal? To limit risk using probability calculations? Do they want to win the game themselves? Or do they want to act as insurers and limit other people's risk of damage?

SLOTERDIJK: This field of play involves various different types and positions: some people play for the sake of the game, and others to win, while a third group wants to play to win profit from others winning. A fourth group doesn't play at all for fear of losing – they are the ones who don't realize they have lost from the beginning. Anyone who hasn't played loses without having had the chance to

[16] Francesco, Petrarch, *Remedies for Fortune Fair and Foul*, trans. C. H. Rawski (Bloomington, IN: Indiana University Press), 1991.

win. The fourth position is that of the eternal conservatives who are still around today, who think they can save their skin in the general competition by staying away from the current games of chance.

RAULFF: Moving upward historically from the medieval emblem of Fortuna – namely, the globe on which the goddess balances – we get to modern techniques of controlling coincidence, from risk minimization to risk elimination. If we go backward from that, we get to the ancient pictures of the distribution of lots.

SLOTERDIJK: On this reading, the Fortune theology of the late Middle Ages and the early modern era would be something like the midpoint between the dark fatalism of the Greeks before the beginning of the first enlightenment, and the apparently complete elimination of risks in modern banking mathematics – although we know by now this can only function as massive deception of oneself and others. That middle position couldn't be held without complications: it was related to the almost insoluble problem of balancing up the fundamental anti-fatalist teachings of Christianity – which assert that after the resurrection of the Lord, Fate has no more dominion – with the persistence of the ancient, popular formulas for neutralizing chance and fate, which were almost indispensable. This is the only reason why Fortuna haunted the Christian Middle Ages, for which she actually had no residence permit. The strongest symptom of this insoluble tension was the Augustine teaching of predestination in which we can retrospectively recognize the matrix of Western neurosis. On the one hand, Augustine understood better than anyone else that faith in Fate is irreconcilable with the triune nature of God. That is why he wanted to sink any idea of Fate in the underworld of vanquished superstition. This, however, didn't eliminate the problem that ancient belief in fate was developed to solve; the unfathomable inequality of human living conditions preoccupied the thoughts of Christians just as much as those of the people of pre-Christian antiquity. The riddle consisted of absorbing the real existing absurdity that yawns at us as we watch human beings wrestling with incredibly blatant inequalities from birth onward. To deal with this, Augustine hit upon a solution that turned out to be even more sinister than ancient fatalism had ever been – the theory of human beings' divine predestination to salvation and perdition. To fend off pagan fatalism, the Church Father plunged into the murkiest adventure in the history of ideas: he invented a monotheist hyper-fatalism called predestination, which literally means the anticipatory determination of fate.

At the same time Augustine firmly adhered to the thesis of human freedom, because otherwise it would have been impossible to defend the penal character of being predestined to damnation. In his philosophy, predestination becomes a medium of divine selectivity that remains incomprehensible. Augustine's finicky God was not a laughing matter. In real terms, the great majority of people have to anticipate belonging to the damned souls from the very beginning. This exactly reflects the ideological situation of late antiquity in which the Church, although it was formally the religion of state from the year 395 onward, barely had any influence on the lives of people in the Empire: the few convinced Christians who existed were well aware that they belonged to a tiny elite and that the gates of heaven would probably remain shut to the great majority. It is true that the Christian God is called the Merciful, and the word 'mercy' describes the exceptional right of the sovereign, but mercy for the many or, indeed, mercy for all, would not be plausible, even for a God that makes exceptions.

The ominous nature of Augustine's version didn't consist in its manifest elitism – Christianity is elitist, or it is not Christian. It was rather a matter of its depressive logic, because it eliminated the possibility of contributing to one's own redemption by making pious efforts. Piety itself is a result of mercy, not its cause. Augustine is formal on this point. Humans cannot obtain merits. Full stop. It took almost a thousand years until Anselm of Canterbury corrected Augustine's erroneous thinking. In Augustine's work, humans remain metaphysically in debit even after the redemption of Christ, because even after their baptism they continue being guilty of original sin, as their debt to God is infinite. This seems to make sense immediately: finite merit can't redeem infinite guilt, because adding a finite plus to an infinite minus yields an infinite minus. The relevant scholastic theorem is: *Inter finitum et infinitum non est proportio.* In other words, one can't bargain with the infinite, and Augustine knew that better than anybody. Yet a false conclusion crept into his calculation, and it was Anselm who first drew attention to it indirectly with his theory of satisfaction in *Cur deus homo*. Anselm presented a discrete kind of theological mathematics that showed the way out of the depressive logic of the Middle Ages. Since then, theologians have been able to calculate differently, as follows – A: the children of Adam brought infinite guilt on themselves; B: the infinite guilt was redeemed by the infinitely satisfying sacrifice of Christ. Consequently, C holds: infinite guilt plus infinite satisfaction equals zero. The revised calculation had an enormous impact: from that time on, human merits have made a difference. They could be chalked up positively because they were no longer directly counterposed to an infinite minus, for the latter is definitively balanced up by the deed of the God-man – and this balance marks the starting position of the believer. The horizon is now free for the active life;

positive deeds count. All at once it is meaningful when Christian people want to make something out of their lives and are not always panting for infinite guilt. From this perspective, the road to the modern world began in an obscure theological tract shortly before the year 1100. Since that time, Augustine's flight from ancient fate into the Christian Super-Fate called predestination has been brought to a standstill, at least wherever possible. That it persisted in Calvinism, and still persists, is a different matter.

RAULFF: What is modern about all this is probably the mathematization or arithmetization of fate, the quantification of guilt and the idea that it is possible to do calculations on the terrain of morality. The ability to add and subtract such factors is typical of the modern age. Fate in antiquity was simply irreparable, and addition, subtraction, etc., were unthinkable.

SLOTERDIJK: These calculations became established at the dawn of the modern age. Each life was linked to an evaluation. The Last Judgement changed its structure. We can see this above all in the emergence of Purgatory in the description of after-death landscapes in the High Middle Ages. The harsh alternative between Heaven and Hell was relativized by the very popular creation of an intermediate region where people would be retrospectively purified, cleansed and upgraded to enable them to share in salvation even if they had accumulated big overdrafts on their moral account which made them strong candidates for Hell. Purgatory marked the beginning of the age of rational repayment procedures.

RAULFF: And the idea of reparability as well.

SLOTERDIJK: We could almost say that the modern therapy society made its debut with the invention of Purgatory. The idea of debt repayment, which had its natural prototype in the beginning of the credit transactions of the High Middle Ages, even pervades human relationships with the heavenly authorities. This offered scope for human initiative and merits. Only then did it really make a difference whether people had behaved well or badly – a difference that would have been impossible otherwise in the Augustinian world, which was deeply paradoxical and impenetrable. In that world, sinners could inexplicably be redeemed at the last minute and the purported saint could remain accursed if, and because, divine predestination had determined that in advance. In contrast, spaces for human achievements were created at the beginning of the modern age and the first approaches to meritocratic thought could take root. One day, towards the end of the eighteenth century, a temple of enlightenment would be erected on Kaisersgracht in Amsterdam with a beautiful Greek facade; on the roof gable were the words *Felix meritis*, 'Happy through merit'. The Dutch were the firstborn members of a world without Hell.

RAULFF: But how does Fortune fit into the picture? Doesn't it stand for the fact that there is still fluctuation in this new arithmetized world, things still see-saw uncontrollably and can be overturned at any time for unknown reasons?

SLOTERDIJK: That is why the message until well into the late Middle Ages was: don't be impressed by Fortune, and be aware that good fortune poses the greater danger. Fortune may seem to favour you, only to let you fall even further later on. Therefore, beware of good luck, but don't be impressed by bad luck either. Petrarch expounded this approach in an immensely diverse manner in his work on medicine: he narrated around 125 stories with admonitory examples on both sides. We can well understand why life training in humanism and literature was so important for people of the fourteenth century. They felt that the message of the Gospels was completely under-determined in terms of modern conditions of life. People became increasingly interested in the supra-temporal or, rather, in the anachronistic elements of the statements of the Gospels. The characters of the New Testament were no longer contemporary, and even Renaissance painting, which persisted in behaving as if the Gospels could be visually actualized whereas they were becoming increasingly remote in moral terms, couldn't change that. The Gospels were hardly relevant in the new world of labour, in emergent politics, in the arts, in the sciences, and at the beginning of global traffic and communications. An intermediary text had to be inserted to develop and express what remained undefined in the Gospels. This became the field of activity for humanist writers at the dawn of the modern age. Think back to the ancient story about Fortuna and Tyche. From the fourteenth century onwards, the near-empty reservoir of knowledge about luck and ideas about risk was refilled. A kind of Stoical-Christian people's press concerned with the specific destiny of famous men and women emerged. Boccaccio's *De claris mulieribus* of 1374 is a model text of the new casuist tendency, as is his most successful collection, *De casibus virorum illustrium*, in which he showed how the unlucky star – *disastro* – is capable of throwing the lives of the great and greatest off track. The whole world was suddenly crazy for case histories, as if people were fed up with the eternal legends of the saints. Perhaps, from a literary perspective, this typifies the whole secret of the modern age: what is interesting outdoes what is edifying. Then Machiavelli arrived on the scene and suddenly the tone changed. His advice to people was no longer to be stoical and show evangelical indifference to good and bad luck. Instead, he openly concluded that the point is to seize luck with both hands. If luck is a woman one shouldn't hesitate for too long. His contemporaries, starting with merchants and adroit princes, understood that immediately. The affairs of Fortune took a great leap forward in the hundred years between Petrarch and Machiavelli. Machiavelli already talked like a trainer who wanted to make contemporary people fit for the really big match, the game of power and luck and success in the world ...

RAULFF: We have to grab the right moment ...

SLOTERDIJK: Machiavelli thought that everything depended on the moment, on *opportunità*, and it depended on the hand that grasps the opportunity – which raises the question of ball technique. Only somebody who is prepared to catch the ball of chance can be in the game at all. From that time on, it didn't help to surrender to the tendency to flee from the world. Let's not forget, people in late antiquity and the Middle Ages were always aware of the option of turning their back on the world. There was still the possibility of settling down in a remote, if uncomfortable, counter-world, in the school of philosophers or the community of saints, whether in the sense of a definitive separation from worldly things or whether one acted to improve the world from the counter-world. These options are not available in the same way to people of the modern age, because they can no longer wholly believe in an existence in the counter-world, but at best they can believe in holidays and emigration. On this point, even Luther who, God knows, was more medieval than the Middle Ages in many ways, scored the modernity goal and cast off his monk's habit. From a philosophical viewpoint, modern philosophy begins with the thesis that human beings are innately a microcosm, an abbreviation of the world as a whole. If human beings themselves are the world in miniature, the idea of flight from the world becomes meaningless because the world is always with me. Where I am, I am completely and utterly the world. The consequence is that the philosophical mentors of modern individuals, the literary life coaches we have mentioned, increasingly convinced their clients to join in the game of the world. This created a new kind of discourse about Fortune. It led to re-evaluation of humankind's being-in-the-world from the perspective of being able to join in the game.

RAULFF: That would mean the advisers are spectators to some extent, giving their clients advance commentaries on their possible fate.

SLOTERDIJK: Literary advisers cast their vote in advance, whereas operative advisers offer counselling on the spot. Of course, it is no coincidence that in the fifteenth century, at the very time when the twilight of Fortune occurred, the career profile of the *secretario* emerged. It was the right name for him, as he was indeed party to the secrets of enterprising modern individuals. We have largely forgotten this because we think of secretaries as people who carry out menial tasks in the boss's office. The job's original high status survives only in titles such as 'secretary of state' or 'general secretary'. The *secretario* of the Renaissance – Machiavelli was the prime example – is, if you like, the temporal version of the *grand aumônier*, the prince's chaplain whom every powerful man had to have at his side, according to the psychogogues of the early modern era. In those days people had already realized that the powerful man simply can't be powerful on his own – Schiller's famous saying 'The strong man is strongest when alone,' is totally wrong. The strong man is strong, and only looks strong, as long as he is surrounded by realistic advisers and efficient ministers, and by his *secretario*, of course. The latter's first task is to keep the prince's conscience intact because it represents the commonwealth's centre of moral strength. A prince who doesn't believe he will be pardoned is lost from the start. As far as I know, the first person to state these ideas explicitly was Eugen Rosenstock-Huessy.[17] According to him, the real state secret is the intact character of the prince's conscience. A prince who saw himself as a criminal would drag the whole state system into disrepute if he doubted himself – and this would particularly apply to a guilty prince who couldn't and wouldn't confess even in his deepest self. Machiavelli understood that being a prince is a profession that cannot be pursued without wrongdoing. This is why the ruler needs a spiritually competent person at his side who is familiar with the sacraments of power. This person must act as a guard to keep the prince's conscience intact in precarious situations – these are the situations we already mentioned, in which people can only choose between different evils. The office was usually performed by clerics – we involuntarily associate this with the archetype of the grey eminence, the notorious Père Joseph who was the spiritual watchdog at the side of Cardinal Richelieu, the most powerful man of the seventeenth century. Père Joseph was a paradigm case of the highest exercise of power from the religious wing. It was he who made the grey of the Capuchin monks' habits the leading political colour in Europe. A glance at the Italian scene shows that this function can also be performed by a secular person who is capable of sharing the prince's secret . . .

[17] Eugen Rosenstock-Huessy (1888–1973) was a German-born American social philosopher and historian of law. He is particularly known for his contribution to Jewish–Christian dialogue.

RAULFF: … sharing and guarding.

SLOTERDIJK: Indeed, 'share and guard' is the secretary's oath. It is both his motto and the basis of his profession. He knows two things that the nation and the court should not know on penalty of losing their power: the first is that exercise of power includes willingness to contravene morality and the law, if necessary …

RAULFF: The willingness to be a criminal …

SLOTERDIJK: Perhaps it must be expressed in such a dramatic way. The second, maybe even more embarrassing secret, is that having power usually means not knowing what to do.

RAULFF: Helplessness increases as power increases?

SLOTERDIJK: That is precisely the secret that has to be shared and guarded. The *secretario* is the person who best understands the difficult position of the mighty. This is the origin of the second source of the modern consultation: it stops giving advice on life from a general literary standpoint and starts providing concrete consultation on power instead. The core idea is the insight that there is no continuity between a plan of action and its execution. When the powerful want to move into action, they are not standing at the beginning of a paved road but in front of a precipice or a wide gap. The break in continuity means we can't walk into action; we can only leap into it. The *secretario* is the person who helps the mighty to find the jumping-off point. There are almost always ditches of indecision, of hesitation, of risk awareness to overcome if we want to act practically, and nobody knows this better than the man in the exposed position. His intimate confidant knows it as well. Having power means always being conscious of how far things can go wrong.

RAULFF: This means we should look up the old literature on the secretary if we want to know what happened to fate once consultants and risk managers became involved in shaping it.

SLOTERDIJK: Recently I happened to look at one of the fundamental books of the dawn of the modern era: Leon Battista Alberti's *Della famiglia – On the Family* – written around 1460. It seems to be a simple text by the father of a family for use by his own offspring. In reality, this book reveals nothing less than the face of the economic modern age that is about to begin, reflected in the language games of classical philosophy. The author was one of the actors who had long since understood that people have to enter the playing field themselves if they expect Fortune's favours – especially if they want to secure its favours on a long-term basis. The fourth part of the book is about friendship, which might make us think that the author is offering nothing but typical contemporaneous variations on the Aristotelian theme of *philía*. At first glance it merely seems to be a free restatement of the subject of friendship, using topical examples. In reality, we are looking at the first theory of networking. Alberti's considerations have a clear starting point: to successfully conclude business in the widening world, the entrepreneur must have friends everywhere in faraway places. What is interesting here is that Alberti didn't envisage the entrepreneur as the Faustian individual but as the active family, the power-conscious clan. At that time, the only method of ensuring the loyalty of employees in nearby and distant places of work consisted of situating one's own family members at key points where possible. We should remember that, as had been common since Greek and Roman antiquity, the family and friendship circles at that time were still closely intertwined, linguistically and in real terms. Loyalty was the greatest asset for people at the centre of entrepreneurial clans. It was the mercantile variant of the classical *philía*. The loyalty and esteem of a house or a firm could only be preserved if the merchants knew that alongside monetary capital and monetary credit there was another, subtle capital, a second kind of credit that was probably more important than the first – a good reputation. The reputation capital ultimately determined the good or bad luck of a firm, that is, a solid, firmly established and viable entrepreneurial unit in the modern markets. In fact, economic relationships between distant partners can't be established and can't flourish in the long term without that good reputation and its carefully nurtured growth. The type of successful long-distance relationships that traders engage in are only possible in the long run if the partners have more reason to trust than to mistrust. Securing trust by making friends is one of the processes for domesticating Fortune. The other successful procedures are in the field of risk management, which was already taking shape at that time. That is what the merchants are talking about on the Rialto in Venice in Shakespeare's *The Merchant of Venice*. This much is clear: a merchant couldn't go far with the Gospels alone. Reflections on Christian teaching couldn't make the new market predictable. That is why, around 1500, a perfectly functioning clandestine system of double theology was established in many places in Europe. For the critical moments in life there was Christianity, and for the business and private spheres there was the cult of Fortune.

RAULFF: In other words, people learned to be Christians and fatalists at the same time.

SLOTERDIJK: Yes, fatalist in the clear sense of the word.

RAULFF: In the entrepreneurial sense?

SLOTERDIJK: In a very practical sense, in which both the businessman and the courtier always did what was necessary to gain and keep Fortune's favours. But, as we have shown, at the beginning of the Enlightenment the suppression of such intellectual constructs had become unavoidable. The eighteenth century tried to break with feudal categories on a broad front, including the favouritism of Fortune. The ideology of equality had as little use for Fortune and its royal court as early Christianity had for Fate.

RAULFF: The early Enlightenment neutralized *amor fati*, while the democracy of the twentieth century doesn't have a clue what to do with it.

SLOTERDIJK: All in all, we can rightly say that the modern age initially had to abolish fate because it brought the dawn of the period in which people decided to direct their own fate. We have discussed how this led to neo-fatalist movements and that it was equally inevitable that they would be clarified in the Enlightenment via enlightenment and counter-enlightenment. Yet the pattern of abolition, return and clarification of the idea of fate is ultimately unsatisfying. I think that the most important thing is missing in this smooth narrative. I admit I have only realized recently what the real fascination of fatalism for people of all periods consists in, and people of the modern age are no exception to this. Fichte once remarked that the philosophy we choose depends on what kind of person we are. He distinguished between determinists, who he regarded as slaves who enjoyed their lack of freedom, and idealists for whom freedom was the most important thing. However problematic this distinction may be, it contains a significant psychological discovery. Strangely enough, there are countless people who see the statement 'There is absolutely nothing we can do' as good news. Whereas others resist this thesis with every inch of their being, fans of fatalism welcome it as absolution from the requirement to do anything.

RAULFF: There is a desire to overcome things that yields a kind of relief. Roland Barthes invented a lovely phrase for it: 'the will to hibernation'.

SLOTERDIJK: The tendency to hibernate at the nadir of the will doesn't only exist in the form of the desire to overcome things. The quietist acceptance of fatality was just as attractive for countless people in the twentieth century. Many people are happy to obtain proof that simply nothing can be done. Everything goes as it goes; everything comes as it comes. I suspect this doesn't only apply to the fatalism of ordinary people who want a quiet life; a large part of the intellectual movements of the twentieth century also felt the longing for hibernation. Switching off the subject is a curious theoretical passion we always have to bear in mind, not only among the mystics of the Middle Ages but also among people of the modern era. The vulgar version of Marxism was a massive kind of fatalism, according to which the revolution simply had to come sooner or later.

RAULFF: The will to fatalism is present both on the left and the right wing. But in the latter case, the role of Fate is often taken by the *homme fatal*, a Duce, the strong figure of an aggressor ...

SLOTERDIJK: ... a personification of world destiny or national appeal. After the Second World War, fatalism changed camps and settled into theories with a quietist structure, without further reference to the strong perpetrator. Since then, fate has anonymously determined the intellectual scene. Let's remember the 1950s, when the 'post-histoire' theories that had been advanced in Cournot's work in the nineteenth century and in the works of de Man and others in the twentieth century reappeared.[18] They argued that we had entered an era of crystallization, the historical alternatives had been exhausted and all that remained were minor variations. Gehlen's phrase, 'movement on a stationary basis', sums up this view. At the same time Kojève once again reintroduced the idea of the end of history in the Hegelian sense.[19] Then came structuralism with its conviction that anonymous structures are ultimately decisive: humans imagine they are doing something, but in reality they aren't doing anything because their internal structures are doing it. Back then, people celebrated the death of the author of structuralism and rejoiced in the expulsion of the subject from the humanities. Still later came system theory made in Bielefeld. It elegantly relegated the whole of the old European semantics of freedom, will, decision-making, commitment and the like to the archive where doctoral candidates are busy with old European phantoms. Finally, our friends the neuroscientists entered the scene and put the lid on old European illusions of action. Maybe Marbach is the ideal place to come face-to-face with these developments. The history of the free subject comes to an end behind steel doors. The excitement is over and the era of shrugging our shoulders and happily saying 'Can't-do-anything-more' can begin. Maybe this is the way we will arrive at the secret last horizon of our topic.

[18] Antoine-Augustin Cournot (1801–77) was a French mathematician and economic theorist and a founder of mathematical economic theory. Paul De Man (1919–83) was a Flemish-born literary theorist and philosopher known as a leading representative of the Yale critics.

[19] Arnold Gehlen (1904–76) was a German philosopher, sociologist and anthropologist and a leading proponent of philosophical anthropology. Alexandre Kojève (1902–68) was a Russian-born French philosopher and statesman whose ideas influenced French philosophy. He was a founding figure of the European Union.

RAULFF: Is this the point where we should stop?

SLOTERDIJK: Yes, but without resignation. The best way to conclude would be to make a proposal to the contradictory spirit of the observer. I'm fond of quoting another statement by Fichte, who once sarcastically remarked that it would be easier to persuade most people to think of themselves as a piece of lava in the moon than as an ego. Fichte understood that naturalism is a kind of hypnosis we can't wake up from without philosophical advice. Nowadays we would say it is easier to convince most people that they are an epiphenomenon of sticky nerve fibres than for them to be prepared to see themselves as free individuals. Anybody who talks about the brain is a traitor to freedom. We have earned the right to this provocative attitude, haven't we?

RAULFF: Wanting to be an individual is very exhausting.

SLOTERDIJK: The individual is a futile passion, but it should still remain a passion.

# 32

# HUMANS IN REPETITION

## The Twenty-first Century Will Be Acrobatic

*For an anthropology of exercises*

*Interview with Philippe Nassif**

NASSIF: When Nietzsche proclaimed that God was dead at the end of the nineteenth century, he prophesied two centuries of nihilism. As a person who sometimes claims to be a proponent of 'left-wing Nietzscheanism', would your outlook for the twenty-first century be equally pessimistic?

SLOTERDIJK: When Nietzsche spoke of nihilism it was because he had understood that at the bottom of things one finds chance, and not the divine and wise necessity that was so highly esteemed from the beginning of time. Our age has caught up with this important intuition. In this sense, the inflation of 'renown' – or, better still, celebrity – which will be accepted as the most important expression of fate in the coming decades and centuries, is very illuminating. In the twenty-first century anybody can become a world star, and can do so for the most unpredictable and often most ridiculous reasons. In other words, it will be the century of the tyranny of chance. Of course, chance was always in power, but it has never been observed in its naked state before. As long as people accepted their fate in relation to what they couldn't control, chance always appeared to them in a religious light, as a revelation of an act of God – *la forza del destino*, as it were. But the second half of the twentieth century produced a human species that is convinced that

* This interview between Peter Sloterdijk and Philippe Nassif appeared under the title 'L'homme dans la repetition/Le XXIe siecle sera acrobatique', in *Cles, Trouver du Sens, Retrouver du Temps*, at: <http://www.cles.com/enque tes/article/le-xxie-siecle-sera-acrobatique>. Interview date: 8 July 2010.

Philippe Nassif is a French philosopher.

the first human right consists of living in a world liberated from the moods of fate. The scandal of chance – that great creator of inequality – will have an increasingly strong effect in a rationalized world. It will be the act of God of the future. We can already see this in the culture of the twentieth century: inequalities, which merely express the reign of chance, evoke the feeling of living in an absurd world.

NASSIF: Still, the present age seems to be turning its back on the absurd. What is being expressed today has more to do with people wanting to create meaningfulness.

SLOTERDIJK: The individualism of the twenty-first century will actually be revealed in the desire to present chance as a deliberate and premeditated act. That will be a new form of eternal mystification. In the past, people lived with the feeling of an all-pervading necessity, a global providence that acted as the great director of the world and of the story of salvation. But then Nietzsche pulled aside the curtain for us: if we get to the bottom of things we find repetition and chance. That is the absolute novelty of modern thought.

NASSIF: A novelty that is difficult to digest.

SLOTERDIJK: It is easier to digest if we consider that alongside the comedy of absolute chance, whose culmination is the world as it is and I myself with all my characteristics, the increasing density of cultures on earth has become the other factor of fate that will shape the future. 'Density' means that the probabilities of encounters and clashes have become almost infinite. At any given moment you can have an encounter that will reshape your life.

NASSIF: In your *Spheres* trilogy you present the iconoclastic idea that the urban dweller is never alone, despite the huge growth of single households.

SLOTERDIJK: My project is based on a philosophical hostility to the ideology of the solitary individual. My thesis is that ultimately the individual does not exist. I reject the fallacious idea of ontological solitude that the society of the modern age is based on. In reality, Being always means being accompanied, but not necessarily by a visible companion. An invisible couple is always hiding in the apparent solitude of the individual. Being single therefore means forming a couple with a hidden Other – even if it is only my unknown 'I'. Modern, urban, available and active subjectivity corresponds perfectly to the idea of the inward-projected couple. The ability to live alone basically implies you have found the means, the media and the exercises to complete yourself self-referentially. I am never alone with my books; never alone with the music I want to hear; never alone with my interior polylogue. I discussed all these things in detail in *Foam*, the third volume of my trilogy. The

Americans are aware of this: when they say 'Take care' to us on leaving, they are addressing our unconscious twin.

NASSIF: The French are more likely to say 'Bon courage' ['Good luck']. Should we take it as a sign that the idea of individual solitude is more entrenched here in Europe than on the other side of the Atlantic?

SLOTERDIJK: Why shouldn't we see courage as a more or less faithful companion? My courage and I, we get on quite well together! Courage is the good spirit of everyday life.

NASSIF: If the public sees psychology as having had a great influence on philosophy in recent decades, could it be because it has proposed a model of the internal couple 'Me and my unconscious' instead of the idea of an autonomous, and therefore solitary, unconscious that philosophers have been tied to for years?

SLOTERDIJK: The whole problem of European First Philosophy stems from the fact that the Greeks called human beings 'mortals'. When the decision is made to emphasize human mortality, the focus is on adults, on the finished version of the human being. Given that humans know they will die, we always have the impression that solitude is the ultimate truth of existence. However, it would be quite conceivable to focus on the other pole of human existence: birth. This theme was only appreciated at a late date in the history of ideas. It was raised in the twentieth century by Heidegger, Hannah Arendt and myself. From this perspective, it is no longer mortality but the fact of being born that is decisive. Yet this has no trace of loneliness: being born means getting involved with a welcome committee. The proto-idea of the newborn human is usually: there are people here. First people, then things. In other words, there are newborn babies, and they experience this profound way of being received into the bosom of the family that shapes what will later become 'the world'. From a philosophical perspective, we experience a great turning point that leads from a priority of mortality to a priority of being born. The people of the twenty-first century will not be mortals but will be people who were born, natal beings. To rethink our state of knowledge in accordance with human rights, we have to imagine a kind of humanity beyond the dictates of pure mortality – a human race whose members express the will to come into the world completely.

NASSIF: Are you telling us to live our lives as a result of birth instead of as little deaths?

SLOTERDIJK: This leads us to take an additional step towards the demystification of fate. To borrow the morose but brilliant term used by the young Heidegger, Fate used to consist of being 'thrown' into the world. But the person who was thrown forward can never appropriate the forces that threw him or her, just as a missile can't take possession of the gun behind it.

NASSIF: Does this mean that demystifying fate allows us to reappropriate the forces that threw us into the world?

SLOTERDIJK: Yes, starting with the biological gun, with sexuality. However, we should use the word 'appropriation' very carefully. It is not by chance that the twentieth century secularized sexuality: it was a matter of halting the destiny that fundamentally consisted in people producing children – and very often producing too many. They didn't know what they were doing in bringing children into the world to whom they couldn't promise what the Americans call 'a decent life'. A decent life – that's exactly what parents should be able to promise their children. In other words, handling procreation is the secret of destiny. Misfortune is usually an inheritance. These mechanisms have never been fully explained, but we now have enough information to know that it is possible to avoid necessarily creating a legacy for our successors from our physical and psychological illnesses. The large range of therapeutic techniques today allows us to break the curse. And that is exactly what is at stake: the Enlightenment is an attempt to sabotage fate. We can interrupt the bad repetition. As we can see in Western countries in the second age of contraception, destiny can also be interrupted by eliminating the overproduction of human beings.

NASSIF: But isn't it continuing everywhere else as it did previously?

SLOTERDIJK: Be careful! The twenty-first century will give rise to a new division of roles between the cultures that produce too many children and those that don't produce enough. Currently, as far as I know, around sixty-two nations are shrinking demographically and around 130 have a positive reproduction rate, whether moderate or excessive. Assuming optimistically that the twenty-first century will not experience a series of terrible catastrophes like the previous century, we can hope that the majority of those 130 countries will soon join the club of those producing fewer children.

NASSIF: Tunisia and Iran, for example, have already fallen to the level of France.

SLOTERDIJK: That's totally surprising, yet totally logical at the same time. Instead of discussing the madness of the ayatollahs, it would be better to talk about the extraordinary rationality shown by Iranian families in producing only two children for every married couple. This is something the ayatollahs have underestimated – a kind of biological strike by Iranian women. By conceiving not more than two children they are robbing the state of its future believers. And in that corner of the world being a believer means you can be sacrificed in a holy war. Still, there will be no holy war in Iran if there are no young men to fight it, even if the country's leaders persist with the idea for some years to come. The Iranians are catching up with the French and Americans, who have long since represented the society of the only son. You can't fight wars that demand heavy sacrifices with armies of only sons – which is why the art of warfare in the West is increasingly turning towards automatic weapons. In the past, a family with six or seven children could sacrifice one or two if need be, because nobody knew what to do with them anyway.

NASSIF: Aren't you painting a very cruel picture of bygone cultures?

SLOTERDIJK: In world history, the second and third sons usually were the great troublemakers. Cultures with only a single son are more peaceful. Why did France abandon the idea of revolution in the 1880s and 1890s? Because it was the first country in Europe, and therefore in the world, that practised the principle of the two-child family. The other nations joked about the French way of love, for example, the way to prevent a third child when having sex. Europe sniggered about anal or oral sexual practices, which were seen as French adult secrets. However, this kind of lovemaking was pure pacifism because it meant people didn't produce further children for waging war. You will object that this didn't stop France from plunging into the First World War. Yet those who ended up in the trenches were actually from the generations born before the demographic change. One of the reasons France lost the Second World War was because the country was in a transitional phase in relation to Germany. The big fall in the birth rate took place somewhat later in Germany, at the beginning of the First World War, in fact. The last massive demographic cohorts, born between 1910 and 1914, were around twenty years old when Hitler came to power. That provided him with 2–3 million young men who were ready for incitement, and he was deeply convinced they were destined for nothing else.

NASSIF: If we see birth as the motif of a philosophy based on privilege, does that mean demographic curves become a fundamental explanatory structure of the evolution of human societies?

SLOTERDIJK: The Greeks said the best fate is not to be born. We can interpret this statement as a confession of optimism. From the perspective of those who are already alive, the best thing in the world is not to populate the earth with people who can't be fed. This elementary act of omission is the true essence of humankind. On this issue, we have to fight against the 'mortalist' ideology embodied by the papacy. The Catholic Church has not achieved the decisive turn towards the modern age: it still wants to protect sperm to reserve it exclusively for procreation. If Italy is one of the countries with the lowest birth rate today, this is despite the Vatican and thanks to Italian women who have decided to delay their wish to have children, risking the chance that there may never be a right moment.

NASSIF: Given the growing opportunities for Asian types of spiritual therapy or psychoanalysis in our affluent societies, aren't we being offered the privilege of experiencing a second birth?

SLOTERDIJK: Take care with the expression 'second birth'. The nineteenth and twentieth centuries were the setting for the end of so-called religions of redemption. From a spiritual viewpoint we are entering a period where what matters is no longer salvation, but relief. Classical redemption proposed a way of healing that tears us out of our world and orients us to another world. In the past, the point was to turn your back on your first life to devote yourself to a radically different lifestyle. But, for several centuries, we have been going through a gigantic spiritual transformation that has led from a spirituality infused with denial of life and the world to a form of spirituality based on affirmation. Consequently, the religion of relief, of alleviation, of easing of life, of well-being or of 'caring' – to adopt a term that, curiously enough, appears in today's politics – will play an essential role in humankind's rituals in the future. There is no second birth for us any more. Everyone will concentrate on the first, which will be quite enough to allow a new spirituality to blossom.

NASSIF: This new way of regarding spirituality – isn't it the subject of your latest book, *You Must Change Your Life*, in which you state that the economic crisis is obliging us to do what politics hasn't managed: to change our life?

SLOTERDIJK: After assessing the results of thirty years of spiritual and physical exercises, I chose the direction of a new kind of philosophical anthropology. In my new book I show that there is a concept missing from the basic concepts of our culture, from our sociologists' classical theory of action. Without this concept it will always be impossible to describe how we live. The classic authors of sociology were concerned with two things: communication on the one hand and work on the other. We can either talk to each other or turn our backs on each other to put our energies into developing a product. But what the modernists have forgotten is the third dimension of our activities, which we can summarize with the concept of 'exercise'.

NASSIF: What do you mean by exercise?

SLOTERDIJK: Exercise consists of repeated operations that result in stabilizing or improving the subject's ability to perform the operation at the next repetition. People who do exercises develop their own form. But we have to understand that humans are beings that aren't in a position not to exercise: they are condemned to repetition. The only alternatives they have are to repeat things consciously or to be pushed into things by routine. Passive habits are simply unconscious exercises, or even dependency or obsessions. By contrast, every culture begins with the discovery that we are able to educate ourselves with specific exercises. Personal culture means having the will to liberate the acrobat inside us.

NASSIF: Doesn't that explain the growing importance of training? Finding somebody who jerks us out of our unconscious exercises and guides us into conscious exercises?

SLOTERDIJK: From the spiritual perspective, I think people's consciousness of this dimension of exercise in human existence will become more clearly emphasized. Unexpectedly, sport was probably the great harbinger in this movement. Due to its relative novelty, sport was the most exciting event in the defining character of modern culture. Its democratization shows that self-referential activities have achieved the highest status. My prophecy is that in twenty years' time sociology will hardly be talking about work, or about communication, but instead about the group of activities we call exercises.

NASSIF: Exercises that are no longer just sport, but will also be spiritual?

SLOTERDIJK: Sport is a metaphor for something that goes far beyond it. Of course, the robust, primitive dimension of sport is evident. But the simplicity of sports professionals shouldn't be an excuse any more for intellectuals to take no interest in sport. In fact, through the mediation of sport we can observe the emergence of a form of spirituality based on affirmation – more precisely, the affirmation of form. But, as we have known since Nietzsche, Being means being-in-form. Moreover, being in form is a more complex phenomenon that covers nearly the totality of what we usually called religion. However, the necessity of getting into form without being compelled to do so by others can only come from daily culture, that is, from a system of good habits. This opens up long-term perspectives for us. On this point we should amend Malraux's dictum: the twenty-first century will be acrobatic or it will be nothing.[1]

NASSIF: Doesn't the consumer culture propagated by the mass

[1] Sloterdijk is referring to a famous saying of André Malraux (1901–76): 'Le 21ème siècle sera spirituel ou ne sera pas.' ('The twenty-first century will be spiritual or it will be nothing.')

media tend to discourage the need for each individual to achieve his or her own form?

SLOTERDIJK: The media that disseminate mass culture are reacting to the need to offer training to those who don't really want to make an effort. That is training for lazy people. We know the outcome: we are heading for a global population in which 50 per cent of people are overweight. Still, an important insight is being communicated, even by the mass media: any kind of wisdom, any kind of personal achievement, starts with the choice of trainer. We are suddenly realizing that we can't train completely on our own. From this perspective, even an instrument can play the teacher's role: a piano, a violin, a drum or a video game.

NASSIF: Aren't you using a rather broad concept of spiritual exercises?

SLOTERDIJK: Looking at things broadly is the only way for us to understand the laws of our cognitive biographies. Let's not forget that a modern spiritual career normally involves several conversions. The classical conversion followed a pattern of people moving from worshipping Roman or Germanic gods to the God of Christianity. Incidentally, Buddha, Mohammed and Christ are the names of the great trainers, and their successors are only second-class trainers, better known under the title of apostle or priest. What people called conversion turns out to have been a change of trainer. Nowadays people often can't be satisfied with a single conversion.

NASSIF: Your daughter, who was born in the mid-1990s, will live most of her life in the twenty-first century. What experiences can you wish for her?

SLOTERDIJK: As she has understood it is not enough to be beautiful, she has made the intelligent choice of a boarding school where she can do all the necessary things to assure her future: friendship exercises, hoping exercises, knowledge exercises and telephoning exercises with her overjoyed parents.

# 33

# WITH THE BABBLE OF BABYLON IN THE BACKGROUND

*Interview with Manfred Osten**

OSTEN: Mr Sloterdijk, your libretto seems like an archaeological work. It has a multitude of different layers. For most people today, the Babylonian world is *terra incognita*. You wrote in your recently published journal collection, *Zeilen und Tage*:

> Mesopotamian studies seem to be in a completely desolate situation. After flourishing briefly around 1900, they contain almost nothing that explains definitively what it was all about between the Euphrates and the Tigris, and this is both troubling and absurd, because two things were discovered there that we couldn't imagine being without in the world we live in today – namely, the week, and friendship.

Another remark concerns the 'background radiation' of the Epic of Gilgamesh that we can feel throughout your libretto. The sensational thing about your project is that you try to rehabilitate Babylon in a sense. Indeed, *Babylon* takes us into contaminated terrain. The Old Testament story has given the Mesopotamian metropolis a negative image. Today it is cursed as the 'Whore of Babylon'.

SLOTERDIJK: I really like the concept of 'background radiation', especially applied to cultural structures. Astrophysicists may rack their brains about what background radiation means in

* This interview between Peter Sloterdijk and Manfred Osten appeared under the title 'Babylon Humming in the Background', in *Max Joseph. Magazin der Bayerischen Staatsoper* 1 (2012/2013): 32–40.

Manfred Osten is a German author, lawyer and art historian.

cosmological terms. However, that there is something like cultural radiation from a darkened background – patterns of order that are so deeply hidden in the oldest things, so strongly embedded in the sediment of what we think is self-evident that they seem to escape any reflection – we can gain experience of that when we get involved in Mesopotamian culture. In doing so, we enter a world much older than that of the Old Testament. We no longer realize what we owe to this world: to this very day we are users of a technique of temporal ordering that was developed in Babylon. We live in the Babylonian week apparently naturally, without thinking that it was predicated on a theology of the Heavenly Seven, that is, on a kind of septemtheism, which means the worship of seven deities. The seven-day week is a cultural creation because, unlike the day, the month and the year, it has no cosmic basis, but represents a freely made decision that fixes the arrangement of social time.

OSTEN: The opera also has seven scenes.

SLOTERDIJK: Jörg Widmann and I played around with this portentous number. We are presenting a planet septet as a stage production for which Widmann has written sublime music. We revive the Babylonian carnival with seven monkeys that play the part of oracle regulators. We have created seven phalli and their female counterparts for the Babylonian carnival, all dramatically larger than life – which gives the theatre audience the opportunity to observe genitalia in the rank of ancillary gods. The stage directions say that the presence of these objects on the stage should give a sacral, solemn impression without a hint of obscenity. In short, the word 'background radiation' has an alternative meaning in this context: it invites us to reflect on an immensely successful proposal for a world order that has come down to us from the culture between the Euphrates and the Tigris. The Mediterranean cultures have picked up on the Babylonian seven, the Jews, the Greeks, the Romans and, following them, all the European peoples.

OSTEN: In the Old Testament the genesis unfolds in a week, as if that time period were also self-evident for the God of the Jews.

SLOTERDIJK: In the last scene of the opera I suggest that even the great Oneness, beside whom you shall have no other gods, has rented a space in the Babylonian week. This is the day on which Jehovah rests after the effort of creation.

OSTEN: Does that mean he lives rent-free in the Babylonian week?

SLOTERDIJK: He is allowed to celebrate his peaceful Sabbath on one of the seven days – Babylonian tolerance is generous enough for that. As we know, the Christians moved the holy day of rest one day further on, and inserted their Lord's Day into the old Sun worship theology. A trace of this still lingers in the German and English names for the days of the week, while the Romance languages scandalously renamed the pagan-sounding day of the Sun as the day of the Lord, the *dies domenica*, from which the French *dimanche* and the Spanish *domingo* derive. That raised the question of whether Sunday is the last or first day of the week: as Sunday, according to astral protocol, takes precedence over the day of the Moon, rest then claimed precedence over activity, whereas in older mythology rest followed after energy had been exhausted. One figure that still understood the original scheme of things very well was Goethe's Mephisto: 'Why, surely, if a god first plagues himself six days / Then, self-contented, Bravo! says / Must something clever be created.'[1]

OSTEN: Another point about the 'background radiation' that emanates from the Gilgamesh epic: the epic describes Gilgamesh's great friendship with Enkidu, his soulmate, whom he follows into the Underworld after the latter's death. A further proof of friendship is crucially important in your libretto: Inanna descends to the Underworld to demand the return of her sacrificed lover, Tammu. Will the audience recognize the deep dimension of this fascinating mirror effect?

SLOTERDIJK: As long as the surface is understandable enough, anyone is free to delve down into a second, third or fourth mythological layer. As regards the phrase 'background radiation', we should bear in mind that time is something that can be translated into spatial relationships. The German language allows us to distinguish between history and the layering of the past [*die Geschichte* and *das Geschichte*]. The latter is spatialized time. It forms the archaeological dimension in which the historian's spade digs when he or she investigates the past that has been deposited. In my opinion the author of a libretto would be well advised only to present understandable surfaces. He or she should never hide behind deeper meanings. Nothing is more boring than a sign that says: *Double meaning!* Signs like that should never stand on a libretto roadside. But that doesn't exclude hidden associations below the surface.

OSTEN: The opera includes overtones and side tones from musical history, ranging from Monteverdi's *Orpheus* to *The Magic Flute*, where Pamina follows her beloved through an 'underworld' of trials.

SLOTERDIJK: With regard to *The Magic Flute*, the librettist, Schikaneder, had no idea where the big snake that follows poor Tamino at the beginning came from – for him it was simply a

[1] Johann Wolfgang von Goethe, *Faust*, VI.

fairy-tale motif he could use for a theatrical beginning. Looking at Mesopotamia, we immediately grasp the reference to the monster that devoured a prince: it is the Tiamat, the female primal dragon whose dismembered parts were once used to create Heaven and Earth.

OSTEN: What is the meaning of the Tiamat?

SLOTERDIJK: The great snake belongs on the side of original chaos and its little relatives behave accordingly. In Mesopotamian mythology the primary difference between chaos and cosmos is embodied in the antagonism between the Tiamat, the dragon of primal chaos, and Marduk, the god of creation. Marduk appears in our opera as the figure of the sacrificial priest god. In terms of mythological psychology, we are playing with the possibility of each figure having a dual identity. Most of the persons in the ensemble are naturally themselves, first of all, but they also embody a mythical figure, sometimes with the same name. Inanna is the priestess that she is, but in the sixth scene she becomes the goddess of the same name.

OSTEN: She mirrors the figure of the rejected love goddess from the Gilgamesh epic, who was also called Inanna.

SLOTERDIJK: We take this even further with Tammu, the male protagonist. At first he is Inanna's lover, a Jewish youth who became friendly with the king, like Joseph and Pharaoh. He is sacrificed during the Babylonian Festival in obedience to the dictates of local myths. At the same time he is a prefiguration of Christ, as he is allowed to return after his sacrificial death, or, as the New Testament says, 'to rise from the dead'. Moreover, he is a revised version of Christ, because for him – and indirectly for us – the point is not to ascend rapidly to heaven but to return to the world of daily life. For this reason, after his return he has not merely forty days on earth like the resurrected Jesus, but a time-span of fifty years to play his part. Even after the miracle he remains a mortal individual who lives out 'a human term'.

OSTEN: What does that mean for our idea of death and life?

SLOTERDIJK: The philosophical punchline is obvious: existence means returning from eternity. To really live, a person must have death behind him or her. As long as we regard death as extermination that lies ahead of everybody, pessimism will engulf us sooner or later. Then the Tiamat, the exterminating chaos that is on our trail, will win out in the end.

OSTEN: That reminds me of Goethe's classic saying: 'Death is the stratagem nature employs for having as much life as possible.'[2]

[2] The quotation is from Goethe's fragment, 'Die Natur' (1780).

SLOTERDIJK: That saying can be accentuated even more – I attempted it in the seventh scene of the opera, where I made the soul, the child and the rainbow septet declare the consequences of the mythological process of Babylon. Human existence can only be understood when the individual has liquidated his or her credit at the bank of illusions about eternity. To really live we must have returned from eternity.

OSTEN: Nonetheless, in your Babylonian story, the path through Hell comes before this existentially affirmative return.

SLOTERDIJK: That happens in the sixth scene, in which Inanna embarks on her journey to the Underworld. The Babylonian myth of Inanna's descent into Hell is probably the oldest example of an Underworld journey in an early high culture. It may give a special thrill to opera lovers because the story of that art form began in the seventeenth century, thanks to the Orpheus legend with the liaison between music and the descent into Hell.

OSTEN: There is one important difference that you introduce into the *Babylon* libretto: to bring Tammu back to the light of day, Inanna must constantly 'keep an eye' on the returnee during his ascent – unlike in the Orpheus story where he wasn't allowed to turn back towards Eurydice.

SLOTERDIJK: In fact, we had to amend something there: at the beginning it is not the singing man who brings his deceased beloved back from the Underworld, but the staunch, loving woman who reclaims her lover. In principle the conventional narrative of the story of Orpheus and his beloved includes a disastrous message. It reveals why the poet ultimately prefers his mourning for Eurydice to the real return of his beloved. The artist clings to his state of melancholy. If Eurydice really rose from the dead, he would have to relinquish it. That is why he must turn round, so that she falls back into the realm of shadows. Poets' love is impossible without poets' lies. We have created an alternative primal scene: it is the eye of the woman that carries the dead man back into the light. Inanna does not need the loss of her lover to be creative. We have to beware of the old web of deceit that binds art to loss and culture to deprivation. Of course, Romanticism cast suspicion on the *topos* of the redemption of man through woman – Gottfried Benn said everything that has to be said about the notorious need that men have for redemption, in the case of neurotics in general and Richard Wagner in particular, when he commented that first they behave like pigs and then they want to be redeemed.

OSTEN: But do things look different in *Babylon*?

SLOTERDIJK: The whole piece is arranged like an appeals procedure against traditional misunderstandings of the myth. We establish the fact that the Babylonian gods had nothing to do with the Flood at all. In the old accounts we read that they fled shivering to the mountaintops to await the end of the catastrophe. First and foremost, the God of Israel had no connection with the Flood – he was only associated with this Mesopotamian story later, in the post-exile period. It follows that he didn't send the Flood and that he had no powers to promise it would never return. In fact, he is completely outside this story – even though people might have perpetuated the false version of it for the past 2,500 years. The real point is that neither the gods of the Babylonians nor the God of Judaism were involved in causing the Flood. The Flood, with all its awe-inspiring astral drama, was an external cosmological event that was later internalized by means of religion and translated into the language of guilt and sacrificial duty. As regards the feeling of guilt, human beings seem to have been sensitive to it already in the Mesopotamia of pre-antiquity.

OSTEN: This means there was already a connection between guilt, sacrifice and willingness to suffer persecution. That disposed the Babylonians to sacrificial acts, even to human sacrifice.

SLOTERDIJK: If we are not wholly mistaken, those people had an unprecedented talent for feeling guilty – even for things they couldn't help. If establishing this fact about a people is a compliment, we can pass it on to the Babylonians, and if it is a reproach, the Babylonians have to accept that as well. We can observe a disposition to exaggerated liability even in those early times. Because Babylon anticipated so much of what later made 'religious' history, I have taken the liberty of dating the father–son relationship familiar to us from the Christian Trinity back to Babylon. I have portrayed the priest-king in such a way that, just like the Father of the Trinity, he sacrifices his best beloved, in this case his young friend from the Jewish guest population, to ward off repetition of the worst case.

OSTEN: You also deal with the abolition of human sacrifice, which was an immense cultural step in the development of humanity. You derive that from a simple cosmological interpretation of the events.

SLOTERDIJK: If the gods weren't involved in the great disaster at all they couldn't have any interest in sacrifices being made to avoid a repetition. The heavens – as understood in cosmological and meteorological terms – constitute a factor beyond divine power. Because God and gods didn't cause the Flood, we don't need to beg them to protect us from another flood. The gods have nothing to do with the cosmic disaster. Consequently, after the end of the Flood there was no need for a new covenant between God and human beings. Whatever could the people on Earth be guilty of? After all, they were at the mercy of a reality in which an ultimate terror like the Flood could happen. The rainbow in the sky after the Flood does not mean that God, after venting his wrath on the sinful mob, returned to calm reflection, as the biblical narrative suggests. If we want to make a symbol out of the rainbow, it stands for people finding the courage to carry on after the worst has happened. It inspires them to unite with each other against blind fate.

OSTEN: Your libretto also says that a Flood can always recur. And – that the old rainbow is obsolete. This corresponds to Nietzsche's insight in *The Gay Science*, telling us we have to learn 'to live dangerously'. Only heightened awareness of finiteness keeps people wakeful.

SLOTERDIJK: Tammu says this *expressis verbis*: the Flood is never over. We have to get used to the idea that life is always in danger. The possibility of being cut short is part of things. It is always about defining the post-Flood situation. Is there a happy, successful life after the catastrophe?

OSTEN: 'Maximal terror' is a key concept, not only of your opera project but also of the general theory of religion. In the end, don't the historical religions base their power on their insistence on fear? I read your libretto as if you wanted to express formal rejection of religious phobocracy, one more time. In your piece, love finally triumphs over fear in operatic style – and at the same time this indicates the end of religion as the hegemony of fear.

SLOTERDIJK: As you rightly say, in operatic style. Modern opera history begins, as we know, with the Orpheus myth – many composers have been fascinated by the story, from Monteverdi to Gluck. In Gluck's version the plot ends with the triumph of love – contrary to the text of the myth, which has Orpheus losing Eurydice again. We reconstruct the Orphic setting by playing it through once more with a changed cast.

OSTEN: In other words, the victory of love gives your opera an affirmative-positive ending?

SLOTERDIJK: One realizes why the happy end is justified if we pursue the question of why love should triumph in European music. We should remember that modern music since the seventeenth century has staged a kind of parallel action to religion and philosophy. From that time on, traditional religion became increasingly self-enlightened: it went through a major historical process of 'undarkening' – becoming less and less dark. It couldn't bear its own darkness any more, shook off its phobocratic mission and became transformed from an object of enlightenment into its vehicle – at least in its best aspects. Its latent theme is lightening up the world. Its mission is to extend the friendship zone. It may be that God is at the beginning of ultimate terror because he not only unleashed Hell on Earth but followed that up by demanding supreme sacrifice. Nevertheless, reformed religion finally got to the point where it could say 'God is love' again.

OSTEN: Does it follow that the development of Christianity after Constantine and Augustus, which was marked by fear, was based on a monstrous distortion of the earlier realization that occurred at some points, particularly in the works of some Jewish prophets, that 'God is love'?

SLOTERDIJK: Enlightenment is actually nothing but the process of critique of myths that results in overcoming the terror of sacrifice. This work on myth began early on in the ancient world. We tune into this work. That's why I have used the key phrase of the Old Testament twice in this piece, in the intermezzo and in the final scene: 'For I desire steadfast love and not sacrifice, the knowledge of God rather than burnt offerings.'[3] Widmann thought a text like this demanded an invisible choir, male voices in octaves, a bass part and a tenor part, lofty, mysterious and magically benign. In Mesopotamia, a world dominated by fear, this message bursts in like a gospel. That is the Enlightenment in the tone of the first millennium before Christ.

OSTEN: In your book *The Aesthetic Imperative*, you wrote that the art of the modern era emerged at the end of the Middle Ages when the wondrous was emancipated from wonder. Isn't that exactly what you have presented once again in your libretto? Why do you describe your opera as a fairy tale?

SLOTERDIJK: As regards categorization, Jörg Widmann and I have disagreed almost from the beginning, and we are very likely to end up with a Solomonic solution by which we are both right. He wants to call the *Babylon* enterprise purely and simply 'An opera in seven scenes'. And he is right, because if you are looking for a kind of operatic musical work that belongs to the improbable category that opera has become in recent years, we can say that *Babylon* is an opera from the first to the last note. As far as I am concerned, if we have to give it a label I would like to point more clearly to the fantastical stage machinery. Widmann's position is clear. What he has composed is grand opera. What I have written is a libretto for an operatic-type marvel, a story that shows how things that are wonderful can achieve miracles on a big stage with technical know-how. Schikaneder, for instance, unashamedly described his *Magic Flute* as a 'mechanical fairy tale'. The generic name shows that people

[3] Hosea 6:6, ESV.

in the eighteenth century had no inhibitions about imagining the machine as the servant of the wondrous. *The Magic Flute* already belonged to the age of special effects.

OSTEN: There are plenty of those effects at the end of your libretto in the sixth and seventh scene. The wondrous really succeeds there. It succeeds because Death makes an exception. And it succeeds because the soul, which seemed to be the great loser to begin with, manages to move beyond the position of loss, finally leaves the melancholic position and is transformed into a sun.

SLOTERDIJK: The wondrous ushers in an exceptional situation. At the decisive moment, Death says, 'You shall have the exception!'

OSTEN: Suddenly a kind of productive madness erupts in Death's mood, a fluctuation which gives rise to the astonishing event. Nonetheless, in the prologue to the story, and in an epilogue, you bring in the disturbing figure of the Scorpion Man who prophesies disaster against the backdrop of a devastated city. What is the meaning of this mysterious figure?

SLOTERDIJK: I go back to this figure from the Epic of Gilgamesh to describe the intervention of the sceptical position into the mythical world, a world in which initially only positive forces and affirmations exist, but where there is no doubt, no distance from ritual and tradition, and no problematic interior world. The Scorpion Man's appearance actualizes the possibilities of the examined life.

OSTEN: In your essay, 'La Musique retrouvée',[4] you suggest that music is the real religion of modernity. It is the medium of a positive relationship to the world, yet at the same time it acknowledges the call of the deep.

SLOTERDIJK: Important music is always related to the rediscovery of lost music – that is the psycho-acoustic thesis I developed many years ago in a different context. Great music of the kind that flourished in Europe from the seventeenth century onward implies friction between what we have already heard and what we have not heard yet. Curious listeners are open to hearing something new, but are searching for a lost sound at the same time. Knowing this immediately gives you a simple guideline for what a modern libretto has to achieve. It should offer the composer the opportunity to explore, in his or her own way, the argument between what we have already heard and what we have not heard yet, between familiar music and new music. I think the cooperation between Jörg Widmann and

[4] Peter Sloterdijk, 'La musique retrouvée', in *Der aesthetische Imperativ* (Berlin: Suhrkamp Verlag), 2014, pp. 8–28.

myself has confirmed this assumption. If I were to characterize our collaboration, I would say it was rather like conceptual chamber music. I think we both know more than we did before about the utopia of listening to one another.

# BERNHARD KLEIN

## Editorial Note

Michel de Montaigne: The most fruitful and natural exercise of the mind, in my opinion, is conversation.[1*]

Friedrich Nietzsche: In a dialogue, there is only one single refraction of thought: this is produced by the partner in conversation, the mirror in which we want to see our thoughts reflected as beautifully as possible.[2*]

Peter Sloterdijk: As paradoxical as all this may sound, these duplications of the ego onto the seeker and what is sought, the questioner and he who answers, the present self and the self that is yet to belong inexorably to the structure of an impassioned existential search for truth.[3*]

Peter Sloterdijk engages in dialogue on many different public platforms. He has given hundreds of interviews in the German and international press, including in Austria, Switzerland, France, Holland, Italy, England, Poland and the USA. His interviews are an important part of his work both as a public intellectual and as a philosopher. He is not shy of attention and is open to, and uses,

1* Michel de Montaigne, *Essays*, Ch. VIII – Of The Art of Conference, at: <https://www.gutenberg.org/files/3600/3600-h/3600-h.htm>.
2* Friedrich Nietzsche, *Human, All too Human – A Book for Free Spirits*, Section 374, Dialogue, 1879, at: <http://www.lexido.com/EBOOK_TEXTS/HUMAN_ALL_TOO_HUMAN_BOOK_ONE_.aspx?S=374>.
3* Peter Sloterdijk, *Thinker on Stage: Nietzsche's Materialism* (Minneapolis: University of Minnesota Press), 1989, p. 22.

all kinds of channels for disseminating his ideas: radio, television, internet, (specialist) periodicals, newspapers, conference paper collections, exhibition catalogues, advertising brochures and newsprint supplements.

Sometimes the present editor had to go to unusual lengths to excavate some of the sources. One memorable occasion was a visit to the underground air raid shelter of the Evangelical Press Archive of Munich University Library.

Sloterdijk has described the interview as a highly artificial form of rhetoric that first has to be refined and polished before it reaches the public:

> I think the interview is a special form that has evolved out of the construct of the rhetorical question. Since the days of oratory in ancient times, the rhetorical question has been a question the speaker asks himself and then usually answers as well. This has only changed in modern times in the sense that the rhetorical question and the rhetorical answer are divided between two people.
>
> (. . .) It usually succeeds when both sides have reworked it enough, in other words, when the last traces of the original situation, which merely creates the raw material for the end product, have been eliminated.[4*]

This kind of reworking for publication fits with Sloterdijk's tendency towards hyperbolical (exaggerated) philosophizing and assertion. He takes a stand against the people who play on understatement in our culture, and he emphasizes that

> by definition, a being with a neocortex can never be overchallenged – because we use fully at most seven to eight per cent of what we have, and even geniuses use only a tiny amount of their potential. In other words the question is how to put an end to the lack of mental challenge of human beings by human beings. For several hundred years, 'enlightenment' was the catchword for saying that the systematic underselling of human beings by human beings is a scandal that can't be maintained any longer if we humans succeed in identifying with the most intelligent members of our species.[5*]

4* Peter Sloterdijk, interview with Christian Thiele in Karlsruhe on 15 January 2010, available at: <https://www.youtube.com/watch?v=_ZKziG1xMw4>.

5* Peter Sloterdijk, 'Baden-Badener Disput', German TV broadcast, November 1992.

Sloterdijk is an exaggerator in the best sense of the term: a person who overstates and surprises, a man with an overview. He is a diagnostician of our times, constantly busy but apparently never over-challenged.

As a protagonist on the existential stage of thought and truth, Sloterdijk often exposes himself to criticism and the risk of failure. His path of development, from his beginnings as a powerfully eloquent writer to an award-winning rhetorician, is admirable.

His book *Kritik der zynischen Vernunft* [*Critique of Cynical Reason*], originally published in German by Suhrkamp Verlag in 1983, is one of the best-selling philosophical works of the twentieth century. This book marked Sloterdijk's entry into a media discourse that has lasted more than thirty years. He is not afraid to engage openly in public discussion about theses that are sometimes tucked away in ornate language and metaphors in his books.

The number of interviews he has given has risen exponentially since the 1980s. While his media presence was relatively easy to track in the 1980s and 1990s, in the 2000s he gave an overwhelming number of interviews.

Looking at the present volume, in formal terms we can distinguish between Sloterdijk's short interviews (e.g., 'Uterus on Wheels'), medium-length interviews (e.g., with Felix Schmidt) and long ones (e.g., with Macho, Raulff). Two of the longer type were previously published separately in German as *Selbstversuch with Carlos Oliveira* (*Conversation with Carlos Oliveira*) 1994, and *Die Sonne und der Tod* with Hans-Jürgen Heinrichs (*The Sun and Death*) 2001.

Sloterdijk's interviews are often linked to publication of his books or related reading tours. They are intended to back up and explain his socio-political position. (At the time of writing he is planning to set up an institute for psycho-political research.)

The interview subjects range from (international) politics, economics and history to topics such as sport, cinema, culture and philosophy.

Below is a short general outline of the interviews, listed as random key topics: global economic crisis, *banlieu*, Tour de France, football world championship, Daniel Goldhagen, spheres, bubbles, globes, world estrangement, cynicism, Crystal Palace, greenhouse, rage, globalization, capital, television, interview, asceticism, design, half-moon men, automobile men, Beethoven, [Helmut] Kohl, the post-war period in Germany, architecture.

When the media start sensationalizing his ideas, Sloterdijk has his own way of analysing how the ensuing debate proceeds.

Players and opponents are often identified as competitors in these debates. Many contemporary German philosophers don't consider it important to intervene in such discussions. They would rather continue as 'thinkers in ivory towers' than be 'thinkers on stage'.

Sloterdijk has initiated the following debates in the German media:

- – the debate on the 'wasted Enlightenment' (*Critique of Cynical Reason*, originally published in German in 1983)
- – the controversy about 'high' versus 'low culture' (*Blick zurück auf Dorn*, [*Look Back at Dorn*], Munich Kammerspiele, Peter Sloterdijk–Julian Nida-Rümelin, 1999)
- – the debate about the lecture 'Rules for the Human Zoo', and subsequently about genetic engineering (Peter Sloterdijk–Jürgen Habermas, started 1999)
- – the 'taxation debate' (Peter Sloterdijk–Axel Honneth, started 2009).

Peter Sloterdijk isn't afraid of getting involved in topical issues by using his gift for formulation to make public statements. He frequently indulges in digressions, inventing new terms or using analogies to illuminate the topic in question. His accurate, captivating power of judgement often enables him to see general events and situations from a totally new perspective (the technique of reversal).

> The author's elaborate language and his artistry in changing his position and perspective provide unusual and convincing insights and revelations. (...) Under Sloterdijk's gaze, familiar aesthetic phenomena are transformed into sources of surprise.[6*]

Sloterdijk's books and his interviews contain subtle neologisms and formulations that journalists and columnists gladly adopt and adapt as catchwords and headlines. This is reflected in many of the titles of the interviews.

Collecting interviews in a book offers the chance to make scattered, ephemeral pieces accessible. The present volume can contribute to rediscovering Sloterdijk as a communicator and provocative thinker. It contradicts the idea that nothing is more boring than yesterday's newspapers or websites. The interviews are entertaining and inspiring to read, and clearly illustrate Sloterdijk's way of thinking. They preserve something that was spoken for the moment – and reveal him as a lively, inventive conversationalist. These 'retrieved media pieces' are gems, fragmentary ideas or surprises waiting to be discovered.

# Appendix

The following is a list of works by Peter Sloterdijk referred to in this book. The works are listed in order of appearance in the original German, with the English edition below.

*Kritik der zynischen Vernunft*. Frankfurt: Suhrkamp Verlag, 1983.
*Critique of Cynical Reason*, trans. Michael Eldred. Minneapolis: University of Minnesota Press, 1988.

*Der Denker auf der Bühne: Nietzsches Materialismus*. Frankfurt: Suhrkamp Verlag, 1986.
*Thinker on Stage: Nietzsche's Materialism*, trans. Jamie Owen Daniel. Minneapolis: University of Minnesota Press, 1989.

*Der Zauberbaum: Die Entstehung der Psychoanalyse im Jahr 1785*. Frankfurt: Suhrkamp Verlag, 1987. No English translation.

*Eurotaoismus: Zur Kritik der politischen Kinetik*. Frankfurt: Suhrkamp Verlag, 1989.
*Eurotaoism: Sketch for the Project of a Critique of Political Kinetics*. Cluj-Napoca, Romania: IDEA, 2004. *Weltfremdheit*. Frankfurt: Suhrkamp Verlag, 1993. No English translation.

*Falls Europa erwacht: Gedanken zum Programm einer Weltmacht am Ende des Zeitalters ihrer politischen Absence*. Frankfurt: Suhrkamp, 1994. No English translation.

*Sphären I – Blasen, Mikrosphärologie*, 1998; *Sphären II – Globen, Makrosphärologie*, 1999; *Sphären III – Schäume, Plurale Sphärologie*, 2004. Frankfurt: Suhrkamp Verlag.

English editions: *Spheres I: Bubbles*, trans. Wieland Hoban, 2011; *Spheres II: Globes,* trans. Wieland Hoban, 2014; *Spheres III: Foam,* forthcoming. Los Angeles: Semiotext(e)/ Foreign Agents.

*Regeln für den Menschenpark: Ein Antwortschreiben zu Heideggers Brief über den Humanismus*, 1999.
'The Elmauer Rede: *Rules for the Human Zoo.* A Response to the *Letter on Humanism*', trans. Mary Varney Rorty. *Environment and Planning D: Society and Space* 27/1 (2009): 12–28. Available at: <http://web.stanford.edu/~mvr2j/sloterdijk.html>.

*Nicht gerettet. Versuche nach Heidegger*, 2001.
*Not Saved: Essays After Heidegger*. Cambridge: Polity, forthcoming.

*Luftbeben. An den Quellen des Terrors.* Frankfurt: Suhrkamp, 2002.
*Terror from the Air*, trans. Amy Patton. Los Angeles: Semiotext(e), 2009.

*Im Weltinnenraum des Kapitals*. Frankfurt: Suhrkamp Verlag, 2005.
*In the World Interior of Capital: Towards a Philosophical Theory of Globalization*, trans. Wieland Hoban. Cambridge: Polity, 2013.

*Derrida. Ein Ägypter*. Frankfurt: Suhrkamp, 2007.
*Derrida, an Egyptian: On the Problem of the Jewish Pyramid*, trans. Wieland Hoban. Cambridge: Polity, 2009.

*Zorn und Zeit.* Frankfurt: Suhrkamp, 2007.
*Rage and Time*, trans. Mario Wenning. New York: Columbia University Press, 2010.

*Gottes Eifer: Vom Kampf der drei Monotheismen.* Frankfurt: Suhrkamp, 2007.
*God's Zeal: The Battle of the Three Monotheisms*, trans. Wieland Hoban. Cambridge: Polity, 2009.

*Scheintod im Denken – Von Philosophie und Wissenschaft als Übung*. Frankfurt: Suhrkamp Verlag, 2010.
*The Art of Philosophy: Wisdom as a Practice*, trans. Karen Margolis. New York: Columbia University Press, 2012.

*Du mußt dein Leben ändern*. Frankfurt: Suhrkamp, 2009.
*You Must Change Your Life*, trans. Wieland Hoban. Cambridge: Polity, 2013.

*Die nehmende Hand und die gebende Seite*. Frankfurt: Suhrkamp, 2010. No English translation.

*Der ästhetische Imperativ*. Frankfurt: Suhrkamp Verlag, 2014.
*The Aesthetic Imperative*. Cambridge: Polity, forthcoming.